Mastering German Vocabulary

Mastering German Vocabulary

A Practical Guide to Troublesome Words

Bruce Donaldson

Routledge
Taylor & Francis Group

LONDON AND NEW YORK

First published 2004
by Routledge
11 New Fetter Lane, London EC4P 4EE

Simultaneously published in the USA and Canada
by Routledge
29 West 35th Street, New York, NY 10001

*Routledge is an imprint of the
Taylor & Francis Group*

© 2004 Bruce Donaldson

Typeset in Sabon and Frutiger by
Florence Production Ltd, Stoodleigh, Devon
Printed and bound in Great Britain by
TJ International Ltd, Padstow, Cornwall

British Library Cataloguing in Publication Data

A catalogue record for this book is available
from the British Library

*Library of Congress Cataloging in Publication
Data*

Donaldson, B. C. (Bruce C.), 1948–
    Mastering German vocabulary: a practical
    guide to troublesome words/Bruce Donaldson.
        p. cm.
        Includes bibliographical references and
        index.
    1. German language – Usage – Glossaries,
    vocabularies, etc.   2. German language –
    Textbooks for foreign speakers – English.
    I. Title.
    PF3460.D66 2004
    438.2′421–dc22   2003015202

ISBN 0–415–26114–7 (hbk)
ISBN 0–415–26115–5 (pbk)

Preface

This book is intended to be of use to those learning German formally at the upper secondary and particularly tertiary level, while at the same time being especially invaluable to the teach-yourself student who more often than not has no proficient speaker of the language to address such issues to. And all categories of learner will often find themselves seriously let down by dictionaries as their only source of information on these matters.

The choice of words covered in this book is inevitably somewhat arbitrary, but it has been based on my own experiences of learning German over a period of forty years, and teaching it and Dutch over a period of thirty years, Dutch lexical difficulties often being similar to those encountered when learning German. I feel confident that this long experience has put me in good stead to recognise the common pitfalls and equipped me to explain them to the keen learner of the language who is continually faced, as was I, with a baffling myriad of detail in the dictionaries. This book is not of course meant in any way to replace a good dictionary (e.g. Collins unabridged German–English, English–German dictionary), but merely to supplement it. Enormous constraints of space apply in dictionaries, endeavouring as good ones do, to list every word in the language, and thus the degree to which they can devote space to elaboration of meanings is inevitably limited. But not all words by any means

need further elaboration. That is the function of the present book, i.e. to take up the story with regard to those commonly occurring words that confront the English-speaking learner with difficult decisions that the dictionaries either do not address at all or do not address in sufficient detail to ensure that those words are correctly used. I am confident that my choice will prove to be useful to the level of student at which it is aimed.

It is *not* the intention of this book to deal with regional differences like **Fleischer, Metzger, Schlachter** where such terms are completely synonymous, i.e. they all mean 'butcher'. At times it was difficult to decide whether a given problem was indeed one of vocabulary or more of grammar (e.g. 'all', 'who', 'that') and here too a degree of arbitrariness has crept into deciding whether to include or exclude a given item.

Where nouns referring to human beings are discussed, it was decided it would have been unwieldy to include both the masculine and feminine forms and thus only the masculine forms have been given, with the exception of adjectival nouns that are indicated as follows: **der/die Bekannte** 'acquaintance, friend'. What is more, feminising masculine agents is more a grammatical than a lexical issue (e.g. **Aussiedler/ Aussiedlerin**) and thus for the sake of brevity and clarity this has not been done.

The reader must be aware that it is not the intention of this book to deal with all the meanings of the German words given here, merely those that correspond to the English word under discussion. For example, the verb **stellen** has a host of meanings but where it is discussed under the heading 'to put', only those functions of the word that equate with this English meaning are relevant and thus dealt with. The German words in question are looked at entirely from an English perspective as this is exactly where the real problem lies with the words that I have chosen to explain in this book. With greater exposure to the language one comes to appreciate more the broad field of meaning of words without compartmentalising their semantics in this way, but one needs to learn to walk before one learns to run and with that this book is intended to help.

It will quickly strike the reader that more entries relate to verbs than to any other part of speech. This is in no mean measure the result of the nuances given to German verbs by the application of prefixes such as **be-**, **ver-**, **er-** and **an-** etc., e.g. **befolgen**, **verfolgen**, **erfolgen**, **folgen**. Such derivatives are dealt with only where their meaning relates to the English key word under discussion (in this case 'to follow'). There may well be other derivatives, formed from other verbal prefixes, but if the resulting verbs do not translate the English key word under discussion, they are not included in the discussion. And if the derived verbs discussed have meanings that do not equate with 'to follow', but are used in some way to express other concepts, those functions are not discussed either as they are irrelevant to how to render the concept 'to follow' in German.

The distinction between transitive and intransitive verbs (abbreviated in this book to 'tr.' and 'intr.') is far less important in English than in German and thus many of the verbal alternatives discussed here, often the result of prefixing, are the result

of the need to distinguish in German between verbs that take a direct object and those that don't. You will notice that some verbs are followed by **lassen** in brackets, e.g. **anbrennen (lassen)**. This means that the verb, which is intransitive, can be made transitive by being used together with **lassen**, e.g. **Die Suppe ist angebrannt**, 'The soup has burnt' (intr.), **Er hat die Suppe anbrennen lassen** 'He has burnt the soup' (tr.).

This book does not attempt to be exhaustive in its explanations of the various ways to render certain English words in German. To have done so would have rendered the book unwieldy and of limited use to the learner battling to get on top of the basics of German. What I offer here is a survival kit to get the learner through the most common vocabulary difficulties that are confronted when one first takes up the mammoth task of learning to speak German well. This is not to say that quite advanced learners will not benefit from this book, but there inevitably comes a point in the acquisition of German vocabulary where prescriptive works such as this must cut the learner loose to pick up the rest through exposure to the living language.

It is true that you can never have enough examples of how to use a given German word and yet a book such as this must by necessity limit the examples it provides the reader with. The reader should therefore find the following website invaluable if further examples are required. The University of Leipzig has put a vast collection of vocabulary on the web consisting of three million words illustrated in 15 million sample sentences under **www.wortschatz.uni-leipzig.de**.

And finally a word on how to find what you are seeking in this book. Although the contents are set out under English key words which are alphabetically ordered, many of the English titles contain multiple words, e.g. the accident, crash. If you had the word 'accident' in mind, you could go to that point in the alphabet and find it, but if you had 'crash' in mind, you would not find it. For this reason all English words occurring in the titles of the individual entries are listed in the 'Index of English words' in the back of the book. Thus in this case, under 'crash' you are told to look up 'accident', which does not refer to 'accident' in the index list, but in the body of the book. Should you by any chance have a given German word in mind, but this will presumably be less common, you can go to the 'Index of German words' at the back of the book. There you will find, for example, that all the words dealt with under 'accident' (i.e. **der Absturz, der Unfall, das Unglück, der Zufall**) are listed alphabetically referring you to 'accident'.

Acknowledgements

First and foremost I would like to thank the many students I have taught over the years for the often astute questions they posed about correct word usage in German. Without their insights into many of the problems dealt with here, this book may never have seen the light of day. I would also like to thank Dr Ana Deumert of the German Department at Monash University in Melbourne for taking the time to answer the many questions I bombarded her with where the dictionaries and other books on the topic left the answers I sought up in the air, which was so often the case. I am also indebted to Guido Ernst from the Department of German and Swedish Studies at my own university for his thorough reading of the manuscript and the many valuable suggestions he made. And finally I thank my employer, the University of Melbourne, for allowing me a sabbatical to Münster in 2000 to be able to finally make a serious start on this book after many years of entertaining the idea of writing it.

Readers are encouraged to write to me with suggestions for the improvement of future editions of this book. All constructive criticism will be very gratefully received and acted upon.

Associate Professor Bruce Donaldson
Department of German and Swedish Studies
University of Melbourne
Parkville, Victoria
Australia 3010
e-mail: bcr@unimelb.edu.au

Abbreviations

acc.	accusative	jdm	jemandem (dat.)*
adj.	adjective/adjectival	jdn	jemanden (acc.)
Am.	American	lit.	literal(ly)
Br.	British	nom.	nominative
coll.	colloquial(ly)	obj.	object
dat.	dative	o.s.	oneself
Eng.	English	sep.	separable verb
etw.	etwas	pl.	plural
fem.	feminine/female	SG	southern German
fig.	figurative(ly)	s.o.	someone
gen.	genitive	s.t.	something
GDR	German Democratic Republic	tr.	transitive
insep.	inseparable verb	wk	weak noun
intr.	intransitive	<	derived from

*   Although it is uncommon in everyday German to use the case forms of **jemand** (i.e. **jemanden** and **jemandem**), it is accepted dictionary practice to use the abbreviations **jdn** and **jdm** to distinguish whether the personal object of a verb is in the accusative or the dative and this practice has been adhered to here, e.g. **jdn über etwas informieren**, 'to inform s.o. of s.t.'.

to abbreviate, abridge, shorten

abkürzen, kürzen, kürzer machen,
verkürzen

Kürzen refers to quantity and is thus used for abridging a book or essay, e.g. **Du musst deinen Aufsatz drastisch kürzen** 'You must shorten your essay drastically', **Das ist die gekürzte Ausgabe des Wörterbuchs** 'That is the abridged edition of the dictionary'. **Kürzen** can often be used interchangeably with **kürzer machen**, which is more usual for items of apparel requiring shortening (commonly **kürzer machen lassen** 'to have shortened').

Verkürzen refers usually to time but can be applied to distance too, e.g. **Die Gewerkschaft strebt verkürzte Arbeitszeit an** 'The union is striving for shorter working hours'. **Kürzen** can be used for time too, but only when there is a disadvantage to those concerned, e.g. **Wegen der schlechten Konjunktur wurde die Arbeitswoche bei VW um 10 Stunden gekürzt** 'As a result of the weak economy the working week at VW was reduced by 10 hours'.

Abkürzen means to abbreviate words, e.g. **Die Bundesrepublik Deutschland kürzt man mit BRD ab/wird mit BRD abgekürzt** 'The Federal Republic of Germany is abbreviated to FRG'. But this verb also refers to shortening a distance (short cutting), e.g. **So können wir den Weg abkürzen** 'This way we can shorten the distance/make a short cut'. And finally **abkürzen** is used for shortening or reducing the duration of s.t., in particular when it was intended to last longer, e.g. **Wegen der Lawine haben wir unseren Aufenthalt in Tirol abgekürzt** 'Because of the avalanche we shortened our stay in the Tyrol'.

about

an, etwa, gegen, rund, über, ungefähr

'About' meaning 'approximately' is most usually expressed by either **ungefähr** or **etwa**, which are synonymous and interchangeable, e.g. **Er hat sich seit ungefähr/etwa einer Woche nicht blicken lassen** 'He hasn't shown himself for about a week'.

Ungefähr can also be used with reference to the hour, e.g. **Er kommt normalerweise ungefähr um vier Uhr nach Hause** 'He normally gets home at about four o'clock', but in this function **gegen** is also commonly heard, **Er kommt immer gegen vier (Uhr) nach Hause.**

But **gegen** is used in other contexts too with the connotation of 'getting on towards, but no more than', e.g. **Gegen drei Millionen Menschen wohnen jetzt in dieser Stadt** 'About three million people now live in this town'. The following is synonymous with **gegen: an die drei Millionen Menschen.**

Rund renders literally 'round about', e.g. **Rund ein Fünftel aller Haiarten sind bedroht** '(Round) about/around a fifth of all shark species are threatened'.

'About' meaning 'concerning' as in 'a book/film about' is **über** + acc., e.g. **Ich habe gerade ein Buch über den Vietnam-Krieg gelesen** 'I have just read a book about the Vietnam War', **Worüber redet ihr?** – What are you talking about? (*see* TO SPEAK) Note the following two important idioms that also express 'about' in this sense: **Dieses Buch handelt vom Ersten Weltkrieg/Es handelt sich in diesem Buch um den Ersten Weltkrieg** 'This book is about the First World War'. In the latter idiom, which is much less common than the former, the subject is always an impersonal **es**, e.g. **Worum handelt es sich in diesem Bericht?** 'What is this report about?' (*see* TO DEAL WITH).

to accept

akzeptieren, annehmen, entgegennehmen, in Kauf nehmen, hinnehmen

The usual word is **annehmen** which can take both a concrete object like payment or a job and a less tangible object such as help or an invitation, but can also be used without an object, e.g. **Ich habe (die Stelle/das Angebot) angenommen** 'I accepted (the job/offer)'. **Akzeptieren** is a somewhat elevated synonym of **annehmen**, e.g. **Das Judentum akzeptiert die Homosexualität** 'Judaism accepts homosexuality'.

In more elevated language where 'to accept' is synonymous with 'to receive' **entgegennehmen** will be encountered, but it is often interchangeable with **annehmen**, e.g. **Er nahm Schmiergelder in Millionenhöhe entgegen** 'He accepted (= received) bribes in the millions', **Der Wissenschaftler hat den Preis im Namen des kubanischen Volkes entgegengenommen** 'The scientist accepted the prize in the name of the Cuban people'.

Where the object of 'to accept' is s.t. to your detriment or dissatisfaction, and thus you accept the inevitable only with resignation or reluctance, **hinnehmen** is required, e.g. **Die Partei wird diese Niederlage einfach hinnehmen müssen** 'The party will simply have to accept this defeat'.

In Kauf nehmen is similar in meaning to **hinnehmen** but implies somewhat less suffering or inevitability, e.g. **Wegen der Protestaktionen haben Fahrer viele Staus auf den Autobahnen in Kauf nehmen müssen** 'Drivers had to accept (contend with) many traffic jams on the freeways as a result of the demonstrations'.

the accident, crash

der Absturz, der Unfall, das Unglück, der Zufall

The most general word for an 'accident' which is not necessarily fatal, is **Unfall**, e.g. **Ich habe einen Unfall im Auto gehabt** 'I've had an accident in the car'. **Unglück**, in addition to meaning misfortune, refers to a serious accident or crash, e.g. **Im Zugunglück von Eschede sind viele Leute ums Leben gekommen** 'Many people died in the Eschede train crash'.

'To crash' with reference to planes is **abstürzen**, from which is derived **der (Flugzeug)Absturz** '(the aeroplane) accident/crash'.

Where accident is synonymous with coincidence or chance, **Zufall** is required, e.g. **Durch/per Zufall haben wir uns im Supermarkt getroffen** 'We met by accident in the supermarket'.

according to

laut, nach, nach Meinung von, so, zufolge

Zufolge (+ dat.), which follows the noun, is possibly the most common way of expressing 'according to' when it is not a person involved, e.g. **Alten Quellen zufolge kostete ein Sklave 306 Gramm Silber** 'According to ancient sources a slave cost 306 grammes of silver'.

Interchangeable with **zufolge** is **laut** (+ dat.), e.g. **Laut Berichten sind über 100 Menschen im Unglück umgekommen** 'According to reports over 100 people died in the accident'.

When a person follows 'according to' and the expression is synonymous with 'in my/your/her opinion' etc., it is best to say just that, e.g. **Ihrer Meinung nach ist er schuldig** 'In her opinion he is guilty'. If the holder of the opinion is a noun, rather than a possessive pronoun as in the previous example, the expression is as follows: **Meine Tante ist der Meinung, dass . . .** 'According to my aunt . . .'. (*see* OPINION)

'According to' in legal parlance (compare in accordance with) is **nach**, e.g. **Nach Artikel 256** 'According to article 256' (in a law). It is commonly used in combination with **Angaben** with reference to the opinion of people, e.g. **Nach Angaben des Zeugen** 'According to the witness', **Die Terrorgruppe hat nach Polizeiangaben bisher 5,5 Millionen Dollar Lösegeld erpresst** 'According to police the terrorist group has so far extorted 5.5 million dollars ransom'.

In journalese **so** often follows reported speech where in English we would say either 'according to x' or 'x said', e.g. **Angeblich, so ein Sprecher der UN, hätten Paramilitärs einen Anschlag auf die Forscher geplant** 'Apparently, according to a UN spokesman (= a UN spokesman said), paramilitaries had planned an attack on the research workers'.

to accuse

anklagen, anschuldigen, beschuldigen, vorwerfen

'To accuse' s.o. of s.t. criminal where there is a connotation of laying charges, is **jdn anklagen**

wegen, e.g. **Sie hat ihn wegen Diebstahls angeklagt** 'She has accused him of theft' (and reported this to the police), **Der Staatsanwalt hat ihn wegen Diebstahls angeklagt** 'The pubic prosecutor has charged him with theft', **Sie hat ihn angeklagt, ihren Ring gestohlen zu haben** 'She has accused him of having stolen her ring' (and reported this to the police).

'To accuse' s.o. of s.t. or doing s.t. without the connotation of laying charges is **beschuldigen**, e.g. **Er hat mich beschuldigt, ihn beleidigt zu haben** 'He has accused me of insulting him', **Die Frau hat ihn des Mordes beschuldigt** 'The woman has accused him of murder'. As illustrated, **beschuldigen** refers to a specific accusation.

Anschuldigen is not common, although the noun **Anschuldigung** is. The two words do not differ markedly from **beschuldigen** and **Beschuldigung** although the former can imply the hurling of general accusations at s.o., e.g. **Die Anschuldigungen, die gegen ihn erhoben werden, sind grundlos** 'The accusations being directed at him are groundless'.

Where 'to accuse' s.o. of s.t. is synonymous with 'to reproach' s.o. with s.t., use **jdm etwas vorwerfen**, e.g. **Er hat ihr vorgeworfen, nicht mithelfen zu wollen** 'He accused her of not wanting to lend a hand' (= reproached her with not wanting to lend a hand), **Er warf mir Undankbarkeit vor** 'He accused me of ingratitude'.

to admit, confess

beichten, bekennen, eingestehen, gestehen, zugeben

Gestehen means 'to confess' s.t. to s.o. in the non-religious sense, e.g. **Er hat (mir) seine Teilnahme an der Tat gestanden** 'He confessed his participation in the act' (to me), **Ich muss gestehen, dass ich mit der Entscheidung sehr unzufrieden bin** 'I have to confess I am very unhappy with the decision'. **Gestehen** is also used for 'admitting/confessing' to a crime, e.g. **Er hat den Einbruch gestanden** 'He admitted/confessed to the burglary'.

Eingestehen too refers to 'confessing' a crime or fault but more fully than **gestehen**, e.g. **Er gestand seine Niederlage/Schuld ein** 'He admitted defeat/He confessed his guilt'.

Sich bekennen zu renders 'to confess/admit to' a sin or crime. This verb is the only possible expression when a criminal (group) claims responsibility for an incident, e.g. **Eine bislang unbekannte Gruppe Terroristen bekannte sich zur Tat** 'A hitherto unknown group admitted to the act'.

Zugeben means 'to admit/confess' in the sense of 'to own up to', e.g. **Er hat es zugegeben** 'He has admitted it', **Er hat zugegeben, nicht gegangen zu sein** 'He admitted to not having gone', **Ich muss zugeben, dass ich nicht sehr begeistert darüber bin** 'I have to admit/confess I am not very enthusiastic about it'.

Beichten is 'to confess' in the religious sense, e.g. **Sie hat ihrem Priester alles gebeichtet** 'She confessed everything to her priest'.

the advertisement; to advertise

die Anzeige, das Inserat, die Reklame, der (Werbe-/Reklame)spot, die Werbung; ausschreiben, inserieren, werben, Werbung machen für

Generally speaking two words, **Reklame** and **Werbe-/Werbung**, refer to commercial advertising, the former being a somewhat colloquial term for what is otherwise officially referred to by either of the latter. A glossy 'advertisement' in a magazine or on a poster or billboard (**eine Werbefläche**) can be called a **Reklame** and a **Reklamebroschüre** or **-zettel** is an 'advertising brochure/leaflet'. 'Advertising' or 'commercials' as a collective on television or in a newspaper is **Werbung** whereas an individual 'advertisement' on television or

radio is a **Werbe-** or **Reklamespot** or simply a **Reklame**; take note of the use of the prefix **Werbe-** in the following examples as it typifies how **Werbe-** is used to render 'advertising': **Handy-Benutzer empfangen immer häufiger Werbebotschaften** 'Mobile phone users are getting more and more advertising messages', **die Werbebranche** 'the advertising industry'. Note too **Er arbeitet in der Werbung** 'He works in advertising'.

A classified 'advertisement' in a newspaper is an **Anzeige**. A more general, but also more formal word for an 'advertisement' in a newspaper is **Inserat**, e.g. **Wir kriegten zehnmal so viel Resonanz als mit einem Zeitungsinserat** 'We got ten times as much response as with an advertisement in the paper'.

Translating 'to advertise' can be tricky. **Inserieren** can be used for placing a classified advertisement in the paper, e.g. **Wir haben das Auto in der Zeitung inseriert** 'We advertised the car in the paper'. For jobs, on the other hand, **ausschreiben** is used, e.g. **Die Stellung wird nächste Woche in der FAZ ausgeschrieben** 'The job is being advertised in the Frankfurter Algemeine Zeitung next week'. A job advertisement is **die Stellenausschreibung** or **das Stellenangebot**.

'To advertise' commercially can be rendered either by **für etwas werben** or **Werbung machen für**, e.g. **Die Koreaner werben in Tschechien für in ihrem Land hergestellte Autos/machen Werbung in Tschechien für in ihrem Land hergestellte Autos** 'The Koreans are advertising cars made in their country in the Czech Republic'.

to advise

abraten, benachrichtigen, beraten, empfehlen, raten, in Kenntnis setzen, verständigen

'To advise' s.o. to do s.t. is **raten**, with the personal object in the dat., e.g. **Mein Makler hat mir** geraten, meine Anteile sofort zu verkaufen 'My broker advised me to sell my shares immediately'. 'To advise' s.o. *against* doing s.t. is **abraten (von)**, e.g. **Er hat mir (davon) abgeraten, die Anteile jetzt zu verkaufen** 'He advised me against selling the shares now', **Er hat mir davon abgeraten** 'He advised me against it'. 'To advise' s.o. (not) to do s.t. is also commonly expressed by **empfehlen**, which is actually the verb 'to recommend', e.g. **Er hat mir empfohlen, nicht mitzugehen** 'He advised me not to go along'.

Beraten, unlike **raten**, takes a direct object and means 'to give s.o. advice', e.g. **Wer hat dich beraten?** 'Who advised you?'. A consultant is thus a **Berater**.

'To advise' in the sense of 'to notify' can be expressed in a number of ways, i.e. by **benachrichtigen, in Kenntnis setzen** or **verständigen** (*see* TO INFORM).

after, afterwards, after that

danach, nach, nachdem, nachher

The difference between these forms hinges on the various parts of speech that 'after' belongs to in English. 'After' can be a preposition, in which function it is rendered by **nach**, e.g. **Wir sehen erst nach dem Abendbrot fern** 'We don't watch television till after supper'. But 'after' can also be a conjunction introducing a whole new clause, not just a phrase, and in this case it is rendered by **nachdem**, e.g. **Wir sehen erst fern, nachdem wir gegessen haben** 'We won't watch television till after we have have eaten'. As an adverb, in which case we normally use 'afterwards' in English, **nachher** is required, e.g. **Wir haben erst nachher ferngesehen** 'We didn't watch television till afterwards'. Similar in meaning to 'afterwards' is 'after that' which is **danach** in German, e.g. **Wir haben erst danach ferngesehen** 'We didn't watch television till after that'.

the age

das Alter, die Ära, die Epoche, das Zeitalter

A person's age is his **Alter**. '*At* the age of' is expressed by **in**, e.g. **In welchem Alter ist er gestorben?** 'At what age did he die?', **Er starb im Alter von 69 (Jahren)** 'He died at the age of 69'. Note also **Sein Neffe ist Anfang/Mitte/Ende Zwanzig** 'His nephew is in his early/mid/late twenties' (for 'middle-aged' *see* MIDDLE).

'Age' in the sense of 'era' is **Zeitalter**, e.g. **Alles ist anders im modernen Zeitalter** 'Everything is different in the modern age'. But 'the Middle Ages' is **das Mittelalter**, a singular, with the adjective **mittelalterlich** (medieval) derived from it, e.g. **Im frühen Mittelalter gab es wenige Städte nördlich der Alpen** 'In the early Middle Ages there were few cities north of the Alps'.

Epoche and **Ära** are used as synonyms of **Zeitalter** in much the same way as 'epoch' and 'era' alternate with 'age' in English.

ago

her, vor

'Three years ago' is **vor drei Jahren** (dat. pl.). **Drei Jahre her** (acc. pl.) is synonymous but can only be used with the present tense of **sein**, e.g. **A: Wann war das? B: Das ist drei Jahre her/Das war vor drei Jahren** 'A: When was that? B: That was three years ago'. **Her** is also required in the following expressions: **Wie lange ist das her?** 'How long ago did that happen?', **Das ist schon lange her** 'It was a long time ago'.

The word **vorhin** means 'a moment/little while ago' as does **vor kurzem** (*see* RECENTLY).

to agree; the agreement

ausmachen, (sich) einig sein (in), sich einigen, einverstanden sein, einwilligen, einer/anderer Meinung sein, übereinkommen, übereinstimmen, vereinbaren, sich verständigen, zustimmen; das Abkommen, die Einigung, die Übereinkunft, die Übereinstimmung, die Vereinbarung

'To agree' is a particularly hard verb to get a grip on, all the more so as use of the various German equivalents often overlaps. A simple solution for agreeing with others is to use the adjective **einverstanden**, e.g. **Ich bin mit dir einverstanden (, dass . . .)** 'I agree with you (that . . .)'. As in English you can even say **Einverstanden? 'Agreed?'** to an arrangement just made. Another simple solution for personal agreement is to use an idiom with **Meinung** ('opinion', *see* OPINION), e.g. **Ich bin mit ihr ganz einer Meinung** 'I fully agree with her', **Ich bin ganz anderer Meinung als sie** 'I don't agree with her at all'.

The first example in the previous paragraph could also be expressed as follows if followed by a **dass** clause: **Ich stimme mit dir darin überein, dass . . .** Übereinstimmen is also the verb required when referring to grammatical agreement, e.g. **Im Deutschen müssen Adjektive und Substantive übereinstimmen** 'In German adjectives and nouns must agree'. The following example shows **übereinstimmen** being used in a way similar to its use in the grammatical context above, but illustrates that its use is broader than that (= to tally/be in keeping with): **Unter den Nazis mussten die Ziele von Forschung und Wissenschaft mit den Zielen der Partei übereinstimmen** 'Under the Nazis the aims of research and science had to agree with the aims of the party'.

Unlike **übereinstimmen**, **übereinkommen** can only refer to people and requires different syntax from

the previous verb– it is always followed by an infinitive clause stating the content of the agreement, e.g. **Beide politische Parteien sind übereingekommen, die Vermögenssteuer abzuschaffen** 'Both political parties have agreed to abolish the wealth tax'. The associated noun is **die Übereinkunft**.

Very common, especially in journalese, is the expression **(sich) einig sein**, e.g. **Alle sind sich (darüber) einig, dass . . .** 'All agree that . . .', **Es war ein wichtiger Tag. Da waren sich alle Teilnehmer einig** 'It was an important day. All participants agreed', **Das muss geändert werden. Darin sind sich alle Länderchefs einig** 'That has to change. All state premiers agree with that'. This expression is mostly but not always used reflexively, e.g. **In diesem Punkt sind die Islamisten und der junge marokkanische König vollkommen einig** 'The Islamists and the young Moroccan king agree entirely on this point'. **Man** is often the subject of **sich einig sein**, e.g. **Man ist sich (darin/darüber) einig, dass . . .** 'We/They/People agree that . . .'.

'Agreeing to', 'approving of' or 'endorsing' policies, particularly at government level, requires the verb **zustimmen**, e.g. **Der Bundesrat muss diesem neuen Gesetz nicht zustimmen** 'The upper house does not have to agree to/pass the new law', **Der Bundestag hat dem Mazedonien-Einsatz der Bundeswehr zugestimmt** 'The Upper House has agreed to/approved the involvement of the army in Macedonia', **einem Kompromiss zustimmen** 'to agree on a compromise'. Use of this word is not necessarily limited to such formal situations, however, e.g. **Ich stimme dir zu, dass . . .** 'I agree with you that . . .'. This verb too has a noun derived from it, e.g. **Die CDU hat dem Vertrag ihre Zustimmung verweigert** 'The conservative party refused/denied the treaty its approval' (= did not agree to it).

When two parties agree *to* or *on* s.t. (especially in a conflict), **sich einigen** is the appropriate word;

it is more formal than **zustimmen**, e.g. **Die beiden größten Parteien haben sich nicht auf eine gemeinsame Steuerreform geeinigt; eine baldige Einigung steht nicht bevor** 'The two largest parties have not agreed to/on a common tax reform'; a speedy agreement is not in the offing.

'To agree' on a time for an appointment requires **vereinbaren**, which has definite connotations of 'to arrange', e.g. **Welchen Tag habt ihr vereinbart?** 'What have you agreed on/arranged?', **Rufen Sie die Firma an, um einen Termin zu vereinbaren** 'Ring the firm to arrange an appointment'. The noun too expresses this dichotomy of meaning, e.g. **die Vereinbarung mit Irak** 'the agreement/ arrangement with Iraq'. **Ausmachen** could be used instead of **vereinbaren** in the first two examples.

A formal political 'agreement' with the status of a treaty, for example, is **das Abkommen**, e.g. **Diese Länder haben das Klimaschutzabkommen von Kioto noch nicht unterzeichnet** 'These countries have not yet signed the Kyoto Climate Agreement', **ein Auslieferungsabkommen mit Australien abschließen** 'to conclude an extradition agreement with Australia'.

Sich verständigen means 'to come to an agreement/understanding' with s.o., e.g. **Sie verständigten sich auf einen Schadensersatz** 'They agreed on compensation for the damage'.

Einwilligen (in + acc.) translates 'to agree' where there are connotations of consenting, e.g. **Junge Mädchen erklären, dass sie ihrem Freund lieber den Laufpass geben, als in Sex ohne Gummi einzuwilligen** 'Young girls declare that they prefer giving their boyfriends their marching orders to agreeing to sex without a condom', **Er hat eingewilligt, sich mit ihr zu treffen** 'He agreed (consented to) meeting with her'.

'To disagree' is merely expressed by negating any of the above expressions by means of **nicht**, e.g.

nicht übereinstimmen mit (a person, opinions), **nicht einverstanden sein mit** (a suggestion), **sich nicht einig sein** (two people).

alive, live (*see* TO LIVE)

leben, lebend, lebendig, lebhaft, zu . . . Lebzeiten, live

Lebendig is the opposite of dead, e.g. **Er ist lebendig begraben worden** 'He was buried alive'. Animals that give birth to live young, as opposed to egglayers, **gebären lebendige Junge**. **Lebendig** also has the fig. meaning of lively/vivid, e.g. **eine lebendige Erinnerung** 'a vivid memory'. Generally speaking, however, this fig. meaning is expressed by **lebhaft** (= vivacious)[1], e.g. **ein lebhaftes Gespräch** 'a lively discussion'.

When 'alive' has the connotation of (that which is) living, **lebend** is the appropriate word, e.g. **die Lebenden** 'the living' (= those who are alive), **ein lebendes Tier** 'a live animal', **ein lebender Zeuge** 'a witness who is still alive', **Man versuchte die Mannschaft des U-Bootes lebend zu bergen** 'They tried to recover the submarine crew alive'.

When asking if s.o. is dead or alive, it is most usual in German to ask **Lebt er noch?** When Goethe was alive, for example, is expressed as **zu Goethes Lebzeiten**.

The loanword **live** is used only of radio and television, e.g. **Der Fußballwettkampf wird live ausgesendet** 'The football match is being broadcast live'.

---

[1] Note that these Latin derived synonyms of lively, i.e. vivid and vivacious, contain the root **viv-** 'life', thus **Leben**.

all

all, all-, ganz

All followed by a mass noun is indeclinable, e.g. **Er hat all sein Geld ausgegeben** 'He's spent all his money'. When followed by a plural noun, both **all** and **alle** are possible, e.g. **Er hat all/alle seine Lehrbücher verbrannt** 'He burnt all his text-books'. Note that 'all the + a plural noun' can be expressed in three ways: **all die Kinder, alle die Kinder** and **alle Kinder**; the fact that the last falls together with 'all children' does not disturb the German.

Whereas **all** is indeclinable in all cases, **alle** has the following case forms: nom. **alle**, acc. **alle**, gen. **aller** and dat. **allem/aller/allen** and adjectives that follow these forms take the ending -en, e.g. **Sie sind mit all/allen ihren kleinen Kindern zum Jahrmarkt gegangen** 'They went to the fun-fair with all their small children', **Er weiß die Namen aller Nachbarkinder nicht mehr** 'He no longer knows the names of all the neighbours' children', **Neunzig Prozent aller Zahnärzte empfehlen es** 'Ninety per cent of all dentists recommend it', **aus aller Welt** 'from all over the world'. **Alle** can also follow the verb, as in English, e.g. **Die Kinder sind alle in der Schule** 'The kids are all at school'.

'All' in combination with expressions of time is rendered by **ganz** (lit. whole), e.g. **Sie ist den ganzen Tag/den ganzen Monat/die ganze Woche/das ganze Jahr krank gewesen** 'She was sick all day/month/week/year'. This use of **ganz** can be extended to replace **all(e) die** in examples such as those in the previous paragraph, e.g. **Er hat die ganzen Kühe (= all[e] die Kühe) selber gemolken** 'He milked all the cows himself'. Note too **Ich bin ganz Ohr** 'I'm all ears', i.e. I'm listening.

Ganz can also be used instead of **all** in the contexts given in the first paragraph, e.g. **Er hat sein ganzes Geld/seine ganzen Bücher weggegeben** 'He's given all his money/books away'.

'No/not/nothing at all' is expressed either by **gar kein/nicht/nichts** or **überhaupt kein/nicht/nichts**, which are synonymous, e.g. **Er hat gar/überhaupt keine Freunde mehr** 'He no longer has any friends at all', **Sie weiß gar/überhaupt nichts darüber** 'She knows nothing at all about it'.

Note that despite appearances **alles** (everything) has nothing to do with **all**, nor does **alle** in the following idiom: **Mein Geld/die Milch ist alle** 'My money/the milk has run out/is all gone'.

to announce, proclaim

ankündigen, bekanntgeben, bekanntmachen

The most everyday words are **bekanntgeben/-machen**, for both official and trivial matters, the latter being less formal than the former, e.g. **Der Außenminister hat heute seinen Rücktritt bekanntgegeben** 'The foreign minister announced his resignation today', **Heidi und Rudolf haben ihre Verlobung bekanntgemacht** 'Heidi and Rudolf have announced their engagement'. These verbs refer to events that have occurred.

Ankündigen means 'to announce' where advance notice of s.t. yet to happen is being given, e.g. **Der General hat eine Feuerpause für nächste Woche angekündigt** 'The General has announced a cease-fire for next week', **Die Preiserhöhung wurde vorher angekündigt** 'The price increase was announced in advance'.

another

ein ander, noch ein

'Another' is ambiguous. For example, if you say 'Please give me another glass' you may mean either 'a different glass' (*see* DIFFERENT) or 'an additional one'; the former is rendered by **ein** anderes and the latter by **noch ein**, e.g. **Geben Sie mir bitte ein anderes Glas/noch ein Glas.**

to answer

antworten, antworten auf, beantworten, erwidern, sich verantworten

Antworten is intr. and thus if answering a question or letter, for example, it must take a prepositional object, the preposition required being **auf** with the acc., e.g. **Sie hat nicht auf die Frage/den Brief geantwortet** 'She did not answer the question/letter'.

Synonymous with the intr. verb **antworten auf** is the tr. verb **beantworten**, e.g. **Sie hat die Frage/den Brief nicht beantwortet**[2] 'She did not answer the question/letter'. An 'answering machine' is thus **der Anrufbeantworter** as it answers calls (**Anrufe**) (*see* TO CALL).

If answering a person, only **antworten** can be used and the personal object goes in the dat., but may also be omitted as in English, e.g. **Er antwortete (mir) nicht/Er gab (mir) keine Antwort** 'He didn't answer (me)'. This is also the verb required after reported speech, e.g. **'Nein', antwortete er** ' "No", he answered'.

'To answer for' in the sense of 'to accept responsibility for' requires **sich verantworten**, e.g. **Er wird sich für diese schreckliche Tat verantworten müssen** 'He'll have to answer for this terrible deed'.

Erwidern (**auf** + acc.) is a more formal synonym of **antworten** similar in connotation to 'to reply/retort'.

any (anyone/anybody, anything, anywhere) (*see* SOME)

etwas, jed-, kein-; etwas/nichts, irgendwo/nirgendwo/nirgends, jemand/niemand

How to render 'any' in German is more a grammatical than a lexical issue but here are a few guidelines.

'Not a/any' is rendered by **kein**, e.g. **Er hat kein Geld** 'He doesn't have any money', **Sie hat kein Fahrrad** 'She doesn't have a bicycle'.

It is a peculiarity of English that when 'some' is used with a negative (see first example in previous paragraph) or in a question, it is replaced by 'any'. Thus, where German leaves 'some' untranslated or uses **etwas** (*see* SOME), German does not translate 'any' either or retains **etwas**, e.g. **Er hat (etwas) Geld** 'He has some money', **Hat er (etwas) Geld?** 'Does he have any money?'. In the following example 'any' can be left untranslated or by inserting **jede** emphasis is added, e.g. **Sie wohnen ohne (jede) Unterkunft** 'They live without any accommodation at all'.

In keeping with what has been said of English above, 'somebody', 'something' and 'somewhere', become 'anybody', 'anything' and 'anywhere' when used with a negative or in a question, or with a negative may become 'nobody', 'nothing' and 'nowhere'; in questions German continues to use **jemand, etwas** and **irgendwo**, as in statements, and in negations uses **niemand, nichts** and **nirgendwo/nirgends**, e.g. **Ich habe jemand hinter der Garage gesehen** 'I saw somebody behind the garage', **Hast du jemand hinter der Garage gesehen?** 'Did you see anybody behind the garage?', **Nein, ich habe niemand gesehen**[3] 'No, I didn't see anybody'; **Er hat etwas in der Hand** 'He

---

[2] Note when comparing this sentence with the one above incorporating **antworten**, that here **nicht** follows the direct definite object, whereas in the first case it precedes the prepositional phrase. This is standard German word order.

[3] In formal written German **jemand** and **niemand** can take case endings, e.g. acc. **jemanden/niemanden**, dat. **jemandem/niemandem**.

has something in his hand', **Hat er etwas in der Hand?** 'Does he have anything in his hand?', **Nein, er hat nichts in der Hand** 'No, he hasn't got anything in his hand'; **Er wohnt irgendwo in der Nähe von Köln** 'He lives somewhere in the vicinity of Cologne?', **Wohnen Sie irgendwo hier in der Nähe?** 'Do you live anywhere near here?', **Er ist nirgendwo/nirgends gewesen** 'He has never been anywhere'.

to appear

erscheinen, scheinen, vorkommen

'To appear' meaning to come into view or existence, i.e. the opposite to 'to disappear' (**verschwinden**), is **erscheinen**, e.g. **Sein neuester Roman ist gerade erschienen** 'His latest novel has just appeared', **Und dann auf einmal ist er erschienen** 'And then all of a sudden he appeared'.

'To appear' in the sense of 'to seem' is **scheinen**, e.g. **Er scheint krank zu sein** 'He appears/seems to be ill'. 'To appear/seem' *to* s.o. is also **scheinen** but can also be expressed by **vorkommen** with different syntax, e.g. **Er schien mir etwas älter (zu sein)/Er kam mir etwas älter vor** 'He appeared/ seemed to me to be somewhat older'. **Scheinen** can be followed by both a **zu** clause, as illustrated, and a **dass** clause, e.g. **Es scheint, dass sie lieber zuhause bleiben** 'It seems/appears (that) they would rather stay home'.

the appliance, device, apparatus

die Anlage, der Apparat, das Gerät

A piece of equipment, device, appliance or utensil is a **Gerät**, e.g. **Fernsehgerät** 'television set', **elektrische Geräte** 'electrical appliances', **Küchengerät** 'a kitchen utensil'. The word **Anlage** usually refers to an (industrial) plant, installation(s) or

equipment, but a couple of household appliances are seen as **Anlagen** too and not as **Geräte**, e.g. **Klimaanlage** 'air conditioner', **Stereoanlage** 'stereo' (installation). But **Apparat** is used in German too where the word apparatus would be quite inappropriate in English, e.g. **der Fotoapparat** 'camera'.

to apply for; the application

einen Antrag stellen, beantragen,
sich bewerben um/bei; der Antrag,
die Bewerbung

'To apply for' a job at/with a firm requires **sich bewerben um**, e.g. **Er hat sich um eine Stelle bei Siemens beworben** 'He has applied for a job at Siemens'. The 'application' is **die Bewerbung**. These two words are used for scholarships too.

In other contexts **beantragen/der Antrag** are used, e.g. **einen Telefonanschluss beantragen** 'to apply for a telephone' (connection), **Die beiden Kurden haben Asyl beantragt** 'The two Kurds have applied for asylum', nevertheless 'asylum seekers' are **Asylbewerber**. In formal contexts you may use **einen Antrag stellen**, corresponding closely to 'to make (an) application for', e.g. **Das Unternehmen hat einen Insolvenzantrag gestellt** 'The firm has applied for bankruptcy', but this could equally be expressed as **Das Unternehmen hat Insolvenz beantragt**.

to approach, come closer

sich annähern, nahen, näher
kommen/rücken, sich nähern

'To approach' in the sense of 'getting closer' can cause problems; you can of course say just that using **näher kommen**, or **näher rücken**, e.g. **Er** kam/rückte mir immer näher 'He got closer and closer to me/He was approaching me'. Synonymous with näher kommen is sich nähern, e.g. Er näherte sich mir 'He came closer to me/was approaching me', Während der Zug sich näherte (= näher kam), fiel auf einmal mein koffer auf die Schienen 'While the train was approaching my suitcase suddenly fell onto the track'.

Sich annähern renders a figurative coming together, i.e. reconciliation, e.g. Nach dem Erdbeben in Griechenland und der Türkei haben sich die beiden Länder angenähert 'Since the earthquake in Greece and Turkey the two countries have come closer to each other', but here too you could say less formally Die beiden Länder sind sich näher gekommen.

Nahen is used for the approaching of time, e.g. Der Sommer naht 'Summer is approaching'. It is commonly used with the optional prefix heran-, e.g. Ostern naht heran 'Easter is approaching', ein herannahendes Gewitter 'an approaching thunderstorm'.

At German railway stations you will hear Der Zug aus Wien und Salzburg hat Einfahrt auf Gleis 5 'The train from Vienna and Salzburg is approaching on platform 5'.

the area

der Bereich, das Gebiet, die Gegend,
die Stelle, das Viertel

The 'area' in which you live is die Gegend and thus it also translates 'neighbourhood' and 'region', e.g. Wir wohnen sehr gern in dieser Gegend 'We like living in this area', Jugendliche aus der hiesigen Gegend 'Young people from the local area'. The area of a town corresponding to a quarter or district is expressed by Viertel, e.g. Sankt Pauli ist das Puffviertel von Hamburg 'Sankt Pauli is Hamburg's brothel area/quarter/district', das

Bankenviertel von Frankfurt 'the banking precinct of Frankfurt' (*see* MUNICIPALITY).

Gebiet covers a larger area than Gegend and can thus mean 'region' but also 'territory', e.g. das Ruhrgebiet 'The Ruhr area/region', das Gewerbegebiet 'the industrial area' (of a town), In diesem ganzen Gebiet kommt Bernstein vor 'Amber is found in this whole area', Das ist deutsches Hoheitsgebiet 'That is German sovereign territory'. It is not difficult to imagine contexts where Gegend and Gebiet could be interchangeable, e.g. In dieser Gegend/diesem Gebiet werden Weintrauben angebaut 'Grapes are grown in this area'. But unlike Gegend, Gebiet can be used figuratively for an area of knowledge, e.g. Ich kenne mich auf diesem Gebiet nicht aus 'I don't know much about this area' (= this is not my area of expertise). In this figurative sense Bereich is synonymous with Gebiet, e.g. Ich kenne mich nicht aus in diesem Bereich der Soziologie 'I am not au fait with this area of sociology' (note the use of auf with Gebiet and in with Bereich). Bereich is not just used figuratively, however, e.g. im Bereich des Rathauses/um das Rathaus 'in the area around the town hall'.

Stelle is used for an area of the body surface, e.g. Diese Stelle ist dann rot geworden 'This area then turned red'.

the army

die Armee, die Bundeswehr, das Heer,
die Wehrmacht, die Wehrpflicht

Although die Armee and das Heer may be used loosely to refer to 'army', the former can in fact have a more general meaning corresponding to 'armed forces', i.e. Streitkräfte, e.g. Australien hat eine Berufsarmee 'Australia has a professional army'. 'The German army' is called die Bundeswehr, which in Nazi Germany was called die Wehrmacht, a term that now only has an historical validity.

Germany is a country that still has conscription, called **die Wehrpflicht/der Wehrdienst**, 'national service'. The sentence **Mein Sohn ist bei der Bundeswehr** can mean either 'My son is in the (German) army' or 'My son is doing his national service' whereas **Er macht gerade seinen Wehrdienst** can only refer to the latter.

to arrive

ankommen, arrivieren, eintreffen, erreichen, kommen

The first problem to address here is which preposition to use with **ankommen**, an elevated synonym of which is **arrivieren**; this depends on the place of arrival, e.g. **Er ist um 10.00 in der Stadt/am Bahnhof/bei Hertie/bei uns angekommen** 'He arrived in the city/at the station/at Hertie/at our place at 10.00' (*see* AT). If in doubt here, **erreichen** (lit. 'to reach'), which takes a direct object and thus needs no preposition, can be an easy way out, e.g. **Wann hat er den Bauernhof erreicht?** 'When did he arrive at the farm?'. In formal contexts **eintreffen** will be heard but it is in fact synonymous with **ankommen**, e.g. **Der Bundesverteidigungsminister ist in Mazedonien eingetroffen** 'The federal minister for defence has arrived in Macedonia'.

Note the following distinction: **Ist die Post schon gekommen?** 'Has the mail arrived yet?' (= Has the postman been?), but **Ist der Brief schon angekommen?** 'Has the letter arrived yet?'.

arts

die Geisteswissenschaften, die Künste

The '(creative) arts' in general are **die schönen Künste**. In Germany a state 'minister for the arts' is a **Kultusminister**, but the portfolio also covers education (*see* EDUCATION). If you are doing 'Arts' at university you are studying **Geisteswissenschaften**, although the faculty is called **die Philosophische Fakultät**.

as

als, so, erst, wie; da, weil

The conjunction 'as' is normally rendered by **wie**, e.g. **Wie du weißt, kann er kein Deutsch** 'As you know, he knows no German'. In 'as . . . as' comparatives the first 'as' is **so** and the second **wie**, e.g. **Ich bin nicht so groß wie er** 'I am not as tall as he', **Er ist genau so alt wie Thomas** 'He is just as old as Thomas'. 'As recently as . . .', which is synonymous with 'only + time', is expressed by **erst**, e.g. **Ich habe ihn erst letzte Woche gesehen** 'I saw him as recently as last week' (*see* ONLY and RECENTLY).

The preposition 'as' is usually **als**, e.g. **Als Kind hat er in Italien gewohnt** 'As a child he lived in Italy', **Er bezeichnete den Schritt als weise** 'He described the step as wise'. In the following example both **als** and **wie** are possible, corresponding to 'as' and like' respectively: **Er hat sie als/wie ein Kind behandelt** 'He treated her as/like a child'.

'As' which means 'since' or because' is rendered by **da** or **weil** respectively, but most usually by the latter, e.g. **Da/weil er total k.o. war, ging er nicht zur Party, sondern blieb zu Hause** 'As he was utterly whacked, he didn't go to the party but stayed at home'.

to ask, demand, request

anfordern, befragen, bitten um, erfordern, fordern, fragen, eine Frage stellen, verlangen

'To ask' as an intr. verb is **fragen**, e.g. **Wie heißt du?, fragte er (mich)** 'What is your name?, he asked (me)'. As a 'question' is **eine Frage**, 'to ask a question' must be rendered by **jdm eine Frage stellen** (i.e. to put a question to s.o.), e.g. **Ich möchte dir eine Frage stellen** 'I would like to ask you a question'. 'To ask' or 'to question' s.o., as in surveys or as a witness, requires **befragen**, e.g. **Die Fernsehmoderatorin befragt Prominente nach der ersten Liebe** 'The television host asks prominent people about their first love'.

'To ask after' s.o. or some place is **fragen nach**, e.g. **Sie hat nach deiner Mutter gefragt** 'She asked after your mother/how your mother is', **Er fragte nach dem Postamt** 'He asked after the post-office/where the post-office is'.

'To ask for' s.t., i.e. 'to request' s.t. as opposed to interrogating s.o., is rendered by **bitten um**, e.g. **Ich habe um ein Zimmer mit Bad gebeten** 'I asked for a room with a bathroom'. 'To ask for' as the asking price of an object, is expressed by **verlangen** (lit. to demand), e.g. **Wie viel verlangt er für seinen alten Audi?** 'How much is he asking for his old Audi?'. **Verlangen** otherwise renders 'to demand' and can thus translate 'to ask' when this connotation is present, e.g. **Du verlangst zu viel von mir** 'You ask too much of me' (= demand too much from me).

Otherwise 'to demand' is most usually rendered by **fordern**, e.g. **Die Rebellen fordern die Freilassung der Gefangenen** 'The rebels are demanding the release of the prisoners'[4] (*see* TO CLAIM). **Anfordern** is a formal synonym of **bitten um**, e.g. **Die Russen hätten sofort Hilfe anfordern sollen** 'The Russians should have asked for/requested assistance straight away'.

Erfordern can translate 'to demand' where this verb is synonymous with 'to require/call for', e.g. **Dieses Projekt erfordert sehr viel Arbeit/Mühe/Zeit** 'This project requires/is demanding a lot of work/effort/time'.

at (*see* TO ARRIVE AT **and** ON)

an, auf, bei, um, zu

It is not possible to cover every translation of 'at' into German but the following covers the majority of cases.

If you buy s.t. 'at' a shop or work 'at' a place, the word you need is **bei**, e.g. **Ich hab's bei Hertie gekauft** 'I bought it at Hertie' (a department store), **Er arbeitet bei Mercedes in Stuttgart** 'He works at/for Mercedes in Stuttgart'. **Bei** expresses 'at' s.o.'s house, e.g. **Er wohnt bei mir/seinen Eltern** 'He lives at my place/at his parents' place' (= with his parents). **Bei**, together with the definite article, is also used for 'at' with mealtimes, e.g. **beim Frühstück/Mittagessen/Abendessen** 'at breakfast/lunch/dinner'.[5]

'At' with reference to public buildings is often **auf**, e.g. **auf der Post/Bank** 'at the post-office/bank', **auf dem Markt** 'at the market' (*see* TO). But there are buildings where **an** is required, e.g. **am Bahnhof** 'at the station'. **An** is also required for university, e.g. **Mein Sohn ist an der Universität** 'My son is at (the) university', i.e. both studying there and physically there at the moment. He is 'at' school, on the other hand, is in both senses **in der Schule** or **auf dem Gymnasium** (*see* SCHOOL).

As **an** means 'on' or 'at' the edge of things (*see* ON where **an** is contrasted with **auf**), it is the word required in the following contexts: **am Tisch** 'at the table', **am Strand** 'at/on the beach', **Er wohnt an der Küste** 'He lives at/on the coast'.

Although 'at' with times of the clock is **um**, **zu** is required for 'at midday' but **um** for 'at midnight', e.g. **um drei Uhr, zu Mittag, um Mitternacht**. 'At' with festive times such Christmas, Easter, Whitsuntide is **zu**, e.g. **zu Weihnachten/Ostern/Pfingsten**.

---

[4] Do not confuse this verb with **(be)fördern**, which is a totally different verb meaning 'to promote/support'.

[5] Note that **zum Frühstück/Mittagessen/Abendessen** means 'for breakfast' etc., e.g. **Was habt ihr zum Frühstück gegessen?** 'What did you have for breakfast?'.

'At home' is **zu Haus(e)**, sometimes written **zuhaus(e)**. The rather formal sounding 'at', as in 'the Roman baths at Bath' where one would normally simply say 'in', can be rendered equally formally in German by the use of **zu**, e.g. **der Dom zu Köln** 'the cathedral at/in Cologne'.

the/to attack

der Anfall, der Angriff, der Anschlag, der Infarkt; anfallen, angreifen, überfallen

A 'heart attack' is either a **Herzschlag, Herzanfall** or a **Herzinfarkt**, the last strictly speaking being a coronary, e.g. **Meine Oma hat einen Herzanfall/-infarkt/-schlag gehabt** 'My grandma has had a heart attack'. All three words can also be used in the fig. sense, e.g. **Ich habe fast einen Herzanfall/-infarkt/-schlag gekriegt** 'I nearly had a heart attack'.

Anfall tends to be limited to the medical field, e.g. **ein Fieberanfall** 'an attack of fever', **ein Anfall von Heuschnupfen** 'an attack of hay fever'.

'The/to attack' in the military or sporting sense is **Angriff/angreifen**, e.g. **Angriff ist die beste Verteidigung** 'Attack is the best form of defence', **Ausländer werden immer noch fast täglich von Rechtsradikalen angegriffen** 'Foreigners are still being attacked almost daily by right-wingers'. These words thus also render 'assault'. In the sense of 'assault' **überfallen** is also common, e.g. **Der Mann ist unterwegs nach Hause von der Arbeit überfallen worden** 'The man was attacked/assaulted on the way home from work'.

An 'attack' or 'attempt' on one's life is an **Anschlag**, e.g. **Es wurde ein Anschlag auf sein Leben gemacht/verübt** 'An attack/attempt was made on his life'. The object of the attack does not necessarily have to be a person. Although there is also a verb **anschlagen**, it does not translate as 'to attack'.

to attract

anlocken, anziehen, hinziehen, locken

'To attract', meaning 'to appeal to', is **anziehen**, e.g. **Er zieht die Mädchen hordenweise an** 'He attracts the girls in hordes', **Die Ausstellung hat viele Besucher angezogen** 'The exhibition attracted many visitors'. Very close in meaning is **anlocken**, which is somewhat more active than **anziehen** (compare 'to entice') – in the first example it might add a slightly sinister flavour, i.e. luring or enticing, but in the second would differ little in meaning from **anziehen**.

'To feel attracted' to s.o. can be expressed using either **angezogen** or less commonly **hingezogen**, but with differing syntax, e.g. **Sie fühlte sich von ihm stark angezogen/zu ihm stark hingezogen** 'She felt really attracted to him'; use of **hinziehen** is more or less limited to this expression.

Anlocken is used for attracting s.o. irresistibly somewhere, e.g. **Dieses schöne Gebiet lockt jedes Jahr 8 Millionen Touristen an** 'This beautiful area attracts 8 million tourists every year' (but **anziehen** is possible here too), **Süßigkeit lockt Insekten an** 'Sweetness attracts insects'.

Locken, without the prefix, is used when the place s.o. or s.t. is being attracted *to* is mentioned, but its most appropriate translation is not always 'to attract', e.g. **Die wunderbare Luft lockte uns hinauf in die Berge** 'The wonderful air attracted/enticed/drew us up into the mountains'.

to avoid

meiden, vermeiden

Meiden is used for avoiding or keeping away from people, places and food, e.g. **Seitdem meidet er mich** 'He has avoided me ever since', **Wegen meiner Allergie muss ich alle Meeresfrüchte**

meiden 'Because of my allergy I have to avoid all seafood'.

The object of **vermeiden** is an abstract like a difficulty, panic or danger, e.g. **Wir wollen jeden Zeitverlust/jedes Missverständnis vermeiden** 'We want to avoid any loss of time/misunderstanding', **Ich gehe nicht, wenn ich es vermeiden kann** 'I am not going if I can avoid it'. If s.o. wants to avoid doing s.t., i.e. an action in '-ing', **vermeiden** not **meiden** must be used, e.g. **Seit dem Unfall vermeidet er, ins Zentrum zu fahren** 'Since the accident he has avoided driving into the city centre', but **Seitdem meidet er das Zentrum** 'He has avoided the city centre ever since'. The idiom 'That can't be avoided' is also expressed with this verb: **Das lässt sich nicht vermeiden.**

bad

böse, schlecht, schlimm, übel

Schlecht is 'bad' as the opposite of 'good' and refers to s.t. being of inferior quality, e.g. **Ich habe ein schlechtes Gedächtnis** 'I have a bad memory', **Er spricht schlechtes Englisch** 'He speaks English badly, **Das ist nicht schlecht, du!** 'That's not bad, you know' (= quite good, said of s.o.'s achievement).

Schlimm implies disaster, e.g. **Es war ein schlimmes Zugunglück** 'It was a bad train accident', **Das ist nicht so schlimm** 'That's not so bad' (= not the end of the world).

Übel is an emphatic word implying great dislike or loathing and often equates with 'nasty', e.g. **Er ist ein übler Bursche** 'He's a bad/nasty guy', **Es ist eine üble Sache** 'It is a bad thing/nasty business'. It is commonly used with **gar nicht** to express s.t. positive, e.g. **Das schmeckt gar nicht so übel** 'That doesn't taste at all bad'.

Böse translates 'bad' in certain common standard expressions, e.g. **Dies sind böse Zeiten** 'These are bad times', **Es sieht böse aus** 'Things look bad', but it can also render 'bad/nasty' of sores and coughs, for example.

the bag

der Beutel, der Koffer, der Sack, die Tasche, die Tüte

A **Tasche** is a 'bag' used for carrying things in. Any bag used for shopping is a **Tasche** or **Tragetasche**, the latter word also being used for the plastic carry bags provided in shops (NB at a price in Germany!). A 'shopping bag' in general is an **Einkaufstasche** and a 'handbag' a **Handtasche**.

A small bag, such as used for packing individual items etc. in, is a **Tüte** (**Plastiktüte, Papiertüte**).

A **Sack** is much larger than a **Tüte** and is generally used where we might also use 'sack' instead of 'bag', e.g. **ein Sack Kartoffeln** 'a bag/sack of potatoes', **ein Schlafsack** 'a sleeping bag'.

A **Beutel** is in fact a 'pouch', but in some contexts renders 'bag', e.g. **Teebeutel** 'tea bag', **Geldbeutel** 'money bag'.

Where you refer to a 'suitcase' as a 'bag', the word required is **Koffer**.

the balance

die Balance, die Bilanz, das Gleichgewicht

Balance (pron. *balangs*) refers to equilibrium, e.g. **Er hat die Balance verloren** 'He lost his balance'. This is synonymous with the native German word **Gleichgewicht**. **Bilanz** refers to balance in the economic sense of balanced books but is also used fig., e.g. **Die Bilanz des Krieges war über 10 000 Tote** 'The balance of the war (= end result) was over 10,000 casualties'.

to bear, endure, stand

aushalten, ausstehen, ertragen, vertragen

Ausstehen, which is always used with **nicht,** is commonly used of people you find hard to bear, e.g. **Ich kann ihn nicht ausstehen** 'I can't bear/stand him'. Such people and things are **unausstehlich** 'unbearable'. Situations that are hard 'to bear' require **aushalten,** e.g. **Er hielt es in dem Zimmer nicht mehr aus** 'He couldn't stand being in that room any longer', **Ich halte es vor Hitze nicht mehr aus** 'I can't stand the heat'.

When you have 'to bear/endure' pain, suffering, s.o.'s moods etc., **ertragen** is appropriate, e.g. **Ich kann diese Schmerzen/seine Launen nicht mehr ertragen** 'I can't bear this pain/his moods any longer'. But you can use **ertragen** instead of **ausstehen** of people too, but it is much stronger than **ausstehen,** e.g. **Ich kann sie nicht ertragen** 'I loathe her/I can't abide her'. Such things and people are **unerträglich** 'intolerable/insufferable'.

Nicht vertragen, although close in meaning to the above, is used in those contexts where 'not to be able to take' is the appropriate translation in English, e.g. **Meersfrüchte verträgt er nicht/kann er nicht vertragen** 'He can't take seafood', **Meine Haut verträgt keine Wolle** 'My skin can't take wool'. **Unverträglich** thus translates as 'incompatible' (with s.t. else) in the medical sense, but also means 'cantankerous/quarrelsome'.

before

bevor, ehe, vor, vorher, (wie) nie zuvor

The difficulty here lies in the fact that 'before' can be a preposition, a conjunction or an adverb and in all three cases German uses a different word.

Vor is a two-way preposition meaning 'before' in both the temporal and locative sense, e.g. **Das war schon vor dem Krieg passiert** 'That had already happened before the war', **Sie ist vor meinen Augen in Ohnmacht gefallen** 'She fainted before (= in front of) my eyes'.

Bevor is a subordinating conjunction and must thus always introduce a whole clause, e.g. **Die ganze Familie wohnte in Bosnien, bevor der Krieg begann** 'The whole family was living in Bosnia before the war began'. Synonymous with **bevor** is **ehe,** but it is less common (*see* **eher** under RATHER).

As an adverb in expressions of time 'before' can be rendered by **davor, vorher** or **zuvor,** e.g. **Er war schon am Tag davor/vorher/zuvor angekommen** 'He'd already arrived the day before', **vier Wochen davor/vorher/zuvor** 'four weeks before'. 'Ever/never before' is best rendered by **je/nie zuvor,** e.g. **Die Opposition im Landtag ist stärker als/denn je zuvor** 'The opposition in the state parliament is stronger than ever before', **Ich hatte ihn nie zuvor gesehen** 'I had never seen him before'. Whenever 'before' means 'previously' or 'before that' use **zuvor** or **davor,** e.g. **Das zeigte, wie wenig sie sich zuvor bemüht hatten** 'That showed how little effort they had made before/previously', **Zuvor besuchte der Außenminister eine Fabrik in der Nähe von Peking** 'Prior to/before that the minister for foreign affairs visited a factory near Peking' (*see* **vorher** under FIRST).

The expression **im Vorjahr** is synonymous with **im Jahr zuvor** (the year before/the previous year), and 'the day before yesterday' is simply **vorgestern,** e.g. **vorgestern Morgen** '(on) Saturday morning' (assuming today is Monday).

bed, to go to bed, be in bed

ins Bett, zu Bett, im Bett

'To go to bed' is usually expressed by **ins Bett gehen** but in colloquial north German you also hear **zu Bett gehen.** The definite article is always required with **in** when going to and being in bed, e.g. **Du solltest dich am besten gleich ins Bett legen** 'You should go straight to bed', **Er liegt noch im Bett** 'He's still lying in bed'.

to begin; the beginning

anfangen, antreten, beginnen; der Anfang, der Beginn

Anfang(en) and **Beginn(en)** are synonymous in intransitive contexts, e.g. **Die Vorstellung hat schon angefangen/begonnen** 'The performance has already begun/started'. **Beginnen** is intransitive but can take a prepositional object using **mit**, e.g. **In Nord-Korea ist mit dem Bau eines Kernkraftwerks begonnen worden** 'The construction of an atomic energy plant has begun in North Korea'. **Anfangen** can be used transitively, e.g. **Er hat den Brief schon angefangen** 'He has already started the letter'.

The noun **Anfang** is more commonly used than **Beginn** and is always used in the following expressions: **der Anfang vom Ende** 'the beginning of the end', **von** (not **vom**) **Anfang an** 'from the beginning/outset', **am Anfang** 'at the beginning/to begin with', **Anfang/Ende des Monats** 'at the beginning/end of the month'.

'To begin' a prison sentence, apprenticeship or job (i.e. to take it up, to take office) is **antreten**, e.g. **Der Mörder hat seine Haftstrafe angetreten** 'The murderer has started his custodial sentence', **Er hat letzte Woche seine neue Stelle angetreten** 'He started his new job last week'.

to behave; the behaviour

sich benehmen, sich verhalten; das Benehmen, das Verhalten

The behaviour of an individual, i.e. his measuring up to certain standards, is his **Benehmen** and thus the corresponding verb is appropriate in such cases, e.g. **Sein Benehmen lässt sehr viel zu wünschen übrig** 'His behaviour leaves a great deal to be desired', **Er hat sich sehr schlecht benommen** 'He behaved very badly', **Benimm dich!** 'Behave yourself!'.

Verhalten and the corresponding verb refer to a person's or animal's behaviour in a given situation, as well as to substances, and is also appropriate when describing an attitude towards a country or government, e.g. **Es gibt keine Instruktionen für die Blauhelmsoldaten, wie sie sich in Afrika zu verhalten hätten** 'There are no instructions as to how the UN soldiers are to behave in Africa', **Sein Verhalten lässt keine andere Erklärung zu** 'His behaviour (i.e. how he acted in this specific situation) permits no other explanation'.

to believe (*see* to think)

glauben an/in, trauen

When the object of **glauben** is personal, it goes in the dat., but an impersonal object goes in the acc., e.g. **Fliegen ist sicherer als Autofahren. Glauben Sie mir!** 'Flying is safer than driving. Believe me!', **Ich glaube dir nicht** 'I don't believe you', **Ich glaube kein Wort davon** 'I don't believe a word of it'. When the object is a person, German often optionally includes the object **es/das** as well, e.g. **Das glaub' ich dir/Ich glaub's dir** 'I believe you'.

The idiom 'not to believe one's eyes/ears' requires the verb **trauen** (+ dat.), e.g. **Er traute seinen Augen/Ohren nicht** 'He couldn't believe his eyes/ears'.

to belong

angehören, hingehören, gehören, zugehören

When items 'belong' to people, the verb required is **gehören**, e.g. **Wem gehört dieses Buch?** 'Who does this book belong to?' (= Whose book is this this?), **Es gehört mir** 'It belongs to me'.

Angehören refers to 'belonging' as a member to a club or organisation, e.g. **Turkmenistan gehört seit 1992 der Organisation für Sicherheit und Zusammenarbeit in Europa an** 'Turkmenistan has belonged to the Organisation for Security and Cooperation in Europe since 1992'. It can also be used figuratively as in the following sentence: **Das alles gehört jetzt der Vergangenheit an** 'All that now belongs to the past'. Note the derived nouns die **Staatsangehörigkeit** 'nationality', **der/die Angehörige** 'relative' (*see* RELATIVE).

Gehören zu refers to 'belonging' to a general group or being part of something, e.g. **Die Internet-Deutschen gehören zu einer neuen sozialen Klasse** 'Internet Germans belong to a new social class', **Rembrandt gehört zu den größten holländischen Malern** 'Rembrandt is one of the greatest Dutch painters', **Zu welchem Land gehört Helgoland?** 'What country does Heligoland belong to (= which country is it part of)?'. You will find **zugehören** in dictionaries but it is antiquated and does not need to be learnt.

Other prepositions (+ acc.) can follow **gehören** when it means 'belonging' in the sense of 'ought to be', e.g. **Dieser Dieb gehört ins Gefängnis** 'This thief ought to be/belongs in prison', **Der Trauring gehört an den dritten Finger** 'The wedding ring belongs on the third finger'.

Hingehören refers to 'belonging' in the sense of something's rightful place, e.g. **Ich wollte aufräumen, wusste aber nicht, wo alles in deiner Küche hingehört** 'I wanted to tidy up but didn't know where everything belongs/goes in your kitchen'.

big, fat, large, tall

dick, fett, fettig, groß, hoch, lang

Groß can mean 'big/large', 'tall' (of people) or 'great', context usually making it clear, e.g. **Napoleon war ein großer Mann** 'Napoleon was a

great man' (as we know he was in fact short), **A: Wie groß bist du? B: Ich bin ein Meter fünfundachtzig** 'A: How tall are you? B: 1.85cm'. But **Helmut Kohl ist ein großer Mann** is ambiguous as this can mean large, tall or great. Likewise die **Größe** can mean 'size' (also and particularly of clothing[6]) as well as 'height' (of people) and 'greatness'. If clothes are 'too big' they are **zu weit**, the opposite being **zu eng** ('too tight/small'; *see* NARROW), but also **zu groß** although this can mean 'too long' as well and not merely the opposite of 'too tight'; in the same way **zu klein**, which can possibly mean 'too short', is not necessarily the same as **zu eng**.

Lang in a few limited contexts can also refer to a person's height, e.g. **Er ist ein langer Lulatsch/eine lange Latte** 'He's a real beanpole'.

'Tall' things are **hoch** not **groß**, e.g. **ein hoher Baum** 'a tall tree', **ein hohes Gebäude** 'a tall building'.

'Fat' people are **dick**; they can also be called **fett**, but this is a very negative word and implies fatter than **dick**. Otherwise **fett** refers to 'fatty' foods, although a 'fatty' or 'greasy' spot, for example, is **fettig**, as is 'greasy hair', **fettige Haare**.

to blow

blasen, wehen

Wehen refers to the blowing of the wind, e.g. **Es weht ein warmer Wind** 'There is a warm wind blowing'. **Blasen** is what you do with your mouth, e.g. **A: Die Kartoffeln sind zu heiß. B: Blas denn drauf!** 'A: The potatoes are too hot. B: Then blow on them!' It is also used for wind instruments.

---

[6]   There are several ways of asking what size s.o. is: **Welche Größe trägst du?** 'What size do you take/are you?', **Welche Größe haben deine Hosen?** 'What size are your pants?', **Welche Hosengröße hast du?** 'What size pants do you wear?'.

Nevertheless, the idiom **Es bläst** can refer to wind but is stronger than **Es weht**, i.e. **Es bläst/weht ein starker Wind** 'There's a strong wind blowing'.

the body

der Körper, der Leib, die Leiche, der Leichnam, der Tote

The most usual word for one's body is **Körper**. **Leib** tends only to be used in standard expressions or religious contexts, e.g. **Gefahr für Leib und Leben** 'Danger to life and limb', **der Leib Christi** 'the Body of Christ', but there are some more everyday contexts in which it is used, e.g. **Leibesübung** 'physical exercise'.

Leiche means 'dead body' and thus corresponds to 'corpse'. A **Leichnam** is also deceased, but is a very formal word, e.g. **den Leichnam begleiten** 'to accompany the body (coffin)', **Fronleichnam** 'the Feast of Corpus Christi'.

the boss, head, manager

der Boss, der Chef, der Direktor, das Haupt, der Manager, das Oberhaupt

The usual word for your 'boss' at work is **der Chef/die Chefin**, an old French loanword, e.g. **Sie ist ihre eigene Chefin** 'She is her own boss'. Lately the English loan **Boss** (no fem. form) has been making inroads, usually used informally.

Where the 'head' or 'boss' of an organisation, for example a bank or insurance company, might be called a 'manager' in English, the same word has been drafted into service in German (no plural ending and fem. form in -in). The older French loan **der Direktor** (fem. form -in) can be used in this sense too, but this is also used to render 'headmaster/mistress' of a school, as is **Schulleiter(in)**.

The 'head of a church' is referred to as **das Kirchenoberhaupt** and the 'head of state' as **das Staatsoberhaupt**, e.g. **Der Papst ist das Oberhaupt der katholischen Kirche und der Bundespräsident ist das Staatsoberhaupt der Bundesrepublik Deutschland** 'The pope is the head of the Catholic church and the federal president is the German head of state'.

Both **Chef-** and **Haupt-** can be prefixed to professions to render the 'main' or 'chief' person, e.g. **Die Chefanklägerin des UN-Kriegsverbrechertribunals in Den Haag ist Italienerin** 'The chief prosecutor of the UN War Crimes Tribunal in The Hague is an Italian', **der Hauptlieferant von Uran in der dritten Welt** 'the main/chief supplier of uranium in the third world'. **Haupt** is of course also prefixed to countless inanimate nouns to render 'main' or 'head', e.g. **das Hauptpostamt** 'the main post office (GPO)', **der Hauptbahnhof** 'the main/central station'.

both

beide, sowohl . . . als (auch)

'Both' as an indefinite pronoun or adjective is rendered by **beide**, e.g. **Beide/beide Kinder möchten mitkommen** 'Both/both children would like to come along'. As a pronoun it is often used in combination with **alle** with no change in meaning, e.g. **Alle beide möchten mitkommen**. Note that **beide** is also commonly used adjectivally after articles and possessives where it usually translates as 'two' rather than 'both', e.g. **die/meine beiden Brüder** 'the/my two brothers'.

The neuter form **beides** refers to two *things* collectively, e.g. **A: Essen wir heute Abend Schweine- oder Rindfleisch? B: Beides** 'A: Are we having pork or beef tonight? B: Both'. Note the singular verbal form when **beides** is the subject of a verb: **Beides ist lecker** 'Both are delicious', **Beides schmeckt gut** 'Both taste good'.

'Both' in the expression 'both . . . and' must be rendered by **sowohl . . . als (auch)**, e.g. **Sowohl seine Mutter als (auch) sein Vater sind mit ihm zum Schulleiter gegangen** 'Both his mother and his father went with him to the headmaster'.

the bottle, jar

die Flasche, das Glas, die Pulle

'Bottle' is usually expressed by **Flasche** but only contains liquids. 'A bottle of olives/capers/cherries', where the word is interchangeable with 'jar', is rendered by **Glas**, rendering a glass container for non-fluids, e.g. **ein Glas Oliven/Kapern/Kirschen**. A colloquial synonym of **Flasche** used for alcoholic beverages is **Pulle**.

the boy, man, bloke, chap

der Bub, der Bursche, der Herr, der Junge, der Kerl, der Mann, der Typ

Mann generally corresponds to 'man', in addition to rendering 'husband'. Where in English we have a tendency to sometimes refer to men as gentlemen, German possibly has a greater tendency to use **Herr**, e.g. **Ein älterer Herr hat Sie eben gesucht** 'A somewhat older man/gentleman was just looking for you', **ein Herren(fahr)rad** 'a man's bike', **ein Herrenfriseur** 'men's/gents' hairdresser'. Toilets are always marked **Herren**, not **Männer** (*see* PERSON for comments on plurals in **-männer/-leute**).

The most usual word for 'boy' is **Junge** which has a pl. in **-n** in standard German but you will often hear people in the north say **Jungs/Jungens**, whereas in the south you commonly hear **der Bub** (pl. **-en**).

'Bloke/chap/guy' etc. are perhaps best rendered by **Kerl**, but **Bursche**, which is also a regional word

for 'boy', is used with this meaning too, as is **Typ**, e.g. **Der Daniel ist ein guter Kerl/ein netter Bursche/ein komischer Typ** 'Daniel is a good bloke/a nice chap/a funny guy'.

the box, tin

die Büchse, die Dose, der Karton, das Kästchen, der Kasten, die Kiste, die Schachtel

A 'tin can' is **die Dose** and thus **Dosen-** expresses 'tinned/canned', e.g. **eine Dose Bier** 'a tin/can of beer', **Dosenmilch** 'tinned/canned milk'. A **Büchse** is also a 'tin can' but seems to be used chiefly in a few standard combinations, e.g. **die Sammelbüchse** 'collection box (for money)', **die Büchse der Pandora** 'Pandora's box', but there are contexts where it is interchangeable with **Dose**, e.g. **Konservenbüchse/-dose** 'tin/can' (for food), **die Sparbüchse/-dose** 'money box' (piggy bank).

A 'letter-box', both your own and a public one for posting letters in, is **der Briefkasten**. Synonymous with **Briefkasten**, but only for a pillar box, is **Postkasten**. **Kasten** can also refer to a 'crate' (e.g. **ein Kasten Bier/ein Bierkasten** 'a crate of beer/a beer crate'), but in this sense is interchangeable with **Kiste**. But **Kiste** can also mean 'box', particularly one made of wood, e.g. **eine Kiste Wein** 'a case of wine', **eine Kiste Zigarren** 'a box of cigars', **eine Schatzkiste = ein Schatzkästchen** (small) 'a treasure chest'. A 'post-office box' in the sense of one you rent at a post-office to receive mail in and thus used in official addresses, is a **Postfach**.

In the following example **Kästchen** is used because the box is made of metal: **Der Voice Recorder ist jenes kleine Kästchen, das alles, was im Cockpit gesagt wird, speichert** 'The voice recorder is that little box that records everything that is said in the cockpit'.

A 'cardboard box' is a **Schachtel** if small and a **Karton** if larger, the dividing line between the two not always being clear; one says for example **Hutschachtel** (hatbox) but **Schuhkarton** (shoebox). Keep in mind that **Karton** is the German word for 'cardboard'. A cigarette or matchbox is a **Schachtel**, e.g. **eine Schachtel Streichhölzer/eine Streichholzschachtel** 'a box of matches/a matchbox', but boxes used for shifting house, for example, are **Kartons**.

the branch

der Ast, die Filiale, die Niederlassung, der Zweig, die Zweigstelle

The 'branch' of a tree is **der Ast**, but **der Zweig** can be used too for a smaller branch as well as a twig.

The 'branch' of a bank or business firm is rendered by **die Zweigstelle** or **die Filiale**, which are more or less synonymous. A larger concern may well refer to its branch as a **Niederlassung**, e.g. **VW hat seit kurzem eine Niederlassung in Argentinien** 'Volkswagen recently established a branch in Argentina'.

The French loanword **die Branche** enjoys enormous frequency in German but refers to a '(branch of) industry' and does not often translate as branch into English, e.g. **Es geht der Autobranche im Augenblick sehr schlecht** 'The car industry is not doing well at the moment'.

the (loaf of) bread, breadroll, sandwich

das Brot, der Laib; das Brötchen, das Rundstück, die Schrippe, die Semmel, die Wecke

'A loaf of bread' is **ein Brot** and **zwei Brote** means 'two loaves of bread' and thus 'a rye/wholemeal loaf' or 'a loaf of rye/wholemeal bread' is ein **Roggen-/Vollkornbrot**. The word **Laib**, literally meaning 'loaf', is not really used in standard German any more.

Because of the importance of breadrolls to German breakfast culture, there is a wide variety of names for breadrolls. Of course some of these words designate various sorts (i.e. flavours) of roll (e.g. **Mohnbrötchen** 'poppyseed roll'), and these are too numerous to list, but some of these words are used regionally to the exclusion of the others. The most general word understood everywhere is **(Frühstücks)brötchen**, but you will also hear **das Rundstück** (north of Hamburg), **die Schrippe** (Berlin), **die Wecke** (Stuttgart), **die Semmel** (Bavaria and Austria).

A 'piece of bread and butter' is **ein Butterbrot** but this can also refer to a 'sandwich', as do **ein belegtes Brot** (or **Brötchen** if made from a roll) and **die Stulle** (in North Germany). German sandwiches are usually lidless by the way.

to build

bauen, erbauen

'To build' is usually **bauen**, e.g. **Wir lassen ein Ferienhaus am Bodensee bauen** 'We are having a holiday home built on Lake Constance'.

Erbauen, in keeping with one of the functions of **er-**, can only refer to s.t. having been built, i.e. the completed action. **Erbaut** can thus be synonymous with **gebaut** but is more elevated; it could not be used in an everyday context such as in the above example but the two are interchangeable in the following example: **Der Aachener Dom wurde unter der Herrschaft Karls des Großen erbaut** 'The Aachen cathedral was constructed during the reign of Charlemagne'. A plaque on an historic building would always read **Im Jahre 1820 erbaut**, for example.

the building

der Bau, das Gebäude, der Plattenbau

Der Bau usually refers to 'building' in the sense of 'construction', e.g. **Wie lange hat der Bau dieser Kirche gedauert?** 'How long did the construction of this building take?'. In compounds, however, it refers to a 'building', e.g. **der Plattenbau**, plural **Plattenbauten**, the large, characterless residential blocks so typical of eastern Germany. The most general word for a 'building' is however **das Gebäude**, e.g. **Dieses Gebäude stammt aus dem siebzehnten Jahrhundert** 'This building dates from the seventeenth century'.

Many Germans do not live in free-standing houses (**Einfamilienhäuser**) but in terrace houses (**Reihenhäuser**) or apartments (**Wohnungen**) or perhaps in edifices with two houses under one roof (**Zweifamilienhäuser**). The building as a whole may be referred to as a house, e.g. **Wie viele Wohnungen gibt es in diesem Haus?** 'How many apartments/flats are there in this building?', **Er wohnt im zweiten Haus von der Ecke** 'He lives in the second building from the corner', where this building might be a block of flats, and not a house in the English sense.

to burn

abbrennen, anbrennen, brennen, niederbrennen, verbrennen

First and foremost you need to be aware that **brennen** is intr. and **verbrennen** tr., thus the former equates to being on fire whereas the latter refers to s.o. burning s.t., e.g. **Ich rieche Rauch. Was brennt?** 'I can smell smoke. What is burning?', **Sie hat all seine Briefe verbrannt** 'She burnt all his letters'. 'To burn yourself' (on s.t.) is **sich verbrennen**. **Brennen** is also used for food burning your mouth, e.g. **Dieser Senf schmeckt mir nicht. Er brennt** 'I don't like this mustard. It burns', but **Ich habe mir den Mund verbrannt** 'I burnt my mouth'. Note **das Sodbrennen** 'heartburn' and the fig. expression **sich** (dat.) **bei etwas die Finger verbrennen** 'to burn your fingers on s.t.'.

Brennen can be used transitively 'to burn' a CD, e.g. **Wirst du mir bitte eine CD davon brennen?** 'Will you please burn me a CD of it?'.

'To burn' something while cooking, i.e. either to turn it black or to let it stick to the pan, is **anbrennen lassen**, e.g. **Er hat die Suppe anbrennen lassen** 'He has burnt the soup'.

'To burn down' (intr.) is **abbrennen** while **niederbrennen** renders 'to burn down' in both tr. and intr. senses, e.g. **Die Dorfskirche ist abgebrannt/niedergebrannt** 'The village church burnt down', **Die Nazis haben die Synagoge niedergebrannt** 'The Nazis burnt the synagogue down'.

to bury

beerdigen, begraben, einbuddeln, vergraben

'To bury' s.o. in the sense of taking them to their grave is **beerdigen** or **begraben**, e.g. **Mein Vater wird heute Nachmittag um vier beerdigt/begraben** 'My father is being buried at four this afternoon'. For all other things use **begraben**, e.g. **Wir haben den Hund unter der Eiche hinten im Garten begraben** 'We buried the dog under the oaktree at the back of the garden'. If a building collapses and buries people this too requires **begraben**.

If s.t. or s.o. (e.g. a murder victim) is 'buried' in secret, **vergraben** is used but this would also apply to a time capsule, e.g. **Er hat das Geld vergraben, und es ist nie wieder gefunden worden** 'He buried the money and it was never ever found'. **Vergraben** is also used for figuratively burying yourself in s.t., e.g. **Er hat sich in Arbeit** (acc.) **vergraben** 'He has buried himself in work'.

In the north you will hear the word **einbuddeln**, a colloquial synonym of **begraben** and thus not used in serious contexts, e.g. **Die Kinder haben sich in den Sand eingebuddelt** 'The kids buried themselves in the sand'.

but

aber, doch, sondern

'But' is usually expressed by **aber**, but where the previous clause contains a negative and the 'but' that follows contradicts that clause, **sondern** must be used, e.g. **Wir sind nicht ins Kino gegangen, sondern an den Strand** 'We didn't go to the movies but to the beach', **Es ist nicht schwarz, sondern dunkelblau** 'It is not black but dark blue'. The following example does not contain a contradiction and thus although 'but' is preceded by a negative, it is rendered by **aber**, e.g. **Diese Leute sind nicht reich, aber freizügig** 'These people are not rich but generous' (i.e. both not rich and generous); compare **Sie sind nicht reich, sondern arm** 'They are not rich, but poor'.

'Not only . . . but also' is rendered by **nicht nur . . . sondern auch**, e.g. **Das Buch ist nicht nur schon erschienen, sondern es ist auch schon ausverkauft** 'The book has not only already appeared, but has already sold out', or **Nicht nur ist das Buch schon erschienen, sondern es ist schon ausverkauft** 'Not only has the book already appeared, but it has already sold out'.

to buy

abkaufen, sich anschaffen, erkaufen, erwerben, (sich) kaufen, lösen

Kaufen is of course the usual verb for 'to buy'. It is commonly used reflexively in exactly the same way we talk of 'buying yourself' a new car, e.g.

Er hat (sich) den neuesten Mercedes gekauft 'He's bought (himself) the newest Mercedes'. Similar in meaning to **sich kaufen** and meaning literally 'to get oneself' s.t. is **sich (dat.) anschaffen**, e.g. **Er hat sich ein neues Auto angeschafft** 'He's bought/got himself a new car'.

Sich anschaffen is an everyday way of expressing 'to acquire (for oneself)', whether by buying it or not, whereas **erwerben** is a more formal synonym and thus equates more or less with 'to purchase', e.g. **Die Partei hat vor kurzem ein neues Hauptquartier in Berlin erworben** 'The party recently bought/purchased/acquired new headquarters in Berlin'.

'To buy' s.t. *from* s.o. is **jdm etwas abkaufen**, e.g. **50 Millionen Kubikmeter Wasser wollen die Israelis den Türken pro Jahr abkaufen** 'The Israelis want to buy 50 million cubic metres of water annually from the Turks'.

When 'buying' a ticket, **kaufen** can be used but you will also hear **eine Karte lösen**, particularly when a ticket is purchased from an automat as on a bus or tram, e.g. **Parkschein hier lösen** 'Purchase your parking ticket here'.

You will see the following in retail businesses: **An- und Verkauf** 'We buy and sell'. **Ankaufen** is best limited to such contexts where a shop or business buys from you to sell on to others.

See TO PAY for **erkaufen**.

careful(ly)

sorgfältig, vorsichtig; Vorsicht

Sorgfältig means to do something with accuracy, e.g. **Man muss Druckfahnen ganz sorgfältig durchnehmen** 'One has to go through galley proofs very carefully'. **Vorsichtig** means taking care not to come to any harm or not to break s.t., i.e. taking caution, e.g. **Auf den Alpenstraßen**

muss man ganz vorsichtig(= mit Vorsicht) fahren 'You have to drive very carefully on alpine roads'. The imperative 'Careful/Take care!' is rendered simply by the noun **Vorsicht!**

the cake, biscuit

der Biskuit, das Gebäck, der Keks, der Kuchen, die Torte

Kuchen is used as a general term for all cakes, like the English word, e.g. **Kaffee und Kuchen am Sonntagmorgen ist eine deutsche Sitte** 'Coffee and cake on a Sunday morning is a German custom'. But when it comes to specific sorts of cakes, the Germans make a broad distinction between **Kuchen** and **Torte**. Plainer 'cakey' cakes are **Kuchen**, whereas cream and custard filled ones are **Torten**, e.g. **der Sandkuchen** 'Madeira cake', **die Schwarzwälderkirschtorte** 'Black Forest cake'.

A 'dog biscuit' is called a **Hundekuchen** and 'ginger bread' **Lebkuchen**, but the usual word for a 'biscuit' is **der Keks** (pl. -e), derived curiously enough from the English word 'cakes'. The word **Gebäck** is used as a collective for 'biscuits' and is thus synonymous with **Kekse**.

Biskuit, despite appearances, means 'sponge (cake)'.

to call, be called, name, rename, ring (up), telephone

anrufen, benennen, heißen, nennen, rufen, telefonieren, umbenennen, zurückrufen

'To call' or 'to ring (up)' is **anrufen**, e.g. **Sie ruft ihre Mutter jeden Tag an** 'She calls/rings her mother (up) every day'. 'To call/ring back' is simply **zurückrufen**, dropping the **an**, e.g. **Warum hast du (mich) nicht zurückgerufen?** 'Why didn't you ring (me) back?'. 'To telephone s.o.' is **mit jdm telefonieren** (actually 'to talk to s.o. on the phone'), e.g. **Ich habe schon mit ihm telefoniert = Ich habe ihn schon angerufen** 'I have already phoned/rung him'.

'To be called' meaning your name requires the verb **heißen**, e.g. **Er heißt Robert** 'His name is Robert', which can also be expressed as **Sein Name ist Robert**. This contrasts with '. . . but he is called Bob (by his friends)' which is expressed by **nennen**, e.g. **Er heißt Robert, aber er wird (von seinen Freunden) Bob genannt**.

Rufen renders the intr. verb 'to call' meaning 'to beckon', e.g. **Die Pflicht ruft** 'Duty calls'.

'To be called after' s.t. or s.o. is expressed by **benannt nach**, e.g. **Der Preis ist nach Leibnitz, dem letzten Universalgelehrten benannt** 'The prize is named after Leibniz, the last universal scholar', **Das Kind ist nach seinem Onkel benannt** 'The child is named after its uncle'. **Benennen** also means 'to name' in the sense of 'to mention', e.g. **Ich könnte Senatoren benennen, die Steuerhinterziehung begangen haben** 'I could name senators who have committed tax evasion'.

'To rename', i.e. to change the name of s.t., is **umbenennen**, e.g. **Nach der Wende sind viele Straßen in Berlin umbenannt worden** 'Many street names were changed in Berlin after the fall of the wall/Many streets in Berlin were renamed after the fall of the wall'.

to cancel, postpone, put off

absagen, annulieren, streichen, verlegen, verschieben

'To put off' s.t. till a later date is expressed by **verlegen auf** (+ acc.), e.g. **Wir haben die Feier auf nächsten Samstag verlegt** 'We have put the party off till next Saturday'. Note that by the addition of the prefix **vor-**, this expression can be used to bring s.t. forward too, in which case it is synonymous with **vorziehen**, e.g. **Wir haben die Feier auf Samstag vorverlegt/vorgezogen** 'We have brought the party forward to Saturday'. If you are simply putting s.t. off, i.e. postponing it without mentioning the new date, use **verschieben**, e.g. **Die Party ist verschoben worden** 'The party has been put off/postponed'. If s.t. is not merely postponed, but cancelled, use **absagen**, e.g. **Der Ausflug wurde wegen schlechten Wetters abgesagt** 'The excursion was cancelled because of bad weather'. If a bus or train is cancelled, use **streichen**, e.g. **Der Zug um 22.30 ist gestrichen worden** 'The 10.30 train has been cancelled'. At airports the word **annulieren** is used for cancelled flights, e.g. **Zwanzig Flüge wurden wegen Nebel annuliert** 'Twenty flights were cancelled because of fog'.

the car, truck, vehicle

das Auto, der Brummi,
der Gebrauchtwagen, die Karosse,
das Kraftfahrzeug, der Kraftwagen,
das Lastauto, der Laster, der Lastwagen,
die Limousine, der LKW, der PKW,
der Schlitten, der Wagen

The most usual word for a 'car' is **Auto**, but **Wagen** is a common synonym and is always used in the compound **Gebrauchtwagen** 'used car'. If using a brand name instead of the generic word for 'car', cars are always masculine, e.g. **Ich fahre einen Porsche/Mercedes** 'I drive a Porsche/Mercedes'.

PKW (pl. **PKWs**) is an official term meaning 'passenger vehicle', commonly used in contrast to **LKW**, 'truck', where vehicles are being assigned to different lanes, for example. The abbreviations stand for **Personen-** and **Lastkraftwagen** but the full form is seldom used.

Fahrzeug and **Kraftfahrzeug** mean '(motor)vehicle' but they too are rather official sounding

words, e.g. **das Nutzfahrzeug** 'commercial vehicle', **die Fahrzeugpapiere** 'vehicle documents', **die Kraftfahrzeugsteuer** 'motor vehicle tax'.

It is not unusual to refer to a 'truck' in general as an **LKW** or **Lkw** but the everyday words are **Laster** or **Lastwagen**. An informal word for 'truck' or 'lorry' is **Brummi**. A 'delivery van/truck' is a **Lieferwagen** and a 'removal van' is a **Möbelwagen**. All sorts of trucks are rendered by **Wagen**, e.g. **Feuerwehrwagen** 'firetruck', **Müllwagen** 'rubbish truck'. A 'railway car/carriage' is also an **(Eisenbahn)wagen**.

Schlitten (lit. 'sleigh') is a colloquial word for a large car, used in much the same way as 'tank' is in English and a **(Nobel)karosse** is a 'limousine' or otherwise a very swank car, whereas **die Limousine** translates 'sedan' in German.

the carpet, rug

der Bodenbelag, der Läufer, die Matte,
der Teppich, der Teppichboden

Teppich means a 'floor/wall rug', as well as a 'carpet', whereas a **Matte** is much smaller, i.e. a 'mat' not a 'rug'. But a **Teppich** must be movable, even if large. A wall to wall carpet (= carpeting) is expressed by **Teppichboden**, whereas **der Bodenbelag** actually means 'floor covering' in general, including carpet(ing). A **Läufer** is an elongated 'rug' as found on stairs or tables, also often called a 'runner' in English.

the castle

die Burg, der Palast, das Schloss

A 'castle' with defensive battlements is a **Burg**. Strictly speaking a **Schloss** is more a 'palace' than a 'castle' but many a German **Schloss** is called a 'castle' in English, e.g. **Schloss Neuschwanstein** in

Bavaria, and the ruined castle in Heidelberg is known as **das Heidelberger Schloss**. The many castles dotted along the Rhine are regarded as **Burgen** and those along the Loire, for example, as **Schlösser**. 'To build castles in the air' is **Luftschlösser bauen**.

As a **Schloss** is a sort of 'palace', you need to know where to draw the line between **Schloss** and **Palast**. **Palast** is used far less frequently in German than **Schloss** and is used mainly with reference to a few particular palaces where use of this word is customary, e.g. **Buckingham Palast, der Palast zu Versailles**. **Palast** is also used fig. and coll. where we might say 'mansion', e.g. **Er hat sich einen Palast gebaut** 'He (has) built himself a mansion'.

to catch

ertappen, erwischen, fangen, nehmen, schnappen

'To catch' a ball or thief requires **fangen**, which explains why a 'prisoner' or 'captive' is **der/die Gefangene**. Coll. **schnappen** can also be used for both balls and thieves. 'To catch' (i.e. see) s.o. doing s.t. is **erwischen**, with which **ertappen** is usually synonymous, e.g. **Der Ladenbesitzer hat das Kind beim Stehlen erwischt/ertappt** 'The shopkeeper caught the child stealing', **Er hat mich bei einer Lüge erwischt/ertappt** 'He caught me telling a lie'.

'To catch' a bus or train requires **nehmen**, e.g. **Welchen Zug nimmst du jeden Morgen?** 'What train do you catch every morning?'.

the chair

die Bank, die Couch, der Hocker, der Lehnstuhl, der Sessel, das Sofa, der Stuhl

The generic word is of course **Stuhl**. An 'armchair' or 'easy chair' is a **Lehnstuhl** or a **Sessel**, but in the south **Sessel** can simply mean a chair (i.e.

replaces **Stuhl**). **Couch** and **Sofa** are synonymous, whereas a **Hocker** is a 'stool', i.e. with no back or arms (< **hocken** 'to crouch, squat'), and **Bank** renders 'bench', both to sit on and to work at.

the chance

die Chance, die Gelegenheit, die Möglichkeit

The French loan **Chance** is pronounced in a variety of ways (e.g. 'schangs'), so pronounce it as in French until experience possibly teaches you otherwise. If you have a chance of doing or winning s.t., **Chance** is the word you need, e.g. **Mein Sohn hat eine gute Chance, ein Stipendium nach Frankreich zu gewinnen** 'My son has a good chance of winning a scholarship to France', **Die besten Chancen auf Sonnenschein gibt es am Freitag** 'The best chances of sunshine are on Friday' (note chance *of* = **auf** + acc.).

To get a chance to do s.t., i.e. where 'chance' is synonymous with 'opportunity', requires **Gelegenheit**, e.g. **Ich habe noch keine Gelegenheit gehabt, ihr zu schreiben** 'I have not yet had a chance to write to her'.

If there is a chance of s.t. happening, i.e. a likelihood, possibility or probability, use **Möglichkeit**, e.g. **Es gibt eine Möglichkeit, dass** (= es ist **möglich, dass . . .**) **die holländische Königin abdanken wird** 'There's a chance that the Dutch queen will abdicate'.

to change, to exchange, to swap

(sich) ändern, austauschen, drehen, kleinmachen, tauschen, umbenennen, umschlagen, umsteigen, umtauschen, (sich) verändern, sich verwandeln, wechseln

This is an extremely difficult verb to render in German, as the wide variety of alternatives illustrates. First and foremost you need to understand how **ändern** and **verändern** are used and when they require the reflexive pronoun. Both these verbs mean 'change' in the sense of transformation. If there is an object, i.e. you need a transitive verb, then stick to **ändern** and you will seldom go wrong, e.g. **Ich möchte die Form der Auffahrt ändern** 'I'd like to change the shape of the driveway'. But more often than not there will be no object, in which case you will need to use **sich ändern**, e.g. **Meine Adresse hat sich geändert** 'My address has changed', **Die Zeiten haben sich geändert** 'Times have changed'.

Although **verändern** can be used transitively, it is much more commonly used reflexively in which case it is usually interchangeable with **sich ändern**, so use the latter if in doubt, e.g. **Die Lage hat sich geändert/verändert** 'The situation has changed'. But with reference to people a subtle distinction is expressed depending on whether you use **ändern** or **verändern**, e.g. **Er hat sich geändert** 'He has changed' (i.e. his character), **Er hat sich verändert** 'He has changed' (i.e. his appearance/character); generally speaking this is the only context where you need to use **sich verändern** and you can otherwise fall back on (**sich**) **ändern**. As a noun **Veränderung** is more common than **Änderung**, e.g. **Chile ist im Prozess der Veränderung** 'Chile is in the process of change', **Ich brauche eine Veränderung** 'I need a change' (i.e. a new environment). **Änderung** equates more with 'alteration', e.g. of clothes, which is another meaning of the verb **ändern** too.

The next most commonly used verb required when 'to change' means to swap s.t. for another example of the same thing, is **wechseln**, e.g. **Windeln wechseln** 'to change nappies/diapers', **das Öl wechseln** 'to change the oil (of a car)', **Dieses Geschäft hat den Besitzer gewechselt** 'This business has changed owner'. **Wechseln** is also used of money, both changing into another currency and changing a note into smaller notes or coins, e.g. **Kann ich hier (Geld) wechseln?** 'Can I change money here?'. **Können Sie €500 wechseln?** 'Can you change €500?' (i.e. into pounds or make it smaller). Changing into another currency can also be expressed by **umtauschen**, while making smaller can be expressed just like that in German too, e.g. **Ich möchte bitte €100 umtauschen** 'I would like to change €100, please', **Können Sie mir €500 bitte kleinmachen?** 'Could you please change €500 for me?' (i.e. into smaller notes).

Tauschen means 'to change/exchange' in the sense of to swap. This is thus the word used when swapping things like stamps, coins and partners. 'Exchanging' s.t. bought in a shop for something else is usually **umtauschen**, e.g. **Gekaufte Waren können innerhalb von zehn Tagen umgetauscht werden** 'Purchased goods can be exchanged within ten days'. An individual changing seats is expressed by **wechseln** (i.e. changing the one for the other) but two individuals changing seats is expressed by **tauschen** (i.e. swapping with each other), e.g. **Ich möchte den Platz wechseln** 'I'd like to change seats', **Wollen wir die Plätze tauschen?** 'Shall we change/swap places?'.

'To exchange' one thing *for* another requires **austauschen** (**gegen**), a rather official sounding word, e.g. **Der Bordcomputer in der Mir wird gegen einen neuen ausgetauscht** 'The on-board computer in the Mir is being exchanged for a new one', **Die beiden Länder tauschen Botschafter aus** 'The two countries are exchanging ambassadors'.

'To change' with reference to trains, buses etc. is **umsteigen**, which is dealt with under 'to get in/out,' but **umsteigen** is also used figuratively when changing or switching over to s.t. else, e.g. **Jetzt umsteigen auf Brother Laser-Technologie** 'Change over now to Brother laser technology' (*see* TO GET IN/OUT).

'To change' of wind and weather requires **umschlagen**, e.g. **Der Wind ist umgeschlagen** 'The wind has changed (direction)', **Die Sonne hat den** ganzen Morgen geschienen und dann auf einmal ist das Wetter umgeschlagen 'The sun shone all morning and then suddenly the weather changed'. **Drehen** can also be used in this sense but only with reference to the wind, e.g. **Der Wind hat gedreht** 'The wind has changed (direction)' (*see* TO TURN).

For 'to change' with respect for items of apparel, *see* TO DRESS.

'To change/turn into s.t.' is expressed by **sich verwandeln in** (+ acc.), e.g. **Im Mittelalter glaubte man, dass Menschen sich in Werwölfe verwandeln konnten** 'In the middle ages it was believed that people could change/turn into werewolves'.

Umbenennen means to change the name of s.t., i.e. 'to rename' it, and is dealt with under TO CALL.

to check

checken, einchecken, kontrollieren, nachsehen

'To check' whether a door is locked or whether s.o. has arrived etc. is **kontrollieren**, e.g. **Geh mal kontollieren, ob . . .** 'Go and check whether . . .'. You will also hear **checken** being used in this sense.

'To check' exams, i.e. to mark them, requires **nachsehen**, e.g. **Diese Klausuren muss ich noch nachsehen** 'I am yet to check/mark these papers' (*see* TO CORRECT).

'To check in' for a flight is **einchecken**.

the chemist

die Apotheke, der Apotheker, der Chemiker, die Drogerie, der Drogist

The person who has studied pharmacy and runs a chemist's shop is **der Apotheker**. The shop is called **die Apotheke**. If you buy s.t. 'at the chemist's', you have two ways of expressing it,

e.g. **Ich hab's beim Apotheker/in der Apotheke gekauft** (*see* SHOP).

In Germany, unlike English-speaking countries, **Apotheken** sell just (prescription) drugs, not other paraphernalia; suntan lotion, soap, deodorant etc. that we can buy at a chemist's are sold in Germany by a **Drogist**, whose shop is called a **Drogerie** (compare the American 'drugstore').

S.o. who has studied the science of chemistry (**Chemie**) is a **Chemiker**.

the chicken, chick

das (Brat)hähnchen, das Brathendl, das (Brat)hühnchen, der Broiler, der Hahn, die Henne, das Huhn, das Küken

The right translation for 'chicken' depends first on whether you are talking about the live animal, **das Huhn** (pl. **Hühner**), or one bought in a shop for consumption, **das Hähnchen**, also called **Brathähnchen** which equates with 'roast chicken' or 'roasting chicken', however you might ultimately cook it; alternative forms that you may come across are **Brathuhn, Brathühnchen, Brathendl** (SG). A 'boiler/boiling fowl' is **das Suppenhuhn**. The best known example of GDR German, and one that is still in use in the east, is **der Broiler** (roast chicken), but this American loanword provokes amusement in the west.

When talking of 'chickens' as live animals, **Hühner** is the collective used to refer to them as a group, **die Henne** is a 'hen', **der Hahn** a 'rooster' and **das Küken** the young, i.e. the 'chick' (of any bird in fact).

to claim

beanspruchen, behaupten, fordern

'To claim' in the sense of to assert that s.t. is the case requires **behaupten**, which is commonly followed by the subjunctive because of the doubt about the validity of the statement, e.g. **Das Land behauptet, es habe keine Massenvernichtungswaffen** 'The country claims it has no weapons of mass destruction'.

When a calamity claims lives, **fordern** is the appropriate verb, e.g. **Der Krieg in Ruanda hat eine halbe Million Tote gefordert** 'The war in Rwanda claimed half a million lives' (*see* TO ASK).

(Für sich) beanspruchen means 'to claim' in the sense of 'to lay claim to', e.g. **Dieses Gebiet wird von den Arabern beansprucht** 'This area is claimed by the Arabs', **Sie beanspruchen dieses Gebiet für sich** 'They claim this area (for themselves)'.

to clean; clean

abputzen, putzen, reinigen (lassen), saubermachen, säubern; clean, rein, sauber

The general word for 'cleaning' is **saubermachen** (lit. 'to make clean'), e.g. **Ich muss nur noch das Badezimmer saubermachen** 'I have only the bathroom to clean now'.

Putzen translates 'to clean' where a degree of rubbing, scrubbing or polishing is entailed, e.g. **das Silber/meine Schuhe/die Fenster/die Badewanne putzen** 'to clean the silver/my shoes/the windows/the bathtub'. But this verb is also used for 'cleaning' or 'brushing' your teeth, e.g. **Ich habe mir die Zähne noch nicht geputzt** 'I haven't yet cleaned/brushed my teeth'. It is also used for 'wiping' your nose, whereas **abputzen** is required for a baby's bottom, e.g. **Putz dir die Nase!** 'Wipe/blow your nose', **Sie hat dem Kind den Hintern abgeputzt** 'She wiped the baby's bottom'.[7]

'To have s.t. dry-cleaned' is **reinigen lassen**, e.g. **Du wirst diesen Mantel reinigen lassen müssen** 'You'll have to have that coat dry-cleaned'; alternatively **den Mantel in die Reinigung bringen** 'to take the coat to the dry-cleaners'.

'To cleanse', commonly heard these days in the phrase 'to ethnically cleanse' is **ethnisch säubern**.

Sauber is 'clean' but **clean** is used in the drugs scene in that very specific sense, e.g. **Er ist jetzt clean**. **Rein**, although normally translating 'pure', can in some limited situations render 'clean', e.g. **Eine Wohnung besenrein verlassen** 'to leave a flat clean and tidy (lit. swept out)', **Meine Hände sind rein** 'My hands are clean (fig.)'.

clever

clever, gescheit, klug, schlau

Klug and **gescheit** are neutral words meaning 'clever/intelligent'. **Schlau** can be synonymous but can also express connotations of shrewdness or craftiness, e.g. **ein schlauer Kerl** 'a crafty devil'. **Clever** has the same double meaning that **schlau** has but can also mean 'sharp (witted)'.

to climb

besteigen, erklettern, erklimmen, ersteigen, hochklettern, klettern, steigen

'To climb' meaning to be going up/rising (intr.) is **steigen**, e.g. **Das Flugzeug/die Temperatur steigt noch** 'The plane/temperature is still climbing'.

'To climb' a mountain can be **besteigen, ersteigen** or **erklimmen**, e.g. **Den Berg wollen wir morgen**

---

[7] Note that when parts of the body, both your own and those of others, are the object of the verb, they are not used with possessive adjectives, as in English, but the definite article is used together with a dative pronoun. If you are doing s.t. to some part of your own body, you use the dative of the reflexive (mir, dir, sich, uns, euch, sich) but if it is the body of s.o. else, you put that person in the dative. **Putz dir die Nase** is an example of the former and **Sie hat dem Kind den Hintern geputzt** an example of the latter.

besteigen 'We are going to climb that mountain tomorrow', **Das ist ein schwerer Berg zu erklimmen/ersteigen** 'That is a hard mountain to climb'. Note that 'mountain climbing' as a past-time is **das Bergsteigen** and the agent is **der Bergsteiger**.

'To climb' where there is an element of clambering up, onto or into s.t. is **klettern** (intr.) e.g. **Der Junge ist in den Baum/auf die Mauer geklettert** 'The boy climbed into the tree/onto the wall'. It can also be synonymous with **steigen**, e.g. **Die Temperatur im Osten klettert heute nicht über 15 Grad** 'The temperature in the east will not climb/rise above 15 degrees today'. **Hochklettern** is a commonly heard compound where the prefix expresses 'up', e.g. **Sie haben die Bergwand erreicht und sind sofort hochgeklettert** 'They reached the mountain face and immediately climbed up (on it)'. But note that **(hoch)klettern** cannot be used with an object so if the previous example were to read ' . . . and immediately climbed (up) it', **besteigen, erklimmen** or **erklettern** would be required, e.g. **. . . und haben sie sofort bestiegen/erklommen/erklettert.**

Erklettern, in keeping with the perfective meaning of the prefix, expresses 'to climb up' (i.e. to scale) and is a tr. verb, unlike **(hoch)klettern**, e.g. **Er hat den Berg/Baum erklettert** 'He climbed to the top of/scaled the mountain/tree'. **Erklettern** and **erklimmen** are more or less synonymous, e.g. **Er hat die Leiter erklommen** 'He climbed the ladder'.

the clock, watch

die Armbanduhr, die Uhr, die Standuhr, die Wanduhr, der Wecker

Uhr means both 'clock' and 'watch', as context usually makes it clear what you mean, e.g. **Er kuckte auf seine Uhr** 'He looked at his watch'. If a distinction needs to be made a '(wrist) watch' is an **Armbanduhr** and a '(wall) clock' a **Wanduhr**, but an 'alarm clock' is a **Wecker** and a 'grandfather clock' is a **Standuhr** (*see* HOUR).

to close, lock, shut; closed, locked, shut

abriegeln, abschließen, schließen, verriegeln, verschließen, zumachen, zuschließen; geschlossen, verschlossen, zu

'To close/shut' of doors and windows is **zumachen** or **schließen** (*see* TO OPEN), where the former is the more everyday expression. If a door is 'shut' it is **zu** or less commonly **geschlossen**, but if used attributively before the noun, **geschlossen** must be used, e.g. **Die Tür ist zu/geschlossen** 'The door is shut/closed', **eine geschlossene Tür** 'a shut/closed door', **Die Gallerie hat montags geschlossen/zu** 'The gallery is closed on Mondays'.

'Locking' as opposed to 'closing' a door or window requires **abschließen**, e.g. **Hast du (die Tür) abgeschlossen?** 'Have you locked up (locked the door)?'. Synonymous but less common is **zuschließen**. **Die Tür verriegeln** means 'to bolt the door' when there is literally a bolt in addition to or instead of a lock.

Verschließen, although similar in meaning to **abschließen**, is not normally used for doors, windows, cupboards etc., but for small things like a jewellery box, while the past participle *is* commonly used as an adjective meaning 'locked' or 'bolted' of doors etc., e.g. **hinter verschlossenen Türen** 'behind closed doors' (standard expression).

the clothes

die Bekleidung, die Kleider, die Kleidung

The difference between **Kleider** and **Kleidung** is more or less the same as that between 'clothes' and 'clothing', thus the former is the more usual word in both cases. **Kleider** also happens to be the plural of **das Kleid** (dress), but context normally makes the meaning clear. **Bekleidung** is more formal (compare 'attire') and can be avoided in everyday usage, e.g. **Bekleidung ist im Ausverkauf liegen geblieben** 'Clothing was left over in the sale'.

cloudy, overcast

bedeckt, bewölkt, wolkig

If it is 'cloudy', it is **bewölkt**, whereas if the sky is 'overcast' it is **bedeckt**. In a weather forecast you may hear it is going to be **bewölkt bis bedeckt** 'cloudy, perhaps overcast' or **wechselnde bis zunehmende Bewölkung** 'variable amounts of cloud, becoming cloudier'. **Wolkig** means there are clouds, but not that it is overcast, e.g. **Es war wolkig/Es gab Wolken am Himmel** 'There were clouds in the sky'.

the coat

der Blazer, die Jacke, das Jakett,
der Mantel, der Sakko, der Überzieher,
die Weste

A full-length coat, i.e. an overcoat, is either a **Mantel** or an **Überzieher**; these terms are synonymous. A waist-length coat, i.e. a parka or anorak is a **Jacke**, therefore a full-length raincoat is a **Regenmantel** and a waist-length one is a **Regenjacke**. A waist-length coat that is part of a suit (a suitcoat or jacket) or the equivalent (a sports coat/jacket), i.e. not put over what you have on for extra warmth or protection like a **Jacke**, is a **Sakko** or **Jackett** (pron. as in French) for men, but a **Blazer** for women. A **Windjacke** is a windcheater (but not in the sense of a sweatshirt). A waistcoat, rare as they are these days, is a **Weste**.

the cold; to get/have a cold

die Erkältung, die Kälte, der Schnupfen;
sich erkälten, erkältet sein, (einen)
Schnupfen bekommen, (einen) Schnupfen
haben, sich (einen) Schnupfen
holen/zuziehen

'Cold' as opposed to heat is **Kälte**, e.g. **Die Kälte in diesen Bergen ist unerträglich** 'The cold in these mountains is unbearable'. 'To catch a cold' can be expressed in several ways: **sich erkälten, erkältet sein, (einen) Schnupfen haben**, e.g. **Ich habe mich erkältet, Ich bin (leicht/stark) erkältet** (a light/bad cold), **Ich habe (einen) Schnupfen**. 'To catch/get a cold' is also expressed in a similar variety of ways: **Ich habe (einen) Schnupfen bekommen/Ich habe mir einen Schnupfen geholt/Ich habe mir eine Erkältung zugezogen** 'I've caught/got a cold'.

the committee, board

der Ausschuss, das Gremium, das Komitee,
der Rat, der Vorstand

A governing or executive committee or board of directors or governors is **der Vorstand**. **Das Gremium** is a rather official sounding word used primarily for government appointed committees or boards to oversee certain responsibilities and is akin to a commission, e.g. **Dieses Gremium soll eine Art Aufsichtsrat für die Hochschulen bilden** 'This committee/commission is intended to form a sort of supervisory board for tertiary institutions'. **Das Komitee** is a good general word if in doubt which word to use; it is more commonly heard than its indigenous synonym **der Ausschuss**. **Der Rat** is strictly speaking a council, e.g. **der Stadtrat** 'city council', **der UN-Sicherheitsrat** 'the UN Security Council'.

the competition

die Konkurrenz, der Wettbewerb,
der Wettstreit, der Wettkampf

'Competition' in the business world is **die Konkurrenz** or **der Wettbewerb**, but a top sportsman has no **Konkurrenz**. A 'competition' in the sense of a 'contest' or '(sporting) match' is **der Wettstreit** or **der Wettkampf**.

the complaint; to complain

die Beschwerde, die Klage; beklagen, sich
beklagen über, sich beschweren über,
klagen über

The syntactical difference between **über etw. klagen** and **etw. beklagen** can be compared to 'to wail/moan about s.t.' and 'to bewail/bemoan s.t.', e.g. **Der Einzelhandel klagt seit Jahren über sinkende Gewinne/Der Einzelhandel beklagt seit Jahren sinkende Gewinne** 'The retail trade has complained for years about sinking profits'. But there is also the verb **sich beklagen über** whose meaning is synonymous with that of non-reflexive **beklagen** and of course both these verbs require an object, e.g. **Über Interessemangel darf sich der Organisator nicht beklagen** 'The organiser can't complain about a lack of interest'. But **sich beklagen** (without **über**) is used without an object, e.g. **Das Geschäft läuft nicht, beklagen sich viele Verkäufer** 'Business is not good, many retailers are complaining'. The standard expression 'I can't complain' meaning 'I mustn't grumble' is both **Ich kann mich nicht beklagen** and **ich kann nicht klagen**.

to concern

anbelangen, anbetreffen, angehen,
anlangen, betreffen

The very common expression 'as far as . . . is concerned' is rendered by a number of synonymous verbs, **betreffen** being perhaps the most usual, e.g. **Was mich/uns/das Land betrifft/anbetrifft/ angeht/anbelangt/anlangt, könnte die Lage nicht besser sein** 'As far as I/we/the country am/are/is concerned, the situation could not be better'. Note that in contrast to the English, the subject of the verb is **was** and thus the verb remains in the singular and German uses **mich** and **uns** in the above example, not **ich** and **wir**.

'To concern' in the expression 'That does not concern you (= that's none of your business)' is **angehen**, e.g. **Was geht mich das an?** 'How does that concern me?', **Das geht dich nichts an** 'That doesn't concern you', **Es geht keinen was an** 'It's no one's business'.

the condition

die Bedingung, der Zustand

If s.t. is in good or bad 'condition', this is its **Zustand**, e.g. **Das Gebäude ist noch in sehr gutem Zustand** 'The building is still in very good condition'. A 'condition' in the sense of a requirement or proviso is **Bedingung**, e.g. **unter der Bedingung, dass . . .**, 'on the condition/proviso that . . .'. In the light of the above, contrary to expectations 'living conditions' is **Lebensbedingungen**, e.g. **Die Lebensbedingungen des Volkes sind erbärmlich** 'The living conditions of the people are pitiful', but **Die Zustände, unter denen das Volk lebt, sind erbärmlich** 'The conditions under which the people are living, are intolerable'.

confident

selbstsicher, zuversichtlich

If you ooze confidence (**das Selbstvertrauen**) you are **selbstsicher**, but if you are confident (i.e. sure) s.t is going to happen, you are **zuversichtlich**, e.g. **Er ist zuversichtlich, dass er die Prüfung bestehen wird** 'He is confident he will pass the exam'.

to confuse

verwechseln, verwirren

'To confuse' two or more things, i.e. to mix them up, is **verwechseln**, e.g. **Ich verwechsle diese beiden Verben** 'I confuse these two verbs'. But if s.t. or s.o. makes you confused, you need **verwirren**, e.g. **Die Berliner U-Bahn verwirrt mich (= Ich finde sie verwirrend)** 'The Berlin underground system confuses me/I find it confusing'.

to continue

fortfahren, fortsetzen

Fortfahren is intr. and **fortsetzen** is tr., e.g. **Fahren Sie bitte fort!** 'Please continue (= carry on)', **Er hat fortgefahren zu arbeiten/Er hat mit der Arbeit fortgefahren** 'He continued working', **Ich setze die Geschichte/Arbeit später fort** 'I'll continue the story/work later', **Wird fortgesetzt** 'To be continued' (at the end of a film or article).

to cook, bake, fry

backen, braten, fritieren, grillen, kochen, schmoren

'To cook' in the general sense is **kochen**, but this verb also means 'to boil' so you cannot use it in contexts for 'to cook' where it might be understood to mean boil, e.g. 'Cook the meat quickly', **Brate/Grille das Fleisch schnell. Auf kleiner Flamme kochen (lassen)** renders 'to simmer'. There is also a verb **sieden** (related to 'seethe') which is chiefly used to render 'to boil' in a fig. sense, e.g. **die siedende Hitze** 'the boiling/seething heat'.

Backen is 'to bake' of cakes, bread etc. but if meat is 'cooked' (i.e. 'roasted') in the oven **braten** is

required, e.g. **der Schweine-/Rinderbraten** 'roast pork/beef'. Potatoes roasted in the oven are called **Ofenkartoffeln** or **Folienkartoffeln** if done in foil. But **braten** translates 'to fry' as well, e.g. **Bratkartoffeln** 'fried potatoes', but a 'fried egg' is **das Spiegelei**. **Fritieren** on the other hand means 'to deepfry', as illustrated in the word **Pommes frites** 'chips/French fries'. **Schmoren** renders 'to braise' or 'pot-roast'.

Germans do not generally 'grill' foodstuffs. The loanword **grillen** thus normally equates with 'to barbecue', e.g. **Dieses Fleisch ist ideal zum Grillen** 'This meat is ideal for barbecuing'.

to cope (with)

sich abfinden, fertigwerden, klarkommen, verkraften, zurechtkommen

'To cope with' meaning 'to come to terms with (reluctantly)' (i.e. to learn to cope with) is expressed by **sich abfinden mit**, e.g. **Russland muss sich endlich damit abfinden, dass Lettland keine sowjetische Republik mehr ist** 'Russia has to finally come to terms with Latvia no longer being a Soviet republic'. More or less synonymous with this are **fertigwerden** and **zurechtkommen** e.g. **Er ist seit zwei Jahren arbeitslos ist aber damit fertiggeworden/zurechtgekommen** 'He has been unemployed for two years but has learnt to cope with it'.

'To (be able to) cope/deal with' s.o. or s.t. is **klarkommen**, e.g. **Kommst du mit deinem neuen Computer klar?** 'Are you able to cope with your new computer?'

'To cope' with meaning 'to be up to' or 'to withstand' is **verkraften**, e.g. **Die Straßen der Stadt können das Verkehrsvolumen nicht mehr verkraften** 'The streets of the city can no longer cope with the volume of traffic'.

to correct

korrigieren, nachsehen

Korrigieren means 'to correct' errors, e.g. **Meine deutsche Mutter korrigiert meine Fehler, wenn ich Deutsch spreche** 'My German mother corrects my mistakes when I speak German'. **Nachsehen** is used of teachers 'correcting' students' work, e.g. **Der Lehrer hat unsere Hausaufgaben noch nicht nachgesehen** 'The teacher has not yet corrected our homework' (*see* TO CHECK and TO IMPROVE).

could; could have (done)

dürfte, konnte, könnte; hätte (machen) können, könnte (gemacht) haben

Ask yourself whether 'could' means 'was able to' or 'would be able to'; with the former meaning **konnte** is required and with the latter **könnte**, e.g. **Er konnte ihr gestern nicht helfen** 'He couldn't help her yesterday', **Er könnte ihr vielleicht helfen (, wenn sie es zulassen würde)** 'He could perhaps help her (if she permitted it)'. **Dürfte**, in addition to its primary meaning of 'would be allowed to' (*see* MUST) is commonly used in lieu of **könnte** when there is a high probability, rather than just a possibility, that something will happen – it comes close in meaning to **werden** (will), e.g. **Dieses Jahr dürfte die Inflationsrate auf 4,5 Prozent steigen** 'This year the inflation rate could rise to 4.5 per cent'.

'Could have (done)', where 'done' stands for any verb, is ambiguous in English but this ambiguity is avoided in German. Where you mean s.o. 'could have done s.t. but didn't', **hätte machen können** is required, e.g. **Er hätte dem Mann helfen können** 'He could have helped the man'. But where 'could have done' means 'may/might have done', **könnte gemacht haben** is required, e.g. **Er könnte dem Mann geholfen haben** 'He could have helped the man (it is possible that he is the one who helped the man)'.

the country (see STATE)

das Ausland, das Land, die Provinz, das Vaterland

'Foreign countries' as a collective are referred to as **das Ausland**, which also renders 'abroad' or even 'overseas', e.g. **Im Ausland kommen rechtsradikale Ausschreitungen selten vor** 'Right-wing riots rarely occur in other countries', **Meine Eltern haben jahrelang im Ausland gewohnt** 'My parents lived abroad/in a foreign country for years'.

A country or foreign state is a **Land,** but this word also renders 'country' in the sense of the 'countryside', e.g. **Meine Kusine wohnt auf dem Land(e)** 'My cousin lives in the country', **Wir fahren morgen aufs Land** 'We're going to the country tomorrow'. The expression **in der Provinz** also means 'in the country' but with a pejorative connotation, i.e. in the backblocks.

The plural of **Land** meaning '(foreign) countries' or 'states' (*see* STATE) is **Länder; Lande** occurs in more poetic contexts and means 'regions', e.g. **Gemüse aus deutschen Landen** 'Vegetables from regions of Germany'.

In patriotic contexts the Germans may refer to their country as their **Vaterland**, e.g. **Liebe zum Vaterland** 'love for one's country' (*see* GERMANY).

the cousin

der Cousin, die Cousine/Kusine, der Vetter

Der Cousin (pron. ku:zeng) and **der Vetter** (pl. -n) are synonymous for a 'masculine cousin', although in fairy tales **Vetter** renders 'Brother/ Brer'; the latter word also happens to occur in **Vetternwirtschaft** 'nepotism'. A 'female cousin' is either **Cousine** or **Kusine**, which is merely a matter of spelling.

to/the cry, scream

beweinen, rufen, schreien, weinen;
der Ausruf, der Ruf, der Schrei

'To cry' in the sense of 'to weep' is **weinen**, e.g.
Warum weinst du? 'Why are you crying?'.
Beweinen, which belongs to a higher register,
means 'to weep (mourn) for', e.g. **Sie beweinen
einen Mann, der jahrelang der Stammesführer
war** 'They are crying for (mourning) a man who
was the leader of the tribe for years'.

Where 'to cry' is poetic language for 'to cry out'
or 'to exclaim', **rufen** or **schreien** must be used,
e.g. **'Hilfe', rief/schrie er** ' "Help", he cried'. 'The
cry', as in the previous example, is **der Ausruf**
(compare **der Hilferuf** 'cry for help') or **der Schrei**,
whereas a 'cry in the dark' is **ein Schrei in der
Dunkelheit** and 'scream' too is rendered by **Schrei**.

curious

gespannt, kurios, neugierig

'Curious' as in showing curiosity is **neugierig**, e.g.
Katzen sind neugierige Tiere 'Cats are curious
animals', but if 'curious' in the previous example
meant 'strange' or 'peculiar', **kurios** would be the
appropriate word. **Gespannt** is required when
being 'curious' is synonymous with wondering,
e.g. **Ich bin gespannt, wie sie darauf reagieren
werden** 'I am curious (= I wonder) how they will
react to that'.

the currency

die Devisen, ausländisches Geld, die
Währung

A country's currency is its **Währung**, e.g.
Südafrika hat eine schwache Währung 'South
Africa has a weak currency'. An official sounding

word used of a country's foreign currency reserves
is **Devisen** (pl.), **Das Land kann nicht zahlen
wegen eines Mangels an Devisen** 'The country
can't pay because of a lack of foreign currency/
reserves'. If you have 'foreign currency' for travelling, what you have is **ausländisches Geld**, e.g.
**Ich habe einen Schuhkarton voll ausländisches
Geld von meiner letzten Reise nach Europa** 'I have
a shoebox full of foreign currency from my last
trip to Europe'.

Note that the sing. of all currencies is used after
numerals, but feminine currencies ending in
-e take a plural -n, e.g. **fünf Euro** (m.), **acht Cent**
(m.), **zehn Mark** (f.), **zwanzig Pfennig** (m.), **drei
Pfund** (n.), **fünf Dollar** (m.), but **eine Krone/
zwanzig Kronen** 'one crown/twenty crowns'.

Ein Euro consists of **100 Cent** and **ein
(Schweizer)franken** (m.) consists of **100 Rappen**
(= centimes). Note the use of the acc. with currencies, e.g. **Es hat einen Cent/Euro/Franken/Dollar
gekostet** 'It cost a/one cent/euro/franc/dollar', **Ich
habe einen Euro dafür bezahlt** 'I paid a euro for it'.

the custom, habit

die Angewohnheit, die Gepflogenheit,
die Gewohnheit, der Gebrauch, die Sitte

The 'customs' of other cultures are their **Sitten** or
their **Gebräuche**, e.g. **Vieles muss noch über das
Leben und die Gebräuche ihrer Vorfahren ermit-
telt werden** 'Much is yet to be ascertained about
the life and customs of their ancestors'.

Gepflogenheit is a more elevated word, positive in
connotation, often referring to customs or norms
of the upper crust, e.g. **Das widerspricht den diplo-
matischen Gepflogenheiten** 'That runs counter to
diplomatic conventions', **die Gepflogenheiten des
Königshauses** 'the customs of the royal family'.

Gewohnheit refers to s.t. that is the result of the
force of habit, either good or bad, e.g. **Er hat die**

Gewohnheit, jeden Abend in die Kneipe zu gehen 'He has the habit/it is his custom to go to the pub every night'.

An **Angewohnheit** is a 'habit' which is negative or strange and is often preceded by a negative adjective, e.g. **die seltsamen Angewohnheiten der Familie** 'the family's strange habits'. The example given for **Gewohnheit** above could also be rendered by **Angewohnheit**, but it would suggest there is some disapproval.

to damage

beschädigen, schaden, schädigen

Beschädigen means to do physical damage to s.t., e.g. **Der Krankenwagen hat den Baum beschädigt** 'The ambulance damaged the tree', **Kriegsbeschädigte**, those injured or wounded as a result of war. **Schädigen** means 'to harm' but is more often than not used adjectivally, e.g. **Flutgeschädigte**, those who have suffered a material or financial loss as a result of flood. Compare this with the previous example; these people are the victims of flood without any physical damage having been done to them.

Otherwise **schaden** (+ dat.) translates 'to damage' where this is synonymous with 'to harm', e.g. **Rauchen schadet der Gesundheit** 'Smoking damages/harms one's health', **Das schadet (dir) nicht** 'It won't do (you) any harm'.

to dare

sich trauen, (sich) wagen

Wagen means to have the courage, e.g. **Ich habe es nicht zu tun gewagt/Ich habe nicht gewagt, es zu tun** 'I didn't dare (to) do it', **Er hat es nicht gewagt** 'He didn't dare (to)'; note the compulsory object in German.

'To dare' meaning to have the confidence to do s.t. requires **sich trauen**, e.g. **A: Warum klopft er nicht an ihrer Tür? B: Er traut sich nicht (, das zu tun)** 'Why doesn't he knock on her door? B: He doesn't dare (to do so)', **Nach dem schweren Erdbeben trauten sich viele Menschen nicht mehr in ihre Häuser zurück** 'After the earthquake many people didn't dare return to their homes'. In the second example the verb **gehen** has been omitted, which is commonly the case with **sich trauen**, e.g. **sich auf die Straße/nach Hause trauen** 'to dare to go out into the street/to go home'.

Sich wagen also occurs and implies a greater fear of doing s.t. than **sich trauen**, e.g. **Sie wagt sich nicht in den Wald** 'She doesn't dare go into the forest'. In the earthquake example above **sich wagen** might well be more appropriate than **sich trauen**, depending on the circumstances.

the date, appointment

das Datum, der Termin, die Verabredung/ verabredet sein, der Wievielte

A 'date' in the sense of an 'appointment', particularly with a doctor or dentist etc. is **Termin**, e.g. **Kann ich bitte einen Termin mit dem Arzt für Montag machen?** 'Can I please make an appointment with the doctor for Monday?' (*see* DIARY).

If you can't do s.t. because you have a prior engagement of whatever kind, this is a **Verabredung**, but can also be expressed adjectivally by **verabredet**, e.g. **Ich kann leider nicht kommen, denn ich habe schon eine Verabredung/denn ich bin schon verabredet** 'Unfortunately I can't come as I already have a date'.

Das Datum refers to a calender date, e.g. **das Geburtsdatum** 'date of birth', **Wir haben uns im Datum geirrt** 'We got the date wrong'. Although **Was für ein Datum haben wir heute?** is a possible way of asking the date, the following expressions are more informal: **Der Wievielte ist heute?/Den Wievielten haben wir heute?** 'What is the date today?', **Heute ist der neunte August/Wir haben heute den neunten August** 'Today is the ninth of August'.

There is not a specific word for a romantic date. This needs to be expressed periphrastically, e.g. **Er geht heute Abend mit ihr aus** 'He has a date with her tonight', **Er geht mit ihr/Sie gehen mit einander aus** 'They are dating'.

to deal with, to be about

gehen um, handeln von, sich handeln um

'To deal with' or 'to be about' as in 'This book is about the war' can be expressed in several ways, all of which are synonymous but require different syntax; the subject of **gehen um** and **sich handeln um** is always **es**, e.g. **Es geht in diesem Buch um den Krieg/Es handelt sich in diesem Buch um den Krieg**, but **Dieses Buch handelt von dem Krieg** 'This book is about the war' (*see* ABOUT).

dear

geehrt, lieb, teuer, verehrt

Letters to friends and loved ones start with **lieber** or **liebe** depending on the gender of the person being addressed. If writing to more than one person of both genders, the following is necessary: **Lieber Dieter, liebe Susanne, liebe Kinder,** 'Dear Dieter, Susanne and children'. These days the first word on the next line has a small letter as **Lieber** is seen as the beginning of the sentence; previously Germans placed an exclamation mark after the name and the next line started with a capital letter, e.g. **Lieber Dieter!**

Impersonal letters to people you are unacquainted with require **Geehrte(r)**, e.g. **Sehr geehrter/Ge-** ehrter Herr Bock 'Dear Mr Bock'. Speeches, however, begin with **verehrte**, e.g. **(Sehr) verehrte Damen und Herren** (Ladies and gentlemen) or simply **meine Damen und Herren**.

'Dear' in the sense of expensive is **teuer**, which drops the **e** when an **-e** or **-er** ending is added, e.g. **ein teures Auto** 'a dear car', **Es war viel teurer als meins** 'It was much dearer than mine'.

the decision; to decide

der Beschluss/beschließen, die
Entscheidung/(sich) entscheiden,
der Entschluss/die Entschließung/sich
entschließen

Personal decisions and deciding between alternatives are most commonly expressed by **Entscheidung/sich entscheiden**, e.g. **A: Was willst du machen? B: Ich kann mich nicht entscheiden (, ob . . .)** 'A: What do you want to do? B: I can't decide (whether . . .)'. **Eine Entscheidung treffen** renders 'to take/make a decision', e.g. **Hast du schon eine Entscheidung getroffen? (= Hast du dich schon entschieden?)** 'Have you made a decision/decided yet?'. **Entscheiden**, without the reflexive pronoun, is used when organisations or bodies 'decide' s.t., not individuals, e.g. **Ende November muss der Bundestag entscheiden** 'The federal parliament must decide at the end of November', **Die Kubaner können selber entscheiden, was sie wollen** 'The Cubans can decide (for) themselves what they want'. **Entscheiden** is also commonly heard in the passive where the use of **sich** is not possible, e.g. **Jeder einzelner Asylantrag muss entschieden werden** 'Every individual application for asylum has to be decided on', **Im Mai wird entschieden, ob . . .** 'It will be decided in May whether . . .'. But whether you use **sich** with **entscheiden** or not can depend on syntax. If followed by a **dass/was** clause, omit **sich**, e.g. **Wir haben entschieden, dass wir miteinander ein neues**

Segelboot bauen 'We have decided that we will build a new yacht together', **Er kann selbst entscheiden, was er möchte** 'He can decide himself what he would like'; compare **Wir haben uns entschieden, ein neues Segelboot zu bauen** 'We have decided to build a new yacht'.

'To decide on/against s.t.' in the sense of opting for or against it in preference to s.t. else, is **sich entscheiden für/gegen**, e.g. **Wir haben uns für das erste Konzept entschieden** 'We have decided on the first concept'. But note that 'to decide *on*' s.t., meaning to decide *about* it, is **entschieden über**, e.g. **Die Regierung will über den Atommeiler erst in 2 Jahren entscheiden** 'The Government only wants to decide on the nuclear power station in two years' time. 'To decide (on) *doing* s.t.' is **sich zu etwas entscheiden**, e.g. **Sie haben sich dazu entschieden, im Frühling zu heiraten** 'They have decided to marry in spring'.

Entschluss/sich entschließen strictly speaking mean 'resolution/to resolve (to do s.t.)/to make up one's mind' and although more or less synonymous with **Entscheidung/sich entscheiden**, are more forceful and **entschließen** is always reflexive, e.g. **Ich habe mich zu diesem Schritt entschlossen, weil** . . . 'I decided on this step because . . .'; (note the use of **zu** where **sich entscheiden** requires **für**), **Ich habe mich dazu entschlossen, den Vertrag zu verlängern** 'I decided to extend the contract' (= I was determined to), **Die Regierung des Landes hat sich nicht freiwillig zu der Öffnung in Richtung Marktwirtschaft entschlossen** 'The country's government did not voluntarily decide on heading towards a market economy'. In addition to **Entschluss** there is also a noun **Entschließung** but it is rare and can be forgotten.

Derived from the same root is the noun **Entschluss** which can translate 'decision' but is more usually rendered in English by 'resolution' or 'intention', commonly with a connotation of firm resolve, e.g.

Er kann zu keinem Entschluss kommen 'He can't make a decision/make up his mind', **Es ist sein fester Entschluss, bei der Firma zu bleiben,** 'It is his firm intention/resolve to stay with the firm'.

Entschlossen as an adjective means 'determined/resolute' but **entschieden** is also used with this meaning.

Beschluss/beschließen are used chiefly for official decisions or decrees, e.g. **Die Regierung hat ein neues Polizeigesetz beschlossen** 'The government has decided on (= passed) a new police law', **Die Wehrpflicht wird abgeschafft. Das hat das französische Parlament beschlossen und das Volk is für den Beschluss** 'Conscription is being abolished. The French parliament has decided on (= passed) that and the nation is for the decision'. This verb is not necessarily only used for official decisions; where it is otherwise used, it simply states the decision made whereas **sich entscheiden** and **sich entschließen** imply a process of deliberation about the alternatives has preceded the decision, e.g. **Er wusste, dass er arbeitslos bleiben könnte und beschloss daher, sich umschulen zulassen** 'He knew he could remain unemployed and decided to have himself retrained'.

to defend

(sich) verteidigen, sich wehren

'To defend yourself' in the combatant sense is **sich verteidigen**, whereas 'to defend yourself' in an argument or against a proposal is **sich wehren** (i.e. to put up a fight against), but how close the two can be in meaning is reflected in the following compound nouns: **etwas in/aus Notwehr tun** 'to do s.t. in self-defence', **die Bundeswehr** 'the federal armed forces', **der Bundesverteidigungsminister** 'the federal minister for defence'.

the department

die Abteilung, das Dezernat, das Institut, das Ministerium, das Ressort, das Seminar

A 'department store' is a **Kaufhaus** or **Warenhaus** (older). An individual 'department' in the shop is an **Abteilung**, which is a general word for a 'department' or subsection of a greater whole.

A government 'department', as in the 'Department of Health', for example, is a **Ministerium**, e.g. **das Verteidigungs-/Bildungsministerium** 'the Department of Defence/Education'. For a subsection of a government department or official body the word **Dezernat** is commonly used. **Ressort** refers to an area of responsibility within a department, thus one's department in the fig. sense, e.g. **Mein Ressort innerhalb des Außenministeriums ist Entwicklungshilfe** 'My department with Foreign Affairs is development aid'.

A university 'department' is a **Seminar** or **Institut**, e.g. **Er arbeitet im Seminar für Germanistik/im germanistischen Seminar** 'He works in the German department'.

to depend on

abhängen von, darauf ankommen, sich verlassen auf

If s.o. or s.t. depends on s.o. or s.t. **abhängen von** is required, e.g. **Sie hängt finanziell sehr von ihren Eltern ab** 'She depends financially very much on her parents', **Es hängt vom Wetter ab, ob wir kommen** 'It depends on the weather whether we'll be coming'. The impersonal 'it (all) depends' requires **darauf ankommen**, e.g. **Es kommt darauf an** 'It depends'. There are many contexts where the two are interchangeable, e.g. **Es hängt davon ab/Es kommt darauf an, welche Laune er hat** 'It depends what mood he is in'.

'To depend on' s.o. or s.t. in the sense of 'to rely on' is **sich verlassen auf**, e.g. **Man kann sich auf ihn verlassen** 'You can depend/rely on him'.

the diary

das Tagebuch, der (Termin)kalender

If you keep a diary of your life, this is a **Tagebuch**, e.g. **Das Tagebuch der Anne Frank** 'Anne Frank's Diary', but a diary in which you note appointments (**Termine**) is a **Terminkalender**, or merely **Kalender** if the context makes it clear what sort of a calender you are referring to, e.g. **A: Kannst du am Montagabend zu uns kommen? B: Moment mal! Ich muss in meinem Kalender schnell mal nachschlagen** 'A: Can you come to our place on Monday night? B: Just a moment. I need to quickly check my diary'.

to die; dead

eingehen, enden, entschlafen, erliegen, ums Leben kommen, sterben, umkommen, verenden, verrecken

German, like English, has an endless array of words meaning 'to die' reflecting various style registers, e.g. **verrecken** 'to snuff it/die like a dog', **ins Gras beißen** 'to kick the bucket', **entschlafen** 'to pass away'. All verbs meaning 'to die' take **sein** in the perfect tense, except **ins Gras beißen**.

Neutral and comparable with 'to die' is **sterben**; 'to die of' a disease requires **an** + dat. but 'to die of' boredom/curiosity etc. (i.e. figurative dying) requires **vor** + dat., e.g. **Seine Mutter ist an Krebs gestorben** 'His mother died of cancer', **Ich sterbe vor Neugierde** 'I'm dying of curiosity'. Very formally people can **erliegen**, where 'of/from' is expressed by the dat., e.g. **Der Polizist ist seinen Verletzungen erlegen** 'The policeman died from his injuries'.

In reports on wars and traffic accidents, for example, you will commonly hear the synonyms **umkommen** and **ums Leben kommen**, e.g. **Es kamen vierzig Menschen im Unfall um/Vierzig Menschen kamen im Zugunglück ums Leben** 'Forty people died in the train accident'.

Eingehen is as formal a word as **erliegen** but is only applicable to plants and animals, not people. **Verenden** is similar, with connotations of 'to perish' and can be applied to both people and things, e.g. **An der deutschen Nordseeküste sind drei Pottwale gestrandet und eingegangen/verendet** 'Three sperm whales got stranded on the German North Sea coast and died'. Similarly **enden**, which is also quite high style, e.g. **Er war schwer verwundet und ist drei Tage später qualvoll geendet** 'He was badly injured and died an agonising death three days later'.

Note that 'dead' is **tot**, while 'stone-dead/dead as a doornail' is **mausetot**. Comparable with 'deceased' is **verstorben**, e.g. **Mein Vater ist verstorben** 'My father is deceased/dead'; compare **Er ist gestorben** 'He (has) died'. **Mein verstorbener Vater** renders 'my late father'; rather archaic sounding these days is **mein Vater selig** or **mein seliger Vater**.

different

ander, anders, unterschiedlich, verschieden

'Different' meaning 'another' as in 'Please give me a different cup' is dealt with under 'another'. 'Different from/to/than' is **ander-/anders als**, e.g. **Ich arbeite in einem anderen Gebäude als er** 'I work in a different building from him', **Das Leben in Australien ist ganz anders als in Deutschland** 'Life in Australia is quite different from Germany'. Note too **etwas Anderes** 'something different'.

As an attributive adjective meaning 'various', 'different' is rendered by **verschieden**, e.g. **Es**

kommen viele verschiedene Tierarten in diesem Wald vor 'A lot of different sorts of animals occur in this forest'. But **verschieden** can also mean 'different from each other', e.g. **Die beiden Schwestern sind ganz verschieden** 'The two sisters are quite different (from each other)'.

Unterschiedlich means 'different' in the sense of 'varied', e.g. **Meine Kinder haben alle unterschiedlich darauf reagiert** 'My children all reacted to it differently'. **A: Was isst man in Deutschland? B: Das ist sehr unterschiedlich, je nachdem wo man wohnt** 'A: What does one eat in Germany? B: That varies/differs/is different depending on where you live'.

to dig (*see* TO BURY)

ausbuddeln, ausgraben, ausheben, buddeln, graben

Graben is the standard word, but in the north in informal speech you often hear **buddeln**, with **ausgraben/-buddeln** rendering 'to dig up', e.g. **Die Kinder buddeln/graben im Garten** 'The kids are digging in the garden'. 'To dig a hole' can be **graben** or **ausgraben**, which actually means 'to excavate', e.g. **Sie haben ein großes Loch hinter dem Schuppen (aus)gegraben** 'They have dug a large hole behind the shed'.

'To dig (out)' a grave or a tree requires **ausheben**.

to disappear

schwinden, verschwinden

Schwinden literally means 'to wane' or 'to dwindle' or 'to be disappearing', while **verschwinden** is the end result and is used to express 'to have disappeared', e.g. **Die Buchenwälder Osteuropas schwinden allmählich, während sie im Westen schon lange verschwunden sind** 'The beech forests of eastern Europe are gradually disappearing while in the west they have long since disappeared'.

the dish, bowl, plate

das Geschirr, der Napf, die Platte, die Schale, die Schüssel, der Suppenteller, der Teller

A flat 'dinner plate' is a **Teller**, but a 'soup bowl' is **ein tiefer Teller** or a **Suppenteller**. Where 'plates' are synonymous with 'crockery' or 'dishes', **das Geschirr** should be used, e.g. **Wirst du das Geschirr bitte wegräumen?** 'Would you please put the plates/dishes away?'. 'To do the dishes', meaning 'to do the washing up' is also **(das Geschirr) abwaschen/spülen**.

A **Platte** is a large plate corresponding more to 'platter', e.g. **Sie hat eine schöne Platte mit Wurst und Käse serviert** 'She served a lovely plate/platter of sausage and cheese'.

The sort of bowl that desserts are served in, i.e. small and shallow, is called a **Schale** but in the south and Austria this word is commonly used instead of **Tasse** for a cup. A **Schüssel** is a 'serving bowl' and an **Obstschale** is a 'fruit bowl'.

A cat or dog 'bowl' is **der Napf**.

the disk

die Diskette, die Festplatte

A computer's 'hard disk' is its **Festplatte**, while a 'floppy disk' is a **Diskette** and it is inserted into a **Laufwerk** (n.) 'disk drive' (*see* TO SAVE).

the distance

der Abstand, die Entfernung, die Ferne

If you can see s.t. 'in the distance' or 'from a distance', you require **Ferne**, e.g. **in der Ferne, aus der Ferne**.

Entfernung can be synonymous with **Ferne**, e.g. **Er hörte etwas aus/in der Entfernung** 'He could hear s.t. in the distance', but in the following context only **Entfernung** will do: **Australien ist ein Land von Entfernungen** 'Australia is a land of distances'.

Abstand is the 'distance' or 'gap' between things, e.g. **mit Abstand fahren** 'to drive keeping a distance between you and the car in front', e.g. **Was ist der Abstand zwischen diesen Bäumen?** 'What is the distance between these trees?'. But the 'distance' between geographical locations is **Entfernung**, e.g. **Die Entfernung zwischen den beiden Städten beträgt 300 Kilometer** 'The distance between the two towns is 300 kilometres'.

to do

hinkriegen, machen, tun

Although **tun** translates as 'to do' and **machen** as 'to make', more often than not **machen** is also used to render 'to do'; the two are however very often interchangeable, and where they are, **machen** is more usual in the spoken language, e.g. **Was tust du/was machst du?** 'What are you doing?'. **Machen** is used for trivial things and more serious actions require **tun**, e.g. **Was machst du da?** 'What are you doing/What are you up to at the moment?', **Was tust du im Büro?** 'What do you do in the office?' (i.e. what is your function?) or 'What are you doing here?' (i.e. what business have you got being here?). Colloquially 'to do' with a nominal object is commonly rendered by **machen**, where in higher style a more precise verb might be used, e.g. **Er hat seinen Aufsatz schon gemacht (= geschrieben)** 'He has already done his essay'. The distinction between **tun** and **machen** remains vague and needs to be closely observed in practice. **Tun** commonly also translates 'to put' in coll. German (*see* TO PUT).

Hinkriegen translates 'to do' in the sense of 'to manage to do', e.g. **Wie kriegt sie das hin?** 'How does she do it?'

the (front-/back-)door, gate(way)

die Haustür, die Hintertür, die Pforte,
das Tor, die Tür, die Vordertür

The 'front-door' of a house is **die Haustür**, but of any other building it is **die Vordertür**, whereas the 'back-door' of any edifice is **die Hintertür**.

A **Tor** is a large 'gate(way)' such as found in medieval towns or sporting stadiums, e.g. **die Tore von Wien** 'the gates of Vienna'. A small garden 'gate' is a **Pforte** but could also be called a **Gartentor**. In fig. language **Pforten** is sometimes used to render 'doors', e.g. **Die Börse hat ihre Pforten zum erstenmal an einem Feiertag geöffnet** 'The stock exchange opened its doors for the first time on a public holiday', but in the following fig. context the word corresponds to 'gates': **die Pforten des Himmels** 'the gates of heaven'. Equally der **Pförtner** is both a 'doorkeeper' of a building or a 'gatekeeper' of a castle, for example.

to/the doubt

anzweifeln, bezweifeln, zweifeln; das
Bedenken, der Zweifel

Bezweifeln presupposes s.t. has just been stated to the contrary, whereas **zweifeln an** + dat. is neutral in this respect, e.g. **Ich bezweifle seine Ehrlichkeit/ Ich zweifle an seiner Ehrlichkeit** 'I doubt his honesty', **Die Echtheit des Bildes muss sehr bezweifelt werden** 'The authenticity of the painting must be seriously doubted' (i.e. contradicting a claim to the contrary).

When followed by a subordinate clause, syntax, not unconnected with the above semantic

distinction, determines whether to use **bezweifeln** or **zweifeln**, i.e. **bezweifeln, dass** and **zweifeln, ob/was** but also **nicht zweifeln, dass**. As **zweifeln** is intr. the presence of a direct object requires **bezweifeln**, e.g. **Ich bezweifle es nicht**, but this can also be expressed as **Ich zweifle nicht daran**.

Anzweifeln is very close in meaning to **zweifeln an**, corresponding to 'to question', but is nearly always used in the passive, e.g. **Die Sicherheit von Kreditkarten wird angezweifelt** 'The security of credit cards is being questioned', **Die Existenz Wilhelm Tells wird von Historikern angezweifelt** 'The existence of William Tell is doubted/questioned by historians'; compare **Historiker zweifeln an der Existenz Wilhelm Tells** 'Historians doubt/question the existence of William Tell'.

'Doubt' as a noun is **der Zweifel**, e.g. **außer Zweifel** 'beyond doubt', **im Zweifel** 'in doubt', **ohne Zweifel/zweifelsohne** 'without doubt'. In the expression 'to have one's doubts about' s.t. both **Zweifel** and **Bedenken** occur, e.g. **Ich habe meine Zweifel/Bedenken über die Sicherheit von Kreditkarten** 'I have my doubts about the security of credit cards'.

to dress, put on, undress, take off, change (one's clothes); dressed

(sich) anziehen, (sich) ausziehen, (sich)
entkleiden, sich kleiden, sich umziehen;
angezogen, bekleidet, gekleidet

The verbs **an-** and **ausziehen** render 'to put on' and 'to take off' items of clothing respectively, e.g. **Es regnet. Zieh einen Regenmantel an!** 'It's raining. Put a raincoat on', **Er hat seine nassen Schuhe ausgezogen** 'He took off his wet shoes'. 'To put on/take off' a hat is **einen Hut aufsetzen/abnehmen** (*see* ON).

When these two verbs are used reflexively they render 'to get dressed' and 'to get undressed', e.g.

Ich geh' mich schnell mal anziehen 'I'm going to quickly get dressed', **Zieh dich aus!** 'Get undressed/Take your clothes off!'.

Sich kleiden renders the far less common 'to dress' which is not synonymous with 'to get dressed, e.g. **Er kleidet sich nach der neuesten Mode** 'He dresses according to the latest fashion'.

The verb **umziehen** is only used reflexively and renders 'to change (one's clothes)/get changed', e.g. **Er hat sich umgezogen** 'He changed (his clothes)'. If you change an item of clothing, this must be expressed by using **anziehen** together with **ander**, e.g. **Er hat einen anderen Pulli angezogen** 'He changed his pullover'.

'Well-dressed' is **gut angezogen**, **gut gekleidet** being a posh synonym, but it cannot be replaced by **angezogen** in the following example: **Die Frauen waren in lustigen Saris gekleidet** 'The women were dressed in cheerful saris'. Note too **eine spärlich bekleidete Tänzerin** 'a scantily dressed dancer' and compare the rather formal sounding **Die Germeinde bittet die Badegäste darum, sich anständig zu bekleiden** 'The council requests that the bathers dress respectably'. **(Sich) entkleiden** is an equally formal sounding word for 'to undress'.

the drink

das Getränk, der Drink, die Limonade,
der Most, die Schorle, der Saft, der Sirup,
der Sprudel

What is rendered by the noun 'drink' in English is commonly expressed verbally in German, e.g. **Ich muss was trinken** 'I need a drink'. Where a general word for a drink, be it alcoholic or otherwise, is required, **Getränk** is best used, e.g. **Dieser Kühlschrank ist zu klein, um Getränke drin kaltzustellen** 'This fridge is too small to store drinks in'. Many large supermarkets in Germany have their drinks section, **der Getränkemarkt**, in a separate building outside the main supermarket.

Presumably under the influence of American movies the word **Drink** (pl. -s) for an alcoholic beverage has made its way into the language, e.g. **Ich mache mir einen Drink** 'I'm going to make myself a drink'.

Schorle is 'spritzer' (i.e. wine or juice mixed with soda, e.g. **Apfelschorle**), whereas **Saft** is 'juice'. **Apfelsaft** is thus 'apple juice' but **Apfelmost** is 'apple cider'.

The closest German comes to a general word for a 'softdrink' is **Limonade** but otherwise you have to name specific forms of soft drink, e.g. **Möchtest du einen Saft/eine Sprite?** 'Would you like a soft-drink? (i.e. a [fruit] juice/lemonade)'. **Sprudel**, in addition to meaning 'fizzy drink' in general (**süßer Sprudel**), is also used for mineral water (**das Mineralwasser**). 'Cordial' is **der Sirup**.

to drown

ertränken, ertrinken

The difference between these two words is simply one of transitivity, the former being tr. and regular and the latter intr. and irregular and taking **sein** in the perfect, e.g. **Mein Vater hat zu meinem Erschrecken die Kätzlein ertränkt** 'To my horror my father drowned the kittens', **Die Kätzlein sind ertrunken** 'The kittens drowned'.

each other, one another

einander, sich

'Each other' can be expressed by either the reciprocal pronoun **einander** or the plural of the reflexive pronoun, (i.e. **uns, euch** or **sich**, depending on the subject), e.g. **Sie haben sich/einander in Köln kennen gelernt** 'They met each other in Cologne'.

Einander is not common in speech unless a preposition precedes in which case it must be used in both speech and writing and it is written together with the preposition as one word, e.g. **Wir sehen uns nächste Woche wieder,** 'We'll see each other again next week', **Die zehn Kinder standen alle hintereinander** 'The ten children were all standing behind each other'.

the east, west, north, south
(*see* GERMANY)

der Osten, der Westen, der Norden, der Süden; Ost, West, Nord, Süd

The four points of the compass are **der Osten** etc., e.g. **Er wohnt im Osten des Landes** 'He lives in the east of the country'. 'East/Eastern' etc. in geographic names are rendered by **Ost-** prefixed to the noun, e.g. **Ostdeutschland** 'East Germany', **Südafrika** 'South Africa', but **im südlichen Afrika** 'in southern Africa'.

'The Far East' is either **Fernost** (without an article) or **der Ferne Osten**, e.g. **Die Märkte in Fernost/im Fernen Osten haben die Wirtschaftskrise durchstanden** 'The markets in the Far East survived the economic crisis'; also **Die Märkte in Ost und West/im Osten und Westen.** Similarly **Nahost** and **der Nahe Osten** 'the Middle East'. As you can see, the forms without -en don't require the definite article, but those ending in -en do; the former are limited to use in standard expressions, e.g. **aus Ost und West** 'from east and west', **von Ost nach West** 'from east to west', **Der Wind kommt aus Ost/dem Osten** 'The wind comes from the east'.

'To the east of' etc. is rendered by **östlich/westlich/nördlich/südlich von** or gen., e.g. **Simbabwe liegt südlich des Äquators und westlich von Mosambik** 'Zimbabwe is situated south of the Equator and west of Mozambique'. Note too **das südafrikanische Land Simbabwe** 'the southern African country of Zimbabwe' and **Westaustralien** 'Western Australia', **Nordengland** 'northern England'.

Note that **Wir fahren in den Osten** means 'We are driving to the east (of the country)', but **Wir fahren nach Osten** means 'We are travelling east (i.e. in an easterly direction)'.

to eat

aufessen, essen, fressen, speisen, verspeisen

The usual word is of course **essen** (see FOOD), but if you eat s.t. up, **aufessen** must be used, e.g. **A: Ist noch was von der Torte übrig? B: Nein, die haben die Kinder aufgegessen** 'A: Is there anything left of the cake? B: No, the kids have eaten it'.

It is usual but not necessary to use **fressen** rather than **essen** when referring to animals, e.g. **Fisch frisst/isst meine Katze nicht** 'My cat does not eat fish'. A degree of subjectivity can influence whether you use **fressen** or **essen** for animals – cute things, or your own pets might **essen**, whereas what a lion does is most definitely **fressen**. **Fressen** can also be used pejoratively of people, e.g. **Er hat alles im Nu aufgefressen** 'He ate (= gobbled up) everything in a flash'.

Speisen is a very formal word akin to 'to dine', e.g. **Rommel speiste am Vorabend der Invasion mit einem berühmten Schriftsteller** 'Rommel ate/dined on the evening before the invasion with a famous author'. **Verspeisen** is an elevated synonym of **aufessen**.

the economy, economics

die Konjunktur, die Ökonomie, die Volkswirtschaft, die Wirtschaft(swissenschaft)

The 'economy' of a country is its **Wirtschaft**, e.g. **Olympia 2000 sollte die australische Wirtschaft ankurbeln** 'The 2000 Olympics were meant to give the Australian economy a boost', **die Wirtschaftskrise** 'the economic crisis'. A more technical word, commonly used by economists when discussing the economy in the media, is **Konjunktur**, e.g. **Die Konjunkturlage ist schlecht** 'The economic situation is bad'.

'Economics' as a university discipline is **Volkswirtschaft**. This is more common than **Ökonomie**, but an 'economist' is either **der Volkswirt, der Wirtschaftswissenschaftler** or **der Ökonom**.

the education, to educate; the training, to train

die Ausbildung, die Bildung, das Bildungswesen, die Erziehung, die Fortbildung, Kultus-, die Pädagogik, die Weiterbildung; ausbilden, aufziehen, erziehen, fortbilden, heranbilden, weiterbilden

The 'education' you get at school and university is your **Ausbildung** and **Du wirst ausgebildet** 'You are being educated/trained'. A 'trainee' or 'apprentice' is referred to as an **Azubi**, an abbreviation of **ein Auszubildender**, but an academic or technical 'trainee' is also called a **Praktikant/ Trainee** and an 'apprentice' in the trades is also called a **Lehrling**. But the government department or ministry in charge of education is called, strangely enough, **das Bildungsministerium**. The minister is called the **Bildungsminister** but the term **Erziehungsminister** occurs too. In a Bundesland the minister in charge of education is **der Kultusminister**, as the ministry covers education and the arts. If referring to a person being 'educated' or 'civilised' the terms **gebildet sein** and **Bildung haben** are used, e.g. **Mein Vater war ein gebildeter Mensch/hatte Bildung** 'My father was an educated man'. Compare **Kinkel ist gelernter Jurist/studierter Sinologe** 'Kinkel is a lawyer/ sinologist by training'.

An **Erziehung** is usually what you get at home from your parents and thus normally equates with 'upbringing' (< **erziehen** 'to bring up/rear') rather than 'education', but the above **Erziehungsminister** is an obvious exception to this. 'Re-education camps' in non-democratic countries are referred to as **Umerziehungslager**, but then it is the whole thinking that is being changed, not merely vocational training.

Almost identical in meaning to **ausbilden** is **heranbilden**, used of 'educating/training' teachers, e.g. **Osteuropa muss so schnell wie möglich mehr Deutschlehrer heranbilden** 'Eastern Europe must train more teachers of German as quickly as possible'. Further vocational training is **Fortbildung**, where **fort** expresses 'continuing/additional', e.g. **Seine Frau möchte sich fortbilden** 'His wife would like to further her education'. **Weiterbildung/ weiterbilden** is similar to the former but implies 'further education' rather than additional training in a field in which you are already employed which is what **Fortbildung/fortbilden** mean.

the employee, the employer, to employ

der/die Angestellte, der Arbeitnehmer/ -geber; anstellen, einstellen

The term **Arbeitnehmer** renders 'employee(s)' but is commonly used where in English we talk of 'the workers'; at the other end of the spectrum is the **Arbeitgeber**, 'the employer(s)'. But there is also the term **der Angestellte**, derived from the verb **anstellen** 'to employ'. All the various people employed to do office work are referred to as **kaufmännische Angestellte**, where the term **kaufmännisch** means 'pertaining to commerce or business'. **Einstellen** means to employ with a connotation of 'taking on' and is the term used on signs of firms with vacancies, e.g. **Wir stellen ein: Dreher** 'We are taking on/looking for turners'.

to encourage

ermuntern, ermutigen

'To encourage' s.o. to do s.t. is both **ermuntern** and **ermutigen,** with a very subtle distinction in meaning. Keeping in mind that **munter** means 'lively' and **Mut** means 'courage', the former is used where the person being encouraged needs to be enticed to do s.t., whereas the latter is used where there is some trepidation and a pep talk is required, e.g. **Mexiko möchte die deutsche Wirtschaft ermuntern, sich in das Land zu engagieren** 'Mexico would like to encourage the German economy to become involved in the country', **Meine Mutter hat mich dazu ermuntert/ ermutigt, Medizin zu studieren** 'My mother encouraged me to study medicine' (either could be used here depending on the connotation). The same distinction applies to the adjectives **ermunternd/ermutigend** 'encouraging'.

to enjoy

sich amüsieren, genießen

'To enjoy oneself' and thus 'to have a good time' is **sich amüsieren,** e.g. **Die Kinder haben sich auf der Geburtstagsfeier riesig amüsiert** 'The kids enjoyed themselves enormously at the birthday party'.

'To enjoy' s.t. is **genießen,** e.g. **Die Kinder haben die Party sehr genossen** 'The kids really enjoyed the party'. This verb is also used fig. in the way that 'to enjoy' is in English, e.g. **Unsere Arbeitnehmer haben eine gute Ausbildung genossen** 'Our employees have enjoyed a good education'.

(to be) enough

genug; ausreichen, genügen, reichen

'Enough' is usually expressed by **genug** which follows adjectives, as in English, but can either follow or precede nouns, e.g. **alt genug** 'old enough', **Geld genug/genug Geld** 'enough money'. But 'enough' is commonly expressed verbally in German. **Reichen** means 'to be enough/sufficient', e.g. **Dieses Mehl reicht für fünf Brote** 'This flour is enough for five loaves', **Reicht das Licht zum Lesen?** 'Is there enough light to read by?', **Das reicht** 'That's enough', **Das reicht mir/mir reicht's** 'I've had enough (= I'm fed up)'. Similar in meaning and usage to **reichen** is **genügen,** but it is not as colloquial, e.g. **Das genügt** 'That's enough', **Das genügt (mir)** 'That's enough (for me)'; this also has the fig. meaning 'I'm fed up'.

Ausreichen means 'to be enough (to do s.t.)', e.g. **Zwei Milliarden Euro würde ausreichen, das Problem zu lösen** 'Two billion euros would be enough to solve the problem', **Die Zeit reicht nicht aus** 'There is not enough time' ('to do s.t.' implied) (*see* TO LAST).

especially, specially

besonders, eigens, vor allem

Where 'especially' means 'particularly' and qualifies an adjective or adverb, **besonders** is required, e.g. **Sie hat besonders gut gesungen** 'She sang especially well'. Where '(e)specially' is synonymous with 'above all', both **besonders** and **vor allem** can be used, e.g. **Es wird überall im Land regnen, besonders/vor allem im Osten** 'It will rain throughout the country, especially in the east'.

Eigens means '(e)specially' in the sense of specifically, e.g. **Diese Autos wurden eigens für die Bonzen des SED-Regimes gebaut** 'These cars were built especially/specifically for the bigwigs of the SED regime' (i.e. GDR).

even

auch, einmal, erst, gar, noch, selbst, sogar

'Even' as in 'Even he has a newer car than I do' is **sogar**, e.g. **Sogar er hat ein neueres Auto als ich.** **Auch** when placed before a subject can mean 'even' as much as it can 'too/also', e.g. **Auch er hat ein neues Auto** 'Even he (= he too) has a new car'. **Selbst** placed before a subject has the same meaning as **sogar**, e.g. **Selbst der Chef hat ein bescheideneres Auto** 'Even the boss has a more modest car'; compare **der Chef selbst** 'the boss himself'.

'Even' followed by the comparative of an adjective or adverb is usually **noch**, but can also be **sogar**, e.g. **Sein Auto ist noch/sogar neuer als meins** 'His car is even newer than mine'. Only **sogar** can be used to modify a verb too, e.g. **Sie hat ihn sogar angerufen** 'She even rang him'.

In more elevated style **gar** can render 'even' but you are advised to adhere to **sogar**, e.g. **Zugelassen oder gar versichert ist in Afghanistan überhaupt kein Fahrzeug** 'No vehicle at all in Afghanistan is registered or even insured'.

'Not even' is **nicht einmal** or **nicht erst**, e.g. **Sogar er hat ein neueres Auto als ich, obwohl er seit Jahren nicht einmal gearbeitet hat** 'Even he has a newer car than I do although he hasn't even worked for years', **Der Präsident wird nicht erst/einmal zum Gipfel in Johannesburg reisen** 'The president will not even be going to the summit in Johannesburg'.

ever

je, jemals, noch

Je and **jemals**, although synonymous, are not always interchangeable. In a question either is possible, e.g. **Bist du je(mals) in Deutschland gewesen?** 'Have you ever been to Germany?'. After a comparative + 'than' **je** is required, e.g. **Die Wachtumsrate ist höher denn je** 'The rate of growth is higher than ever'. 'Never ever' is rendered by **noch nie** (*see* NEVER).

'Ever' in the expressions 'whatever', 'whoever', 'wherever' etc. is expressed by **(auch) immer**, i.e. **was/wer/wo (auch) immer**, e.g. **Wo er sich (auch) immer auf der Welt befindet, wird Interpol ihn aufspüren** 'Wherever he is in the world, Interpol will track him down'.

the exam, test (*see* TO PASS, TO FAIL and TO TEST)

das Examen, die Klassenarbeit, die Klausur, die Prüfung, der Seminarschein, das Staatsexamen, der Test

The most usual word for an 'exam' is **Prüfung**, e.g. **eine mündliche/schriftliche Prüfung** 'an oral/written exam'.

An **Examen** (pl. **Examina**) is quite an important affair being used chiefly for university finals. The basic degree from a German university that qualifies you to teach is called, for example, **das Staatsexamen**, e.g. **Er hat das Staatsexamen an der Universität Köln absolviert** 'He graduated from the university of Cologne'.

A **Klausur** is an 'exam' written under examination conditions, but also refers to the physical papers requiring correction, e.g. **Ich habe das ganze Wochenende Klausuren korrigiert** 'I marked exams/examination papers all weekend'.

A 'test' at school or university which does not count towards one's final result is a **Test** whereas a **Klassenarbeit** is a grander affair that does count. **Test** is used for medical tests etc.

German universities issue **Seminarscheine**, certificates of attendance at individual courses for one semester; there are **benotete** and **unbenotete Seminarscheine** where usually mere attendance is sufficient for the latter.

except (for), besides, apart from

abgesehen von, ausgenommen für, außer, außerdem

As prepositions **außer** (+ dat.) and **abgesehen von** are synonymous, with the former being more common, e.g. **Außer dir/abgesehen von dir kenne ich hier niemand** 'I know no one here apart from you'. Note **abgesehen davon** 'besides/apart from that'. Synonymous with **außer** and **abgesehen von**, but less common, is **ausgenommen** but note what cases it governs, e.g. **niemand, ausgenommen du = niemand, du oder dich ausgenommen** 'no one except for/apart from you'. In the following examples taken from signs only **ausgenommen** can be used: **Eintritt verboten ausgenommen für Badegäste** 'Entry prohibited except for bathers', **Täglich offen ausgenommen montags** 'Open daily except for Mondays'. Also **Ausgenommen, wenn/dass . . .** 'Except when/that . . .'.

'Besides' as an adverb, i.e. meaning 'in addition', is **außerdem**, e.g. **Sie will nicht ins Kino mitkommen und außerdem kann sie es sich nicht leisten** 'She does not want to come to the movies with us and besides, she can't afford it'.

the/to experience

die Erfahrung, das Erlebnis; durchmachen, erleben, mitmachen

The 'experience' you accumulate while working is **Erfahrung**, e.g. **Haben Sie viel Erfahrung in dieser Branche?** 'Do you have much experience in this industry?'. Thus **(un)erfahren** renders '(in)experienced'. An individual great/bad experience is an **Erlebnis**, e.g. **Das war ein einmaliges Erlebnis** 'That was a once in a lifetime experience'.

'To experience' s.t. is **erleben**, e.g. **Ich habe in Japan viel erlebt** 'I experienced a great deal in Japan'.

If 'to experience' has a connotation of having 'to endure/go through' s.t. you can use either **erleben** or **durch-/mitmachen**, e.g. **Was er alles durchgemacht/mitgemacht hat, ist unglaublich** 'What he has had to experience/go through is unbelievable'.

to fail

durchfallen (lassen), nicht durchkommen, fehlschlagen, nicht gelingen, misslingen, platzen, scheitern, versagen, versäumen

'To fail' an exam has to be expressed periphrastically as there is no tr. verb with this meaning, thus you must use either **durchfallen** or **nicht durchkommen** (in + dat.), e.g. **Ich bin (in Deutsch) durchgefallen, Ich bin (in Deutsch) nicht durchgekommen** 'I failed (German)'.[8] In the German schools system, however, where marks 1 to 6 are given and a 5 or more is a fail it is usual to say **Ich habe eine Fünf in Deutsch bekommen** 'I got a five for German' (= I failed German) (*see* MARK). But if a teacher 'fails' a student, **durchfallen** is required and in order to be able to let it take an object, it must be used with **lassen**, e.g. **Ich habe ihn leider durchfallen lassen** 'I failed him'.

When machinery or human endeavour 'fails', **versagen** is the appropriate word, e.g. **Der automatische Pilot hat versagt und das Flugzeug ist abgestürzt** 'The automatic pilot failed and the plane crashed', **Die Ursache des Unfalls war technisches Versagen** 'The cause of the accident was technical failure'.

Not necessarily interchangeable but very similar in meaning to **versagen** is **scheitern** and its

---

8 Of course it is also possible to express 'to fail' by using the tr./intr. verb 'to pass', **bestehen**, in the negative, e.g. **Ich habe (Deutsch) nicht bestanden** 'I failed (German)' (*see* TO PASS).

colloquial synonym **platzen,** but both have connotations of 'to break down' or 'fall through', e.g. **Ihre Ehe ist gescheitert/geplatzt** 'The marriage has failed' (= broken down), **Der Putsch ist gescheitert/geplatzt** 'The coup failed' (= fell through), but the following mean more or less the same thing: **Die Regierung hat kläglich versagt/ Die Regierung ist kläglich gescheitert** 'The Government has failed miserably' (in negotiations).

'To fail' in the sense of 'to go wrong' is **fehlschlagen,** e.g. **Der erste Raketenstart schlug fehl/ist fehlgeschlagen** 'The first rocket launch failed', **Wenn friedliche Maßnahmen fehlschlagen . . .** 'When peaceful measures fail . . .'. But **scheitern** would be possible in both these examples too.

'To succeed' is **gelingen** and the reverse, which in many contexts is synonymous with 'to fail', can be expressed by **misslingen** or **nicht gelingen,** e.g. **Es ist ihnen nicht gelungen, die U-Boot-Matrosen zu bergen**[9] 'They failed (= did not succeed) to rescue the submariners', **Das Experiment ist misslungen** 'The experiment failed'. **Misslingen** can also be followed by a clause, but less commonly so than **nicht gelingen.**

'To fail' to do s.t., meaning to neglect to do s.t., is **versäumen,** e.g. **Er hat versäumt, mir zu sagen, dass er an dem Abend nicht zuhause wäre** 'He failed to tell me that he would not be at home that night' (*see* TO MISS).

the farm; the farmer

der Bauernhof, die Farm, das Gehöft, die Länderei; der Bauer, der Farmer, der Landwirt

A small scale 'farm' as found in Europe is a **Bauernhof,** whereas the 'farmstead', if a distinction needs to be made, is **das Gehöft.** If the context makes it clear, a 'farm' can be referred to simply as a **Hof,** e.g. **Wegen Maul- und Klauenseuche stehen etliche Höfe unter Quarantine** 'As a result of foot and mouth disease several farms are under quarantine'.

The 'farmer' is **der Bauer** (wk) and his wife **die Bäuerin,** but these words also translate 'peasant' in historical contexts. In higher style a 'farmer' may be referred to as a **Landwirt** (< **Landwirtschaft** = agriculture). In the New World, where 'farms' are seldom such minute, cosy entities as in Europe, it is common to use the words **Farmer** (pl. –) and **Farm** (pl. -en), which behave entirely as German words, as their plurals indicate, e.g. **Die weißen Farmer in dem afrikanischen Land wollen ihre Höfe nicht aufgeben** 'The white farmers in that African country do not want to give up their farms'.

to fear (for), be afraid (of)

Angst haben um/vor, Angst machen, ängstigen, sich ängstigen um, bangen um, befürchten, fürchten (um), sich fürchten vor

'To be afraid of' is most commonly expressed by **Angst haben vor** + dat., e.g. **Rotkäppchen hatte Angst vor dem Wolf** 'Little Red Riding Hood was afraid of the wolf'. Less commonly this can be expressed by **sich fürchten vor** + dat., e.g. **Sie fürchtete sich vor dem Wolf.** This can also have a clause as its object, e.g. **Ich fürchte mich davor, dass . . .** 'I fear that . . .' (a real fear, in contrast to **Ich fürchte, dass . . .**).

Angst machen and **ängstigen** render 'to frighten/make afraid', e.g. **Dieses chemische Zeug macht uns Angst/ängstigt uns** 'This chemical stuff frightens us'.

Fürchten renders 'to fear' where the subject of the sentence is afraid of what the object may do to it and is used for expressing awe and dread of

---

[9] Note that both **misslingen** and **gelingen** are unusual verbs in that they are irregular (**gelang/gelungen**), take **sein** in the perfect and the English personal subject stands in the dative in German.

things, e.g. **Vor allem ältere Leute fürchten die Rückkehr der Randalierer** 'Especially older people fear/dread the return of the hooligans', **Diese Sekte fürchtet Gott** 'This sect fears god'.

Where you fear or feel uneasy about possible developments in the future, **befürchten** is appropriate, e.g. **Sie brauchen nichts zu befürchten** 'You don't need to fear anything' (= that anything untoward will happen), **Wir befürchten das Schlimmste** 'We fear the worst', **Ich befürchte, dass es Nachbeben geben wird** 'I fear that there are going to be aftershocks'; also in the more figurative sense of 'thinking' where there is no question of a literal fear, e.g. **Ich befürchte, dass er recht hat** 'I fear he is right', but in speech **Ich fürchte, dass . . .** is also heard, especially after **ich**. There are many instances where the two are interchangeable.

'To fear for' s.t. is expressed by both **fürchten um** and **bangen um**, but also **Angst haben um**, e.g. **Alle fürchteten/bangten um ihr Leben/die Zukunft** 'Everyone feared for his life/the future'. But this can also be expressed by **Angst haben um** which also expresses 'to be worried about' s.o. or s.t. (i.e. to fear for), e.g. **Die Eltern hatten alle Angst um ihre Kinder** 'The parents all feared for their children/were worried about their children'. **Sich ängstigen um** is another possible synonym here.

far (*see* DISTANCE)

fern, unweit, weit (. . . entfernt)

Fern tends to be used chiefly in standard expressions and can refer to both temporal and spacial distance, e.g. **Der Tag ist nicht mehr fern, wo . . .** 'The day is not far off when . . .'. Note too **im Fernen Osten** 'in the Far East'. By far the more usual word is **weit**, e.g. **Wie weit ist Hamburg?** 'How far is Hamburg?'. When a place is a certain distance *from* another, **weit** is used in combina-

tion with **entfernt**, e.g. **A: Wie weit von der Stadt entfernt wohnt ihr? B: Wir wohnen sehr weit von hier entfernt** 'A: How far from town do you live? B: We live a long way from here'.

Unweit + gen. renders 'not far from', e.g. **Wir wohnen unweit der Grenze und fahren oft nach Holland** 'We don't live far from the border and often go to Holland'.

'How far' meaning 'to what extent' is both **inwiefern** and **inwieweit**, just as 'in as far as' is both **(in)sofern als** and **(in)soweit als**, e.g. **Inwiefern hat er dir dabei geholfen?** 'To what extent did he help you with it?'. **Er hat mir geholfen, soweit er konnte** 'He helped me as far as he could'.

Note that the expression 'As far as I know' is expressed as follows in German: **Sofern ich weiß**, where **sofern** is interchangeable with **soviel**.

to feel

abtasten, anfühlen, betasten, empfinden, (sich) fühlen, Lust haben, spüren, tasten

Fühlen is the general word for both emotional and physical feeling, e.g. **Ich fühle die Kälte** 'I feel the cold', **Sie fühlte etwas auf der Schulter** 'She felt something on her shoulder'. **Empfinden** refers to one's sensitivity or ability to discern feelings, e.g. **Ich habe sein Benehmen als Beleidigung empfunden** 'I felt his behaviour to be an insult'.

The expression 'to feel hot/cold' is expressed by **sein** + dat., e.g. **Mir ist heiß/kalt** 'I feel hot/cold'. 'To feel sick' in the sense of 'to feel like vomiting' is expressed similarly, e.g. **Mir ist schlecht**, but otherwise if you feel sick, happy, sad etc. **fühlen** is the verb and it must be used reflexively, e.g. **Ich fühle mich krank** 'I feel sick'. If s.t. feels good to you, i.e. it imparts a tactile sensation on you, **sich anfühlen** is required, e.g. **Die Sonne fühlt sich wunderbar an** 'The suns feels wonderful'.

'To feel like doing s.t.' is expressed by **Lust haben zu**, e.g. **Hast du Lust, spazieren zu gehen?** 'Do you feel like going for a stroll?'. **Danke, ich habe keine Lust dazu** 'No thanks. I don't feel like it'.

'To feel' meaning 'to sense' s.t. is **fühlen** or **spüren**, e.g. **Er fühlte/spürte ihren Atem auf der Haut** 'He felt her breath on his skin'.

Tasten refers to feeling in the sense of touching with your hands, in particular searching for s.t., e.g. **Franz tastete im Dunkeln nach der Türklinke** 'Franz felt (around) in the dark for the door handle'. **Betasten** means 'to feel' or 'touch' s.t. in several places, e.g. **Er betastete das Sofa hat aber nichts gefunden** 'He felt the couch but couldn't find anything'. **Abtasten** means 'to feel' all over as in a body search, e.g. **Alle Fluggäste werden abgetastet, bevor sie einsteigen dürfen** 'All airline passengers are felt all over (body searched) before they are allowed to embark'.

'To feel' in English is often synonymous with thinking or believing s.t., e.g. I feel things will get better; see TO THINK for ways to express this as **fühlen** cannot be used in this way in German.

to/the fight

bekämpfen, erkämpfen, fechten, kämpfen, streiten um, sich zanken

Kämpfen is used for fighting in wars, boxing or fighting against adversity, e.g. **Er hat im zweiten Weltkrieg gekämpft** 'He fought in the Second World War', **bis zuletzt kämpfen** 'to fight to the last'. 'To fight against' is **kämpfen gegen**, e.g. **Wir kämpfen gegen den Rechtsradikalismus** 'We are fighting against right-wing radicalism'; likewise the noun: **der Kampf gegen die Lehren der Kirche** 'the fight against the teachings of the church'.

Fighting against s.t., meaning to oppose it, is best expressed by the tr. verb **bekämpfen** rather than by **kämpfen gegen**, e.g. **Wir müssen alles Mögliche machen, das organisierte Verbrechen zu bekämpfen** 'We must do everything possible to oppose/combat organised crime'; **die Verbrechensbekämpfung** 'fighting/combatting crime', compare **der Kampf gegen das Verbrechen** 'the fight against crime'.

Erkämpfen renders to win or secure s.t. by figuratively having fought for it, e.g. **Den Wettbewerb, den wir in der Wirtschaft hart erkämpft haben, brauchen wir auch in der Politik** 'The competition which we fought hard for in the economy, we also need in politics'.

Fechten with the meaning of 'to fight' is a rare, elevated synonym of **kämpfen** but the noun **das Gefecht**, does have a certain frequency but corresponds more to 'battle' or 'skirmish', e.g. **Während der Gefechte haben sich die beiden Erzfeinde mit dem Atomschlag gedroht** 'During the fighting/battles/skirmishes the two arch enemies threatened each other with a nuclear strike'.

When two people fight in the sense of argue with each other, **sich streiten (um etwas)** is the verb, e.g. **Die Jungen streiten sich ständig (um das Fahrrad), wenn ihr Vater nicht dabei ist** 'The two boys continually fight (about the bike) when their father is not around'. The corresponding noun is **der Streit** 'fight/argument'. Similar in meaning to **sich streiten** is **sich zanken**.

When two people have a fight which comes to blows, **sich prügeln (um etwas** 'about/for s.t.') is more appropriate than **sich streiten/zanken**, e.g. **Der beiden Männer haben sich um das Mädchen geprügelt** 'The two men fought over the girl'. **Er hat sich geprügelt** means 'He got into a fight'.

'To put up a fight against' can be expressed by **sich wehren gegen** (*see* TO DEFEND), e.g. **Man kann an der Tür sehen, dass der Mann sich gewehrt hat** 'You can see from the door that the man put up a fight'. But this is not just limited to a physical fight, e.g. **sich gegen den Vorschlag wehren** 'to (put up a) fight against the suggestion'.

to find

auffinden, bergen, fallen, finden, halten von

Finden, apart from referring to finding things that have been lost, can be used to express a judgement (= to consider to be), e.g. **Ich habe die Prüfung sehr leicht gefunden** 'I found the exam quite easy', **Ich finde es heiß** 'I find it hot'. Note the interrogative in the following example can be expressed either by **finden** or **halten von**: **Ich fand den Film sehr gut. Wie hast du ihn gefunden?/Was hast du davon gehalten** 'I found the film really good. How did you find it' (= what did you think of it? (*see* TO THINK).

Fallen + dat. commonly expresses 'to find' with reference to experiences, e.g. **Es fiel mir schwer, ihm helfen zu müssen** 'I found it hard to have to help him', **Ihm fallen Sprachen leicht** 'He finds languages easy'.

'To find' in the sense of to discover is **auffinden**, e.g. **Zwei der Entführten wurden lebend aufgefunden** 'Two of the abducted people were found alive'. Compare **Zwei der Entführten wurden gefunden** 'Two of the abducted people were found'.

'To find/recover/retrieve' bodies from accidents and disasters is **bergen**, commonly used in the passive, e.g. **Bislang sind zwei Leichen geborgen worden** 'So far two bodies have been found'.

to finish, end, cease

absolvieren, aufhören, beenden, enden, zu Ende sein/gehen, kein Ende nehmen, fertig, Feierabend machen

The most general tr. verb for expressing finishing doing something is **fertig** used with a verb appropriate to the action, e.g. **fertig packen** 'to finish packing', **sich fertig anziehen** 'to finish getting dressed', **fertig bauen** 'to finish building', e.g. **Sie muss ihren Koffer noch fertig packen** 'She still has to finish packing her suitcase'.

Zu Ende lesen/schreiben means 'to finish writing/reading', e.g. **Ich muss das Buch noch zu Ende lesen/den Brief noch zu Ende schreiben** 'I still have to finish reading the book/writing the letter'. The same concept can be expressed by **fertig lesen/schreiben** 'to finish reading/writing' s.t., e.g. **Ich habe das Kapitel noch nicht fertig gelesen** 'I haven't finished reading the chapter yet', just as **fertig essen** renders 'to finish eating' (no object), e.g. **Hast du fertig gegessen?** 'Have you finished eating?'.

But **fertig** can also render 'ready', e.g. **Ich bin fertig; wir können jetzt gehen** 'I am ready/finished; we can go now', **Das Essen ist fertig** 'The dinner is ready'.

Very often simply **fertig**, used with **sein**, suffices, e.g. **Bist du fertig?** 'Have you finished?' (writing, reading, sewing, preparing the meal etc.).

Beenden is tr. and thus means 'to bring to an end', e.g. **Die Rebellen haben das alte Regime beendet** 'The rebels ended (= brought an end to) the old regime', **Der Bundeskanzler hat seine Bosnien-Reise beendet** 'The Chancellor has finished his Bosnia tour'.

Enden is intr. and renders 'to finish' when it means 'to end', e.g. **Das Konzert endete um 11 Uhr** 'The concert finished at 11 o'clock'. But **enden** sounds a little bookish and in speech it is more common to express this with either of the next two verbs.

Zu Ende sein/gehen are intransitive like **enden** which they commonly replace, e.g. **Die Ferien sind am 23. Oktober zu Ende** 'The holidays finish on 23rd October', **Die Ferien gehen jetzt zu Ende** 'The holidays are finishing now' (= coming to an end).

The idiom **kein Ende nehmen** translates 'not to end/to be endless', e.g. **Die Ausschreitungen gegen den Atommülltransport nehmen einfach kein Ende** 'The riots against nuclear waste transportation simply don't end/are endless'.

'Finished' meaning 'all gone/used up' is expressed very idiomatically by **alle**, e.g. **Die Torte ist alle/muss alle werden** 'The cake is finished/must be finished', **Mein Geld ist alle/zu Ende** 'My money's finished/run out/all gone'.

Feierabend means 'knock-off time from work' and thus **Ich mache jetzt Feierabend** 'I'm finishing work now/knocking off now/calling it a day'.

Aufhören means 'to end' in the sense of 'to stop/cease', e.g. **Der Regen hat aufgehört** 'The rain has finished', **Es hat aufgehört zu regnen** 'It has finished/stopped raining' (*see* TO STOP).

Absolvieren means 'to finish' school or university and can thus also render 'to graduate', e.g. **Meine Tochter hat gerade die Grundschule/Universität/ ihr Studium absolviert** 'My daughter has just finished primary school/university/her studies'.

the fire

der Brand, das Feuer

'Fire' as an element is **Feuer**, e.g. **Feuer ist gefährlich** 'Fire is dangerous', **Die Pfadfinder haben ein Lagerfeuer gemacht** 'The scouts made a campfire', but when the firebrigade (**die Feuerwehr**) is called to a fire, what they go to is a **Brand**, e.g. **Es hat gestern Nacht nebenan einen Brand gegeben** 'There was a fire next-door last night'. Compare also **der Feuerlöscher** 'fire extinguisher', but **der Brandstifter** 'arsonist', **der Waldbrand** 'forest/bush fire'. 'Fire!' as an imperative with reference to guns is also **Feuer!**, which is also used as an exclamation when fire breaks out.

first(ly)

erst, erstens, vorher, zuerst, zunächst (einmal)

'First' as an attributive adjective is **erst**, e.g. **Meine erste Frau hat inzwischen wieder geheiratet** 'My first wife has married again meanwhile'. This is also used to express 'Who was/came first?', **Wer war der erste?**

'First, second, third' etc. is **erstens, zweitens, drittens** etc., but 'first' when not part of such a list, is most usually rendered by the very common expression **zunächst (einmal)**, e.g. **Es ist zehn Uhr. Die Nachrichten. Zunächst die Übersicht** 'It is ten o'clock. The news. First the summary (on television)', **Sie haben mehr Gepäck mitgenommen als zunächst geplant** 'They took more luggage with them than first planned'.

More or less synonymous with **zunächst** is **zuerst**, both of which mean something like 'first of all' (before going on to do s.t. else), e.g. **Bevor ich ausgehen kann, muss ich zuerst duschen** 'Before I can go out I first have to shower'.

'First . . . second' can be synonymous with 'on the one hand . . . on the other (hand)' in which case it is best to use **zum einen . . . zum andern**, e.g. **Meine Tochter möchte unheimlich gerne nach Australien, zum einen weil sie das Land schon immer gereizt hat und zum anderen, weil sie einfach gerne Englisch perfekt sprechen können will** 'My daughter would love to go to Australia, first because the country has always fascinated her, and second because she would simply like to be able to speak perfect English'.

Where 'first' is synonymous with 'beforehand', use **vorher**, e.g. **Ruf uns bitte vorher an, wenn du auf Besuch kommen willst** 'Please ring first if you want to come and visit'.

to flee

entfliehen, die Flucht ergreifen, (sich) flüchten, fliehen

'To flee' as executed by refugees (**der Flüchtling**) from wars etc. can be expressed either by **fliehen** or **flüchten vor** (+ dat.), e.g. **Die ganze Bevölkerung ist vor dem Feind geflohen/geflüchtet** 'The whole population fled from the enemy'. 'To flee' a town or country (i.e. a tr. verb) can also be expressed by both these words, e.g. **Sie sind aus der Stadt geflohen/geflüchtet** 'They fled the town'.

Flüchten, unlike **fliehen**, is also used reflexively to render 'to seek refuge', e.g. **8000 Moslims flüchteten sich in die nächste Stadt** '8000 Muslims fled to the next town'.

Die Flucht ergreifen is an elevated synonym of **fliehen/flüchten** when there is no direct object or anything to flee from, e.g. **Panikartig ergriffen die Zuschauer im Stadion die Flucht** 'The spectators in the stadium fled in panic'.

'To flee from' danger or temptation is rendered by **entfliehen** (+ dat.), e.g. **Sie entflohen der Gefahr des Brandes, indem sie ins Schwimmbad sprungen** 'They fled the danger of the fire by jumping into the swimming pool'.

the floor

das Erdgeschoss, die Etage, der Fußboden, das Geschoss, der Keller, das Parterre, der Stock, das Stockwerk, das Souterrain

The 'floor' of a room is **der (Fuß)boden** (*see* GROUND), but 'floor' in the sense of the 'storey' of a building is somewhat complicated in German. A multi-storied building consists of several **Stockwerke**, but you say **Ich wohne im zweiten Stock** 'I live on the second floor'. A synonym of **Stockwerk** is **Etage** and you can also say **Ich wohne auf der zweiten Etage**. But there can be a distinction in meaning, e.g. **Er wohnt im 3. Stock und bewohnt die ganze Etage** 'He lives on the second floor and occupies the whole floor'. **Stock** is never used in the plural, e.g. **Er wohnt zwei Stock/Stockwerke/Etagen höher** 'He lives two floors up'.

A two/three/four-storied building is **ein zwei-/drei-/vierstöckiger** or **ein zwei-/drei-/viergeschossiger Bau**.

The 'ground floor' is called either **das Erdgeschoss** or **das Parterre** and the 'basement' is **der Keller, das Kellergeschoss** or **das Souterrain**. Consequently German lifts might use **E, P, K** or **S** as abbreviations for the above.

The word **Geschoss**, which means 'floor/storey', only occurs in compounds, thus in addition to the above also in **Ober-/Untergeschoss** 'upper/lower storey'.

Americans should note that in Germany the ground floor is not the first floor.

In a private house the 'top floor' is **der Dachboden**, which is synonymous with loft or attic. Most German houses have both a **Keller** and a **Dachboden**.

to follow

befolgen, erfolgen, folgen, verfolgen

'To follow' somebody physically is **folgen**, which takes a dat. object and **sein**[10] in the perfect, e.g. **Der liebe, kleine Hund ist ihrer Tochter nach Hause gefolgt** 'The dear little dog followed her daughter home'. 'To follow on from' in a temporal sense is **folgen auf** + acc., e.g. **Auf Regen folgt**

---

10 **Folgen** can take **haben** but then it means 'to do as one is told/obey', e.g. **Der Bub hat seinen Eltern nicht gefolgt** 'The boy didn't do what his parents told him to'.

Sonnenschein 'Sunshine follows rain', **Auf Georg den Sechsten folgte Elisabeth die Zweite** 'Elizabeth II followed (on from) George VI'. **Folgen** is most commonly used intr. as follows: **Die Tagesschau folgt** 'The news follows', **wie folgt** 'as follows'. **Folgen**, but then usually in combination with **können**, can also mean, as in English, to understand, e.g. **Ich habe den Vorlesungen nicht folgen können** 'I wasn't able to follow the lectures'.

'To follow' rules is **befolgen**, e.g. **Malaysia befolgte die IWF-Rezepte nicht**[11] 'Malaysia did not follow the directives of the IMF', **Wer befolgt noch die Zehn Gebote?** 'Who still follows the Ten Commandments?'. **Folgen** is possible in this sense too but **befolgen** is stronger; with **befolgen** you do so because you must, whereas **folgen** implies willingness to do so, e.g. **Die Botschaft des Papstes war deutlich, und die deutschen Bischöfe sind seinem Wort gefolgt** 'The pope's message was clear and the German bishops followed his command'.

'To follow' a course, proceedings, etc. is **verfolgen**, e.g. **Der Journalist hat den Prozess aufmerksam verfolgt** 'The journalist followed the trial attentively', **Das sind Länder, die eine protektionistische Politik verfolgen** 'Those are countries that follow a protectionist policy', **Er hat das Fußballspiel im Fernsehen verfolgt** 'He followed the football match on television'. But **verfolgen** often equates with 'to pursue', both people and aims, e.g. **Jemand hat mich verfolgt** 'Someone was pursuing me', **Welche Ziele verfolgt er?** 'What goals is he pursuing'.

There is also a verb **erfolgen**, an elevated word seldom meaning 'to follow' as such but more 'to ensue, occur', e.g. **Die ersten Auszahlungen des Entschädigungsgeldes an die Opfer können dann erfolgen** 'The first payments of reparations to the victims can then ensue/occur'.

---

[11] Der IWF – der Internationale Währungsfonds.

the food

das Essen, die Kost, die Lebensmittel, die Nahrung, die Nahrungsmittel, der Proviant, die Speise

The most general word for 'food' is **Essen**, e.g. **Wie ist das Essen in Südafrika?** 'What is the food like in South Africa?'. **Das deutsche Essen schmeckt mir nicht** 'I don't like German food'. As **Essen** is also the verb 'to eat', it can cause stylistic difficulties (*see* LUNCH).

Lebensmittel (always plural) should be used when 'food' is synonymous with 'groceries', e.g. **Ich muss noch Lebensmittel für das Wochenende kaufen** 'I still have to buy food for the weekend'.

Nahrung means 'food' in the sense of 'sustenance' and is thus more technical and formal and is used for '(animal) food', e.g. **Nahrung gibt es hier für die Tiere in Überfluss** 'There is food in profusion for the animals here', **Die meisten Einwohner des Landes können sich nicht einmal die Grundnahrungsmittel leisten** 'Most of the inhabitants of the country can't even afford basic food items', **Der Mais ist ein wichtiges Grundnahrungsmittel in Afrika** 'Maize is an important staple food in Africa'. Note: **Der Welternährungsfonds sorgt für Nahrungsmittelhilfe in Entwicklungsländern** 'The World Food Organisation provides developing countries with food aid', where the name of the body is derived from **ernähren** (to feed, provide food for).

Proviant is used in some contexts where 'food' is synonymous with 'provisions/supplies', e.g. **Wir müssen noch Reiseproviant kaufen** 'We still have to buy food for the journey'.

Speise, although meaning 'food', is mainly used in set compounds, e.g. **die Götterspeise** 'food of the gods, jelly/jello', **die Speisekarte** 'menu', **der Speisesaal/-raum** 'restaurant/dining-room' (in a public building).

'Seafood' is expressed by **Meeresfrüchte** (pl.).

Kost means 'food' in the sense of fare. Its use is generally speaking limited to set phrases, e.g. **vegetarische Kost** 'vegetarian food', **Tiefkühlkost** 'frozen food(s)', **freie Kost und Wohnung** 'free board and lodgings'.

for (with expressions of time)
(see SINCE)

Translating 'for' in expressions of time is tricky but can be summarised as follows.

If 'for' precedes a period of time in the past, leave it untranslated, e.g. **Er war 10 Tage/einen Monat in Wien** 'He was in Vienna for 10 days/a month' (NB acc. case), **Er war monatelang in Wien** 'He was in Vienna for months'. Note that this applies to the question too: **Wie lange war er in Wien?** 'How long was he in Vienna (for)?'. Despite the advice given here, **für** is not unknown in such phrases referring to the past, e.g. **In den Kasematten von Petrovsrdin wurde Tito 1914 für einige Tage gefangen gehalten** 'In 1914 Tito was held prisoner for some days in the casemates of Petrovsrdin'.

If 'for' precedes a period of time in the future, it is rendered either by **für** or **auf** (more formal), e.g. **Wir fahren für/auf drei Wochen nach Rhodos** 'We are going to Rhodes for three weeks'. This applies to the question: **Für/auf wie lange fahrt ihr?** 'How long are you going for?'.

If you have been doing s.t. for a certain length of time and still are, you use the present tense and 'for' is expressed by either **seit** (followed by dat.), **schon** (followed by acc.) or **schon seit** (followed by dat.), e.g. **Er wohnt seit 10 Jahren/schon 10 Jahre/schon seit 10 Jahren in Deutschland** 'He has been living in Germany for 10 years'. Note that 'for' in the following example is also expressed by **seit: Das war der schwerste Anschlag seit Jahren** 'That was the heaviest attack for years'.

the force, power, strength, violence; forceful, powerful, strong, violent

die Gewalt, die Kraft, die Macht, die Stärke, der Zwang; allmächtig, gewaltig, kräftig, kraftvoll, mächtig, stark

To have the 'strength' to do s.t. is **die Kraft**, e.g. **Ich habe keine Kraft mehr in den Händen** 'I no longer have any strength in my hands'. The corresponding adjective **kräftig** means 'strong' or 'powerful' with reference to a whole range of things such as taste, voice or even men.

Stärke refers to the strength of metals etc. rather than to personal strength although a person can of course be **stark**, 'strong'. Note also **Lautstärke**, the 'volume (knob)' on a television or radio.

Political 'power' is **Macht** and s.o. who is 'powerful' is **mächtig**. 'All-powerful', i.e. omnipotent, but also 'almighty' is **allmächtig**. But 'powerful language' is **kraftvolle Sprache**. If s.t. is within s.o.'s power to do s.t., it is **in seiner Macht**.

Gewalt translates both 'violence' and 'force', e.g. **Gewalttaten** 'acts of violence', **nackte Gewalt** 'brute force', **mit Gewalt** 'by force', **Gewalt anwenden** 'to use force', **die Gewalt des Sturmes** 'the force of the storm'. In this sense it causes no problems but it can also translate 'power' and you thus need to be aware where it is required and not **Macht**; power over s.o. or s.t. is **Gewalt**, e.g. **jdn in seiner Gewalt haben** 'to have s.o. in your power', **Gewalt über Leben und Tod haben** 'to have power (i.e. control) over life and death'. The adjective **gewaltig** can be used for a 'violent' storm but it commonly renders 'tremendous, massive, colossal' (also fig.) as well, e.g. **Er hat sich gewaltig geändert** 'He has changed enormously'.

'To force/compel' is **zwingen** from which der **Zwang** (force) is derived, but this 'force' refers to the pressure you exert on s.o. to do s.t., **Sie hat keinen Zwang auf mich ausgeübt** 'She didn't use any force on me/exert any pressure on me', **der Zwang des Gesetzes** 'the force of the law'.

A country's 'armed forces' are its **Streitkräfte** (*see* ARMY).

the foreigner, foreign

der Ausländer, der Fremde; ausländisch, fremd

A 'foreigner' in the sense of s.o. from another country is an **Ausländer**, and a 'stranger' is a **Fremder** (*see* STRANGE), but 'foreign' can be expressed by both **ausländisch** and **fremd**, normally by the former (e.g. **ausländische Währungen** 'foreign currencies'), but in compound nouns sometimes by the latter, e.g. **Fremdsprachen** 'foreign languages', **Fremdarbeiter** 'foreign workers', **die Fremdenlegion** 'foreign legion', **fremdenfeindlich** 'hostile to strangers/foreigners'.

free

frei, gratis, kostenlos, umsonst

'Free' as in freedom is **frei**, e.g. **Mandela war nach 27 Jahren Gefangenschaft endlich frei** 'Mandela was finally free after 27 years imprisonment'.

'Free' in the sense of not having to pay for something is **gratis** or **kostenlos** (also used as an adj. before a noun), but **umsonst** (lit. 'in vain') is commonly used adverbially with this meaning too, especially to express 'for free/nothing', e.g. **Der Eintritt war gratis/kostenlos/umsonst** 'Entry was free', **ein Gratisabonnement/ein kostenloses Abonnement** 'a free subscription', **Ich habe dieses Handy gratis/kostenlos/umsonst bekommen** 'I

got this cell phone for nothing'. As illustrated, as **gratis** cannot take an ending, it is usal to prefix it to the noun which it qualifies.

to freeze, frozen

abstürzen, frieren, einfrieren, erfrieren, gefrieren, vereisen, zufrieren

Both meteorological 'freezing' and the figurative use of 'to freeze' as in 'to be very cold', are expressed by **frieren**, e.g. **Ich friere/habe gefroren** 'I am/was freezing', **Es friert** 'It's freezing' (both lit. and fig.).

With reference to liquids, use **gefrieren**, e.g. **Wenn die Temperatur unter null Grad fällt, gefriert das Wasser in den Leitungen** 'When the temperature falls below zero, the water freezes in the pipes'. 'Freezing point' is **der Gefrierpunkt**, e.g. **unter dem Gefrierpunkt** 'below zero' (*see* FREEZER).

Erfrieren means 'to freeze to death' (lit. and fig.), e.g. **Die Tomatenpflanzen sind erfroren** 'The tomato plants have been killed by the frost', **Ohne Heizdecke wäre ich erfroren** 'I would have frozen to death without an electric blanket'.

'To freeze over' of stretches of water is **zufrieren**, e.g. **Dieser See/Bach friert im Winter sehr oft zu** 'This lake/stream often freezes over/up in winter'.

'To freeze/ice over/ice up' of roads and windows is **vereisen**, e.g. **Die Straße ist vereist** 'The road has frozen over/There is ice on the road'. This is also used as a tr. verb in the medical sense of having a wart etc. 'frozen (off)', e.g. **Der Arzt hat den Fleck auf meiner Wange vereist** 'The doctor froze off the mark on my cheek'.

'To freeze' food requires **einfrieren (lassen)**, e.g. **Dieses Produkt lässt sich gut einfrieren** 'This product freezes well', **Ich habe die Reste eingefroren** 'I have frozen the left-overs'. Note too **Der Schwan ist in dem See eingefroren** 'The swan got frozen into the lake'. **Tiefkühl-** or

tiefgekühlte/tiefgefrorene Produkte are frozen products and **die Tiefkühlkost** is frozen food (*see* FREEZER).

Einfrieren is also used for 'freezing' wages, e.g. **Alle Löhne sind für sechs Monate eingefroren worden** 'All wages have been frozen for six months'.

'To freeze' of computers is expressed by the same verb as 'to crash', i.e. **abstürzen**, e.g. **Auf einmal ist mein Computer abgestürzt** 'Suddenly my computer froze/crashed'.

the freezer

das Gefrierfach, der Gefrierschrank, die Gefriertruhe; das Tiefkühlfach, die Tiefkühltruhe, der Tiefkühlschrank

The two prefixes **Gefrier-** and **Tiefkühl-** are synonymous. The trick here is to decide whether the freezer you are referring to is a **Fach** (small compartment in a fridge), a **Truhe** (a chest) or a **Schrank** (an upright model).

the friend

sich anfreunden, sich befreunden; der/die Bekannte, der Freund, die Freundin, der Kumpel

The Germans make a clearer distinction between 'acquaintances' and 'friends' than we do in English. Only really close friends are **Freunde** (fem. **Freundin**), while all other 'friends/acquaintances' are **Bekannte**. Generally speaking **Freunde** are addressed with **du**, thus the word **Duz-Freund**, s.o. you are on **du** terms with. **Freund/Freundin** also render 'boy-/girlfriend', context usually making this clear, e.g. **Im Augenblick hat sie keinen Freund** 'She hasn't got a boyfriend at the moment', **meine Freundin** 'my girlfriend', **eine Freundin von mir** 'a (female) friend of mine'.

Your 'circle of friends' is **der Freundeskreis**. There is also the useful phrase **befreundet sein mit**, e.g. **Ich bin mit ihm (gut) befreundet** 'We are (good) friends'. 'To become friends with s.o.' is expressed verbally by **sich anfreunden**, e.g. **Wir haben uns letztes Jahr auf Rhodos angefreundet** 'We became friends last year in Rhodes'. Identical is **sich befreunden**, which occurs in two separate but synonymous constructions, e.g. **Wir haben uns befreundet** 'We have become friends', **Ich habe mich mit ihr befreundet** 'She and I have become friends'.

'Friendship' is **die Freundschaft** as an abstract, whereas **Bekanntschaft** is a collective for all your friends and acquaintances, i.e. **deine ganze Bekanntschaft** 'all your friends and acquaintances'. It also renders 'acquaintance' in the abstract sense, e.g. **Ich bin froh, dass ich ihre Bekanntschaft gemacht habe** 'I am pleased to have made your acquaintance'.

Der Kumpel (pl. **-s**) is a colloquial synonym of **Freund** rendering 'chum', 'mate' or 'buddy'.

the garage

die Garage, das Parkhaus, die Tankstelle, die Werkstatt

A **Garage** is what you park your car in at home, as well as in town, i.e. a **Hoch-/Tiefgarage** is an 'above/below ground multi-storied car park', also called a **Parkhaus**. Where you buy petrol/gas is a **Tankstelle**, but where you have your car serviced is a **(Reparatur)werkstatt**.

the German language

(das) Deutsch, das Deutsche

The language is referred to generally as **Deutsch**, e.g. **Sie lernt Deutsch in der Schule** 'She is learning

German at school'. This is also the case for 'German' in a specific context, often preceded by an article, and always when preceded by an adjective, e.g. **das Deutsch Thomas Manns** or **Thomas Manns Deutsch; Er spricht sehr gut Deutsch** 'He speaks German very well', **Er spricht gutes Deutsch** 'He speaks good German'. If **können** (*see* TO KNOW) is used instead of **sprechen** the adjective is used adverbially and thus remains uninflected, e.g. **Er kann sehr gut Deutsch** 'He speaks good German' (lit. He knows German well).

When the language is referred to in a general sense it is very common to treat it as a neuter adjectival noun preceded by the definite article, e.g. **etwas aus dem Deutschen ins Englische übersetzen** 'to translate s.t. from German into English'. This applies of course to all languages and dialects, which end in -isch, eg. **aus dem Türkischen ins Ungarische** 'from Turkish into Hungarian'. This form can never be used when **Deutsch** is preceded by an adjective, e.g. **die Rechtschreibung des Deutschen** but **des modernen Deutsch(s)** 'the spelling of modern German'.

Deutsch, or any language, as the object of **sprechen/reden** has long been seen as functioning as an adverb and has been written with a small letter, e.g. **Hat er mit dir deutsch gesprochen?** 'Did he speak German to you?'. Under the new spelling **Deutsch** is capitalised here, as well as in the expression **auf Deutsch**, where it was previously written with a small letter. **In Deutsch**, synonymous with **auf Deutsch**, is becoming quite common but **in** is always used when an adjective follows, e.g. **in schönstem Amtsdeutsch** 'in perfect officialese'. **Im Deutschen** can translate 'in German' where the meaning is 'in the German language', e.g. **Es gibt heutzutage viele englische Lehnwörter im Deutschen/in der deutschen Sprache** 'There are many English loanwords in German these days'. There is also a formal idiom **in deutscher Sprache**, e.g. **Das Buch erscheint Ende Mai in deutscher Sprache** 'The book is appearing in German (translation) at the end of May'.

The expression **auf gut Deutsch gesagt** means 'to put it bluntly'.

Germany

die Bundesrepublik (Deutschland), Deutschland, Westdeutschland, Ostdeutschland, die alten/neuen Bundesländer

The official name of the country is **die Bundesrepublik Deutschland** 'the Federal Republic of Germany'. Although Germans commonly refer to their country as **Deutschland**, it is also very common for them to simply call it **die Bundesrepublik**, e.g. **Wie lange wohnen Sie schon in der Bundesrepubik?** 'How long have you been living in Germany?'. Historically (i.e. 1949–1990) Germans did not refer to East Germany as **Ostdeutschland** but called it **die DDR** (< **Deutsche Demokratische Reuplik**), but since reunification the term has gained some frequency, alternating with the equally common **die fünf neuen Bundesländer** (also called **der Osten**), referring to West Germany either as **Westdeutschland** or **die alten Bundesländer**.

to get, to receive

bekommen, empfangen, erhalten, kriegen, werden

'To get' can mean so many things in English that it can be quite tricky deciding on the appropriate translation. We'll start with its literal meaning of 'to receive'. The most everyday word is **kriegen**, a somewhat more formal synonym of which is **bekommen**, e.g. **Fritz hat Hundert Euro von** seinem Opa zum Geburtstag gekriegt/bekommen, 'Fritz got 100 euros for his birthday from his grandpa'.

Where 'to get' means 'to be awarded/given' as of a prize or prison sentence, for example, **erhalten** can be used but is interchangeable with **bekommen**, e.g. **Der amerikanische Präsident hat in dem Jahr den Karlspreis erhalten** 'The American President got/received the Charlemagne Prize in that year'. It is also used for getting a permit, e.g. **Er hat seine Aufenthaltsgenehmigung immer noch nicht erhalten** 'He still hasn't got/received his residence permit'. **Erhalten** can also be used for receiving mail etc. in which sense it is also interchangeable with **bekommen** and **kriegen**, but far less usual.

Empfangen also means 'to receive' but usually in the more formal sense of receiving or welcoming a guest, but also of television and radio, e.g. **Er wurde sehr herzlich empfangen** 'He was very heartily received', **Wir können die BBC hier nicht empfangen** 'We can't receive the BBC here'.

Note that where 'to get' stands for 'to buy', **kaufen** is often used instead of **kriegen** or **bekommen** with which it is interchangeable, e.g. **Wo hast du dieses wunderbare Laptop gekauft?** 'Where did you get this terrific laptop?'.

Where 'to get' does not mean 'to receive/obtain' it often stands in for 'to become' and in such contexts must be rendered by **werden**, e.g. **Es wurde sehr früh dunkel** 'It got dark very early', **Du bist dick geworden. Wie willst du jetzt in deine Jeans kommen?** 'You have got fat. How do you expect to get into your jeans?'. As the second 'get' in the previous example illustrates, 'get' can have a host of other meanings other than 'to receive' and 'to become', in which case you have to look to rephrasing it in German. The range of options is too diverse to be treated here.

to get in/out, to get on/off

aussteigen, besteigen, einsteigen, steigen, umsteigen, zusteigen

'To get into' a car, bus, train, tram etc. can be rendered either by **steigen in** + acc. or **(hin)einsteigen in** + acc. (**stieg/ist gestiegen**), e.g. **Er ist in den Zug gestiegen/(hin)eingestiegen** 'He got into the train'; the latter puts just a little more emphasis on the motion of the action, and even more so with the addition of **hin**.

Exactly the same choice exists with regard to 'to get out', e.g. **Er ist aus dem Zug gestiegen/ (her)ausgestiegen** 'He got out of the train'.

A more elevated synonym of **einsteigen** is **besteigen**, which is a tr. verb (compare 'to alight'), e.g. **Er bestieg den vollbesetzten Bus**.

In German trains the conductor (**der Schaffner**) walks though the carriages crying out **Ist irgendjemand zugestiegen?** 'Has anyone just got in?', the connotation of the **zu** being 'joined those who were already here and thus haven't been checked yet'.

Umsteigen is used for 'changing' buses, trains, trams etc. Whereas in English we mention the mode of transport, if changing from bus to bus, train to train or tram to tram it suffices to say in German **Er ist in Hannover umgestiegen** 'He changed trains in Hanover'. But if changing the mode of transport, you can say **Er ist in Hannover in den Bus umgestiegen** 'He changed to the bus in Hanover/He got into the bus in Hanover' (*see* TO CHANGE).

(Auf)steigen auf + acc. and **(ab)steigen von** render 'to get on/off' bicycles and horses, e.g. **Er stieg auf sein Fahrrad (auf)** 'He got on his bike', **Er stieg von seinem Fahrrad (ab)** 'He got off his bike'; it is more usual not to use the prefixes.

to give

bescheren, geben, schenken, verschenken, weggeben

Geben is of course the most usual verb. When you give s.o. s.t. as a present, you use **schenken** in German avoiding all the ambiguity inherent in English 'to give' as to whether you have given the thing for keeps or not, e.g. **Ich habe zwei Exemplare von diesem Buch. Ich schenke dir eins** 'I have two copies of this book. I'll give you one'.

Verschenken renders 'to give away' (lit. and fig.) and thus in its lit. meaning is synonymous with **weggeben**, e.g. **Er hat all sein Geld verschenkt/ weggegeben** 'He has given all his money away'.

Bescheren is used specifically for the giving (out) of Christmas presents, i.e. **jdn (mit etwas) bescheren**, e.g. **Sie hat mich beschert** 'She gave me a Christmas present', **Seine Eltern haben ihn mit einem Auto beschert** 'His parents gave him a car for Christmas'.

to go (*see* TO WALK)

gehen, fahren, Auto fahren, Rad fahren, radeln

Very often 'to go' must be rendered by **fahren** in German, for example whenever the mode of transport is mentioned, i.e. **mit dem Auto/Fahrrad/Zug, mit der Straßenbahn/Bahn fahren** 'to go by car/bike/train/tram/train', e.g. **Wir fahren morgen mit dem Zug in die Schweiz** 'We are going to Switzerland by train tomorrow'. But if the mode of transport is not mentioned and the reference is merely to 'going' somewhere, **gehen** can be used, despite the fact that a vehicle of some sort is clearly being used, e.g. **Wir gehen sehr oft nach Polen** 'We often go to Poland', **Wir gehen nach Deutschland zurück** 'We're going back to Germany' (suggesting for good, i.e.

emigrating, not merely going on a trip). Compare **Wir fahren am Wochenende nach Deutschland zurück** 'We're going back to Germany on the weekend', where the connotation is one driving or taking the train back.

'To go cycling/cycle' is **Rad fahren** or more informally **radeln**, e.g. **Wir sind während der Ferien viel Rad gefahren/geradelt** 'We went cycling a lot during the holidays'. Note however that when the emphasis is on the mode of transport as a means of getting from A to B, rather than on the action of cycling itself, it is necessary to use **mit dem (Fahr)rad fahren**, e.g. **Wir sind mit dem Rad in die Stadt gefahren** 'We cycled to town'. Similarly with **Auto fahren** and **mit dem Auto fahren**.

'To go shopping/fishing/walking' etc. is rendered quite simply by **einkaufen/fischen/spazieren gehen**, e.g. **Marianne ist einkaufen gegangen** 'Marianne has gone shopping'.

'Was/were going to' can mean 'had the intention of (but didn't)'. This is rendered in German by **wollte(n)**, e.g. **Er wollte während der Ferien seinen Führerschein machen, hat's aber nicht geschafft** 'He was going to go for his driver's licence during the holidays, but didn't make it'.

goodbye

auf Wiederhören/Wiedersehen/ Wiederschauen, bis gleich/später/morgen, servus, pfüti/pfüteuch, tschau, tschüs

The most usual formal expression is **auf Wiedersehen**, which in the south commonly has the form **auf Wiederschauen**.[12] When saying 'goodbye' on the phone, possibly to s.o. you do not know and will never see, the appropriate greeting is **auf Wiederhören**.

---

12 Note that natural pronunciation demands the dropping of the e in the ending, i.e **Wiedersehn/-schaun**.

But often the above are more than is required for a mere 'bye, bye' or 'see ya'. You might settle for **tschüs** 'bye', or **bis gleich/später** 'see you later' (some time on the same day) or **bis morgen/Freitag** 'till tomorrow/Friday'; all these expressions with **bis** are likely to be preceded or followed by a **tschüs** as well just for good measure.

Where **tschüs** is predominantly a northern expression, which is also used in the south, the south has its own variant which is not used in the north, namely **pfüti** (to s.o. you are on **du** terms with) with a plural form **pfüteuch**.

Servus is another predominantly southern form which can be used for both coming and going (*see* HELLO) in a similar way to the Italian 'ciao', whereas **tschau** (< It. ciao) in German is only used for going.

the government, parliament

der Bundesrat, der Bundestag, der Landtag, das Parlament, die Regierung

'Government' in the sense of a given regime is rendered by **Regierung** or **Bundesregierung** 'federal government'. 'Parliament', in particular with reference to any foreign country's, is **das Parlament**. The Germans will normally refer to decisions of **der Bundestag**, the federal lower house, or **der Bundesrat**, the federal upper house. These two concepts with reference to foreign countries, are referred to as **das Unter-/Oberhaus**, given that they can be called a host of things in other languages and cultures. Thus if referring to the House of Lords in Britain, **das Oberhaus des britischen Parlaments** will express the concept in a way that means s.t. to a German, while the Germans refer to the lower house of the US congress as **das Repräsentantenhaus** 'the House of Representatives'.

The parliament of a German state is **der Landtag**.

the grain, corn (*see* SEED)

das Getreide, das Korn, der Mais, das Popcorn

The best general word for 'grain' or 'cereal' is **Getreide** but **Korn** is commonly used with this meaning too, as is the word 'corn' in some parts of the English-speaking world, e.g. **der Kornspeicher** 'grain silo/granary', **die Kornmühle** 'mill for grinding grain'. But where 'corn' refers to 'maize' or 'sweet corn' (no distinction in German), the word required is **Mais**, e.g. **der Maiskolben** 'corn cob'. 'Popcorn' is **das Popcorn**.

the ground, earth, soil, land, floor, bottom

der Boden, die Erde, der Fußboden, der Grund, das Grundstück, die Parzelle

The planet 'earth' is called **die Erde**. 'Earth' in the sense of 'soil' is **der Boden**, e.g. **Lehmboden** 'clay soil', **Hier liegt alles Mögliche im Boden begraben** 'There is every possibly thing buried in the earth/ground here'. **Bodenschätze** renders 'mineral resources'. Note, however, that 'to cover s.t. with soil' is **etwas mit Erde bedecken**.

The 'floor' is der **Fußboden**, but where context makes it clear that you are referring to a 'floor' and not the 'ground' or 'soil', **Boden** suffices, e.g. **Die Zeitung liegt auf dem Boden neben dem Sofa** 'The paper is lying on the floor next to the couch'.

Grund generally refers to 'land' which one occupies or buys and sells, and a given 'block of land' is a **Grundstück** or **Parzelle**. The word **Land** generally means 'province' or 'country' and only translates 'land' where this is synonymous with a country (*see* COUNTRY). Thus die **Grundsteuer** renders 'property tax' or 'rates' and **das Grundwasser** 'ground water'. **Grund und Boden** are commonly used together to refer to the 'land' or 'ground', particularly in set expressions, e.g **ein Dorf in Grund und Boden bomben** 'to bomb a village into the ground'. But both **Grund** and **Boden** can render 'bottom' of a valley, barrel or the sea, e.g. **der Meeresgrund/Meeresboden** 'sea bed, bottom of the sea', **Der Frosch lag tot auf dem Boden des Eimers** 'The frog was lying dead in the bottom of the bucket'.

to grow

anbauen, anpflanzen, anwachsen, aufwachsen, erwachsen, großwerden, heranwachsen, wachsen, werden, ziehen, züchten

'To grow' as an intr. verb is **wachsen**, e.g. **Mit 13 hat er angefangen zu wachsen** 'He started to grow at 13'. Where 'growing' is synonymous with getting bigger, exactly that can be said in German, e.g. **Was bist du gewachsen/Was bist du großgeworden!** 'Boy, how you have grown!' When it means 'to grow up' in a given place or in a given way, the word is **aufwachsen**, e.g. **Er ist Deutscher, ist aber in Amerika aufgewachsen** 'He is a German but he grew up in America'.

Erwachsen in the sense of 'to grow' is an adjective, e.g. **Ihr Sohn ist jetzt erwachsen** 'Their son is now grown-up', **Mein Gott bist du erwachsen geworden** 'Gee, how you have grown up'. **Der/die Erwachsene** 'the grown-up/adult'.

Anwachsen renders 'to grow' where it is synonymous with to increase, e.g. **Das Team der Inspektoren ist inzwischen auf 30 Mitglieder angewachsen** 'The team of inspectors has meanwhile grown to 30 members'.

Heranwachsen with reference to people means 'to grow (up) into' (i.e. to turn into), e.g. **Ihr Sohn ist zu einem intelligenten jungen Mann herangewachsen** 'Her son has grown into an intelligent young man'.

But 'to grow' is ambiguous in English as it is also used as a tr. verb meaning 'to grow' plants etc. This too is expressed by a variety of words: **anbauen, anpflanzen, ziehen** and **züchten**. **Anbauen** is used in agriculture whereas **züchten** has connotations of cultivating/breeding and is thus used of animals too, e.g. **In Australien wird überall Weizen angebaut** 'Wheat is grown everywhere in Australia', **Ich züchte Rosen** 'I grow roses', but **Ich habe diesen Blumkohl selbst angepflanzt** 'I grew this cauliflower myself'.

And finally, 'to grow' can be used figuratively in the meaning of 'getting/becoming' and in such contexts must thus be rendered by **werden**, e.g. **Es wurde dunkel** 'It was growing dark' (*see* TO GET).

the guard

der Wächter, der Wärter

The two words are synonymous but usage has determined that one or the other is preferred for particular professions. **Wächter** is used for night watchman, museum or parking area guard or attendant; compare **Wachhund** 'guard-/watchdog'. **Wärter** on the other hand is used for animal or lighthouse keeper as well as prison guard/warder.

to guess

erraten, raten

Raten is used to express 'to have a guess' whereas **erraten** expresses 'to have guessed (correctly)', e.g. **Rat mal, was ich in der Hand habe!** 'Guess what I have in my hand', **Ich habe erraten, wo er sich damals befunden hat** 'I guessed where he was at the time', **Wie hast du das erraten?** 'How did you guess that?'.

the gun

die Flinte, das Gewehr, die Pistole, der Revolver, die Schrotbüchse, die Schusswaffe

Schusswaffe is a generic word for 'gun'. A **Gewehr** is a 'rifle', as is a **Flinte**. A **Luftgewehr** is an 'air-rifle' and **Schrotbüchse** a 'shotgun'. **Pistole** and **Revolver** are self-explanatory.

the handle

der Griff, der Henkel, die Klinke, der Stiel

A 'handle' which is gripped, such as a door which has a handle rather than a knob (**der Türknopf**), is a **Griff** or **Klinke**, the latter being exclusive to doors, whereas a long handle such as a frying pan has, is a **Stiel** and thus this word is used for a broomstick too for example, but the handle of a knife is a **Griff**. The rounded handle of a cup, jug or bucket is a **Henkel**.

to hang

(sich) aufhängen, auflegen, (sich) erhängen, hängen

Part of the problem here has to do with whether 'to hang' is used as a tr. or an intr. verb. In the former case **hängen**, a regular verb is used, e.g. **Ich hänge/er hängt das Bild, ich hängte/er hängte das Bild, ich habe/er hat das Bild gehängt** 'I hang/he hangs the picture etc'. A variant of this identical in meaning to 'to hang up' is **aufhängen**. As an intr. verb you must use the strong verb **hängen** (i.e. **es hängt, es hing, es hat gehangen**), e.g. **Diese Bild hing jahrelang an der Wohnzimmerwand** 'This picture hung on the loungeroom wall for years'. Note that in the present tense these two verbs are identical.

The intr. verb **hangen** is now obsolete, having been replaced by **hängen** (*see* TO PUT).

Erhängen relates to the hanging of people and is used reflexively in the case of suicide by hanging, e.g. **In diesem Land wird man sogar wegen Diebstahls erhängt** 'In this country one is even hanged for robbery', **Ihr Sohn hat sich erhängt** 'Her son hanged himself'; **sich hängen** is also possible here. **Sich aufhängen** is used coll. with this meaning too, but **aufhängen** is also the verb used for 'hanging up' on the phone, in which case it is synonymous with **auflegen**, e.g. **Sie hat (den Hörer) aufgehängt/aufgelegt** 'She hung up (put the receiver down)'.

to happen, occur, take place

sich ereignen, geschehen, passieren, stattfinden, vorkommen, zustoßen

Passieren and **geschehen**, which are synonymous, are the most usual way of rendering 'to happen', the French loanword strangely enough being more common than the indigenous German word.[13]

How you translate 'to happen to s.o.' depends on the connotation, e.g. **Wenn mir was zustößt, rufe ich euch an** 'If anything happens to me (= befalls), I'll ring you'; but **geschehen** and **passieren** could all be used here, all followed by the dative. But where the sense is not 'to befall' but 'to become of', **werden von** is used, e.g. **Was ist von ihm geworden?** 'Whatever happened to him?' (i.e. What became of him?).

The question 'What's happened?' meaning 'What's up/what's the problem?' can be rendered colloquially by **Was ist los?**

Sich ereignen, from which is derived **das Ereignis** (event), is a more formal sounding word

---

13 Note that all the verbs that render 'to happen' require **sein** in the perfect tense, except **sich ereignen** which, like all reflexive verbs, takes **haben**.

corresponding more with 'to occur', e.g. **In Norwegen hat sich ein schweres Zugunglück ereignet** 'A serious train accident occurred in Norway'. But **vorkommen** also renders 'happen' in the sense of 'to occur' in more everyday language, e.g. **Das kommt öfter vor** 'That occurs from time to time'; **sich ereignen** would sound ridiculous in this simple sentence.

There is one idiomatic use of 'happen' where it means 'to chance', in which case the verb has to be expressed periphrastically, e.g. **Er hat sie zufällig am Wochenende gesehen** 'He happened to see her on the weekend'.

happy, lucky

froh, fröhlich, glücklich, Glück haben, Schwein haben, zufrieden

Das Glück means 'luck' but 'to be lucky' is expressed by **Glück haben**, e.g. **Du hast Glück gehabt** 'You were lucky'. A colourful colloquial synonym is **Du hast Schwein gehabt.**

Glücklich means 'happy' in the sense of full of happiness, e.g. **Meine Tochter wohnt seit Jahren in Australien und ist sehr glücklich da drüben** 'My daughter has been living in Australia for years and is very happy over there'.

'Happy' when it does not mean 'full of happiness' but rather 'glad' or 'pleased' is usually rendered by **froh**, e.g. **Ich bin froh, dass meine Kinder alle in der Nähe wohnen** 'I'm happy/glad/pleased all my children live in the vicinity'. **Fröhlich**, on the other hand, means 'merry' and can thus render 'happy' in this sense, e.g. **A: Und wie war er? B: Ganz fröhlich** 'A: And how was he? B: Quite jolly', **frohe/fröhliche Weihnachten** 'Happy/ Merry Christmas'.[14]

'Happy/pleased with' s.t. is **zufrieden mit** (lit. satisfied with), e.g. **Mein Onkel hat vor kurzem eine digitale Kamera gekauft und ist sehr zufrieden damit** 'My uncle bought a digital camera recently and is very happy with it'. Of course the concept can also be expressed by using one of the various words meaning 'to like', e.g. **Seine neue Kamera gefällt ihm sehr** 'He's very pleased with his new camera' (*see* TO LIKE).

hard

fleißig, hart, schwer, schwierig

'Hard' as the opposite of soft (**weich**) is **hart**, e.g. **ein hartgekochtes Ei** 'a hard-boiled egg', **hartes Holz** 'hard wood'. Like its English counterpart, this word can also be used figuratively as the opposite of mild (**mild**), e.g. **ein harter Winter** 'a hard/harsh winter'.

'Hard' meaning 'difficult' is **hart**, **schwer** or **schwierig**, but most usually **schwer**. In this sense the three words are interchangeable, but **schwer** also means 'heavy' and 'severe', e.g. **eine harte/schwere/schwierige Übung** 'a hard exercise' (note that **leicht** too can mean either 'easy' or 'light[weight]'), **Dieser Koffer ist verdammt schwer** 'This suitcase is bloody heavy', **ein schwerer Sturm** 'a severe storm'. There are contexts where either **hart** or **schwer** might be interchangeable, e.g. **ein hartes/schweres Leben** 'a hard life', **ein harter/schwerer Winter** 'a severe winter'. A 'difficult' person is **schwierig**, but 'it is difficult to (say/measure)' is usually **es ist schwer zu (sagen/messen)**.

To work 'hard' is rendered by **hart** or less commonly by **fleißig** (lit. industrious[ly]), e.g. **Er hat während des Jahres sehr fleißig gearbeitet und hat**

---

14 The salutation 'happy birthday' on the other hand is rendered idiomatically, i.e. either by (**Herzlichen**) **Glückwunsch** or by **Gratuliere** (lit. I congratulate you), but

'Did you have a happy Christmas/birthday?' is expressed **Hast du schöne Weihnachten/einen schönen Geburtstag gehabt?**

vier Einsen für sein Abi bekommen 'He worked really hard during the year and got four A's for his school leaving exam' (*see* MARK).

to heal, cure

ausheilen, auskurieren, gesundmachen, heilen, kurieren, verheilen

Heilen is both a tr. and an intr. verb, e.g. **Diese Salbe hat die Wunde geheilt** 'This salve healed/cured the wound', **Die Wunde ist geheilt** 'The wound has healed', **Der Patient ist geheilt** 'The patient is cured'. As a tr. verb with reference to people **gesundmachen** is also possible, e.g. **Dieser Arzt hat mich geheilt/gesundgemacht** 'This doctor healed/cured me'. **Kurieren** is synonymous with **heilen** and could be substituted for it in all the above examples.

Ausheilen as an intr. verb with reference to a wound is interchangeable with **heilen**, e.g. **Die Wunde ist ausgeheilt; geheilt** is also possible here.

Verheilen is only used intr. with reference to wounds and in common with the intr. use of both **heilen** and **ausheilen**, with which it is synonymous, it requires **sein** in the prefect tense, e.g. **Seine Wunden sind verheilt** 'His wounds have healed'.

to hear

erfahren, erhören, hören

Don't bother to use **können** with **hören** when asking s.o. if they can hear s.t.; verbs of perception in German do not require it but can use it, e.g. **Hörst du das/Kannst du das hören?** 'Can you hear that?'.

Erhören is used specifically for prayers being 'heard' or 'answered' and usually occurs in the passive, e.g. **Ihre Gebete sind erhört worden** 'Her prayers have been heard/answered'. Note that **unerhört,** derived from the past participle of this verb has the same fig. meaning as the English 'unheard of' (i.e. outrageous).

'To (get to) hear of/about' is **erfahren**, e.g. **Als seine Mutter das erfuhr, wurde sie wütend** 'When his mother heard/got to hear about that, she was furious'.

to heat (up); to warm (up)

beheizen, erhitzen, heiß machen, heizen; aufwärmen, (sich) erwärmen, vorwärmen, warm werden

Heizen is used as a tr. and intr. verb for 'heating' a room, e.g. **Wir heizen das Wohnzimmer aber nicht die Schlafzimmer** 'We heat the lounge but not the bedrooms', **Wir heizen gar nicht im Herbst** 'We don't heat at all in autumn' (*see* HEATER, HEATING). As a tr. verb **heizen** and **beheizen** alternate, with the latter sounding more official, e.g. **Diese Räume können nicht geheizt/beheizt werden** 'These rooms can't be heated', **Das Horner Schwimmbad ist ungeheizt/unbeheizt** 'The swimming pool in Horn is not heated'.

Everyday heating of food or water is **heiß machen** whereas **erhitzen** is a more technical term used for heating to a certain temperature, e.g. **Hast du die Würstchen schon heiß gemacht** 'Have you heated the sausages yet?', **Das Wasser muss auf 60 Grad erhitzt werden** 'The water has to be heated to 60 degrees'.

'To warm' food up is **aufwärmen**, in which case this verb is synonymous with **heiß machen** (compare TO HEAT and TO WARM UP). The intr. verb 'to warm up' (lit. and fig.) is **warm werden**, e.g. **Der Tag ist warm geworden** 'The day has warmed up'.

'To preheat' an oven is **vorheizen** and 'to heat/warm' dinner plates is **vorwärmen**, e.g. **Hast du den Ofen vorgeheizt/die Teller vorgewärmt?** 'Have you preheated the oven/heated the plates?'.

Sich aufwärmen (to warm [o.s.] up) can refer either to doing so to ward off the cold or in the sporting sense.

Erwärmen is usually used reflexively in a technical sense, e.g. **Die Welt erwärmt sich allmählich** 'The world is gradually getting warmer', **die globale Erwärmung** 'global warming'.

the heater, heating

die (Zentral)Heizung, der Heizkörper, der Kamin, der Ofen, der Radiator

The 'heating' found these days in nearly all German homes is **(Zentral)Heizung** '(central) heating'. The 'central heating element' up against the wall of the room is called a **Heizkörper**. A one or two bar 'electric heater' is a **Radiator** (pl. **Radiatoren**). An 'open fireplace' is a **Kamin**. In older German houses, for example in a typical farmhouse, you may find a large tiled structure protruding through the wall from the kitchen, where it is the oven, into the lounge where it is the heater – this is a **(Kachel)ofen**.

hello

grüezi, grüß dich/euch, grüß Gott, guten Morgen/Tag/Abend, hallo, moin, servus

The most usual, reasonably formal greeting is **(schön) guten Morgen** or **(schön) guten Tag** during the morning and **guten Tag** in the afternoon,[15] and **guten Abend** after 5.00pm; there is

no equivalent of 'good Afternoon'. **Guten Tag** is also the accepted greeting when meeting someone for the first time, regardless of the time of day. It is uttered as you put your right hand out to shake hands, usually while mumbling your name at the same time, e.g. **Guten Tag – Karl Schmollgruber** 'How do you do! My name is Karl Schmollgruber'.

A colloquial greeting akin to 'hi' in the south is **grüß dich** or **grüß euch**, if those being greeted are plural, but **servus** is common in the south too, and like 'ciao' in Italian, can be used for both 'hi' and 'bye'. As northern as **servus** is southern, is the expression **moin**, often said double, **moin moin**, which is dialect for 'morning' but is used at all times of the day for 'hello'. The Sie-form of **grüß dich/euch**, which is not at all particularly coll. but the most commonly heard greeting in the south, is **grüß Gott**! The Swiss use the very handy **grüezi** as an all purpose 'hello'.

The German form of 'hello' is **hallo**, pronounced as spelt with more stress on the first syllable than is the case in English where the stress is clearly on the second syllable.

to hide

(sich) verbergen, (sich) verstecken

Verstecken renders 'to hide' when it is intended that s.t. or s.o. should not be found, e.g. **Er versteckte seine Brieftasche in der Schublade** 'He hid his wallet in the drawer', **Er versteckte sich unter dem Bett** 'He hid under the bed'. Thus a 'hiding place' is **das Versteck**.

Verbergen is 'to hide' in the sense of conceal, not revealing, e.g. **Ich habe nichts zu verbergen** 'I have nothing to hide', **Sie versuchte ihre Hand zu verbergen** 'She tried to hide her hand' (keep it out of sight), **Hier liegen Opale verborgen** 'Opals are lying hidden here'.

---

15 Colloquially one often hears the following when greeting a group of people: **guten Morgen/Tag (alle) miteinander** 'Good Morning/Day everybody'.

the holiday(s)

der Feiertag, die Ferien, der Urlaub

Ferien (pl.) and **Urlaub** are synonymous in many contexts but it is worth noting the use of **Urlaub** in the following standard expressions: **in/im/auf Urlaub sein** 'to be on holidays', **in Urlaub fahren** 'to go on holiday'. School or university holidays are always **(Schul)ferien**, whereas workers get **Urlaub** (e.g. **einen Tag Urlaub nehmen** 'to take a day's holiday/leave'), but this is not to say that expressions like **Ferien haben** (to be on holidays) and **Ferien machen** (to [take a] holiday) cannot be used with reference to workers too.

A 'public holiday' is a **Feiertag**, e.g. **Wir haben jeden Tag auf, außer feiertags/an Feiertagen** 'We are open every day except on public holidays', **Der 3. Oktober ist ein Feiertag in Deutschland** 'The third of October is a (public) holiday in Germany'.

to hope

sich erhoffen, hoffen, hoffentlich

Hoffen often requires a syntax that is quite different from English. Here are some examples: **Ich hoffe sehr, dass . . .** 'I really hope (that) . . .', **Ich hoffe es** 'I hope so', **Ich will nicht hoffen, dass er das macht** 'I hope he doesn't do that', **Wir wollen hoffen, dass . . .** 'We can only hope that . . .'. But it is often simpler to avoid the verb **hoffen** by using the adverb **hoffentlich** (hopefully), e.g. **Hoffentlich kommt er zurück** 'I hope he'll return', **Hoffentlich** 'I hope so', **Hoffentlich nicht** 'I hope not'.

'To hope for' s.t. requires **auf** (+ acc.), e.g. **Man hofft auf eine Lösung** 'We're hoping for a solution', but there is also a verb **sich erhoffen** which means 'to expect', e.g. **Worauf hoffen sie?** 'What are they hoping for?', **Was erhoffen sie sich davon?** 'What are they expecting (= hoping to gain)?'.

the hospital

die Klinik, das Krankenhaus, das Lazarett, das Spital

The usual word is **Krankenhaus**, but a 'university/academic hospital' is a **(Universitäts)klinik**. In Austria and Switzerland **Spital** is used instead of **Krankenhaus** but is obsolete in Germany. A 'field hospital', but also a 'military sick bay', is a **Lazarett**.

the hour

die Uhr, die Stunde

Uhr normally translates 'clock' and 'watch' (*see* CLOCK) but it also renders 'o'clock' when telling the time, e.g. **um achtzehn Uhr** 'at six o'clock'. 'Hour' is rendered by **Stunde**, e.g. **Der Film hat zweieinhalb Stunden gedauert** 'The film lasted two and a half hours'. German also has an adjectival derivative, **-stündig**, e.g. **ein zweistündiges Konzert.** 'a concert of two hours' duration'.

the house, (at) home, the apartment

das Apartment, die Bleibe, der Bungalow, das Ein-/Zweifamilienhaus, das Heim, die Heimat, das Reihenhaus, das Wohnhaus, die Wohnung, das Zuhause; zu/nach Hause

Many more Germans live in an 'apartment' or 'flat', **Wohnung**, than is the case in English-speaking countries; the word **das Apartment** also occurs. Even when they do live in a house, there may well be either one or two houses under one roof, called an **Ein-** or **Zweifamilienhaus** respectively. A 'free-standing house', relatively rare in Germany, is called **ein freistehendes Haus** whereas a 'terrace/town house' is a **Reihenhaus**. A **Bungalow** is also a free-standing house but it must have a flat roof. The word **Wohnhaus**, 'residential building', serves to distinguish such a building from one used for other purposes, e.g. **Parkhaus** 'a multi-storied carpark'.

Your own 'home' is your **Zuhause**, which *can* be used as a noun but it is more usual to say **Hier bin ich zu Hause** 'This is my home' (house or town or country in which you live). The adverbial expression 'at home' is **zu Hause** whereas 'home',[16] in 'I am going home' is **Ich gehe nach Hause**. Southern equivalents of **zu Hause** and **nach Hause**, which are regarded as High German, are **daheim** and **heim** respectively, e.g. **Ich bin hier daheim/Ich gehe heim**.

Das Heim as a noun renders 'home' in the sense of 'hostel', i.e. **Studentenwohnheim** 'student residence', **Alten-** or **Altersheim** 'old people's home', **Kinderheim** 'children's home'. It can refer to one's own home, e.g. **ein neuartiges Alarmsystem für Eigenheime** 'a new type of burglar alarm for private homes'.

Heimat expresses 'home' is the sense of 'homeland' or 'home town', e.g. **Nach dem Krieg haben viele Deutsche ihre Heimat in Ost-Europa verlassen müssen** 'After the war many Germans had to leave their home(land) in eastern Europe'. **Heimat** and **Heimatland** are synonymous with reference to the country from which one hails; these words have a folkloristic ring to them.

'Homeless' is **obdachlos** and thus 'the homeless person' is **der/die Obdachlose**.

Note that 'housework' is expressed by **die Hausarbeit**, while 'homework' is **die Hausaufgabe(n)**.

---

16 Note that the expression 'at home' (**zu Hause**), which is distinguishable from 'home' (direction towards, i.e. **nach Hause**), can dispense with the 'at', e.g. **Es scheint, dass sie lieber zu Hause bleiben** 'It seems that they would rather stay (at) home'. Don't let this confuse you in deciding between **zu Hause** and **nach Hause**.

humid, moist

drückend, feucht, schwül

A 'humid' or 'muggy' day or weather is **schwül**, but weather and heat can also be **drückend** (**heiß**). Meteorologically speaking 'humidity' is **die (Luft)feuchtigkeit**, while the adjective **feucht** normally means 'moist' rather than 'humid', not referring to weather, e.g. **Die Socken sind noch feucht** 'The socks are still moist'.

to hurt; the pain, ache

kränken, schmerzen, wehtun; das Weh, der Schmerz, die Schmerzen

'To hurt' both as a tr. and an intr. verb is **weh tun**, e.g. **Er hat mir weh getan** 'He hurt me', **Das tut weh** 'That hurts'. When parts of the body are hurting, express it as follows: **Mir tun die Hände weh** 'My hands are hurting', **Ihm tut der Magen weh** 'His stomach is hurting'. **Schmerzen** is synonymous with **wehtun** with reference to hurting body parts e.g. **Mein Bein schmerzt/Mir schmerzt das Bein** 'My leg is hurting'.

'Pain' is expressed either by **das Weh** or **die Schmerzen** (pl.) and these words are interchangeable when used in compounds with parts of the body, e.g. **Ich habe Kopfweh/Kopfschmerzen** 'I have a headache', **Sie hat Bauchweh/Bauchschmerzen** 'She has (a) stomach ache'. **Schmerz** is not commonly used in the sing. but does occur, e.g. **stechender Schmerz** 'stabbing pain', **Ich kann den Schmerz/die Schmerzen nicht mehr ertragen** 'I can no longer bear the pain'.

'To hurt' s.o.'s feelings is **kränken**, e.g. **Ich habe sie leider gekränkt** 'Unfortunately I hurt her feelings', **Er war sehr gekränkt** 'He was very hurt/His feelings were badly hurt'.

to hurry, be in a rush

sich beeilen, eilen, Eile haben, in (großer) Eile sein, es eilig haben

'To hurry (yourself) up' is **sich beeilen**, e.g. **Ach Gott, es ist schon zehn Uhr. Ich muss mich beeilen** 'Crikey, it is ten o'clock already. I'd better get a move on/hurry up'. This is also the verb for ordering s.o. else to hurry up, e.g. **Beeil dich!** 'Hurry up!'.

'To be in a hurry/rush' can be expressed in any of three ways using **Eile haben, in (großer) Eile sein** and **es eilig haben**, e.g. **Ich habe Eile, Ich bin in (großer) Eile, Ich habe es eilig** 'I'm in a hurry/ rush'. Note **Nur keine Eile!** 'Don't rush!'.

Eilen is 'to hurry/rush', e.g. **Er eilte sofort herbei** 'He rushed over immediately'.

if (*see* WHEN)

ob, wenn

When 'if' is interchangeable with 'whether', it must be translated by **ob**, e.g. **Ich weiß nicht, ob er morgen zurückkommt** 'I do not know if/whether he's returning tomorrow'. When it does not mean 'whether' it must be rendered by **wenn**, e.g. **Du kannst zum Abendbrot bleiben, wenn du willst** 'You can stay for supper if you wish', **Was wäre, wenn?** 'What if?'.

to imagine

sich einbilden, sich vorstellen

Sich vorstellen means 'to picture' s.t. to o.s., e.g. **Ich kann es mir nicht vorstellen** 'I can't imagine it' (lit. and fig.), **Stell dir vor, du wohntest in Indien** 'Imagine you lived in India', **Der Mann sah**

so aus, wie Eva sich ihn vorgestellt hatte 'The man looked the way Eva had imagined he would'.

Sich einbilden refers to an illusion, e.g. **Er bildet sich ein, dass er der Chef ist** 'He imagines he is the boss', **Ich habe es mir nur eingebildet** 'I merely imagined it'.

to immigrate, emigrate; the immigrant, emigrant

abwandern, auswandern, einwandern, emigrieren, immigrieren, zuwandern; der Asylant, der Asylbewerber, der Aussiedler, der Auswanderer, der Einwanderer, der Gastarbeiter, der Zuwanderer

Auswandern/emigrieren and **einwandern/immigrieren** are synonymous couplets but the indigenous German words are more common. The same applies to the nouns **Auswanderer/Emigrant** and **Einwanderer/Immigrant**. **Zuwandern** is another verb meaning 'to immigrate' but with connotations of 'to join those who are already there' (see **ein-** and **zusteigen** under TO GET IN), e.g. **Der Bundesinnenminister will die Zuwanderung nach Deutschland neu regeln** 'The federal interior minister wants to reorganise (further) immigration into Germany'. Consequently the new law to encourage controlled immigration to Germany is called **das Zuwanderungsgesetz**. Note: all the above verbs take **sein** in the perfect.

As Germany has until very recently never seen itself as a country of immigration, despite having been one since the arrival of the first guest or migrant workers (**Gastarbeiter**) over 40 years ago, where in English-speaking countries foreign compatriots might be called 'immigrants', in Germany other names are used, depending on their origins. **Aussiedler** is used for people of German ethnic origin *returning* to live in

Germany after centuries in eastern Europe, chiefly the former Soviet Union. These days many of the latest arrivals are **Asylbewerber**, 'asylum seekers', many of whom will end up with the status of immigrant. The term **Asylant** is tricky; for some it is synonymous with **Asylbewerber**, for others it applies to s.o. who has already been granted asylum, but these days it also tends to be used by right-wingers who oppose the presence of these people in Germany.

Abwandern (Abwanderung) also renders 'to emigrate' but with the connotation of population drain, e.g. **Ostdeutsche Jugendliche wandern ab in den Westen** 'East German youth is emigrating to the west'.

immediate(ly)

gleich, sofort, unmittelbar

'Immediately' in the literal sense of 'straight away' is **sofort**, e.g. **Komm sofort hierher** 'Come here immediately'. In combination with other adverbs, **gleich** is used, e.g. **gleich danach** 'immediately after that', **gleich am Anfang** 'right at the beginning'. But **gleich** on its own does not mean 'straight away', but 'directly', i.e. soon, e.g. **Ich komme gleich** 'I'll be there in a moment/directly', whereas **Ich komme sofort** means 'I'm coming right now'.

Unmittelbar when used adverbially is synonymous with **gleich**, e.g. **unmittelbar nach dem Krieg** 'immediately after the war', but it can also be used adjectivally, unlike **sofort**, in which case its meaning is somewhat figurative, e.g. **in unmittelbarer Nähe** 'in the immediate vicinity', **Indien ist unmittelbarer Nachbar von Pakistan** 'India is an immediate neighbour of Pakistan'. The adjectival derivative of **sofort** renders the more literal meaning of 'immediate', e.g. **Man erwartete eine sofortige Reaktion** 'They were expecting an immediate reaction'.

to impress; impressive

beeindrucken, einen Eindruck machen auf, imponieren; beeindruckend, eindrucksvoll, imponierend, imposant

'To impress' s.b. is expressed either by **beeindrucken** or **imponieren** but the latter verb takes the dat., e.g. **Ihr Sohn hat mich sehr beeindruckt/mir sehr imponiert** 'Her son impressed me very much'. If there is no object, use **imponieren**, e.g. **Das neue Gebäude imponiert, nicht?** 'The new building impresses (= is impressive), doesn't it?'. 'Impressive' is otherwise expressed by **beeindruckend, eindrucksvoll** or **imponierend**, but also **imposant** (lit. imposing) which is not negative as 'imposing' can be in English.

to improve

besser gehen/machen/werden, sich bessern, nachbessern, (sich) verbessern

Bessern is usually reflexive and suggests an ongoing process of improvement, e.g. **Ihr Bruder hat sich mittlerweile gebessert** 'Her bother has improved meanwhile' (i.e. his character), **Die Lage hat sich etwas gebessert** 'The situation has improved somewhat'.

Verbessern means 'to improve (on)' or 'to bring closer to perfection', e.g. **Das Buch ist in vielen Hinsichten verbessert worden** 'The book has been improved in many respects', **Die Firma versucht, die Qualität ihrer Produkte zu verbessern** 'The firm is trying to improve the quality of its products'. With regard to people **sich verbessern** particularly refers to improving achievement, e.g. **Ihr Sohn hat sich in der Schule verbessert** 'Her son has improved at school'.

Verbessern also renders 'to correct' or 'remove errors', particularly with reference to the written word, e.g. **Werden Sie meinen Aufsatz bitte**

verbessern? 'Will you please correct my essay?' (*see* TO CORRECT).

With reference to s.o.'s health 'improving' **besser gehen** is best used, e.g. **Ihm geht es wieder besser** 'He has improved', but note **Gute Besserung** 'I hope you get well soon'. You will often find that **besser machen/werden** will suffice to render improve (tr./intr.), e.g. **Das hat die Lage besser gemacht** 'That improved the situation', **Das Wetter ist besser geworden** 'The weather has improved'.

Nachbessern means 'to retouch/make improvements to', but with reference to a law, a context in which it is commonly heard, it renders 'to amend', e.g. **Wir wollen den Balkon nachbessern** 'We want to make some improvements to the balcony', **Der Bundestag hat das Zuwanderungsgesetz endlich nachgebessert** 'Parliament has finally amended the Immigration Act'.

independent

unabhängig, selbstständig

Unabhängig von (independent from) is the opposite of **abhängig von** (dependent on), e.g. **Er ist jetzt finanziell unabhängig von seinen Eltern** 'He is now financially independent of his parents'. This is also the word used to express political 'independence', e.g. **Die Vereinigten Staaten haben im 18. Jahrhundert Unabhängigkeit von Großbritannien erworben** 'The US obtained independence from Great Britain in the 18th century'.

Selbstständig(keit) refers to independence in the sense of standing on one's own two feet, e.g. **selbstständig handeln** 'to act independently/on one's own', **Er arbeitet/ist jetzt selbstständig** 'He's now independent/on his own' (i.e. in business). Under the old spelling this word was written **selbständig**.

to inform

benachrichtigen, (sich) informieren, mitteilen, (sich) unterrichten, verständigen

'Informing s.o. of s.t.' is both **jdn über etwas informieren** and **jdn von etwas unterrichten** where the preposition rendering 'of' differs, e.g. **Er hat mich darüber informiert/Er hat mich davon unterrichtet** 'He informed me of it'. **Sich informieren/unterrichten über** (+ acc.) renders 'to inform o.s. about s.t.', e.g. **Ich habe mich über die Schließung des Kernkraftwerkes informiert/unterrichtet** 'I've found out about the closure of the nuclear power station'.

Synonymous with **jdn informieren** is **jdm mitteilen**, e.g. **Er hat mich informiert, dass . . . /Er hat mir mitgeteilt, dass . . .** 'He informed me that . . .', **Ich wurde informiert, dass . . ./Mir wurde mitgeteilt, dass . . .** 'I was informed that . . .'.

'To inform' where the meaning is 'to advise' or 'notify' can be expressed in three ways e.g. **die Polizei informieren/benachrichtigen/verständigen** 'to inform/notify the police'.

the inhabitant, resident

der Anlieger, der Anrainer, der Anwohner, die Anwohnerschaft, der Bewohner, der Einwohner

The 'inhabitant' of a town or country is **der Einwohner**, but the 'inhabitant' of a building is a **Bewohner**, lit. a 'resident'. The 'residents' of a given area are **Anwohner**, e.g. **Anwohner des Flughafens/der Weser** 'people residing in the vicinity of the airport/the Weser River'; **die Anwohnerschaft** is a collective with the same meaning. **Anrainer** is a synonym of **Anwohner**, e.g. **Flughafenanrainer** 'those living in the vicinity of the airport'. Both words commonly occur on signs in Germany to point out that parking, thoroughfare etc. is only permitted for those who reside there, e.g. **Parkplatz – nur für Anwohner/ Anrainer**. Synonymous with both these words and usually only encountered on signs is **Anlieger**, e.g. **Anlieger frei** 'Residents only' (no thoroughfare).

to inherit (*see* hinterlassen and vermachen under TO LEAVE)

beerben, erben, vererben

'To inherit' from s.o. is **erben**, e.g. **Ich habe von meiner unverheirateten Tante geerbt** 'I inherited from my maiden aunt'.

Beerben means 'to inherit s.o.'s estate', always with a personal object and means the same as **erben von**, e.g. **Ich werde meine Tante beerben/von meiner Tante erben** 'I will inherit my aunt's estate/from my aunt'.

'To leave' or 'bequeath' s.t. to s.o. is **vererben**, e.g. **Sie vererbte mir ihr ganzes Vermögen** 'She left me her entire fortune/all her assets'.

to intend

beabsichtigen, die Absicht haben, vorhaben

Beabsichtigen and **die Absicht haben** are synonymous, with the latter sounding somewhat more everyday, e.g. **Wir beabsichtigen/haben die Absicht, dem Land zu helfen** 'We intend to help the country', **Hatten Sie das beabsichtigt/War das Ihre Absicht?** 'Was that your intention?'. The question 'What do you intend doing?' cannot be expressed by either of these verbs but must be rendered by **vorhaben**, e.g. **Was hast du (heute) vor?** 'What do you intend doing (today)?'.

interested in, an interest in

ein Interesse haben an, sich interessieren für, interessiert sein an

'To be interested in' can be expressed relatively literally by **interessiert sein an** + dat., e.g. **Er ist sehr an Vögeln interessiert** 'He is very interested in birds'. But completely synonymous is the somewhat idiomatic formulation **sich interessieren für**, e.g. **Er interessiert sich sehr für Vögel**. Less usual, but nevertheless synonymous is **ein Interesse haben an** + dat., e.g. **Er hat ein großes Interesse an Vögeln** 'He has a great interest in birds'.

the job, labour, work, employment

die Anstellung, die Arbeit, der Arbeitsplatz, der Job, die Stelle, die Stellung, das Werk

'Work' in general is **Arbeit** as well as one's own job, but where we use the noun 'work', German commonly utilises the verb **arbeiten** (*see* TO WORK), e.g. **Ihr Mann ist arbeiten** 'Her husband is at work', **Er ist arbeiten gegangen** 'He has gone to work', **Mein Mann kommt bald von der Arbeit nach Hause** 'My husband will soon be coming home from work', **Ich muss jetzt zur Arbeit gehen** 'I must go to work now', **Ihr Mann ist auf der Arbeit** 'Her husband is at work', **Ich muss gestehen, dass ich meine Arbeit immer noch sehr genieße** 'I must admit I still enjoy my job/work very much'.

Arbeit also renders 'labour', e.g. **der Tag der Arbeit** 'Labour Day', **Zwangsarbeit** 'forced/hard labour'. **Arbeit** also often translates 'employment', e.g. **arbeitslos** 'unemployed', **das Arbeitsamt** 'employment office/job centre'. Note that **Hausarbeit** renders 'housework' and **Hausaufgaben** (usually pl.) renders 'homework'.

In certain standard expressions **Arbeit** is used where we might use the word 'job', e.g. **Ich suche**

Arbeit 'I am looking for a job', **Er hat keine Arbeit** 'He hasn't got a job'. **Er hat Teilzeitarbeit** can be translated as 'He has part-time work' or 'a part-time job', but **Er hat den Arbeitsplatz verloren** renders 'He has lost his job'. Note too **Er ist an der Arbeitsstelle/am Arbeitsplatz** 'He is at work'.

There are, however, several other words that translate 'job': **der Job, die Stelle**, and **die (An)stellung. Job** is mostly used with reference to a part-time **Job** that a student might have, for example, but it is also possible for a full-time member of the workforce (**die Arbeiterschaft**) to refer to his work as a **Job**. But **jobben**, a German verb derived from the English noun, only relates to casual or part-time working, e.g. **Er muss in den Sommerferien jobben, um seine Lehrbücher kaufen zu können** 'He has to work/get a job in the summer holidays to be able to buy his textbooks'. A normal full-time 'job' is called either a **Stelle** or **(An)stellung**, the former being the more usual word and the latter having connotations of 'one's position'. Where **Stellen** refers to 'jobs' in the work force, **Arbeitsplätze** is synonymous, e.g. **Der Vorstand von VW will Stellen/Arbeitsplätze abbauen** 'The management of VW wants to reduce the number of jobs'.

Werk refers to the 'work' of authors, artists and scientists, i.e. the fruits of their labours, e.g. **Mir gefällt dieses Werk von Bach** 'I like this work of Bach's'. It, like 'works' in this sense in English, also commonly occurs in the plural, e.g. **die gesammelten Werke der Gebrüder Grimm** 'the collected works of the Brothers Grimm'.

to judge

beurteilen, einschätzen, schätzen, urteilen

The intr. verb **urteilen über etwas** refers to lofty judging or giving of opinion of s.t., e.g. **Er will nicht darüber urteilen** 'He does not want to give an opinion about it/judge it'. **Urteilen** is the word required in the expression 'to judge by/judging by', e.g. **Nach seinem Aussehen zu urteilen, ist er ein Penner** 'Judging by his appearance he is a tramp'.

Much more common is the tr. verb **beurteilen**, e.g. **Ich kann die Qualität des Buches nicht beurteilen** 'I can't judge/assess the quality of the book', **Er beurteilt die Lage im Westjordanland als ruhig** 'He judges/assesses the situation on the West Bank to be peaceful'.

Einschätzen is more or less synonymous with **beurteilen**, e.g. **Wie ich die Lage einschätze . . .** 'As I judge the situation . . .', but where some mathematical assessment is required **schätzen** is more appropriate, e.g. **Ich schätze den Abstand auf 400 Meter** 'I judge the distance to be 400 metres'.

just

eben, genau, gerade, gerecht, (so)eben

The adverb 'just' meaning s.t. has 'just' happened is either **(so)eben** or **gerade** with no distinction in meaning, e.g. **Ich habe eben/soeben/gerade mit ihm telefoniert** 'I just talked to him on the phone'. But **gerade** also means 'just at this/that very moment', e.g. **Er kommt gerade** 'He's just coming'.

'Just' meaning 'exactly' is either **gerade** or **genau**, e.g. **Es ist gerade/genau sechs Uhr** 'It is just six o'clock'.

The adjective 'just' meaning 'fair' is **gerecht**, e.g. **Es war ein gerechtes Urteil** 'It was a just verdict'.

to keep

aufbewahren, aufheben, beibehalten, behalten, bewahren, einhalten, erhalten, (sich) halten, vorenthalten, wahren

Bewahren means 'to keep' valuables in a safe place, e.g. **Er bewahrt seine Münzsammlung im**

Keller 'He keeps his coin collection in the cellar' (compare **halten** below where both the idea of valuables and a safe place is lacking). **Bewahren** can also mean 'to keep' or 'maintain' s.t. abstract, particularly under difficult circumstances, e.g. **Nur die Überweisungen von Verwandten aus Amerika bewahren viele kubanische Familien vor dem Absturz in die totale Armut** 'Only the transfers of funds from relatives in America keep many Cuban families from succumbing to utter poverty'.

'To keep' meaning 'to store' or 'put away' in a safe place is also **aufbewahren** but unlike **bewahren**, the implication is that it is only for a shortish period and that the item is to be called on later, e.g. **Ich kann Ihren Pass für Sie aufbewahren, wenn Sie wollen** 'I can keep your passport for you if you wish', **Diese Medikamente müssen kühl aufbewahrt werden** 'This medication must be kept in a cool place'.

'To keep' in the sense of 'to preserve' in certain standard expressions is **wahren**, e.g. **Die Europäer wollen ihr Gesicht wahren** 'The Europeans want to keep face', **Sie tun alles in ihrer Macht, den Schein zu wahren** 'They are doing everything in their power to keep up appearances'.

Aufheben is similar in meaning to **aufbewahren** but with the emphasis being on not throwing away or not losing rather than being stored in a particular place, e.g. **Heben Sie die Quittung auf!** 'Keep the receipt', **das Beste bis zum Schluss aufheben** 'to keep the best till last'.

'To keep' in one's possession is **behalten**, e.g. **Du kannst den Schirm behalten** 'You can keep the umbrella', **Wir möchten die neue Sekretärin behalten** 'We would like to keep the new secretary', **Ich kann das alles nicht im Kopf behalten** 'I can't keep all that in my head', **Er hat das Geheimnis für sich behalten** 'He kept the secret to himself'.

'To maintain' or 'to keep' s.t. in one position is **halten**, e.g. **Er hält Kontakt mit seinem Dozenten** 'He keeps in touch with his lecturer', **Sie hielt die Hand hinter dem Rücken** 'She kept her hand behind her back', **Halte den Finger da!** 'Keep your finger there', **Sie hält ihm sein Essen warm** 'She is keeping his dinner warm for him', **das Gleichgewicht halten** 'to keep one's balance'. It is also used in the standard expressions **ein Versprechen halten** (to keep a promise) and **dein Wort halten** (to keep your word). 'To keep' of domestic animals is also **halten**, e.g. **Wir halten keine Ziegen mehr** 'We don't keep goats any more'. 'To keep to the left/right' is **sich links/rechts halten**.

When food 'keeps' well/badly **(sich) halten** is required, e.g. **Brombeeren halten (sich) nicht gut bei diesem Wetter** 'Blackberries don't keep well in this weather', **Sie halten (sich) noch eine Woche** 'They'll keep for another week'.

Erhalten means 'to keep' from deteriorating, dying or decaying where emphasis is on the result, e.g. **jdn am Leben erhalten** 'to keep s.o. alive', **Sie hat ihre Figur gut erhalten** 'She has kept her figure well', **Die Regierung will die Wehrpflicht erhalten** 'The government wants to keep conscription'.

Aufrechterhalten means 'to keep' or 'maintain' at a certain level or standard, e.g. **den Frieden aufrechterhalten** 'to keep the peace', **Die alten Stammessitten werden noch aufrechterhalten** 'The old tribal customs are being kept up', **Gute Beziehungen zu Russland werden von der Regierung aufrechterhalten** 'Good relations with Russia are kept up/maintained by the government'.

Einhalten means 'to keep/stick to' of obligations between two or more parties, e.g. **Sie haben den Termin/die Vereinbarung eingehalten** 'They kept the date/stuck to the agreement'. Compare **ein Versprechen/dein Wort halten** above where there is only one person involved.

'To keep/withhold' s.t. from s.o. is **vorenthalten**, e.g. **Das wollte die Regierung dem Volk vorenthalten** 'The government wanted to keep that from the people'.

Beibehalten means 'to retain' or 'stick to' s.t., e.g. **Amerika will seinen harten Kurs gegen den Terrorismus beibehalten** 'America wants to retain its hard line against terrorism'.

to kill, murder

ermorden, hinrichten, killen, morden, töten, (sich) umbringen

The everyday word is **töten**, which is used with reference to people and animals, but a common synonym for people is **umbringen**, which is the usual word with reference to killing oneself, e.g. **Er hat die Schlange getötet** 'He killed the snake', **Er hat sich/seine Mutter umgebracht** 'He killed himself/his mother'.

Killen and **der Killer** have made their way into German via American films but only refer to the killing or murdering of people. The indigenous words are **morden** (intr.), **ermorden** (tr.) and **der Mörder** – note that the last word means 'murderer' and **der Mord** renders 'the murder', e.g. **Bewaffnete Banden in Ruanda mordeten hemmungslos** 'Armed gangs in Rwanda were murdering in an unrestrained fashion', **Die Rebellen haben ihre Geiseln ermordet** 'The rebels murdered their hostages'.

Note how the prefix **er-** in the following verbs changes the meaning of the root verb to one of 'killing by means of', i.e. **schlagen** is 'to hit/beat' but **erschlagen** is 'to beat to death'; similarly **schießen** 'to shoot' and **erschießen** 'to shoot dead', **stechen** 'to stab' and **erstechen** 'to stab to death', e.g. **Man muss schon unglaublich gefühlskalt sein, um jemanden einfach zu erschlagen** 'You have to be unbelievably cold-blooded to simply beat someone to death'[17] (*see* TO HANG).

Hinrichten means to execute.

to know

sich auskennen, erkennen, kennen, können, (Bescheid) wissen

'To know' in the sense of 'to be acquainted/familiar with s.o. or s.t.' is **kennen**, e.g. **Kennst du meinen Bruder?** 'Do you know my brother?', **Er kennt Rom sehr gut** 'He knows Rome very well'. 'To know' a fact is **wissen**, e.g. **Weißt du, wie er heißt?** 'Do you know what his name is?'. The following examples sum up the difference between these two verbs: **Kennst du den Weg? Weißt du, wohin der Weg läuft?** 'Do you know the way/path? Do you know where the path goes?', **Kennst/Weißt du den Autor des Buches?** 'Do you know the author of the book?' (the former means are you acquainted with him and the latter means do you know who he is), **Ich weiß den Weg dahin, aber ich kenne ihn nicht** 'I know how to get there but I have never taken the route'. See TO MEET for **kennen lernen** 'to get to know s.o.'.

Wissen is commonly combined with **Bescheid** adding a connotation of 'being informed about', e.g. **Er weiß schon Bescheid, denn ich habe es ihm gestern gesagt** 'He knows already as I told him yesterday', **Weißt du über Computer Bescheid?** 'Do you know about computers?'.

But there are contexts where the theoretical distinction between **kennen** and **wissen**, i.e. acquaintance versus knowledge, is not always obvious. **Kennen** can, for example, also express 'to know of' and is thus synonymous with **wissen von**, e.g.

---

[17] Prefixed to other verbs **er-** can mean 'to die by' (i.e. intr.) rather than 'to be killed by' (tr.), **ersticken** 'to suffocate' (and die in the process), **ertrinken** 'to drown', but **ertränken** 'to drown' as a tr. verb.

Die Parteiführenden kannten seine Aktivitäten (= wussten von seinen Aktivitäten) 'The party leaders knew of his activities'. The following also require **kennen**, not **wissen: Sie haben den Hunger nie gekannt** 'You have never known hunger', **Ich kannte seinen Namen** 'I knew his name (I'd heard it before)'; compare **Ich wusste seinen Namen** 'I knew his name (I knew what it was)'.

'To know' a language, i.e. '(to be able) to speak' a language is rendered by **können**, e.g. **Er kann gut Deutsch** 'He knows/speaks German well', **Er kann kein Deutsch** 'He knows/speaks no German'.

'To know one's way around a place' is expressed by **sich auskennen**, e.g. **Kennen Sie sich hier aus?** 'Do you know your way around here?', which is a good way to address s.o. when asking directions in a foreign place; it is tantamount to asking people if they are locals. But this expression is also applied to expertise in a given field, e.g. **Am Kaiserstuhl kennt man sich mit Rebensaft aus** 'At Kaiserstuhl they know everything there is to know about grape juice', **Er kennt sich in der Chemie aus** 'He knows about chemistry'.

the knowledge

die Erkenntnis, die Kenntnis(se), das Wissen, die Wissenschaft

'Knowledge' in the sense of without s.o.'s knowledge is **Wissen**, e.g. **ohne sein Wissen** 'without his knowing'. 'He had no knowledge of it' can be expressed simply as **Er wusste nichts davon** or alternatively **Er hatte keine Kenntnis davon**. **Kenntnis**, most often used in the plural, is used for 'knowledge' in the sense of something learnt, e.g. **Er will in England seine Sprach-/Englischkenntnisse auffrischen** 'He wants to brush up his knowledge of the language/of English in England'.

In a few compounds 'knowledge' is rendered by **Erkenntnis**, a word which otherwise means 'recognition/realisation', e.g. **der Erkenntnisdrang** 'thirst for knowledge', **die Erkenntnistheorie** 'theory of knowledge (epistemology)'.

'Knowledge' in the sense of learning is **Wissenschaft**, e.g. **der Fortschritt der Wissenschaft** 'the advance of knowledge'.

to last

andauern, ausreichen, dauern, halten

'To last' as in how long a film etc. lasts or how long it takes to do s.t. is rendered by **dauern**, e.g. **Wie lange hat der Krieg gedauert?** 'How long did the war last?', **Wie lange hat es gedauert, ihn zu beruhigen?** 'How long did it take to calm him down?'.

'Lasting' in the sense of 'continuing on' is **andauern** or **anhalten**, e.g. **Der Regen wird nicht andauern/anhalten** 'The rain won't last'.

'To last' in the sense of standing the test of time is rendered by **halten**, e.g. **Ihre Beziehungen mit Jungen halten nie** 'Her relationships with boys never last'.

'To last' meaning 'to be sufficient' is **ausreichen**, e.g. **Normale Packungen reichen nicht aus** 'Normal packs don't last' (= are too small) (*see* ENOUGH).

last

letzt, vergangen, vorig; zum letztenmal

'Last' in 'last week/month/spring/year' is most usually rendered by **letzt**, e.g. **letzte Woche/letzten Monat/letzten Frühling/letztes Jahr**, all in the accusative case. **Vergangen** and **vorig** are completely synonymous with **letzt** in these expressions but are stylistically higher, e.g. **im August (des) vergangenen Jahres** 'in August last year', **Im vorigen Juli wurde eine zehnprozentige Mehrwertsteuer eingeführt** 'Last July (but also 'in the previous July') a 10% VAT was introduced', **in den letzten/vergangenen drei Tagen** 'in the last three days' (*see* PERIODS OF THE DAY for 'last night'). **Vorletzt/vorvergangen** renders 'last but one' and **vorvorletzt/vorvorvergangen** 'last but two', e.g. **Am vorletzten/vorvergangenen Montag hatten die Rebellen ihr Quartier verlassen** 'Last Monday week the rebels had left their quarters'.

'Last year', as mentioned above, is normally **letztes Jahr** but can be expressed more formally by **im Vorjahr**, e.g. **Es gab dieses Jahr weniger Bewerbungen um Asyl als im Vorjahr** 'There were fewer applications for asylum this year than last year'.

'Last' as in 'When did they last see each other?' is **zum letztenmal**, e.g. **Wann haben sie sich zum letztenmal gesehen?** This German sentence is in fact ambiguous as it can also mean 'When did they see each other for the last time?' (*see* TIME). In the former sense **zuletzt** is very commonly used, e.g. **Wo haben Sie zuletzt gearbeitet?** 'Where did you last work?'. Compare too **Er kam zuletzt** 'He was the last to come'. In combination with **bis** this word renders 'to the last', e.g. **bis zuletzt kämpfen** 'to fight to the last', **bis zuletzt bleiben** 'to stay to the very end'.

'To come last' in sport or a competiton is expressed as follows: **Er war letzter/der letzte** 'He came last'.

(at) last(ly), finally

endgültig, endlich, letztens, letztendlich, letztlich, schließlich, zum Schluss, zuletzt

When listing, as in 'firstly, secondly and finally', the appropriate word for 'finally' is **letztens**, but

here you could also say **schließlich** or **zum Schluss**, e.g. **erstens, zweitens und letztens/schließlich/zum Schluss**.

Expressing relief at s.t. having 'finally' occurred requires **endlich**, e.g. **Und um sechs Uhr ist er endlich nach Hause gegangen** 'And at six o'clock he finally went home'. 'Finally' (and also 'eventually') without this connotation of relief is expressed by **schließlich/zum Schluss**, as in 'after all/when all is said and done', which is also the meaning of **letztlich**, e.g. **Es ist letztlich/schließlich/zum Schluss egal** 'It comes down to the same thing in the end/when all is said and done'.

'Finally' where there is a connotation of 'definitively/once and for all' can be rendered by **endgültig**, e.g. **Jetzt sind wir ihn endgültig los** 'We are finally rid of him (for good)'.

Letztendlich renders 'at (long) last', e.g. **Letztendlich hat er sich entschieden, die Stelle anzunehmen** 'At long last he has decided to accept the job'.

(to be) late

zu spät kommen, sich verspäten, verspätet sein, Verspätung haben

'To be late for s.t.' is **zu spät kommen (zu etwas)**, e.g. **Sie ist zu spät zur Vorlesung gekommen** 'She was late for the lecture'.

The subject of **Verspätung haben** is never a person but a train, plane etc., e.g. **Der Zug hat (10 Minuten) Verspätung** 'The train is (10 minutes) late'. This can also be expressed adjectivally by **verspätet**, e.g. **Der Zug ist verspätet** 'The train is late'. But **verspätet** can also be used for people, e.g. **Er ist verspätet (= zu spät) angekommen** 'He arrived late'.

Sich verspäten can mean either 'to be late' or 'to be delayed', e.g. **Wir mussten auf ihn warten, weil er sich verspätet hat** 'We had to wait for him because he was late/delayed', **Der Frühling hat sich verspätet,** 'Spring is late'.

to laugh (at), smile (at)

anlachen, anlächeln, auslachen, belachen, lachen über, sich lustig machen über, zulachen; belächeln, lächeln, zulächeln

'To laugh' and 'to smile' are simply **lachen** and **lächeln** (e.g. **Er lachte/lächelte** 'He laughed/smiled') but rendering 'to laugh/smile *at* s.o. or s.t.' is problematical. If you 'laugh at s.o.' in the sense of ridiculing them, you need **sich über jdn lustig machen** or **auslachen**, e.g. **Warum macht ihr euch lustig über mich/Warum lacht ihr mich aus?** 'Why are you laughing at me (= mocking me)?'. **Belächeln**, 'to smile at s.o.' has the same connotation as **auslachen**, e.g. **Der Beamte belächelte ihn** 'The official smiled at him (condemningly)'. If you need to make a distinction between 'laughing at' s.o. (i.e. ridiculing) and 'laughing with' s.o., **lachen mit** is used, e.g. **Ich lache dich nicht aus; ich lache mit dir** 'I'm not laughing *at* you but *with* you'.

'To smile at s.o.' positively is **jdn anlächeln**, e.g. **Der Beamte lächelte ihn an** 'The official smiled at him'. **Anlachen** has the same positive connotation in German but in English 'to smile at' is usually positive, whereas 'to laugh at' is always negative and thus 'to laugh at' is not really an appropriate translation of **anlachen**; it also renders 'to smile at', e.g. **Sie lachte mich freundlich an** 'She smiled at me in a friendly fashion/She gave me a friendly laugh'. **Jdm zulächeln/zulachen** are synonymous with **jdn anlächeln/anlachen** but are less commonly heard, e.g. **Sie lächelte/lachte mir freundlich zu.**

the law; the lawyer

das Gesetz, Jura, das Recht, die Rechtswissenschaft; der Jurist, der Notar, der Rechtsanwalt

An individual 'law' is a **Gesetz** and 'to pass a law' by the parliament is **ein Gesetz verabschieden.** The German constitution is called **das Grundgesetz** 'the Basic Law'. 'Sound laws' in linguistics are **Lautgesetze**. But the 'law' (i.e. 'legal system') of a given nation is its **Recht**, e.g. **Nach deutschem Recht ist so was nicht möglich** 'According to German law something like that is not possible'.

Rechtswissenschaft renders 'jurisprudence' but when studying 'law' as a discipline at university you study **Jura** (no article) and you are a **Jurist**. A qualified 'lawyer' with a practice is a **Rechtsanwalt/-anwältin**, which renders both 'solicitor' and 'barrister'. The Germans distinguish between a **Rechtsanwalt** and a **Notar**; the latter does not appear in court but deals with forms and documents and is thus in some ways comparable to a solicitor. In some Bundesländer **Rechtsanwälte** can also be **Notare**.

to lead; the leader

anführen, führen, leiten; der Anführer, der Führer, der Leiter

Führen means to 'lead' or 'to guide', e.g. **Er hat uns nach Hause geführt** 'He led/guided us home', **Sie führte die alte Dame über die Straße** 'She led/guided the old lady across the road'. A 'tourist guide' is a **Fremdenführer** whereas a **Reiseführer** (travel guide) might be either a person or a book. **Führen** is also required for paths, doors, steps etc. 'leading' somewhere, e.g. **Dieser Weg führt zu einem See** 'This path leads to a lake', and it is also used in fig. contexts such as **Der Krieg führte zu**

Armut im ganzen Land 'The war led to poverty throughout the country'.

Leiten in the sense of 'leading' rather than 'guiding' differs little from **führen** except that **führen** is usual in military and political contexts, whereas in business **leiten** prevails, e.g. **Er leitet unsere Zweigstelle der Deutschen Bank/unsere Schule** 'He runs our branch of the Deutsche Bank/our school'. The noun **Führer** has unfortunate connotations and although found in compounds (e.g. **Geschäftsführer** 'manager') , 'leader' is better rendered by **Leiter, der Leiter der Gruppe = der Gruppenführer/-leiter** 'the leader of the group', **der Schulleiter** 'headmaster/school director'.

The adjectives **führend** and **leitend** diverge more in meaning than the verbs from which they are derived; **leitend** means 'in a managerial position' whereas **führend** means the best in its category, e.g. **ein leitender Angestellter** 'an employee in a managerial position', **Volvo ist Schwedens führendes Auto** 'Volvo is Sweden's leading car'.

Anführen means 'to be at the head of' a group etc. in the literal sense. The noun **Anführer** has negative connotations similar to those of 'ringleader' and is used for the leader of gangs etc.

to learn (*see* TO STUDY)

lernen, erfahren, erlernen, verlernen

'To learn' in the sense of acquiring knowledge or a skill is **lernen**, e.g. **Wo hast du so gut Deutsch gelernt?** 'Where did you learn (to speak) German so well?'. Note how you express 'learning to do s.t.': **Sie hat schwimmen gelernt/zu schwimmen gelernt** 'She (has) learnt to swim'.

Erlernen is a more elevated synonym of **lernen** that can however only be applied to the finished process of having learnt s.t., e.g. **Manch ein Gastarbeiter hat schon Deutsch erlernt/gelernt** 'Many a guest worker has already learnt German; compare **Sie lernen Albanisch** where **erlernen** is not possible.

Verlernen renders 'to unlearn' s.t. but is usually translated by forgetting how to do s.t., e.g. **Er hat das Tanzen/seine Deutschkenntnisse verlernt** 'He's forgotten how to dance/how to speak German'.

'To learn' meaning 'to hear' is **erfahren**, e.g. **Er hat dann erfahren, dass seine Frau den ersten Preis im Lotto gewonnen habe** 'He then learnt that his wife had won first prize in Lotto', **Das habe ich im Fernsehen erfahren** 'I learnt that from television/I heard that on television'.

(at) least, the least

mindestens, am wenigsten, wenigstens, zumindest, zumindestens

Mindestens, wenigstens und **zumindest** are synonymous, with the first being the preferred form in the south, the second in the north and the last gradually becoming the most common form in the standard language, e.g. **Durch die Überflutungen kamen wenigstens/mindestens/zumindest 200 Menschen ums Leben** 'At least 200 people died as a result of the floods', **So ein Konzert kann ganz schön anstrengend sein, wenigstens/mindestens/zumindest für die Techniker** 'A concert like that can be quite taxing, at least for the technicians'. The hybrid form **zumindestens**, although not officially recognised, is commonly heard, even from the mouths of well educated people.

'The least' or '(the) least of all', the superlative of **wenig**, is rendered by **am wenigsten**, e.g. **Sie wurde von der Sache am wenigsten berührt** 'She was moved the least/least of all by the matter'.

to leave

abfahren, abfliegen, abgehen, abreisen,
auslaufen, gehen, hinterlassen, lassen,
losfahren, überlassen, verlassen, vermachen,
weggehen, zurücklassen

At the heart of the problem here is the difference
between 'leaving' s.t. alone or behind (= forgetting) and 'departing'. The former requires **lassen**,
e.g. **Lassen Sie mich in Ruhe** 'Leave me alone/in
peace'. It is commonly also possible to use **liegen**
or **stehen** in combination with **lassen** in the sense
of forgetting s.t., e.g. **Ich habe meine Kamera im
Kino gelassen/liegen lassen** 'I (have) left my
camera in the cinema', **Wo hast du dein Auto
gelassen/stehen lassen?** 'Where have you left
(= parked) your car?'.

'To leave behind' (i.e. as a consequence of an event
or action) is **zurücklassen**, e.g. **Der Sturm hat Tote
zurückgelassen** 'The storm left fatalities in its
wake'. 'To leave behind' in the sense of 'to be
survived by' after a death is **hinterlassen** (insep.),
e.g. **Er hinterlässt drei Kinder** 'He leaves three children behind/he is survived by three children'; also
**Als er starb, hinterließ er (seinen Kindern) ein
Vermögen** 'When he died he left (his children) a
fortune'. But 'to leave' s.t. to s.o. in one's will can
also be expressed by **vermachen**, e.g. **Er hat seinen
Kindern keinen Pfennig vermacht** 'He did not
leave his children a penny' (*see* TO INHERIT).

'To leave' it to s.o. else to do s.t. requires **überlassen**, e.g. **Das überlasse ich dir** 'I'll leave that to
you/in your hands'.

'To leave' in the sense of departing requires that
you distinguish between tr. and intr. use, the
former being **verlassen**, e.g. **Wann habt ihr die
Party verlassen?** 'When did you leave the party?',
Er hat seine Frau verlassen 'He has left his wife'.
Intransitively, i.e. all those contexts where 'leave'
can be replaced by 'depart', can be expressed in
a variety of ways, most usually by **(weg)gehen** or

abfahren, e.g. **Er ging ohne ein Wort zu sagen** 'He
left without saying a word', **Er ist gleich nach dem
Abendessen weggegangen/abgefahren** 'He left
straight after dinner'; **abfahren** puts more emphasis on leaving by means of a vehicle rather than
simply leaving without comment on the mode,
thus **Wann fährt der Zug ab?** 'When is the train
leaving?'. With reference to planes **abfliegen** is
used, e.g. **Wann fliegst du ab?** 'When are you
leaving?'. When departing on a longer journey
you can also use **abreisen**, e.g. **Wann reist du ab?**
Note that in some contexts **abfahren von** can
alternate with **verlassen**, e.g. **Wann seid ihr von
Berlin abgefahren/Wann habt ihr Berlin verlassen?** 'When did you leave Berlin?'.

'To leave for' a place is best rendered simply by
fahren/fliegen nach, e.g. **Wie fahren morgen nach
Frankreich** 'We leave for France tomorrow'; **auslaufen nach** is used specifically for ships, e.g. **Das
Schiff ist nach Grönland ausgelaufen** 'The ship
has left for Greenland'.

Die Schule verlassen/von der Schule abgehen
render 'to leave school', i.e. finish school.

But there are even more ways of expressing
'leaving' in the sense of 'departing', e.g. **Wie spät
gehst du morgens aus dem Haus?** 'At what time
do you leave home in the morning?', **Wann willst
du losfahren?** 'When do you want to leave (= set
off)?', **Er geht jeden Morgen um 7.00 zur Arbeit**
'He leaves for work at 7.00 every morning'.

the lecture, university class
(*see* LESSON)

das Referat, das Seminar, die Vorlesung,
der Vortrag

'Lectures' that form part of a course are
Vorlesungen. A one-off lecture, not forming part
of a tertiary course, is a **Vortrag**. 'To give a
lecture' is **eine Vorlesung/einen Vortrag halten**.

Seminar, in addition to referring to a university department (*see* DEPARTMENT), means what it does in English with the Germans making the following distinction: a **Proseminar** is an introductory seminar course for students in their first and second year and a **Hauptseminar** is one for advanced students. To present a seminar paper is **ein Referat halten/vortragen.**

to lend, borrow, loan

ausleihen, borgen, entlehnen, entleihen, leihen, pumpen, verleihen

The most usual word for both 'lending' (i.e. to give to s.o.) and 'borrowing' (i.e. to take from s.o.) is **leihen**, e.g. **Er hat mir ein Buch geliehen** 'He has lent me a book', **Ich habe (mir) ein Buch von ihm geliehen** 'I have borrowed a book from him'. It can also be used of money. In the sense of borrowing this verb is optionally reflexive (i.e. a dat. reflexive) in the same way that **kaufen** is (*see* TO BUY).

Synonymous with **leihen** in both senses of 'borrowing' and 'lending', although more formal, is **borgen**, i.e. **jdm etwas borgen** (to lend s.o. s.t.) and (**sich** dat.) **etwas bei/von jdm borgen** (to borrow s.t. from s.o.); the latter is optionally reflexive in the same way that **leihen** is, e.g. **Ich habe ihm meine Kamera geborgt** 'I've lent him my camera', **Er hat (sich) meine Kamera geborgt** 'He's borrowed my camera'.

Pumpen is a colloquial word and is chiefly used with reference to 'lending/borrowing' money, as illustrated by the expression **auf Pump** 'on credit', e.g. **Er kauft alles auf Pump** 'He buys everything on credit', **Er pumpt (sich) immer wieder Geld von seinem Bruder** 'He's always borrowing money from his brother'. As with **leihen** and **borgen**, in the sense of 'to borrow' this verb is optionally reflexive.

Verleihen (**an** + acc.) (compare **vermieten** under TO RENT) meaning 'to lend out to' s.o. is synonymous with **ausleihen**, which is the more everyday verb, e.g. **Ich verleihe mein Auto ungern/Ich leihe mein Auto ungern aus** 'I don't like lending my car'. **Ausleihen** can also render 'to borrow' and is the word used for 'borrowing' books from a library, as is **entleihen**, e.g. **Dies ist nur eine Präsenzbibliothek; man darf die Bücher nicht ausleihen** 'This is only a reading library; you are not allowed to borrow the books', **Ich habe das Buch aus der Universitätsbibliothek entliehen** 'I have borrowed the book from the university library'.

Entlehnen (**aus**) renders 'to borrow from' in the fig. sense, e.g. **Deutsch hat das Wort 'fit' aus dem Englischen entlehnt** 'German has borrowed the word 'fit' from English'.

the lesson, class

die Klasse, die Lektion, die Stunde, der Unterricht

Unterricht actually means 'instruction' (*see* TO TEACH) but is often used where in English we would say 'classes/lessons' (i.e. as a collective), e.g. **Was kostet der Klavierunterricht?** 'What do the piano lessons cost?', **Wie viel Unterricht hast du in der Woche?** 'How many classes do you have per week?'.

A **Stunde**, in addition to meaning an 'hour' also renders a 'class', e.g. **Wie viele Stunden unterrichtest du in der Woche?** 'How many classes/hours do you teach per week?'. Note **die Nachhilfestunde/der Nachhilfeunterrricht** 'private lesson/lessons'.

Klasse refers to a 'class' only as a group of people, e.g. **Wie viele Schüler türkischer Abstammung gibt es in dieser Klasse?** 'How many students of Turkish descent are there in this class?'.

Lektion is used chiefly for a 'lesson' in a book (i.e. a chapter in a textbook), e.g. **Lektion 5 beginnt auf Seite 85** 'Lesson 5 starts on page 85'. It is also used in the idiom **jdm eine Lektion erteilen** 'to teach s.o. a lesson' (fig.).

the letter

der Brief, der Buchstabe, die Letter

A 'letter' of the alphabet is der **Buchstabe**, e.g. **ein großer/kleiner Buchstabe** 'a captital/small letter', **'Auf Deutsch' schreibt man heutzutage groß**, 'These days you write "auf Deutsch" with a capital letter' (*see* SPELLING).

Die Letter is used in the printing trade and corresponds more with 'character', e.g. **Der Buchdruck mit beweglichen Lettern machte es möglich, Informationen schnell zu verbreiten** 'Printing with movable letters/characters made it possible to disseminate information quickly'.

Der Brief refers to a postal letter.

to lie (i.e. to tell a lie)

anlügen, belügen, erlügen, lügen

'To lie' and 'to tell a lie' are both rendered by **lügen**, e.g. **Er hat gelogen** 'He lied/told a lie'. There is a noun, **die Lüge**, but it is not used to express 'to tell a lie', e.g. **Das ist bestimmt eine Lüge** 'That's a lie for sure'.

'To tell s.o. a lie' or 'to lie to s.o.' are both **jdn anlügen**, e.g. **Die Wissenschaftler haben die Waffeninspektoren angelogen** 'The scientists lied to the inspectors'. **Belügen** is more or less synonymous with **anlügen**, although the latter can be more emphatic or blatant.

Erlügen means 'to fabricate' or 'make up' and thus its past participle used as an adjective can

correspond to 'to lie', e.g. **Das ist eine erlogene Geschichte** 'That story is a fabrication/lie', **Das ist erlogen** 'That is a lie'.

to lie (down), lay

legen, liegen, sich hin-/niederlegen

The confusion here is partially caused by so many English speakers not knowing the difference between 'lie' and 'lay' – the two are never confused in German. **Legen** (to lay) is a tr. verb and is regular in both languages (**legt/legte/hat gelegt** 'lays/laid/has laid'), e.g. **Er legte das Tuch auf den Tisch** 'He laid the cloth on the table' (*see* TO PUT). **Liegen** (to lie) is an intr. verb and is irregular in both languages (**liegt/lag/hat gelegen** 'lies/lay/has lain'), e.g. **Sie lag zu lange in der Sonne (hat . . . gelegen)** 'She lay/has lain in the sun too long'.

Despite the above, however, 'to lie down' in German is either **sich hinlegen** or **sich niederlegen**, i.e. both being formed from **legen**, not **liegen**, e.g. **Sie fühlte sich müde und hat sich eine Stunde hingelegt/niedergelegt** 'She felt tired and (went and) lay down for an hour' (*see* TO SIT DOWN). Both **hin-** and **niederlegen** are also used as tr. verbs meaning to 'lay/put down' (*see* TO PUT).

the light

die Ampel, die Glühbirne, die Lampe, die Laterne, das Licht

'Light' as opposed to 'dark' is **Licht**, e.g. **Ich brauche mehr Licht** 'I need more light'. It can also indirectly refer to the device that makes light, e.g. **Das Licht ist noch an/brennt noch** 'The light is still on/still burning'. The emphasis in the previous example is still on a light as a source of light, not on the light as a device in which case **Lampe** is more usual, e.g. **Wir müssen eine Lampe** für die Ecke kaufen 'We must buy a light for that corner'. A 'streetlight' is **die (Straßen)laterne** and a 'fluorescent light' is **die Leuchtstoffröhre**. Where the word 'light' stands for 'light bulb', this must be stated in German, e.g. **Diese (Glüh)birne ist durchgebrannt** 'This light/globe has blown'. **Ampel** is a 'traffic light', e.g. **Halte an der nächsten Ampel!** 'Stop at the next (traffic) light(s)'.

to like

finden, gefallen, gern haben/tun, lieben, mögen, schmecken

One common way of rendering 'to like' s.t. is with **mögen**; it can be used for liking people or things, e.g. **Wir mögen sie (nicht)** 'We (don't) like them', **Sie mag keine Meeresfrüchte** 'She doesn't like seafood', **Manche Mögen es Heiß** 'Some Like it Hot (the movie)'. The past tense is **mochten/ haben gemocht**, e.g. **Auch in Deutschland haben viele Leute diese Schauspielerin gemocht** 'A lot of people in Germany also liked this actress'. **Gern** can be used together with **mögen** but is optional, e.g. **Ich mag meine Schwiegermutter sehr (gern)**. **Mögen/können** are often used in combination with **leiden** with reference to people to render 'to like', e.g. **Ich mag/kann ihn (gut) leiden** 'I like him (a lot)', **Ich mag/kann ihn nicht (gut) leiden** 'I don't like him', but a thing could also be the object of these sentences.

Möchte(n), a subjunctive form, is derived from **mögen** and renders 'would like', e.g. **Was möchten Sie?** (in a shop, but also **Was darf es sein?**) 'What would you like?'. **Ich möchte gern(e) einen Kaffee (haben)** 'I would like a cup of coffee' (**gern** optional). An alternative to this is: **Ich hätte gern eine Tasse Kaffee** (**gern** not optional). **Gerne** is a common alternative form of **gern**, e.g. **Ich möchte (gern[e]) einen deutschen Pass (haben)** 'I would really like (to have) a German passport'.

Gefallen generally speaking has the same meaning as **mögen**, although the two are not always necessarily interchangeable, and is used for both people and things with aesthetic appeal. As with **schmecken** (see below), the thing or things that you like form the subject of the sentence (= literally 'It/they are pleasing to me'), e.g. **Es gefällt mir/sie gefallen mir** 'I like it/them'. Note: **Es gefällt uns (gut) hier** 'We like it here'.

Gern haben is a good general verb meaning 'to like' and is used for things rather than people, e.g. **Ich habe Deutsch sehr gern**. Note that **lieber haben** renders 'to prefer', e.g. **Ich habe Deutsch gern, aber ich habe Französisch lieber** 'I like German but I prefer French' (*see* TO PREFER).

When you like doing something, you use the relevant verb + **gern**, e.g. **Ich schwimme gern** 'I like to swim/swimming', **Ich lerne gern Deutsch** 'I like learning German'. **Lieber** + verb renders 'to prefer doing' s.t., e.g. **Ich lerne gern Deutsch, aber ich lerne lieber Französisch** 'I like learning German but I prefer learning French' (*see* TO PREFER).

Schmecken is used for liking food on one occasion, e.g. **Dies schmeckt (mir gut/schlecht)** 'I like this/don't like this', **Schmeckt's?** 'Do you like it?'. **Mögen** and **gern essen** refer to liking food generally, e.g. **Ich mag Schokolade/Ich esse gerne Schokolade** 'I like chocolate'.

Finden plus an adjective of approval (or disapproval for dislike) is another not uncommon way of expressing 'to like' of people, food and other things, e.g. **Ich finde ihn sympathisch/Er ist mir sympathisch** 'I like him (= likeable)', **Ich habe den Film super gefunden** 'I liked the film a lot', **Ich finde die Torte sehr lecker** 'I really like the cake'.

Lieben is used far less than 'to love' is in English, e.g. 'I love to swim' and 'I love the beach' are more usually expressed by one of the above verbs meaning 'to like', not **lieben**.

to listen to

sich anhören, belauschen, hinhören, hören, hören auf, lauschen, zuhören

The most usual term is **zuhören**, which applies to listening passively, e.g. **Ich habe nicht zugehört** 'I wasn't listening', **Ich hörte ihm zu, ohne ihn verstehen zu können** 'I listened to him without being able to understand him', **Hör mal gut zu!** 'Listen closely!'.

Sich (dat.) **anhören** means 'to listen' attentively and must have an object, e.g. **Der Verbrecher musste sich anhören, was ihm vorgeworfen wurde** 'The criminal had to listen to what he was being accused of', **Hör dir das mal an!** 'Listen to that!'.

Anhören is used together with **mit** and an optional reflexive pronoun meaning 'to be forced to listen to' s.t., i.e. when not being directly addressed, e.g. **Sie musste sich dreckige Witze im Bus mit anhören** 'She had to listen to dirty jokes in the bus' (i.e. being told by others to others, not to her).

'To listen to' music or the radio is **Musik/Radio hören**, e.g. **A: Was machst du? B: Ich höre Musik/Radio/CDs** 'A: What are you doing? B: I'm listening to music/the radio/cds'. **Hören** can also render 'to listen' in the imperative, e.g. **Hör mal!** 'Listen!'.

'To listen to' meaning 'to pay heed to' is **hören auf**, e.g. **Ich habe nie auf meine Mutter gehört** 'I never listened to (took any notice of) my mother'.

Hinhören means 'to listen' closely so as to catch s.t. that is being said, e.g. **Ich habe nicht hingehört** 'I wasn't listening/I didn't catch what was being said'.

Jdm/etwas lauschen refers to listening either secretly (i.e. listening in surreptitiously), e.g. **Sie versuchte unserem Gespräch zu lauschen** 'She tried to listen (in) to our conversation'. **Belauschen** (+ a direct object) also renders 'to eavesdrop on', e.g. **Sie hat unser Gespräch belauscht** 'She eavesdropped on our conversation'. But **jdm/etwas lauschen** can also refer to listening attentively, e.g. **Wenn der amerikanische Präsident spricht, lauscht die ganze Welt** 'When the American president speaks, the whole world listens'.

literally

buchstäblich, wörtlich

'Literally' meaning the exact words used is **wörtlich**, e.g. **A: Was hat er wörtlich gesagt? B: Er nannte mich wörtlich 'ein Schwein'** 'A: What did he actually say? B: He literally called me a pig'. Where the word is used figuratively, **buchstäblich** is required, e.g. **Johannesburg ist buchstäblich aus dem Nichts entstanden** 'Johannesburg literally sprang up out of nothing'.

to live (*see* ALIVE)

bewohnen, leben, wohnen

The usual difficulty here lies in distinguishing between **leben** and **wohnen**. The former means 'to spend one's life' and the latter 'to dwell' or 'to reside', e.g. **Hitler hat von 1898 bis 1945 gelebt** 'Hitler lived from 1898 till 1945', **Es lässt sich hier gut leben** 'One can live well here', **Meine Tante wohnt seit 60 Jahren in dem Haus** 'My aunt has been living in that house for 60 years'. However, there are numerous cases where the distinction is not clear-cut, e.g. **Er hat jahrelang hier gelebt/gewohnt** 'He lived here for years', or it can depend on what you mean, e.g. **Wie hat er gewohnt/gelebt?** 'How did he live?' (**wohnen** = the sort of accommodation he had, and **leben** = how he spent his life).

Wohnen is intr. whereas **bewohnen** is tr. and thus if used to render 'to live in/on', no preposition is required, e.g. **Wir bewohnen einen Bauernhof am**

Ortsrand = Wir wohnen in einem Bauernhof am Ortsrand 'We live on a farm on the edge of town' (*see* INHABITANT).

Animals **leben** even when referring to where they reside, e.g. **Dachse leben unter der Erde** 'Badgers live underground', **Was lebt in diesem Baum?** 'What lives in this tree?'. Note too **im Exil leben** 'to live in exile', **leben und leben lassen** 'live and let live'.

(as) long as

sofern, solang(e)

The subordinating conj. 'as long as' in the temporal sense is **solang(e)**, e.g. **Du kannst bei uns wohnen, solange du willst** 'You can stay with us as long as you wish'.

Where 'as long as' means 'provided that', **sofern** is required, e.g. **Es kann sehr wohl Demokratie geben ohne ein Mehr-Parteien-System, sofern Bürger Handels- und Meinungsfreiheit haben** 'There can very easily be democracy without a multi-party system as long as citizens have freedom of trade and thought'.

to look (at), to watch

gucken, sehen, schauen (auf); (sich) angucken, (sich) ansehen, (sich) anschauen; blicken, hinsehen, wirken, zugucken, zuschauen, zusehen

This is one of the hardest verbs of all to correctly translate into German. 'To look', as opposed to 'to look at', can be rendered by three synonymous verbs, **gucken**,[18] **sehen** and **schauen**; the first is

colloquial North German and the last South German as well as Hochdeutsch, whereas **sehen** is neutral, e.g. **Er guckte/sah/schaute aus dem Fenster** 'He looked out of the window', **Guck/ sieh/schau mal!** 'Look!' (also **Sieh/schau her**), **Schauen/sehen Sie** 'Look ([fig.] as in 'Look, this is the situation . . .'), **Es ist schwierig den Leuten in die Augen zu gucken und zu sagen, dass sie sicher sind** 'It is difficult to look people in the eye and say that they are safe'.

'To look at' with reference to glancing at a clock or watch to find out the time, is expressed by **blicken/schauen/sehen auf** + acc., e.g. **Sie hat auf die Uhr geblickt/geschaut/gesehen** 'She looked at her watch/the clock'. In fact, if you briefly glance at anything, these are the verbs to use. But these verbs can express more than mere glancing. In the following examples **blicken/schauen/sehen auf**, although translated as 'to look at', implies 'looking in the direction of': **Im Jahre 2000 zur Zeit der Olympischen Spiele blickte/schaute/sah die ganze Welt auf Australien** 'In 2000 during the Olympic Games the whole world was looking at Australia', **Er blickte/schaute/sah hinüber auf die Berge** 'He looked across at the mountains'. The preposition may vary depending on the context, e.g. **Sie blickte/schaute/sah in das Zimmer** 'She looked into the room', **Jetzt blicken/schauen/ sehen wir nach Asien** 'Now we'll look at Asia' (weather map on television).

In all other contexts, however, 'to look at' is rendered by **(sich) ansehen/angucken/anschauen**, with the same regional variation applying as explained above. The trick is to know when to use these verbs reflexively. When looking at things intensively, i.e. studying them or taking a good look at them, the reflexive is required, e.g. **Sieh dir dies mal an!** 'Take a (good) look at this', **Ich will mir sein neues Auto/seine Bilder ansehen** 'I want to take a look at his new car/ pictures'; compare **sich etwas genau ansehen** (to take a close look at s.t.), where **genau** necessitates

---

[18] This verb is usually written **gucken** but nearly always pronounced **kucken**, which is sometimes found in writing too.

the use of **sich**. Compare **Sieh mich mal an!** 'Look at me' (always non-reflexive when the object is a person), **Sie schaute ihn voll Interesse an** 'She looked at him full of interest'.

German does not make the distinction between 'looking' and 'watching' that we make, i.e. watching is more prolonged and intensive than looking; 'to watch' is rendered by the same verbs as 'to look (at)', e.g. **Morgen Abend will ich mir unbedingt das Spiel gegen Inter-Mailand ansehen** 'Tomorrow night I definitely want to watch the match against Inter-Milan'; the reflexive form is needed as watching is intensive looking. 'To watch television' is **fernsehen**, e.g. **Die Kinder haben den ganzen Tag ferngesehen** 'The kids watched television all day'. 'To watch football' etc. is **Fußball gucken/schauen**, where the name of the sport can be substituted, e.g. **Tennis gucken/schauen**. In similar fashion you can also say **einen Krimi gucken/schauen** 'to watch a who-dunnit', but also **Fernsehen gucken** 'to watch television'.

'To watch' or 'look on' while s.o. does s.t is **zugucken/-sehen/-schauen**, e.g. **Er hat tatenlos zugesehen, wie der Pavian das Kind angefallen hat** 'He watched helplessly while the baboon attacked the child', **Es ist schlimmer als Gras beim Wachsen zuzusehen** 'It is worse than watching grass grow', **Er sah den Soldaten bei der Arbeit zu** 'He watched the soldiers working/looked on while the soldiers worked', **Vielen Dank fürs Zusehen** 'Thank you for watching' (television announcer). From **zuschauen** is derived the word **der Zuschauer** 'spectator'.

When you 'take a second/better look' at s.t., this is expressed by **hinsehen**, e.g. **Dann habe ich genauer/noch einmal hingesehen** 'I then took a better/second look'.

For 'to look' meaning 'to have the appearance of', see TO LOOK LIKE.

to look after, to take care of

aufpassen auf, sich kümmern um,
sorgen für

'To look after' s.o. or s.t. in the sense of watching over them is **aufpassen auf** + acc., e.g. **Wer passt denn auf die Kinder auf, wenn du bei der Arbeit bist?** 'Who looks after the kids when you are at work?'.

Sich kümmern um renders 'to look after' in the sense of to take care of s.o. in the nursing sense, e.g. **Niemand kümmert sich in diesem Land um die Geisteskranken** 'In this country no one looks after the mentally handicapped'.

Sorgen für can mean the same as the previous word but in addition to the 'nursing' sense, it can also mean 'to take care of' in the sense of taking it upon yourself to do s.t., e.g. **Er sorgt wunderbar für seine Mutter** 'He looks after his mother very well', **Ich sorge für die Getränke und du kannst für das Essen sorgen** 'I'll take care of (provide/organise) the drinks and you can take care of the food'.

to look around

sich umsehen, um sich herumsehen

Sich umsehen means 'to look around' in the sense of 'to turn your head', e.g. **Er hörte etwas hinter sich und sah sich sofort um** 'He heard something behind him and immediately looked around'. **Sich umsehen** also translates 'to look around' in the sense of to go nosing, as in shops, e.g. **Sehen Sie sich ruhig um!** 'Do look around', **Ich möchte mich nur mal umsehen** 'I'm only looking' (in a shop), **Wir sehen/schauen uns nach etwas Passendem um** 'We're looking around (= searching) for something appropriate'. This verb can however be used with a meaning similar to **um sich herumsehen** (see next paragraph), e.g. **Ich sah mich um – wir**

waren in einer gottverlassenen Gegend 'I looked around – we were in a godforsaken area'.

Um sich herumsehen means 'to look all around', e.g. **Er stand in der Mitte des Hofs und sah verwundert um sich herum** 'He stood in the middle of the courtyard and looked around amazed'.

to look like

ähneln, ähnlich sehen/sein, aussehen, (sich) gleichen, wirken

'To look like' in the sense of 'to look as if' is **aussehen nach**, e.g. **Es sieht danach/so aus, als ob . . .** 'It looks like/as if . . .', **Es sieht nach Regen aus** 'It looks like rain', **Das sieht nach einem guten Versteck aus** 'That looks like a good hiding place', **Sie sollten sich entschuldigen, aber danach sieht es nicht aus** 'They should apologise but it doesn't look like that is going to happen'. This is often more or less synonymous with 'to seem' and can thus also be rendered by **scheinen**, e.g. **Es scheint, dass es ihm gefällt** 'It looks as if he likes it/It seems he likes it', **Die Mitgliedschaft dieses Landes in der Nato scheint nur noch eine Frage der Zeit (zu sein)** 'That country's membership of NATO seems to be just a question of time' (= It looks as if . . .).

'To look like' s.o., i.e. 'to resemble', is **ähneln** + dat., e.g. **Er ähnelt seiner Mutter sehr** 'He looks very much like his mother'. This can also be expressed adjectivally, e.g. **Sie sind sich ähnlich** 'They look alike', but this can also refer to character, i.e. They are similar. More elevated in style, but synonymous with reference to appearance, is **gleichen** (+ dat.), e.g. **Die ganze Region gleicht einer Seenlandschaft** 'The whole region looks like a landscape of lakes'. Also **sich gleichen** 'to be like each other/resemble each other' (see next paragraph).

'To look' meaning 'to have the appearance of' is **aussehen**, e.g. **Er sieht krank aus** 'He looks sick',

Er sah aus wie ein zerbrechlicher, alter Mann 'He looked like a fragile old man'. This verb can also be used as a synonym of **ähneln**, e.g. **Du siehst wie deine Mutter aus** 'You look like your mother'. This can also be expressed by **jdm ähnlich sehen**, e.g. **Sie sehen dem Bundespräsidenten verdammt ähnlich** 'You do look like the federal president'.

More or less synonymous with **aussehen**, but not nearly as common, is **wirken**, e.g. **Sie wirkt immer noch sehr jung** 'She still looks very young' (= gives the impression of being).

to look up

aufsuchen, nachschlagen

'To look up' s.t. in a reference/telephone book etc. is **nachschlagen**, e.g. **Schlag's im Wörterbuch nach!** 'Look it up in the dictionary'.

'To look up' s.o., i.e. to visit them, is **aufsuchen**, e.g. **Als wir vor kurzem in Tirol waren, habe ich meinen alten Deutsch-Lehrer vom Gymnasium aufgesucht** 'When we were in Tyrol recently I looked up my old German teacher from high school'.

to lose (one's way)

sich verirren, sich verlaufen, verlieren, sich verfahren

'To lose' s.t. is **verlieren**, e.g. **Ich habe meinen Schlüsselbund verloren** 'I have lost my key ring'.

'To lose one's way' is translated differently depending on whether one is walking or driving, the former being **sich verlaufen** and the latter **sich verfahren**, e.g. **Wir haben uns im Schwarzwald verfahren** 'We got lost in the Black Forest', where it is obvious you were driving when you got lost as opposed to **Wir haben uns auf der Insel verlaufen** 'We got lost on the island' (while walking). **Sich**

verirren is synonymous with both the above but is neutral, the mode of movement not being relevant.

the lunch, lunchtime (*see* MEAL)

(zu) Mittag, Mittag essen, das Mittagessen, mittags

'Having lunch' is expressed periphrastically in German to avoid the double mention of **essen** in **Mittagessen essen**. Here's how it can be avoided: **Was hast du zu Mittag gegessen?** 'What did you have for lunch?', **Er isst (zu) Mittag zu Hause** 'He has lunch at home', **Er kommt mittags zum Essen nach Hause** 'He comes home for lunch', **Da esse ich jeden Tag Mittag** 'That's where I have lunch every day'. **Mittagessen** can be used as the name of the meal when it is not necessary to express 'eating lunch', e.g. **Das war ein wunderbares Mittagessen, Mutti** 'That was a wonderful lunch, mum'. It should be noted that **das Mittagessen** is traditionally the main meal of the day in Germany and is thus assumed to be a hot meal, as opposed to **das Abendbrot**, which is not. Where 'lunch' is not a hot meal, the concept can be expressed by avoiding all mention of the time of day, e.g. **Ich gehe schnell was essen** 'I'll shoot off and have lunch', **Hast du gegessen?** 'Have you had lunch?'.

the magazine, journal

die Illustrierte, das Magazin, die Monatsschrift, die Wochenschrift, die Zeitschrift

Zeitschrift can be used as a general term for 'magazine' or it can refer to a '(scientific) journal' (**Fachzeitschrift**). **Das Magazin**, although possible in both senses, is not common. A glossy (womens') magazine is most usually **die Illustrierte** (adj. noun). A weekly or monthly magazine/journal is a **Wochenschrift** or **Monatsschrift** respectively.

the mark

der Fleck(en), die Marke, die Note

A 'mark', 'stain' or 'spot' on your clothing, for example, is a **Fleck** or **Flecken** (pl. of both being **Flecken**), e.g. **Dieses Zeug macht Flecken** 'This stuff makes marks/stains'.

A school or university 'mark/grade' is a **Note**. At German schools marks or grades are given out of six where **eine Eins** (**zwei Einsen**) is the best score and **eine Sechs** the worst, e.g. **Ich habe eine zwei in Mathe bekommen** 'I got a 2 for maths'. **Eine Fünf** and **eine Sechs** are both fails (see TO FAIL). Synonymous with the six grades are the following: **1 – ausgezeichnet/sehr gut, 2 – gut, 3 – befriedigend, 4 – genügend/ausreichend, 5 – mangelhaft, 6 – ungenügend**.

the marriage, wedding

die Ehe, die Heirat, die Hochzeit, die Trauung, die Vermählung

The institution of marriage is **die Ehe**, e.g. **Die Schwulenehe ist im Kommen** 'Homosexual marriage is on its way', **Sie haben eine schlechte Ehe** 'They have a bad marriage'. Note too **ein Ehepaar** 'a married couple'.

Heirat is the word that most commonly occurs in compounds referring to 'marriage', e.g. **Heiratsantrag/-anzeige/-urkunde** 'marriage proposal/advertisement/certificate', **heiratsfähig** 'marriageable', **An eine Heirat zwischen den beiden ist nicht zu denken** 'The marriage of those two is unimaginable'.

The 'wedding feast' is **die Hochzeit**, which also renders 'silver/golden etc. wedding anniversary', e.g. **Unsere Hochzeit haben wir in einem Restaurant gefeiert** 'We celebrated our wedding in a restaurant', **die goldene Hochzeit** 'the golden wedding anniversary'.

The 'marriage/wedding ceremony' is **die Trauung,** e.g. **Die Trauung ist am nächsten Freitag** 'The wedding ceremony is next Friday'.

Vermählung is a very formal word rendering 'marriage' (*see* **vermählen** under TO MARRY).

to marry

anheiraten, heiraten, trauen, verheiratet sein, (sich) verheiraten, vermählen

Both 'to marry' (tr.) and 'to get married' (intr.) are **heiraten,** e.g. **Er hat sie geheiratet** 'He married her', **Er hat geheiratet** 'He got married'. A somewhat more elevated variant in the latter meaning is **Er hat sich vor zwei Jahren schon verheiratet** 'He got married two years ago'. But most usually you will only need to use the adjective **verheiratet** 'married', e.g. **Er ist mit ihr verheiratet** 'He's married to her'.

Trauen (tr.) is what the priest does, e.g. **Pastor/Pfarrer**[19] **Liebenberg wird uns trauen** 'Reverend/Father Liebenberg is going to marry us'. It also occurs in the more elevated expression **sich trauen lassen** which is synonymous with **heiraten/sich verheiraten.**

Vermählen is a very formal word comparable to 'to wed', e.g. **vermählt mit** 'wedded to'. It is to be avoided in everyday language.

Anheiraten is usually only found in adjectival form, **angeheiratet,** where it means related by marriage, e.g. **Er ist ein angeheirateter Neffe des amtierenden nepalesischen Königs** 'He is a nephew by marriage (nephew-in-law) of the ruling Nepalese king'.

---

[19] The former is usually protestant (**evangelisch**) and the latter catholic (**katholisch**).

the meal(time) (*see* LUNCH)

das Abendbrot, das Abendessen, das Frühstück, die Mahlzeit, das Mittagessen

Note that the definite article is used with the names of the three daily meals. **Beim Abendessen/Frühstück/Mittagessen** express 'while having dinner/breakfast/lunch' while **zum Abendessen/Frühstück/Mittagessen** express 'for dinner/breakfast/lunch', e.g. **Heute beim Frühstück hat Vati bekannt gemacht, dass er sich scheiden lassen will** 'At breakfast today dad announced he wants to get a divorce', **Was gibt's zum Abendessen?** 'What's for dinner?'.

'Morning/afternoon tea' has to be expressed periphrastically as in Germany it is not the institution it is in Anglo-Saxon countries, e.g. **Kommen Sie morgen gegen 11 herüber zum Kaffee/zu Kaffee und Kuchen** 'Come over for morning tea tomorrow at about eleven o'clock'.

The main meal of the day for many Germans is lunch (*see* LUNCH), which explains why the lighter bread based meal eaten in the evening is called **Abendbrot.** A more elaborate hot evening meal is called **das Abendessen.**

Dictionaries give the word **das Mahl** for 'meal'. Forget it as it is not in common use. The general word for a 'meal' is **Mahlzeit,** e.g. **Wann sind die Mahlzeiten in dieser Jugendherberge?** 'When are the meals in this youth hostel?'. The word does not in the first instance mean 'mealtime', despite appearances. It is also used for 'hello' or as a general 'enjoy your lunch' in the work environment at about lunchtime. 'To have a meal' is expressed quite simply by **essen,** e.g. **Wir haben zusammen am Bahnhof gegessen** 'We had a meal together at the station'.

The idiosyncrasies associated with 'having lunch' are dealt with under LUNCH.

to mean (*see* TO THINK)

bedeuten, besagen, heißen, meinen, sollen

When words and events have a meaning or significance, this is their **Bedeutung**, e.g. **Was bedeutet dieses Wort?** 'What does this word mean?', **So eine schöne Dämmerung bedeutet morgen schönes Wetter** 'Such a beautiful twilight means good weather tomorrow'. **Was soll das (bedeuten)?** 'What's that supposed to mean?' is a commonly heard idiom where **bedeuten** is often omitted. A person cannot be the subject of **bedeuten** unless there is reference to that person's significance, e.g. **Sein Neffe bedeutet ihm sehr viel** 'His nephew means a lot to him'.

Particularly with reference to the meaning of words, **heißen** is commonly used instead of **bedeuten**, e.g. **Was heißt 'au revoir' (auf Deutsch)? Das heißt 'auf Wiedersehen'** 'What does "au revoir" mean (in German)? It means "goodbye"'.

But the use of **heißen** as a translation of 'to mean' can go beyond words, e.g. **Er weiß, was es heißt, ständig in Gefahr zu leben** 'He knows what it means to constantly live in danger'.

The subject of **meinen** is nearly always a person, e.g. **Was meinen Sie (damit)?** 'What do you mean (by that)?', **Meinst du das (im Ernst)?** 'Do really mean that?/Are you serious?' (*see* SERIOUS), **Sie meinen es gut** 'They mean well'. Note that although **die Bedeutung** means 'meaning/significance', **die Meinung** never translates as 'meaning' but usually as 'opinion' (*see* OPINION), which is related to the fact that **meinen** is very often translated by 'to think' (*see* TO THINK).

Besagen tends to be exclusively used in the idioms **Das besagt nichts/viel** '(I haven't heard from him but/and) That means nothing/a lot', **Das besagt nicht, dass . . .** 'That does not mean that . . .'.

meats

der Aufschnitt, das Gehackte, das Hackfleisch, das Hammelfleisch, das Kalbfleisch, die kalte Platte, das Lammfleisch, der Rinder-/Schweinebraten, das Rindfleisch, der Schinken, das Schweinefleisch, die Wurst/das Würstchen

The array of meats and meat products available in German-speaking countries can be bewildering, but here are a few of the main types. The 'sliced' or 'cold meats' (i.e. smallgoods) so integral to a German **Abendbrot** (*see* MEAL) are referred to by the collective **Aufschnitt**, e.g. **Ich habe vergessen, heute Aufschnitt zu kaufen** 'I forgot to buy cold meats today'.

The meat of various animals is expressed by compounds of the word for 'meat', **das Fleisch**, but watch out for the idiosyncrasies of compounding, e.g. **Kalbfleisch** 'veal', **Lammfleisch** 'lamb', **Hammelfleisch** 'mutton', **Rindfleisch** 'beef', **Schweinefleisch** 'pork'. **Hackfleisch** or **Gehacktes** (adj. noun) is 'minced meat'.

A German staple is of course sausage. The word **Wurst** is compounded with a host of other nouns to describe the wide variety of German sausages, **Blutwurst** 'black pudding', **Leberwurst** 'liverwurst', **Mettwurst** 'smoked beef/pork sausage' etc. An individual sausage to be eaten by one person, as opposed to a large one which you take slices from, is usually referred to as a **Würstchen**, rather than a **Wurst**.

'Roast beef/pork/veal' is **der Rinder-** or **Rindsbraten, der Schweinebraten** and **der Kalbsbraten**, e.g. **Heute gibt's Schweinebraten zum Mittagessen** 'We're having roast pork for lunch today'. 'Roast chicken' is **Brathähnchen/-hendl** (*see* CHICKEN).

the medicine, drug(s)

das Arzneimittel, die Droge, das Medikament, die Medizin, das Rauschgift

'Drugs' in the sense of marijuana, hash etc. are **Drogen**, but **Rauschgift** is also used as a collective noun in this sense. 'Drugs' in the medical sense are **Medikamente**, a noun that is usually used in the plural, e.g. **Das kann der Arzt mit Medikamenten behandeln** 'The doctor can treat that with medicine/drugs'. **Medizin** can be used as a synonym of **Medikament(e)**, e.g. **Nimm deine Medizin/ Medikamente!** 'Take your medicine'. **Medizin** also renders 'medicine' as an academic discipline. **Arzneimittel** translates 'drugs' in the more formal sense of 'pharmaceuticals' (= **Pharmazeutika**).

to meet; the meeting

begegnen, kennen, kennen lernen, tagen, (sich) treffen, (sich) versammeln, zusammentreffen; die Begegnung, die Tagung, das Treffen, die Versammlung

'To meet' s.o. in the sense of making their acquaintance for the first time is **(sich) kennen lernen**, e.g. **Wo habt ihr euch kennen gelernt?** 'Where did you meet (each other)?', **Ich habe sie in Warschau kennen gelernt** 'I met her in Warsaw'.

Begegnen means 'to meet' in the sense of bumping into s.o. unexpectedly. The verb takes **sein** and its object is in the dat., e.g. **Ich bin ihm heute in der Stadt begegnet** 'I met him in town today', **Wo bin ich dieser Frau schon einmal begegnet?** 'Where have I come across this woman before?'. The noun **Begegnung** more often than not corresponds to 'encounter', e.g. **eine Begegnung der dritten Art** 'an encounter of the third kind'.

(Sich) treffen[20] is to meet s.o. by appointment but can also render meeting s.o. by chance (see

---

[20] The reflexive pronoun, as with **sich kennen lernen**, expresses 'each other' when no other object is present.

begegnen above), e.g. **Wo treffen wir uns denn?** 'Where shall we meet then?', **Ich habe ihn ganz zufällig in der Straßenbahn getroffen** 'I met him quite by accident in the tram today', **Per Zufall trafen wir uns im Bus** 'I met him by chance in the bus'. A variation of this, **sich treffen mit**, implies quite the reverse to an accidental meeting, e.g. **Ich treffe mich heute Abend mit ihm in der Gaststätte** 'I'm meeting him in the pub tonight', **Er wollte sich mit mir treffen** 'He wanted to meet up with me'.

Similar in meaning and style to 'to meet with', is **zusammentreffen mit**, which requires **sein** in the perfect, unlike **treffen**, e.g. **Der Kanzler ist mit dem pakistanischen Präsidenten in Islamabad zusammengetroffen** 'The chancellor met with the Pakistani president in Islamabad'.

'To meet each other' meaning 'to meet head on/ clash' is **aufeinander treffen**, e.g. **Wo Menschen und Bären aufeinander treffen, verlieren immer die Bären** 'Where people and bears meet head on, the bears always lose out'.

'To meet' as of club or board members getting together is **sich versammeln** and thus that sort of a meeting is a **Versammlung**, e.g. **Die Mitglieder versammeln sich jeden zweiten Dienstagabend in der Pfarrkirche** 'The members meet every second Tuesday evening in the parish church', **eine Bürgerversammlung** 'a meeting of the citizens'. At a more official level meetings are referred to as **Treffen**, e.g. **ein Treffen der Verteidigungsminister der EU-Länder** 'a meeting of the ministers of defence of the countries of the European Union', **das Gipfeltreffen** 'summit meeting'.

Tagen is 'to meet' or 'to sit' as at conferences, e.g. **In diesem Hotel wird regelmäßig getagt** 'Meetings/conferences are often held in this hotel', but this verb is used for the 'meeting' of boards, councils and commissions too, e.g. **Zur Krise im Nahen Osten tagte heute der Sicherheitsrat** 'The Security Council met today to discuss the crisis in the Middle East'. The meetings or sessions are **Tagungen**. The same root is found in the name of the lower house of the German parliament, **der Bundestag**, lit. federal assembly.

The fig. 'to meet' a challenge is **sich einer Herausforderung stellen**.

the memory

die Erinnerung, das Gedächtnis, der Speicher

'A pleasant memory' of s.t. ist **eine angenehme Erinnerung**, which word also renders 'momento', e.g. **eine schöne Erinnerung an** + acc. 'a nice momento of'. If you have trouble remembering things, the appropriate word is **Gedächtnis**, e.g. **Ich habe ein sehr schlechtes Gedächtnis** 'I have a very bad memory'. A computer's memory is its **Speicher**.

the middle, centre

inmitten, die Mitte, der Mittelpunkt, mitten in, mittlere, der Stadtkern, das Zentrum

The 'middle' or 'centre' of s.t. is **die Mitte**, e.g. **in der Mitte des Waldes** 'in the middle of the forest'. **Das Zentrum** means 'city centre' and is synonymous with **die Stadtmitte**, which in turn is synonymous with **die Innenstadt** and **der Stadtkern** or **die Ortsmitte** in the case of a small town. Note too **Mitte nächster Woche/nächsten Monats** 'the middle of next week/month'.

More or less synonymous with **in der Mitte von/gen.** is the phrase **mitten in** + dat., e.g. **mitten in Kairo** 'in the centre of Cairo', **mitten im fruchtbaren zentralrussischen Tiefland** 'in the centre of the fertile central Russian lowlands'. It is also used with reference to time, e.g. **mitten in der Nacht** 'in the middle of the night', **mitten in der Arbeit** 'while I/he/she etc. was in the middle of

working'. **Mitten** can be followed by prepositions other than **in**, e.g. **Er bahnte sich einen Weg mitten durch die Menge** 'He made his way through the middle of the crowd'. Note that **inmitten** + gen. renders 'amidst' and is as formal sounding as its English equivalent, e.g. **Die alte Frau stand nach dem Erdbeben inmitten der Trümmer ihres Hauses da** 'The old woman stood there after the earthquake amidst the ruins of her house'. **Mitten drin** is used adverbially to render 'in the middle of', e.g. **Sie befanden sich mitten drin (im Guerillakrieg)** 'They found themselves in the middle of it/in the middle of the guerilla war'.

The word **Mittel** on its own never renders 'middle/centre/central' but it regularly has this meaning in compounds, e.g. **der Mittelsmann** 'middle man', **der Mittelfinger** 'the middle finger'. It occurs in many geographical names, e.g. **Mitteleuropa** 'central Europe', **Mittelamerika** 'Central America' and even **das Mittelmeer** 'the Mediterranean Sea'.

The adjective **mittlere** is used in a few isolated instances in geographic names, e.g. **der Mittlere Westen** 'mid-west' (of USA), but the Middle East is **der Nahe Osten** and **Nahost** in compounds, e.g. **der Nahostkonflikt** 'the conflict in the Middle East'; you will however occasionally see the term **der Mittlere Osten**.[21] Otherwise **der/die/das mittlere** means 'the middle one' with reference to a previously mentioned noun, e.g. **Du wirst deine Socken in der mittleren Schublade finden** 'You'll find your socks in the middle drawer'. 'Middle age' is **das mittlere Alter** and a phrase like 'a middle-aged lady' is expressed as follows: **eine Dame mittleren Alters/in den mittleren Jahren**. The 'Middle Ages', on the other hand, are **das Mittelalter** (sing.). Note too **Sie war Mitte Zwanzig** 'She was in her mid-twenties', **Er war ein Mittvierziger** 'He was a man in his mid-forties'.

---

[21] Particularly, but not exclusively in historical contexts, 'the (Middle) East' is rendered by **das Morgenland** (= the Levant) and thus Europe and the West in general by **das Abendland**.

the mind

die Gedanken, das (Ge)hirn, der Geist, das Gemüt, die Meinung, der Sinn, der Verstand

How to render 'mind' in German can be elusive as the English word covers such a wide field. It is hard to give guidelines here and thus some typical examples are possibly the best way to learn how the concept is rendered in German: **aus den Augen aus dem Sinn** 'out of sight out of mind', **Das kam mir in den Sinn** 'That came to mind', **Das ist ein Beispiel eines kranken Gehirns** 'That is an example of a sick mind' (lit. brain), **ein beschränkter Geist** 'a limited mind', **Sie ist nicht recht bei Verstand/Sinnen** 'She is out of her mind/not in her right mind'. The word **Gemüt**, which dictionaries give as meaning mind, is a very elevated concept in German and will seldom be the word you will require.

'To change one's mind' is **seine Meinung ändern** (**über** + acc.) or **es sich anders überlegen**, e.g. **Ich habe meine Meinung über ihn geändert** 'I have changed my mind about him', **Ich habe es mir anders überlegt** 'I have changed my mind'. It might also be expressed as **Ich bin jetzt anderer Meinung** (*see* OPINION).

to miss

fehlen, missen, verfehlen, vermissen, verpassen, versäumen

'To miss' a bus or train is **verpassen**, e.g. **Ich habe den Bus zum zweiten Mal verpasst** 'I missed the bus for the second time'. This is also used for 'missing' a class or appointment. In one of its various meanings **versäumen** is a less common synonym of **verpassen**, e.g. **Er soll die Chance nicht versäumen, die Welt zu sehen** 'He shouldn't miss the chance to see the world' (*see* TO FAIL).

'To miss' a person, i.e. to pine for s.o., is **vermissen**, e.g. **Ich habe dich furchtbar vermisst** 'I missed

you dreadfully'. The same idea can be expressed quite idiomatically by **fehlen** + dat., e.g. **Du hast mir sehr gefehlt** 'I missed you a lot', **Frank Sinatra ist tot; er wird uns fehlen** 'Frank Sinatra is dead; we will miss him'. This verb must be used in the following context: **Was/wer fehlt noch?** 'What/who is still missing?', **Die Milch fehlt** 'The milk is missing/There is no milk' (on the table).

Vermissen is also used in the passive to express that s.o. is missing, e.g. **Sie wird vermisst** 'She is missing/has gone missing'. There is also a verb **missen** but this does not usually equate to Eng. 'to miss', e.g. **Die Freiheit eines eigenen Autos möchten die Deutschen nicht missen** 'Germans would not like to make do without their cars'.

'To miss' a target is **verfehlen**, e.g. **Viele der Raketen haben ihr Ziel verfehlt** 'Many of the rockets missed their target', **Das abgestürzte Flugzeug verfehlte nur knapp ein Wohnhaus** 'The plane that crashed only narrowly missed a dwelling'.

(at the) moment

im Augenblick, augenblicklich, derzeit, im Moment, momentan, zur Stunde, zurzeit

All these expressions are more or less synonymous. **Im Augenblick** and **im Moment** are stylistic variants, as are the two adverbs **augenblicklich** and **momentan** derived from these nouns. **Derzeit** and **zurzeit** are completely synonymous, stylistically too, whereas **zur Stunde** has the connotation of 'as we speak'.

the mood

die Gemütslage, die Laune, die Stimmung

A (good/bad) 'mood' is a **Laune** but this word requires idiomatic syntax, e.g. **Du bist (in) guter/schlechter Laune** 'You are in a good/bad mood', **Du hast gute/schlechte Laune** 'You are in a good/bad mood'.

Stimmung can be synonymous with **Laune** but if so it occurs in set collocations, e.g. **Wir sind in Stimmung** 'We are in a good mood/in high spirits', **Ich bin nicht in der Stimmung zum Mitmachen** 'I am not in the mood for joining in'. But generally speaking **Stimmung** refers to a 'mood' in the sense of ambiance or atmosphere, e.g. **Wie war die Stimmung auf der Konferenz?** 'What was the mood of the conference like?', **In der Stadt herrschte zu Weihnachten eine Geisterstimmung** 'A ghostly mood prevailed in the city at Christmas time'. But it is also possible in coll. German for **Laune** to render the meaning of atmosphere, although it is normally reserved for individuals' moods, e.g. **Wie war die allgemeine Laune in Bethlehem?** 'What was the general mood in Bethlehem like?'. **Gemütslage** can render 'mood' where there are connotations of 'state of mind', e.g. **Die Gemütslage aller Teilnehmer am Gipfeltreffen war sehr positiv** 'The mood of all participants at the summit meeting was very positive'.

most, mostly

äußerst, höchst, meist, meistens;
am -sten, -st

As an intensifier of adjectives and adverbs **höchst** is used, e.g. **Das ist höchst wichtig** 'That is most important'. More or less synonymous with this is **äußerst** (lit. 'extremely'). Not to be confused with this is the superlative of the adjective/ adverb which in German, unlike English, is consistently expressed by the ending -**st** added to adjectives of any length, e.g. **Das ist das interessanteste Buch** 'That is the most interesting book' (of all of them); compare **Das ist ein höchst/äußerst interessantes Buch** 'That is a most interesting book'.

Particularly confusing is the distinction between **der/die/das interessanteste** and **am interessantesten**, where **interessant** represents any adjective. The superlative of the adverb is always the latter,

e.g. **Wer ist am schnellsten gelaufen** 'Who ran (the) fastest?'. The superlative of the adjective is the former, e.g. **Ich habe das schnellste Auto** 'I have the fastest car (of the three)'. After the verb 'to be', however, either form is possible where a noun is understood, e.g. **Wer war am schnellsten/der schnellste?** 'Who was fastest/Who was the fastest (runner/person)?'. Where no noun can be understood only the adverbial form is possible, e.g. **Wann sind deine Rosen am schönsten?** 'When are your roses (the) prettiest?'. As a rough rule of thumb, if 'the' can be omitted, as in the two examples above where it is bracketed, you are dealing with the comparative of the adverb and thus the **am -sten** form is required.

'Most' followed by a plural noun is **die meisten + noun**, e.g. **Die meisten Mitglieder sind zufrieden** 'Most members/most of the members are satisfied'. Note that this is also how you express in German 'most of the + plural noun'; similarly 'most of the time' is **die meiste Zeit**, but this is synonymous in English with 'mostly' which is in turn **meistens** in German but is always temporal, e.g. **Er ist meistens bei seinen Eltern** 'He is mostly/usually at his parents'. However, where 'mostly' means 'generally', it is rendered in German by **meist** or **zumeist** in higher style, e.g. **Es wird heute im Süden meist trocken sein** 'In the south today it will be mostly dry', **In Südafrika wird die Afrikanisierung der zumeist aus der Kolonialzeit stammenden Ortsnamen geplant** 'In South Africa the africanisation of place names mostly dating from the colonial era is planned'.

to move, shift

(sich) bewegen, rücken, sich verlagern,
umziehen, versetzen, ziehen

'To move' or 'to shift house' is **umziehen**, e.g. **Wir sind umgezogen** 'We have moved'. Related are **ein-** and **ausziehen** rendering 'to move in' and 'to move out' respectively, e.g. **Wir sind noch nicht** eingezogen 'We have not moved in yet'. **Ziehen** without a prefix can also mean 'to move/shift house', usually when the town or country being moved to is mentioned, e.g. **Mein Bruder zieht nach Japan** 'My brother is moving to Japan' (compare **versetzen** below).

'To move' a part of the body is **bewegen**, e.g. **Er konnte den rechten Arm nicht mehr bewegen** 'He could not move his right arm any more', and **sich bewegen** refers to 'moving yourself', e.g. **Er blieb auf dem Sofa sitzen und hat sich den ganzen Tag nicht bewegt** 'He remained seated on the couch all day and did not move'.[22]

Bewegen also renders 'to move' s.o. emotionally, i.e. 'to be moved', e.g. **Sein Brief hat mich sehr bewegt** 'His letter moved/touched me greatly'. 'To move/drive/inspire' s.o. to do s.t. is also **bewegen** but in this sense it occurs as both a weak and a strong verb, e.g. **Das Buch hat mich bewegt/ bewogen, nach Italien zu fahren** 'The book inspired me/to go to Italy'.

'Moving' s.t. from one position to another is **versetzen**, e.g. **Wir versuchten die schwere Kiste zu versetzen** 'We tried to move the heavy chest'. This is also used of people being 'transferred', e.g. **Mein Bruder ist nach Japan versetzt worden** 'My brother has been moved/transferred to Japan'.

Sich verlagern refers to the 'moving' of the centre or focus of s.t., e.g. **Das Tief über der Ostsee hat sich seit gestern verlagert** 'The low pressure trough over the Baltic has moved since yesterday'.

Rücken means 'to move' in stages or jerks from one position to another, e.g. **Das Land rückt näher an den Westen** 'This country is moving towards the west', **Sie rückte ihren Stuhl näher zu meinem** 'She moved her chair closer to mine'.

the municipality, shire

der Bezirk, die Gemeinde, die Kommune, der Kreis

Your local municipality is your **Kommune** so that when local government elections are held, these are called **Kommunalwahlen**. The three tiers of government in Germany are thus **Kommune** (municipality/shire), **Land** (state) **Bund** (federal) (*see* GOVERNMENT).

Less official sounding with connotations of the 'local community' is **die Gemeinde**, which also renders a church 'parish'.

Bezirk is a district within a **Kommune**. It is similar in meaning to **Viertel** but is an official administrative entity (*see* AREA), e.g **das Bezirksgericht** 'district/county court'. Similar in meaning is a **Kreis**; you will see it on place name signs, for example, **Appelbüren, Kreis Münster**, which means that Appelbüren is an outlying village forming part of greater Münster.

must, have to, need (not)

brauchen, dürfen, müssen

'To have to' or 'must' is of course expressed by the forms of **müssen**. Problems arise when this verb is negated. In English there is a semantic difference between 'You mustn't do it' (= I advise you not to do it/You are not allowed to do it) and 'You don't need/have to do it' (= There is no compulsion to do it). The former in German is **Du darfst es nicht machen**, and the latter is either **Du brauchst es nicht (zu) machen** or, and this is the the trick, **Du musst es nicht machen**.

Note the difference between **Ich habe viel zu tun** 'I have a lot to do', and **Ich muss viel tun** 'I have to do a lot'. Nevertheless, in higher style **haben zu** occurs with the meaning 'it is incumbent on/required of the doer of the verb to', e.g. **In**

---

[22] Note that **bewegen** in the sense of 'to move' is weak but there is also a strong verb **bewegen** (bewog/bewogen) that is used more figuratively, i.e. **jdn zu etwas bewegen** 'to induce or persuade s.o. to do s.t.', e.g. Was hat dich dazu bewogen? 'What induced you to do it?'.

Marokko haben die Frauen auch beim Baden Trachten und Schleier zu tragen 'In Morocco women have to (= are required to) wear traditional dress and veils even when bathing', **Du hast mir nicht zu befehlen** 'It is not up to you to order me around'.

narrow

eng, schmal

'Narrow' in the literal sense of lacking width is **schmal**, e.g. **ein schmales Bett** 'a narrow bed', **ein schmaler Weg** 'a narrow path'.

Eng renders 'narrow' in the fig. sense but also literally where the emphasis is on how cramped a space is, e.g. **im engeren Sinn des Wortes** 'in the narrow sense of the word' (always comparative in German), **Ich finde den neuesten VW Polo etwas eng** 'I find the new VW Polo a bit narrow/cramped', **Der Weg ist hier sehr eng** 'The path is too narrow (= restricted) here'. Because of this connotation of **eng** it also renders 'tight' of clothes, e.g. **Diese Hose ist zu eng** 'These pants are too tight', **eine Hose enger machen** 'to take a pair of trousers in'.

near(by), close

bei, nahe, neben, in der Nähe

'Near' as a prep. meaning 'in the vicinity of' is most usually precisely that, i.e. **in der Nähe von/+ gen.**, e.g. **Unser Haus befindet sich in der Nähe von Aldi/des Bahnhofs** 'Our house is near Aldi/the station'. Followed by nothing **in der Nähe** translates the adverb 'nearby', e.g. **Er wohnt in der Nähe** 'He lives nearby'.

When standing 'near' s.t., where in English 'in the vicinity of' is inappropriate, German requires **bei**, e.g. **Sie stand beim Fenster** 'She was standing near the window' (compare **am Fenster** 'at the window'). **Bei** can also be synonymous with **in der Nähe von**, e.g. **Unser Haus liegt beim Bahnhof**. **Bei** is commonly used to indicate that villages and small towns are near larger, better known places, e.g. **Sie wohnt in Rudersdorf bei Basel** 'She lives in Rudersdorf near Basel'.

Nah is the adjective 'near(by)', e.g. **die nahe Zukunft** 'the near future', **Die Kambodschaner sind ins nahe Thailand geflohen** 'The Cambodians fled (in)to nearby Thailand'. The comparative and superlative of **nah** are **näher** and **am nächsten** and thus **nächst** in German translates both 'nearest' and 'next', e.g. **Die Türkei ist das Afghanistan am nächsten gelegene Land der Nato** 'Turkey is the nearest/closest Nato country to Afghanistan', **Wer war Napoleon am nächsten?** 'Who was closest to Napoleon (fig.)?'.

Noun/pronoun (dat.) + **nahe** renders 'close to' s.o. in the fig. sense, e.g. **Die Schwester meines Vaters stand mir sehr nahe** 'My father's sister was very close to me (i.e. a close friend)'. The last example in the previous paragraph is the superlative of this. But in higher style **nahe + dat.** also renders 'near/close to' of geographical entities, e.g. **Birecik ist eine staubige türkische Stadt nahe der Grenze zu Syrien** 'Birecik is a dusty Turkish town close to the border with Syria', **Der Unfall ereignete sich in Buxtehude nahe Hamburg** 'The accident occurred in Buxtehude near Hamburg'. It is synonymous with **in der Nähe von**.

Strictly speaking **neben** means 'next to' rather than 'near (to)', e.g. **Er saß neben mir**, 'He was sitting next to me'. You will find **neben** on occasions rendering 'near' but stick to **in der Nähe von** to translate 'near' and there will never be any ambiguity.

necessary (*see* TO NEED)

erforderlich, nötig, notwendig, (nicht) unbedingt

The main trick here is to distinguish between **nötig** and **notwendig**. **Nötig** is the most usual word, e.g. **Es war gar nicht nötig, so früh anzukommen** 'It was not at all necessary to arrive so early', **Hast du das Nötige mit?** 'Have you got all the necessaries with you?', **Wenn nötig** 'If necessary/need be'. **Notwendig** is stronger than **nötig** implying inevitability, e.g. **Das war die notwendige Folge seines Benehmens** 'That was the necessary consequence of his behaviour', **Krieg ist ein notwendiges Übel** 'War is a necessary evil'. Despite the theoretical difference in connotation between the two words, there are many contexts where either will suffice, e.g. **Es ist nicht nötig/notwendig, dass du kommst** 'It is not necessary for you to come'. Note however that **nötig**, unlike **notwendig**, is commonly used in combination with **haben** to render 'to need' (*see* TO NEED).

'Necessary' meaning required (for a particular purpose) is **erforderlich**, e.g. **Sie hat die erforderlichen Kenntnisse für diese Stelle** 'She has the necessary expertise for this job'.

The adverbial expression 'not necessarily' requires none of the above but rather **nicht unbedingt**, e.g. **Das ist nicht unbedingt der Fall, weißt du?** 'That is not necessarily the case, you know'.

to need

bedürfen, benötigen, brauchen, nötig haben

The most usual verb to express 'to need' is **brauchen** used both as a tr. verb and as a modal auxiliary (see MUST), e.g. **Er braucht Geld** 'He needs money', **Du brauchst mir nicht (zu) helfen** 'You don't need to help me/You needn't help me'.

Nötig haben is a not uncommon synonym of tr. **brauchen**, e.g. **Das habe ich nicht nötig (= Das brauche ich nicht)** 'I don't need that', but **nötig haben** must be used in the following ironical sense: **Das haben wir gerade nötig!** 'We really need that!' (i.e. like a hole in the head).

Synonymous with both **brauchen** and **nötig haben** as tr. verbs, but less common than both, is

benötigen (= to require); it is more often than not used adjectivally, e.g. **Die Flüchtlinge benötigen Informationen in ihrer Sprache** 'The refugees need/require information in their own language', **Er konnte das benötigte Geld nicht rechtzeitig verdienen** 'He was not able to earn the money needed/necessary money in time'.

Bedürfen + gen., like all verbs that take the gen., belongs to very high style, e.g. **Die Sache bedarf einer richtigen Formel** 'The matter requires an appropriate formula'.

the need

der Bedarf, das Bedürfnis, -bedürftig, die Not

'Need' in the sense of want in dire situations is **Not** and as in English can be used in the plural (**Nöte**), e.g. **In Äthiopien herrscht zurzeit bittere Not** 'Dire need prevails in Ethiopia at the moment'.

Bedürfnis (**nach** = for) refers to subjective want or desire, both physical and emotional, e.g. **Ich fühle das Bedürfnis nach Schlaf** 'I feel the need for sleep', **Auch ich habe Bedürfnisse** 'I too have needs'. Quite handy is the adjectival suffix **-bedürftig** meaning 'in need of', e.g. **renovierungsbedürftig** 'in need of renovation', **reparaturbedürftig** 'in need of repair'.

Bedarf (never pl.) refers to a 'need' or 'demand' for things, e.g. **Der Frankfurter Lufthafen hat Platzbedarf** 'Frankfurt airport needs space', **der Reformbedarf in der Bundeswehr** 'the need for reform in the German army'.

never

(noch) nie, niemals

Nie and **niemals** are synonymous (*see* EVER), e.g. **Er lässt sich nie(mals) die Haare schneiden** 'He never has his hair cut'. **Nie**, but not **niemals**, is more often than not used in combination with

noch, which enforces it somewhat (compare 'never ever' in Eng.), but **noch** can only be used when the verb is in the past tense, e.g. **Er hat sich noch nie die Haare schneiden lassen** 'He has never had his hair cut'. It is not possible, for example, to use **noch** in the following sentence, as it is not in the past tense: **Diese Straße wird nie benutzt** 'This street is never used'.

the news

die Nachrichten, Neues, das Neueste, die Neuigkeit, die Tagesschau

'The news' in general is **die Nachrichten**, e.g. **Ich hab's heute Morgen in den Nachrichten gehört** 'I heard it on the news this morning' (radio or television). The programme in which **die Nachrichten** are televised on one particuar channel (**ARD**) is called **die Tagesschau**, which can be used as a synonym for 'the news' (on television), e.g. **Ich hab's in der Tagesschau gehört** 'I heard it on the (television) news', **die Tagesschau um drei** 'the three o'clock news (on television)'. Note that **Nachrichten** is used in the plural here; in the singular it can mean 'a piece of news' but often corresponds to 'message', e.g. **Ich habe eine Nachricht für dich von Dieter** 'I have a message for you from Dieter', **keine Nachricht ist gute Nachricht** 'no news is good news'.

'The news' in the sense of 'the latest' is **das Neueste**, e.g. **Hast du das Neueste über die Tour de France gehört?** 'Have you heard the news about the Tour de France?'. Similar but corresponding more to 'What's new?' is **Neues**, e.g. **Was gibt's Neues, Gibt es etwas Neues?** 'Is there any news?'. **Neuigkeit(en)** is very close in meaning to **das Neueste**, in the singular rendering 'a piece of news', like **eine Nachricht**, but it does not have the connotation of 'message', e.g. **Das ist die beste Neuigkeit seit langem** 'That is the best news for ages'.

nice (*see* TO LIKE)

angenehm, freundlich, herrlich, lecker, nett, schön, sympathisch

This oh so simple English word can be quite tricky to translate into German. Some of the problems are related to the difficulty of rendering 'to like' in German (*see* TO LIKE). Because 'nice' is such a colourless word in English, you need to ask yourself whether 'nice' in a given context means 'delicious', 'beautiful', 'friendly' or 'pleasant' etc. and then translate it accordingly, e.g. **eine herrliche/ leckere Tasse Kaffee** 'a nice cup of coffee', **ein schönes Zimmer** 'a nice room'. 'Nice weather' or 'a nice day' require **schön**, but weather can also be **freundlich**. Most students learn 'nice' as being **nett**, but this is mostly used of people, e.g. **Das ist sehr nett von Ihnen** 'That is very nice of you', **ein netter Mann** 'a nice man', **Nett, dass ihr alle gekommen seid!** 'So nice of you all to come'. It is not however hard to find contexts where the use of **nett** goes beyond people but it tends to be a bit of a downtoner in such cases, e.g. **A: Wie war der Film? B: Ganz nett** 'A: How did you find the film? B: It was alright', **Es war ein nettes Essen** 'It was an okay meal'. If expressing that you find s.o. particularly 'nice', i.e. you like them a lot, **sympathisch** is commonly used, e.g. **Er ist mir sehr (un)sympathisch** 'I think he's really nice (not nice)'.

no, not a/any/one

kein-, nicht ein, nein, nee

'No' as the opposite of 'yes' is of course **nein**, but colloquially in the north you often hear **nee** (*see* YES). 'No' in front of a noun is **kein**, e.g. **Er hat kein Geld/keine Kinder** 'He has no money/no children'. But the previous example also translates as 'He hasn't got any money/children' and thus when confronted with 'not any', you have to realise that **kein-** is the appropriate word, e.g. **Er spricht kein Deutsch** 'He doesn't speak any German', but this can also be translated as 'He doesn't speak German'; compare also **Ich esse keine Nüsse** 'I don't eat (any) nuts'.

Kein- also translates 'not a', e.g. **Er hat keinen Sohn** 'He does not have/hasn't got a son'. **Nicht ein** is used to render 'not one' (which **kein-** can also render), but it is used when there is a certain emphasis, e.g. **Von all diesen Verbrechen ist bislang keiner/nicht einer/kein einziger/nicht ein einziger aufgeklärt worden** 'Of all these crimes not (a single) one has been solved to date'.

to notice

anmerken, bemerken, merken

The main problem here is distinguishing between **merken** and **bemerken**. **Merken** translates 'to notice' s.t. abstract, often corresponding to 'to realise', e.g. **Ich merkte, dass sie müde war** 'I noticed (= saw) she was tired', **Sie merkte einen scheußlichen Geruch** 'She noticed (= smelt) a dreadful smell', **Ich merkte an seinem Gesichtsausdruck, dass . . .** 'I noticed from his expression that . . .' (compare **anmerken** below).

See TO REMEMBER for **sich merken**.

Bemerken is required when 'noticing' is synonymous with 'becoming aware of' s.t., usually by seeing, e.g. **Seine Frau bemerkte eine schreckliche Gespanntheit in seinem Gesicht** 'His wife noticed a terrible tension in his face', **Er hat die Straßenbahn rechtzeitig bemerkt** 'He noticed the tram just in time'. Only **bemerken**, not **merken**, can have a person as its object, e.g. **Er bemerkte seine Schwester unter den Zuschauern** 'He noticed his sister among the spectators'. **Bemerken** is a more formal word than **merken**.

Despite the above attempt to define the difference between these two verbs, there are many contexts where it is immaterial which you use, e.g. **Hast du gemerkt/bemerkt, dass . . . ?** 'Did you notice that . . .?', **Ich habe es nicht bemerkt** 'I didn't notice it', **Ich habe nichts davon gemerkt** 'I didn't notice anything'.

Anmerken, where the personal object stands in the dat., expresses 'to notice' s.t. by looking at s.o., e.g. **Wir merkten ihm seine Aufregung an** 'We noticed (= could see) how excited he was', **Ich habe es dir angemerkt, dass du nicht gut geschlafen hattest** 'I noticed (= I could see) that you had not slept well'.

now

heutzutage, jetzt, nun

The word for 'now' in the sense of 'at this very moment' is **jetzt**, e.g. **Was machen wir jetzt?** 'What are we going to do (right) now?'. **Nun** renders both a not so immediate 'now' as well as a non-temporal 'now', i.e. the exclamation similar in meaning to 'well', e.g. **Nun, was machen wir jetzt?** 'Now/well, what are we going to do now?', **Was machen wir nun?** 'What'll we do now?', **Was nun?** 'What now?', **A: Warum hat er das getan? B: Es gibt nun verschiedene Gründe dafür** 'A: Why did he do that? B: Now there are various reasons for it'.

We sometimes use 'now' to mean 'nowadays/these days' in which case **heutzutage** is the appropriate translation, e.g. **Heutzutage geht keiner mehr in die Kirche** 'People now no longer go to church'.

the number, numeral

die Anzahl, die Nummer, die Zahl, das Zahlwort, die Ziffer

A 'number' is most usually expressed by the word **Nummer**, e.g. **Albertstraße Nummer 10** 'Number

10 Albert Street', eine Telefonnummer 'a telephone number'.[23]

Zahl, often used in the plural, expresses 'figures', e.g. **Die Arbeitslosenzahlen sinken ständig** 'The unemployment figures/number of unemployed are dropping continually', **Die (Verkaufs)zahlen sehen nicht gut aus** 'The (sales) figures don't look good'. In the sing. it refers to a definite quantity (in contrast to **Anzahl** below) or the total number, e.g. **Die Zahl der Mitgliedsländer der EU wird auf 25 steigen** 'The number of member states of the EU will rise to 25'.

A vague, indefinite 'number' of s.t. is **Anzahl**, e.g. **eine Anzahl Polizisten/Bücher** 'A number of policemen/books'. This word is always preceded by the indefinite article and the following noun can either take the same case as **Anzahl** or the gen. or be preceded by **von**; what is more, when **eine Anzahl** + pl. noun is the subject of the sentence, the verb can be either in the sing. agreeing with **Anzahl** or in the plural agreeing with the noun that follows it, e.g. **Eine Anzahl neugierige Leute hat/haben zugeschaut** (+ nom.) or **Eine Anzahl neugieriger Leute hat/haben zugeschaut** (+ gen.) 'A number of inquisitive people looked on'.

A 'numeral' is a **Zahlwort**, e.g. **Die französischen Zahlwörter ab sechzig sind ulkig** 'French numbers/numerals from sixty on are weird'.

Ziffer, in addition to translating 'cypher', can also render 'number' or 'figure' and in this sense is interchangeable with **Zahl** or **Nummer**, e.g. **Manche glauben, dass 7 eine magische Ziffer/Zahl/Nummer ist** 'Many believe 7 is a magical number/figure'.

---

[23] Note that the prefix for a country or town is called **die Vorwahl(nummer)** and the individual's number, if the distinction needs to be made, is **die Rufnummer**.

obviously, apparently

anscheinend, deutlich, offenbar, offenkundig, offensichtlich, scheinbar

'Obviously/clearly/evidently', i.e. there is no doubt about it, is **offenbar**, **offensichtlich** or **offenkundig**, e.g. **Es ist offenbar/offensichtlich/ offenkundig, dass . . .** 'It is obvious that . . .', **Offenbar/offensichtlich/offenkundig hat *er* es getan** 'Obviously *he* did it'.

The literal word for 'clear(ly)' is **deutlich**, which can be used where Eng. uses 'clear(ly)', i.e. when there is no doubt whatsoever, e.g. **Es ist deutlich, dass er das Verbrechen begangen hat** 'It's clear/ obvious that he committed the crime'.

Scheinbar, similar to 'seemingly', means that what is being suggested is in reality not the case, whereas **anscheinend** leaves the matter open, e.g. **Er hörte (nur) scheinbar interessiert zu** 'He gave the appearance of listening' (where **nur** emphasises this was not the case, **Er war anscheinend dafür** 'He was apparently in favour of it' (= I am assuming he was, but am not 100% sure). In practice, however, it is not uncommon for Germans to use **scheinbar** where they mean **anscheinend**.

to offer

anbieten, bieten

Anbieten is used when 'offering' s.t. to s.o. is to be utilised, e.g. **Er hat mir eine Zigarette/eine Stelle/seine Freundschaft/sein Auto angeboten** 'He offered me a cigarette/a job/his friendship/his car', **Darf ich Ihnen ein Glas Sekt anbieten?** 'Can I offer you a glass of champagne?'.

Bieten is used for more abstract things that are not available for immediate use, and thus often equates with 'providing' or 'presenting', e.g. **Die Stadt hat viel zu bieten** 'The city has a lot to offer',

Das Internet bietet neue Möglichkeiten, die Welt kennen zu lernen 'The internet offers new possibilities to get to know the world'.

the office

das Amt, das Arbeitszimmer, das Büro, die Geschäftsstelle

Your 'office' at home is an **Arbeitszimmer**. In a government or business institution an 'office' is a **Büro**. A 'post office' is a **Postamt**, but **die Post** often suffices, e.g. **Ich muss zum Postamt/auf die Post gehen** 'I have to go to the post office'. This word **Amt** occurs in many compounds referring to government 'offices' or departments (*see* DEPARTMENT), e.g. **Arbeitsamt** 'employment office', **Finanzamt** 'tax office', **Kanzleramt** 'office of the chancellor', **Jugendamt** 'youth welfare department', **Verkehrsamt** 'traffic office/branch', **Sozialamt** 'social welfare office' etc. **Amt** also renders 'office' in the figurative sense of holding 'office', e.g. **sein Amt niederlegen** 'to resign from office', **Es ist ihm gelungen, eines der mächtigsten Ämter des Landes zu erobern** 'He succeeded in acquiring one of the most powerful offices in the country'. From **Amt** is derived the word **Beamte** 'civil/public servant' (*see* OFFICIAL).

the official, officer

der Beamte/die Beamtin, der/die Bedienstete

Any 'official' working for a government department is a **Beamter** (adj. noun), e.g. **der Staatsbeamte** 'civil servant', **der Zollbeamte** 'customs officer/official', **der Polizeibeamte** 'police officer', **Sie ist Beamtin** 'She is a civil/public servant', **ein kleiner Beamter** 'a petty official'. A seemingly synonymous term in the sense of 'civil servant' is **der/die Bedienstete**, but there is a technical difference between the rights and privileges accorded to **Beamten** as opposed to **Bediensteten**, the former enjoying greater privileges.[24]

on

an, auf, in, um

With the meaning of 'on' the basic distinction between **an** and **auf** is that the former indicates vertical and the latter horizontal position, e.g. **Das Bild hängt an der Wand** 'The picture is hanging on the wall', **an der Wandtafel** 'on the blackboard', **Die Illustrierte liegt auf dem Tisch** 'The magazine is lying on the table'. But **an** also translates 'on' the edge of things, as well as very often rendering 'at' (*see* AT), e.g. **an der Küste** 'on the coast', **an der See** 'at the sea(side)'. But there are many idiomatic uses of both prepositions that don't clearly fit the above definition of the distinction between the two, e.g. **am Montag** 'on Monday', **auf hoher See** 'at sea', **auf dem Heimweg** 'on the way home', **auf dem Markt** 'at the market'. Note that items of apparel, when you have them 'on', can be **an** (Hose, Hemd), **auf** (Hut, Mütze, Brille, Ring) or even **um** (Uhr, Gürtel), although it is most usual in German to render having s.t. on by using **tragen** (to wear), e.g. **Sie trug ein wunderschönes Kleid** 'She had a lovely dress on'.

Note that 'on the radio/on television' is expressed by **in**, e.g. **Ich hab's gestern im Radio/Fernsehen gehört** 'I heard it on the radio/on television yesterday'. If a television or radio etc. is 'on', it is **an** in German too, e.g. **Ist das Radio noch an?** 'Is the radio still on?'.

---

[24] Note that although both **Beamter** and **Bediensteter** are adjectival nouns and as such are inflected as adjectives, the fem. form of **Beamter** is not an adj. noun whereas **die Bedienstete** is.

once

einst, einmal, früher, das Mal

The adverb 'once' meaning 'one time/occasion' is **einmal**, e.g. **Ich bin nur einmal in der Schweiz gewesen** 'I have only been to Switzerland once', **noch einmal** 'once more/one more time'. Fairy-tales starting with 'Once upon a time there was . . .' start in German with **Es war einmal. . . .** But 'once upon a time' can also be a more elevated way of saying 'formerly'; the same bookishness is expressed by the word **einst**, e.g. **Es waren einst die Bolschewisten, die so auftraten** 'Once upon a time it was the Bolshevists who acted like that', **Die einst blutigen Rassenunruhen von Malaysia gehören der Vergangenheit an** 'The once bloody racial riots of Malaysia now belong to the past'.

Where 'once' is synonymous in everyday language with 'formerly/previously', use **früher**, e.g. **Er hat früher hier gewohnt** 'He once lived here'.

In certain fixed expressions 'once' is expressed nominally by **das Mal**, e.g. **nur das/dieses eine Mal** 'just (the/this) once', **ein einziges Mal** 'just once', **kein einziges Mal** 'not once'.

one

ein, ein(e)s, eins

As a straight numeral not followed by a noun 'one' is **eins**, e.g. **eins, zwei, drei** 'one, two, three'. In telling the time 'one' is **ein** when followed by **Uhr** and **eins** when this is left unmentioned, e.g. **Es ist ein Uhr,** 'It is one o'clock', **Er kommt um eins/um Viertel vor eins,** 'He's coming at one/at a quarter to one'.

When **ein-** is inflected before a noun it can be ambiguous whether it means 'a' or 'one', although in speech the latter would be emphasised, e.g. **Er hat ein Kind** 'He has a/one child', **Er hat nur ein Kind** 'He has only one child'. Note the following:

Sie hat auch nur ein(e)s 'She only has one too', where **ein(e)s** acts as a pronoun, and **eins** is a contracted form of **eines**. This pronominal form varies according to gender and case, e.g. **Ich habe einen Mercedes und sie hat auch einen** 'I have a Mercedes and she has one too', **Das Erdbeben war eines der stärksten der letzten Jahre** 'The earthquake was one of the strongest of the last years'. Note also **Eines weiß ich schon** 'I already know one thing' (*see* THING).

The pronominal form of 'one' that follows an adjective remains untranslated in German, the inflected adjective sufficing, e.g. **Ich habe einen roten Mercedes und meine Frau einen dunkelblauen** 'I have a red Mercedes and my wife a dark blue one', **Welche Tasse meinst du? Die kleine** 'Which cup do you mean? The little one'.

Another form of **ein-** meaning 'one' that is declinable is the following which illustrates 'one' being used adjectivally: **auf der einen Seite** 'on the one hand', **Der eine Mann hatte nur eine Hand** '(The) one man had only one hand'.

The indefinte pronoun 'one', which is usually replaced by 'you' in speech (**du** is possible here too in German but is not as common as Eng. 'you' in this sense) is **man**; its case forms are **einen** and **einem** and its possessive is **sein**, e.g. **Die richtigen Freunde sind diejenigen, die einen anrufen, wenn man einsam ist und die einem helfen, wenn man Hilfe braucht** 'Real friends are those who ring one when one is lonely and help one when one needs help', **seine Freunde** 'one's friends'.

The indefinite pronoun 'one' (e.g. One shouldn't say such things) is also dealt with under PEOPLE.

only

bloß, einzig, erst, lediglich, nur

The usual adverb 'only' is **nur**, e.g. **Er hat nur ein Kind** 'He only has one child'. **Bloß** and **lediglich** in the sense of 'only' are synonymous with **nur**, the latter commonly standing at the beginning of a sentence, e.g. **Ich habe bloß noch einen Fünfeuroschein in meiner Brieftasche** 'I only have one five euro note left in my wallet', **Lediglich Senioren wird damit geholfen** 'Only senior citizens are being helped by this'.

'Only' can also be an adverbial conjunction in which case it is also translated by **nur**, e.g. **Sie ist bei weitem die Dümmste, nur ist es ihr noch nicht aufgefallen** 'She is by far the dumbest only it hasn't struck her yet'.

It is important to note that an 'only' occurring in expressions of time is always **erst**, never **nur**, e.g. **Es ist erst sechs Uhr** 'It is only six o'clock', **Der Junge ist erst zehn Jahre alt** 'The boy is only ten years old', **Die Familie wohnt erst seit einem Jahr in Hamburg** 'The family has only lived in Hamburg for a year', **Es ist erst gestern passiert** 'It only happened yesterday/It did not happen till yesterday'. Note that in the previous and the next example 'only' can be replaced by 'not until', which must always be rendered by **erst**: **Er kommt erst am Montag wieder** 'He is only coming back on Monday/He isn't returning till Monday'. It is of course possible to say **Er kommt nicht vor Montag wieder** but strictly speaking this translates as 'He won't be returning before Monday'.

Less commonly, **erst** can also express non-temporal 'only' where the connotation is 'the first of more to come', e.g. **Fünfzig Leute haben das Buch bestellt. Erst zehn haben es bislang erhalten.** 'Fifty people ordered the book. Only ten have so far received it'.

Einzig translates 'only' as an adjective, e.g. **Peter ist mein einziges Kind** 'Peter is my only child'. Note also **Er ist ein Einzelkind** 'He is an only child'.

to open, (to be) open (*see* TO CLOSE)

aufdrehen, aufmachen, eröffnen, öffnen, aufschließen; auf, geöffnet, offen

The most usual verb for 'opening' doors and windows is **aufmachen**, the opposite of **zumachen**, e.g. **Mach die Tür bitte auf!** 'Please open the door', **Mach auf!** 'Open up'. **Öffnen** is a more elevated synonym, the opposite being **schließen**, but both these verbs are also used for 'opening' and 'shutting' computer files (**Dateien**), e.g. **Die Geschäfte öffnen um 8 Uhr = Die Geschäfte machen um 8 Uhr auf** 'The shops open at 8 o'clock'.

'To be open' of doors can be expressed in two ways, e.g. **Die Tür ist auf/steht offen** 'The door is open'.

Sich öffnen is used when things seemingly 'open' of their own accord (i.e. an intr. usage), e.g. **Die Türen dieser Klinik öffnen sich nur für Privatpatienten** 'The doors of this clinic only open for private patients'. **Aufgehen** can render this meaning of 'to open' too, e.g. **Auf einmal ging die Tür auf** 'All of a sudden the door opened'.

The past participle of **öffnen** is used adjectivally as a more formal synonym of **offen**, e.g. **Diese Apotheke ist auch sonntags geöffnet** 'This chemist shop is also open on Sundays'. In speech one might ask **Sind Sie sonntags offen?** or **Haben Sie sonntags auf?** 'Are you open on Sundays?'.

Eröffnen refers to 'opening' a new building, monument, bridge, events etc., e.g. **Der Bundespräsident hat das neue jüdische Museum eröffnet** 'The federal president opened the new Jewish museum', **Ich erkläre diese Ausstellung für eröffnet** 'I declare this exhibition open'. But this verb can also be used as an intr. verb with the same meaning of 'opening for the first time'. **Gerade hat in Paderborn eine hochmoderne Fabrik eröffnet** 'A highly modern factory has just opened in Paderborn'. **Eröffnen** is also the verb required for 'opening' a bank account, e.g. **Er hat ein Konto bei der Dresdner Bank eröffnet** 'He's opened an account at the Bank of Dresden'. In addition, the same verb renders 'to open fire' with a weapon, e.g. **Ohne Vorwarnung zog der Geiselnehmer eine Schusswaffe und eröffnete das Feuer** 'Without any forewarning the hostage taker drew a weapon and opened fire'.

Aufschließen, the opposite of **ab-/zuschließen**, as well as **aufsperren**, the opposite of **zusperren**, render 'to open (up)' in the sense of 'to unlock'.

'To open up' a new area for oil exploration or an area of forest for exploitation of its timber, for example, is expressed by **erschließen**, e.g. **Man hat vor kurzem ein neues Ölfeld südlich von Bagdad erschlossen** 'Recently a new oilfield was opened up south of Baghdad'.

'To open' a tap, i.e. 'to turn on' a tap is **einen Hahn aufdrehen**; the opposite is **zudrehen**.

the opinion

die Ansicht, die Auffassung, das Erachten, die Meinung

The usual word for 'opinion' is **Meinung**, e.g. **Was ist deine Meinung?** 'What is your opinion?', **meiner Meinung nach** 'in my opinion', **Ich bin der Meinung, dass . . .** 'I am of the opinion that . . .', **Die Opposition ist anderer Meinung** 'The opposition is of a different opinion'. The last three examples show the word being used in standard expressions.

Nach Ansicht + von/gen. is an alternative way of expressing 'in s.o.'s opinion', e.g. **Nach Ansicht von Experten/der Experten sollte das Schiff ausgemustert werden** 'In the opinion of (the) experts the ship should be withdrawn from service', **meiner Ansicht nach** 'in my opinion'.

'I am of the opinion that . . . ' can be expressed in the following three ways: **Ich bin der Meinung/Ansicht/Auffassung, dass. . . .**

Meines/seines Erachtens is an elevated synonym of **meiner/seiner Meinung/Ansicht nach**.

In formal contexts where a professional 'opinion' is required, **Gutachten** is the appropriate word, e.g. **Wir brauchen das Gutachten eines Experten** 'We need the opinion (= report) of an expert'.

opposite

der Gegensatz, das Gegenteil, gegenüber

When two things are 'opposites', they are **Gegensätze**, as **Gegenteil** cannot be used in the plural. If the word opposite in the sing. is followed by 'to be' **Gegenteil** must be used, e.g. **'Leider' ist das Gegenteil von 'glücklicherweise'** ' "Unfortunately" is the opposite of "fortunately" ', **Er ist genau das Gegenteil von seinem Bruder** 'He is the exact opposite of his brother'. In the following example too only **Gegenteil** is permissible as nothing follows: **Sie war sehr freundlich und er das Gegenteil** 'She was very friendly and he the opposite'. **Gegensatz** also means 'contrast' (**im Gegensatz zu** 'in contrast to/as opposed to') and as such can imply antagonism, e.g. **Das ist der Gegensatz zu dem, was ich redlich nenne** 'That is the opposite of what I call reasonable'.

'Opposite' is also a preposition, in which case it is rendered by **gegenüber** + dat. in German, but this is a preposition with a difference; it follows the noun or preposition when it refers to a person, but usually precedes it when the noun is non-personal, e.g. **Er saß mir gegenüber/Er wohnt der alten Dame gegenüber** 'He sat opposite me/He lives opposite the old lady', **Die Bäckerei befindet sich gegenüber dem Postamt** 'The bakery is opposite the post office'.

original(ly)

original, originell, ursprünglich

The adverb 'originally', i.e. meaning 'initially/in the beginning', is always **ursprünglich**, but this is also used as an adjective to render 'original' in the sense of 'the first', e.g. **Wo kommst du ursprünglich her?** 'Where do you come from originally?', **Das sind die Reste der ursprünglichen Stadt, die hier gestanden hat** 'Those are the remains of the original town that stood here'.

Original, which is generally prefixed to nouns, is synonymous with **ursprünglich** as an adj., e.g. **eine Originalausgabe** 'a first edition', **in der deutschen Originalfassung** 'in the original German version'.

If s.o. or s.t. is 'original' in the sense of being unique, the word required is **originell**, e.g. **Seine One-Man-Show habe ich ganz originell gefunden** 'I found his one-man-show very original'.

otherwise

anders, ansonsten, sonst, sonstig

Ansonsten and **sonst** are synonymous but the latter is the more everyday word, e.g. **Ich musste. Was hätte ich sonst tun können?** 'I had to go (i.e. to the toilet). What could I have done otherwise?', **Der ansonsten sich so volksnah gebende britische Regierungschef ließ sich nicht blicken** 'The British prime minster, who otherwise likes to show he is close to the people, was nowhere to be seen'. In the previous examples it is the informality of the former and the formality of the latter that determine usage; in the latter case **sonst** would be acceptable too, but **ansonsten** would not be possible in the former. After you have ordered s.t. from a shop assistant, you will inevitably be asked **Sonst noch etwas?** 'Anything else?'; this too is never **ansonsten**.

There is also an adj. derived from **sonst, sonstig**, which can be a handy stylistic variant, e.g. **Montags und dienstags ist er in Köln, aber an sonstigen Tagen in Essen/aber sonst arbeitet er in Essen** 'Mondays and Tuesdays he works in Cologne but otherwise/on other days in Essen'.

If 'otherwise' means 'in a different way', it is expressed by **anders**, e.g. **Das kann man auch anders machen** 'That can also be done otherwise'.

outside/inside

außerhalb, (nach) draußen, heraus, hinaus; (nach) drinnen, herein, hinein, innerhalb

As a preposition, i.e. 'on the outside of', **außer-** and **innerhalb** (+ gen. or **von**) are used, e.g. **Beuteltiere kommen auch außerhalb Australiens/ außerhalb von Australien vor** 'Marsupials also occur outside Australia', **Es gibt Fresken sowohl innerhalb wie außerhalb (der Kapelle)** 'There are frescos on both the inside and the outside (of the chapel)'.

As adverbs of place **draußen/drinnen** render 'inside/outside', e.g. **Die Kinder spielen draußen im Garten** 'The kids are playing outside in the garden', **Sie ist den ganzen Tag drinnen geblieben** 'She stayed inside all day'.

'To come/go outside' is most usually **herauskommen/hinausgehen**,[25] e.g. **Komm bitte raus!** 'Please come outside', **Er ging dann hinaus** 'He then went outside'. Similarly to 'to come/go in(side)' are **hereinkommen/hineingehen**, e.g. **Komm bitte (he)rein!** 'Please come in(side)', **Geh sofort hinein/rein!** 'Go inside immediately'. Alternatives

---

[25] Although **her-** as a verbal prefix expresses towards the speaker and **hin-** away from the speaker, in spoken German forms such as **raus, rein, rüber** etc. are considered abbreviations of both **her-** and **hin-**, e.g. **Sie ist sofort rausgegangen = Sie ist sofort hinausgegangen** 'She went outside immediately' (*see* footnote to UPSTAIRS).

to the above are **nach draußen/drinnen**, e.g. **Er ging nach draußen** 'He went outside', **Geh nach drinnen!** 'Go inside'.

over

über, übrig, vorbei, vorüber

The preposition 'over', i.e. 'above', is **über**, e.g. **Das Düsenflugzeug flog über die Stadt/über der Stadt hin und her** 'The jet flew over the city/back and forth over the city'. This is a two-way preposition taking acc. or dat. depending on whether motion from a to b is indicated or not.

'Over' as an adverb meaning 'past' is rendered by **vorbei** or **vorüber**, e.g. **Die Weihnachtsferien sind jetzt vorbei/vorüber** 'The Christmas holidays are now over'.

'Over' as an adverb or adjective meaning 'left (over)' is **übrig**, e.g. **Ich habe was gegessen und getrunken und hatte nichts übrig von fünfzig Euro** 'I ate and drank something and had nothing left (over) from 50 euros'.

the owner

der Besitzer, der Eigentümer, der Inhaber

The 'owner' of s.t. can be either **der Besitzer** or **der Eigentümer**, but the latter is especially used of houses, e.g. **Wer ist der Eigentümer der Wohnung, die ihr mietet?** 'Who's the owner of the flat you are renting?'. Otherwise **Eigentümer** sounds like officialese, e.g. **Wer ist der Eigentümer dieses Autos?** 'Who's the owner of this car?'.

The standard expression 'Who's the owner of . . . ?' is usually expressed verbally in German, e.g. **Wem gehört dieser Regenmantel?** 'Who's the owner of this raincoat?'.

The 'owner' of a shop, restaurant or bar is **der Inhaber**.

to pack, unpack

auspacken, einpacken, packen, verpacken

'To pack' a suitcase or the car is **packen**, e.g. **Ich habe meinen Koffer/das Auto gepackt** 'I've packed my suitcase/the car'. Also use **packen** when there is no object, e.g. **Hast du schon gepackt?** 'Have you packed yet?'. 'To pack' clothes is **einpacken**, e.g. **Ich habe vergessen, einen Pyjama einzupacken** 'I forgot to pack a pair of pyjamas'.

'To unpack' a suitcase or the car is **auspacken**, e.g. **Marianne hat die Koffer ausgepackt** 'Marianne unpacked the suitcases'.

Verpacken refers to commercial 'pack(ag)ing', e.g. **Die Pralinen waren sehr schön verpackt** 'The chocolates were very nicely packed/packaged'.

to paint, the painter

anmalen, anstreichen, ausmalen, malen, streichen; der Anstreicher, der Maler

Streichen and **anstreichen** are synonymous and mean 'to put paint on' s.t., e.g. **Er hat die Haustür (grün) gestrichen/angestrichen** 'He painted the front door (green)', **ein Zimmer anstreichen/streichen lassen** 'to have a room painted', but the warning 'Wet paint' is always **Frisch gestrichen**.

Malen and its derivatives refer to artistic painting therefore Rembrandt was a **Maler** (painter, artist),[26] e.g. **Vermeer hat das damalige Holland gemalt** 'Vermeer painted Holland as it was then', **Er malte Ölgemälde** 'He painted oil paintings'. Something which is 'hand-painted' is **handgemalt**.

---

[26] Funnily enough a 'house painter' is a **Maler** too (and also an **Anstreicher**) but can be called a **Malermeister** to avoid any confusion with an artist.

Bemalen is to decorate by painting s.t. on s.t., e.g. **Sie hat ihre Küchenschränke bemalt** 'She painted/decorated her kitchen cupboards', **Die Eingeborenen von Australien bemalten sich früher den Körper** 'The natives of Australia used to paint their bodies'. **Anmalen** is similar in meaning to **bemalen** but suggests less skill is entailed, e.g. **Frau Müller hat das Gesicht von allen Kinder auf der Feier angemalt** 'Mrs Müller painted the faces of all the children at the party'. It can even simply refer to 'colouring in', as children do, which is what **ausmalen** means too, but this implies the work is done more meticulously. Note that **malen** refers to both the painting and the drawing that children do, e.g. **Der Bub hat ein Haus gemalt** 'The lad painted/drew a house'.

the pants, trousers

die Hose(n), der Slip, die Strumpfhose, die Unterhose

A 'pair of pants/trousers', both for men and for women, is **die Hose** or **die Hosen** (pl.) – the two forms are interchangeable with reference to one pair, but **Hosen** can of course refer to two or more pairs. This applies to derivatives too, e.g. **eine kurze Hose/kurze Hosen** 'a pair of short pants', **zwei kurze Hosen** 'two pairs of shorts/short pants', **eine Lederhose/Lederhosen** 'a pair of leather pants'.

A 'pair of underpants' (for males and females) is **eine Unterhose;** here the plural can only mean two or more pairs although **ein Paar Unterhosen** is also possible. **Der Slip** (pl. -s) can refer either to a man's (pair of) briefs or to a woman's panties; **Damen-/Herrenslip** are possible if a distinction needs to be made, whereas **eine Strumpfhose** is a 'pair of tights' or 'pantyhose' (**der Strumpf** = stocking).

the paper(s)

das Papier/die Papiere, die Unterlagen, die Zeitung, der Zettel

The material is called **Papier**, e.g. **Diese Karten sind aus Altpapier hergestellt** 'These cards are made from waste paper'. In the plural this word is synonymous with English 'papers' meaning 'documents', e.g. **Vor einer Reise ins Ausland sollte man immer schauen, dass alle Papiere in Ordnung sind** 'Before a trip abroad you should always check that all papers are all right'. But 'papers' in the sense of documents is also expressed by **Unterlagen** (always pl.).

When 'paper' is merely an abbreviation of 'newspaper' you must say **Zeitung**, e.g. **Wo hast du die Zeitung liegen lassen?** 'Where did you leave the paper?'.

A 'sheet of (writing) paper' is **ein Blatt Papier** and a 'note' or 'piece of (note) paper' is a **Zettel**, e.g. **Was steht auf dem Zettel geschrieben?** 'What's written on that piece of paper?'. A 'piece of scrap/jotting paper' is a **Schmierzettel**.

the part, share

die Aktie, der Anteil, der Teil, das Teil

Anteil is that which is due to you or from you, e.g. **Das war mein Anteil des elterlichen Vermögens** 'That was my share of the parental fortune'. **Anteile** also translates 'shares' in the stockbroking sense, although these are commonly called **Aktien** too.

Der Teil means 'part' and **das Teil** means 'share', but this distinction does not help in remembering the gender of the many compounds formed from **Teil**, e.g. **der erste Teil von Goethes Faust** 'the first part of Goethe's Faust', **Ich möchte meinen Teil**

der Rechnung bezahlen 'I would like to pay my part/share of the bill', **der Nachteil** 'disadvantage', **der Vorteil** 'advantage', but **das Abteil**, '(railway) compartment', **das Ersatzteil** 'spare part', **das Gegenteil** 'opposite', **das Urteil** 'judgement'.

to pass

bestehen, durchkommen, überholen, vergehen, vorbeifahren/-gehen an, vorübergehen

'To pass' an exam (tr.) is **bestehen**, e.g. **Sie hat ihre Deutsch-Prüfung bestanden** 'She passed her German exam'. 'To pass' an exam when no object is mentioned (i.e. intr.) can be expressed by both **bestehen** and **durchkommen**, e.g. **Hat sie bestanden?** 'Did she pass?', **Ist sie (in der Prüfung) durchgekommen?** 'Did she pass (the exam)?' (*see* TO FAIL).

The 'passing' of time is **vergehen**, e.g. **Wie die Zeit vergeht!** 'How time passes/flies', **In dem Land vergeht kein Tag ohne Gewalt** 'No day passes in that country without violence'.

When things 'pass', i.e. pass into oblivion, **vorübergehen** is required, e.g. **Alles geht vorüber** 'Everything passes'.

'To pass' someone in a car, i.e. 'to overtake', is **überholen** (insep.), e.g. **Er hat den Porsche zu überholen versucht** 'He tried to pass the Porsche'.

'To pass' s.t. in a car etc. in the sense of 'driving past' it is **vorbeifahren**, and the object being passed must be preceded by the preposition **an** + dat., e.g. **Wir sind dann an der Kirche vorbeigefahren** 'We then passed (= drove past) the church'. The same action on foot requires **vorbeigehen**, e.g. **Sie sind dann am Dom vorbeigegangen** 'They then passed (= walked past) the cathedral'.

the passenger

der Beifahrer, der Fahrgast, der Insasse, der Mitfahrer, der Passagier, der Reisende, der Sozius

Passagier is used for ships and planes, as illustrated in the words **Passagierflugzeug** 'passenger plane', **Passagierliste** 'passenger list'. The word **Fahrgast** is an official sounding word for 'passengers' in public transport and taxis; similarly **Fluggast** is used as an alternative for **Passagier** in a plane. It is possible for train passengers to be referred to as **Reisende** 'travellers'.

S.o. accompanying a driver in a car can be called an **Insasse**[27] or a **Mitfahrer**, e.g. **Der Fahrer und die beiden Mitfahrer sind noch am Leben** 'The driver and the two passengers are still alive'. **Insasse**, however, can refer to all occupants of a vehicle, plane or train including the driver, e.g. **Alle vier Insassen des Autos waren betrunken** 'All four occupants of the car were drunk'. The person sitting next to the driver can be called a **Beifahrer**, which can also refer to pillion passenger on a motorbike, another word for which is **der Sozius**.

the party

die Feier, das Fest, die Partei, die Party

A political 'party' is a **Partei**. A festive 'party' can be both a **Party** and a **Feier**, e.g. **Kommst du zu meiner Geburtstagsparty/zu meiner Geburtstagsfeier?** 'Are you coming to my birthday party?'. Although **Fest** normally equates more with 'festival' or 'feast', in certain limited contexts it can be synonymous with **Feier**, e.g. **das Hochzeitsfest** 'wedding reception'. Note that the 'wedding party', i.e. the collective of people, is called **die Hochzeitsgesellschaft**.

---

[27] **Insasse** is not limited to vehicles but can also refer to the occupants of a prison or institution.

to pay

sich auszahlen, bezahlen, sich bezahlt
machen, einzahlen, erkaufen, heimzahlen,
zahlen, zurückzahlen

First and foremost you need to distinguish
between **zahlen** and **bezahlen**. It is true that **zahlen**
often has no object and **bezahlen** frequently does,
e.g. **Ich möchte bitte zahlen/die Rechnung
bezahlen** 'I would like to pay/the bill'. But both
words occur as both tr. and intr. verbs. **Zahlen**
expresses the handing over of money and is used
for fees, taxes, subscriptions etc., e.g. **Ich habe
eine hohe Geldbuße zahlen müssen** 'I had to pay
a hefty fine'. For a firm that pays well, **zahlen** is
also required.

Bezahlen is used when the object is a person, but
zahlen *can* be used if what is paid for is mentioned, but then the personal object takes the dat.,
e.g. **Ich habe ihn schon bezahlt** 'I have already
paid him', **Ich habe ihm das Mittagessen/€5
gezahlt/bezahlt** 'I paid for his lunch/him 5 euros'.

'To pay for' s.t. can be expressed by **bezahlen** (+
direct object,), **bezahlen für** or **zahlen für**, e.g. **Ich
habe das Mittagessen bezahlt/dafür bezahlt/dafür
gezahlt** 'I paid for the lunch/for it', **A: Wie viel
haben Sie dafür bezahlt/gezahlt? B: Ich habe €58
bezahlt/gezahlt** 'How much did you pay for it? I
paid €58'.

In fig. contexts only **bezahlen für** can be used, e.g.
**Er hat für sein schlechtes Benehmen bezahlen
müssen** 'He had to pay for his bad behaviour'.

'To pay (s.o.) back' (lit. and fig.) is **zurückzahlen**,
e.g. **Er hat mir das Geld zurückgezahlt** 'He paid
me back the money', **Das werde ich ihm noch
zurückzahlen** 'I'll pay him back for that' (fig., i.e.
to get one's own back). This fig. meaning can
also be expressed by **heimzahlen**, e.g. **Das werde
ich ihm noch heimzahlen** 'I'll pay him back for
that'.

'To pay off' a debt is **abbezahlen**, e.g. **Wir haben
unsere Hypothek schon abbezahlt** 'We have
already paid off our mortgage'. But when s.t.
pays off, i.e. was worth doing, this can be
expressed in a variety of ways, e.g. **Der hohe
Anschaffungspreis hat sich schon bezahlt
gemacht/hat sich schon ausgezahlt** 'The high purchase price has already paid off'.

'To pay' money into an account, i.e. to deposit it,
is **einzahlen**, e.g. **Er hat €500 auf mein Konto
eingezahlt** 'He paid €500 into my account'.

The relatively rare verb **erkaufen** renders 'to pay
(dearly)' for s.t. in a fig. sense, e.g. **Seinen Erfolg
hat er teuer erkauft** 'He paid dearly for his
success'.

the pen, pencil

der Bleistift, der Füller, der Füll(feder)halter,
der Filzstift, der Kugelschreiber, der Kuli,
der Stift

A (lead) pencil is a **Bleistift** (**das Blei** = lead), a
coloured pencil is a **Buntstift** and a crayon a
Wachsstift (**der Wachs** = wax), whereas a **Filzstift**
is any pen with a felt tip. A ballpoint pen or
biro is a **Kugelschreiber**, commonly abbreviated
to **Kuli** but **Stift** is commonly used too as a
general word for 'pen' (or pencil). A 'fountain
pen' is a **Füller**, a coll. abbreviation of **der
Füll(feder)halter**.

the people

die Leute, man, die Menschen,
die Personen, das Volk

A 'person' or a 'human being' (i.e. man[kind]) is
der Mensch and thus **die Menschen** refers to a
number of human beings, e.g. **Wie viele Menschen
wohnen hier?** 'How many people live here?', So

sind die Menschen 'That's the way people are' (note the use of the definite article here), **Alle Menschen müssen sterben** 'All people have to die'. **Menschen**, as opposed to **Leute**, stresses the individuals in a given group and it is a weightier word than **Leute**.

Leute refers to people seen to be belonging to a specific class or group, e.g. **Die Leute nebenan sind sehr ordinär** 'The people next-door are very common', **All die Schüler in der Klasse waren ganz begeistert** 'All the pupils in the class were really enthusiastic'.

'Some/many/most people' as the subject of a sentence is best rendered by indefinite pronouns in German with no attempt to translate 'people', e.g. **Manche/viele/die meisten sind dafür** 'Some/many/most people are in favour of it' (*see* SOME and MOST).

It is not uncomon in German for the words 'man/woman/person/people', when preceded by an adjective, to be expressed by adjectival nouns, e.g. **ein Blinder** 'a blind man/person', **eine Blinde** 'a blind woman/person', **die Blinden** 'blind people/the blind'. In theory any adjective can be nominalised in this way, e.g. **der Tote** 'the dead man/person', **der Kranke** 'the sick man/person', etc.

Man literally means 'one' but is commonly used in German where in spoken English we use 'people' to avoid this rather posh sounding word, e.g. **Was wird man dazu sagen?** 'What are people going to say about it?'. **Leute** is sometimes used in this way in German too, **Die Leute haben (= man hat) sehr negativ auf die Nachrichten reagiert** 'People reacted very negatively to the news'. Note that **man** has case forms, i.e. **einen** (acc.) and **einem** (dat.), and its possessive form, 'one's', is rendered by **sein**, e.g. **Es tut einem weh, wenn man krank ist und seine Feunde rufen einen nicht an** 'It hurts one when one is sick and one's friends don't ring one'.

Die Person/die Personen is similar in meaning to **der Mensch/die Menschen** with reference to people as individuals but has in addition that official sounding connotation that 'persons' has in English, e.g. **Über 50 Personen/Menschen wurden verhaftet** 'More than 50 persons/people were arrested'.

The 'people' meaning the 'nation' is **das Volk**, e.g. **Das Volk hat gesprochen** 'The people have spoken'. The 'League of Nations' was **der Völkerbund** whereas the 'United Nations' these days is **die Vereinten Nationen (die UN)**. Although 'the German people' is most likely to be translated as **das deutsche Volk**, 'German people' in general is **die Deutschen** – this applies to all nationalities.

periods of the day: afternoon, evening, morning, night

der Abend, der Morgen, der Nachmittag, die Nacht, der Vormittag; gestern, heute, morgen, übermorgen, vorgestern; abends, morgens, mittags, nachmittags, nachts/des Nachts, tagsüber, vormittags; heutig, gestrig, morgig

The following are all adverbs in German and are thus written with a small letter: **gestern** 'yesterday', **heute** 'today', **morgen** 'tomorrow', **übermorgen** 'the day after tomorrow', **vorgestern** 'the day before yesterday'. They are used in combination with the nouns **Abend, Morgen, Nachmittag** and **Nacht**, which are thus written with capital letters but were written with small letters under the old spelling, e.g. **gestern Abend** 'last night' (before lights out), **morgen Nachmittag** 'tomorrow afternoon', **vorgestern Morgen** 'the morning of the day before yesterday' (we'd be more likely to say 'Tuesday morning' etc.). Note that 'tomorrow morning' can only be expressed by **morgen früh** whereas 'this morning' can be **heute Morgen** or **heute früh**.

Both **heute Abend** and **heute Nacht** mean 'tonight' but the former must be used when referring to 'this evening', i.e. that period of the night up till bed-time; **heute Nacht** is the period between going to bed and sunrise, e.g. **Was machst du heute Abend?** 'What are you doing tonight?'. The same applies to **gestern Abend** 'last night'; if referring to the wee hours of last night, this is **letzte Nacht** or **heute Nacht**,[28] e.g. **Bist du auch letzte/heute Nacht durch das Gewitter geweckt worden?** 'Were you woken up last night by the thunder storm too?'.

All the above periods of the day can be compounded with the names of the days of the week, previously written as two words but as one under the new spelling, e.g. **am Dienstagabend** 'on Tuesday evening', **am Mittwochmorgen** 'on Wednesday morning'. **Mittwoch früh** is synonymous with the previous expression.

The following are all adverbs: **abends** 'in the evening', **morgens/vormittags** 'in the morning', **nachmittags** 'in the afternoon', **nachts** 'at night', **tagsüber** 'during the day'. All but **tagsüber** are used with the names of the days of the week, which are then written with small letters as the new compound is also an adverb, e.g. **dienstagabends** 'on Tuesday evenings/on a Tuesday evening', **mittwochmorgens** 'on Wednesday mornings'. Note too **wochentags** 'on weekdays'.

See LUNCH for **mittags**.

German has adjectives derived from the adverbs **heute**, **gestern** and **morgen**, namely **heutig**, **gestrig** and **morgig** and these are used where in English we have no choice but to say 'today', 'yesterday' and 'tomorrow', e.g. **die gestrige Zeitung** 'yesterday's paper', **Die Nachricht vom heutigen Montag ist sehr positiv** 'The news from today, Monday, is quite positive'.

---

[28] The tense of the verb makes it clear whether **heute Nacht** means 'last night' or 'tonight'.

to permit, allow

erlauben, genehmigen, zulassen

'To give permission' to s.o. to do s.t. (i.e. to allow) is **jdm etwas erlauben**, e.g. **Er hat mir erlaubt, seinen Parkplatz zu benutzen** 'He permitted/allowed me/gave me permission to use his parking spot'. **Das wird der Richter nicht erlauben** 'The judge will not permit that'. 'To permit/allow' yourself s.t. is **sich etwas erlauben**, e.g. **Er erlaubt sich jeden Tag ein Glas Rotwein** 'He permits himself one glass of red wine a day'.

'To permit' meaning to passively let s.t. happen is **zulassen**, e.g. **Dieses Ergebnis lässt keine andere Erklärung zu** 'This result does not allow for/leave any other explanation'. But also **Ich lasse nicht zu, dass . . .** 'I won't permit/allow' (s.t. to happen).

Genehmigen is used for the approving of official bodies authorising s.t., e.g. **Die Gemeinde hat den Umbau genehmigt** 'The municipality has approved the alterations'. Thus **die Arbeits-/Aufenthaltsgenehmigung** 'work/residence permit'.

to persuade, convince

überreden, überzeugen

Überzeugen is 'to persuade' in the sense of convincing s.o. of s.t., e.g. **Er hat mich davon überzeugt, dass er unschuldig ist** 'He has persuaded/convinced me that he is innocent', **Ich bin fest (davon) überzeugt** 'I am firmly convinced (of it)'.

Überreden renders 'to persuade' where you talk s.o. into doing s.t., e.g. **Er hat mich überredet mitzugehen** 'He persuaded/convinced me to go along'.

the pipe

die Leitung, die Pfeife, die Pipeline, die Röhre, das Rohr, die Rohrleitung

A household '(water) pipe' is a (**Wasser)leitung**. A larger municipal 'pipe' carrying water, gas or sewage past your door is a **Rohr**, e.g. **das Kanalisationsrohr** 'sewage pipe'. 'To pipe' oil etc. is **in Rohren leiten** from which is derived the synonym of **Rohr, die Rohrleitung. Die Pipeline** has also been adopted into German for an 'oil pipeline'. The 'drainage pipe' leading from a sink, bath or shower is an **Abflussrohr**.

There is also the word **Röhre**, but it more usually translates as 'tube' rather than 'pipe' – exception **die Luftröhre** (windpipe).

A 'smoking pipe' is **die Pfeife,** the indefinite article being omitted from the phrase 'to smoke a pipe', e.g. **Er raucht Pfeife** 'He smokes a pipe'.

the place

der Ort, der Platz, die Stelle

An inhabited locality or scene of an event is an **Ort**, e.g. **Celle ist ein schöner Ort** 'Celle is a nice place' (*see* TOWN), **Ihr Geburtsort/Wohnort?** 'Your place of birth/residence?', **An diesem Ort haben wir uns kennen gelernt** 'We met each other for the first time in this place', **der Tatort** 'the place where it happened/scene of the crime'.

Stelle, unlike **Ort**, refers to an exact spot, and must be used for the body, a 'place' in a book or speech etc. **An dieser Stelle ist es passiert** 'It occurred on this very spot' (here **Ort** would not be as specific), **Ich kann die Stelle nicht mehr finden** 'I can't find the spot any more' (on body, in a book).

Platz refers to the natural 'place' for s.o. or s.t., e.g. **Dein Platz ist an meiner Seite** 'Your place is at my side', **Hier ist nicht der richtige Platz für so was** 'This is not the right place for something like that'. **Platz** also means 'space' or 'room' (for s.o. or s.t.), e.g. **Gibt es noch Platz für mich?** 'Is there still room for me?'. **Platz** is used to render 'place' or 'square' in proper names, e.g. **am Bahnhofplatz** 'at Station Square'.

the powder

der Puder, das Pulver

'Powder' for the body is **der Puder**, e.g. **der Baby-/Talkumpuder** 'baby/talcum powder'.

Explosive 'powder' is **das Pulver**, e.g. **das Schießpulver** 'gun powder', **Dieser Teil der Welt ist ein Pulverfass** 'This part of the world is a powder keg'. **Pulver** also occurs in the following compounds: **Waschpulver** 'washing powder', **Pulverschnee** 'powdered snow', **Pulverkaffee** 'instant coffee' (coll.).

the prawn, shrimp, crab, lobster, crayfish

die Garnele, der Hummer, die Krabbe, der Krebs, die Languste, die Langustine

There are several complications associated with the correct use of these words, not the least of which is that the English equivalents mean different things in different parts of the English-speaking world.

A 'crab' is a **Krebs** and is therefore also the word for 'cancer', both the disease and the constellation, thus **der Wendekreis des Krebses** 'the Tropic of Cancer'. **Krabbe** on the other hand is a small 'shrimp', such as occurs in the North Sea, which is a North German speciality. A larger 'prawn' (called a shrimp in the USA) is a **Garnele**, while a 'lobster/crayfish/crawfish' is a **Hummer**.

You may also hear people speaking of **Langusten** or **Langustinen,** both of which are Mediterranean specialities in the prawn/shrimp family.

to prefer

bevorzugen, lieber + verb, vorziehen

'To prefer' one thing to another where both are mentioned can be expressed by **vorziehen** (note the use of the dat.), e.g. **Ich ziehe deinen Bruder deiner Schwester vor** 'I prefer your brother to your sister'. Where only what is preferred is mentioned, a construction with **lieber** is best used (*see* TO LIKE), e.g. **Ich habe Aquarelle lieber (als Ölgemälden)** 'I prefer water colours (to oil paintings)'. The following would also be possible: **Ich ziehe Aquarelle Ölgemälden vor.** Whenever you prefer *doing* s.t., **lieber** plus the appropriate verb is the simplest solution, e.g. **Ich tanze lieber (als turnen)** 'I prefer dancing [= to dance] (to doing gymnastics)', **Ich trinke lieber Vodka** 'I prefer (drinking/to drink) vodka'.

Bevorzugen has connotations of 'to give preference/preferential treatment to', e.g. **Jugendliche unter 21 werden bevorzugt** 'Young people under 21 are preferred (preference is given to)'.

to prepare

vorbereiten, zubereiten

'To prepare yourself for' any eventuality is **sich vorbereiten auf** + acc., e.g. **Wir müssen uns auf ihren Besuch vorbereiten** 'We'll have to prepare for a visit from them'. From the same verb is derived the adj. **vorbereitet,** e.g. **Darauf war ich nicht vorbereitet** 'I wasn't prepared for that'.

'Preparing' meals and medicines requires **zubereiten,** e.g. **Er hat ihr zu diesem Anlass eine wunderbare Mahlzeit zubereitet** 'He prepared her a wonderful meal for this occasion'.

to prevent

behindern, hindern, verhindern, vorbeugen

'To prevent' s.t. is **verhindern,** e.g. **Das schlechte Wetter hat die Rettung verhindert** 'The bad weather prevented the rescue'. 'To prevent' s.t. (from) happening is **verhindern, dass . . . ,** e.g. **Die Geiselnehmer verhindern, dass die Menschen fliehen** 'The hostage takers are preventing people from fleeing'. **Verhindern** is only used with reference to people in the expression **Er kann nicht kommen. Er ist verhindert** 'He can't come. He is indisposed' (= prevented from coming for some unnamed reason).

'To prevent' s.o. from doing s.t. is **jdn daran hindern, etwas zu tun,** e.g. **Die Krankheit meiner Mutter hat uns daran gehindert zu kommen** 'My mother's illness prevented us from coming', **Er hat sie daran gehindert, die Schienen zu überqueren** 'He prevented her from crossing the railway line'; compare: **Er hat verhindert, dass sie die Schienen überquerte. Mach was du willst. Ich kann dich leider nicht hindern** 'Do as you like. I can't stop/prevent you', **Was hindert dich?** 'What's stopping/preventing you?'.

Behindern means 'to prevent' in the sense of impeding or standing in the way of, e.g. **Die Sanitäter wurden bei ihrer Arbeit behindert** 'The ambulance men were being prevented from doing their work/impeded in their work (people were standing in their way)'.

'To prevent' by taking precautionary measures is **vorbeugen** (+ dat.), e.g. **Den meisten tropischen Krankheiten können heutzutage vorgebeugt werden** 'Most tropical diseases can be prevented these days'.

the priest

der Geistliche, der Pastor, der Pfarrer,
der Priester

The everyday word for a '(parish) priest', be he **katholisch** or **evangelisch**,[29] is **Pfarrer**; this is also used as a title, e.g. **Pfarrer Schmidt** 'Father Smith/Reverend Smith. A **Pastor** may be protestant or catholic depending on the region and this word can also be used as a title before a surname. A **Priester** is a general term meaning a 'catholic cleric' which cannot however be used as a title, e.g. **Er ist Priester/Pfarrer** 'He is a priest', **Er ist Pfarrer** 'He is a priest/a minister' (of religion). **Geistlicher** means 'clergyman/cleric', but is also used in compounds to render 'chaplain', e.g. **der Militärgeistliche** 'army chaplain', **der Gefängnisgeistliche** 'prison chaplain'.

the prime minister

der Bundeskanzler, der Ministerpräsident,
der Premier, der Premierminister

The German prime minister is called the **Bundeskanzler,** or **Kanzler** for short; the latter is also used for the Austrian prime minister. The political head of a Bundesland is called a **Ministerpräsident,** which can be used for the 'prime minister' of foreign countries such as Britain or Australia too but they can also be called **Premierminister** or simply **Premier** (pron. as in French).

the professor, associate/assistant professor, lecturer

der Assistent, der Dozent, der Hilfswissenschaftler, der Lektor, der Privatdozent, der Professor

The hierarchy of positions at German universities is bewildering for those who only know the Anglo-Saxon system. Crucial to the distinctions outlined below are whether the person concerned has a doctorate or also a **Habilitation,** a sort of second doctorate required to qualify for consideration for a **Professur** (a chair).

A **(wissenschaftlicher) Assistent** has a Ph.D. and is doing his **Habil** (a common abbreviation) and teaching **Proseminare** (*see* THE LECTURE).[30] On becoming **habilitiert,** he becomes a **Privatdozent** and may teach **Hauptseminare** but does not yet have a chair. A **Dozent** has a Ph.D. and teaches but is not doing a **Habilitation.**

A **Lektor** only exists in Arts. He teaches language classes only and thus the 'lecturers' sent abroad by the **Deutscher Akademischer Austauschdienst (der DAAD)** are called **Lektoren.**

A **Hiwi** (< **Hilfswissenschaftler**) has not yet completed the basic degree, i.e. a **Magister** in Arts or **Diplom** in science or engineering, and thus does minor work for a **Professor.**

The **Habilitation** is on its way out in Germany. This has led to a new position, that of **Juniorprofessor/-assistent,** who is s.o. who has done a Ph.D., is not required to do a **Habi** and holds a four-year untenured lecturing position.

The best general word for a 'lecturer' in the British sense is **Dozent,** which would also translate what in America is a non-chair-holding 'professor'.

---

[29] In the nineteenth century the Lutheran and Calvinist churches in Germany amalgamated to form the **Evangelische Kirche,** which means **evangelisch** best equates to 'protestant'.

[30] For the sake of brevity I refer only to the masculine here but of course all these positions can be feminised, e.g. **Assistentin, Dozentin** etc.

the property

der Besitz, das Eigentum, das Grundstück, die Immobilie

'Property' in the sense of s.t. that belongs to you is **dein Eigentum**, but the word might just as likely be avoided in practice by using the verb **gehören**, e.g. **Das gehört mir** 'That is my property' (= belongs to me) (*see* TO BELONG).

'Property' meaning real estate can be expressed by **Haus** or **Wohnung**, if the context permits it, or otherwise **Besitz**, e.g. **Ich habe ein Haus in Tirol** 'I have a property in Tyrol', **Dieses Haus ist ein wertvoller Besitz** 'This house is a valuable property'. The term used in the real estate world for 'property' is **Immobilie**, e.g. **der Immobilienmarkt** 'the property market', **Er hat sein Geld in Immobilien angelegt** 'He has invested his money in property/real estate'; in the sing. this word refers to one particular property and in the pl. to property as a collective.

to protect

beschützen, schützen

'To protect' some*thing* is **schützen** (**gegen** = against, **vor** + dat = from), e.g. **Die Markise schüzt die Waren im Schaufenster gegen die Sonne** 'The awning protects the articles in the shop window against the sun'. But 'to protect' some*one* or an animal requires **beschützen**, e.g. **Al Capone konnte nicht vor seinen Feinden beschützt werden** 'Al Capone was not able to be protected from his enemies'.

to prove

(sich) beweisen, sich bewähren, erweisen, sich erweisen, nachweisen

'To prove' s.t. in the sense of providing evidence is **beweisen**, e.g. **Ich weiß, dass das so ist, kann es aber nicht beweisen** 'I know that is the case but I can't prove it'. 'To prove' your worth or courage also requires this verb, e.g. **Er hat seinen Mut bewiesen** 'He proved his courage', but 'to prove oneself' (also a plan, method, investment etc.) is expressed by **sich bewähren**, e.g. **Diese Anteile haben sich bewährt** 'These shares have proven themselves/paid off'. Synonymous with **sich bewähren**, but then only with respect to people proving themselves, is **sich beweisen**, e.g. **Er ist noch jung und unerfahren. Er muss sich noch beweisen** 'He is still young and inexperienced. He still has to prove himself'.

'To prove to be', i.e. to turn out to be, is expressed by **sich erweisen als**, e.g. **Er hat sich als ein Schurke erwiesen** 'He proved/turned out to be a scoundrel'. The past participle is commonly used as an adjective translating 'proven', in which case it is interchangeable with **bewiesen**, e.g. **Das ist noch nicht erwiesen/bewiesen** 'That has not yet been proven', **eine erwiesene/bewiesene Tatsache** 'a proven fact'. As a non-reflexive verb **erweisen** has other meanings not related to 'to prove'.

Nachweisen means 'to establish proof of' which takes a personal object in the dat., e.g. **Die Polizei hat ihm nichts nachweisen können** 'The police was not able to prove a thing against him', **Er möchte nachweisen, dass er für die Menschenrechtsverletzungen in der Gegend keine Verantwortung trägt** 'He would like to prove (= provide proof) that he is not responsible for the infringement of human rights in the region'.

the pub, hotel, inn

das Gasthaus, der Gasthof, die Gaststätte, die Herberge, das Hotel, die Kneipe, das Lokal, die Raststätte, die Wirtschaft, das Wirtshaus

German has a host of terms for drinking venues: **das Gasthaus, der Gasthof, die Gaststätte, die**

Wirtschaft and **das Wirtshaus** are all more or less synonymous and refer to a place where one can both eat and drink, as well as often spend the night, and as such are comparable with a British pub. Every village has at least one **Gasthaus** or **Gasthof** etc., often with names like **Gasthaus zum Wilden Hirsch/zum Weißen Rössl** 'The Wild Stag/The White Horse'. **Raststätten** are only found along autobahns and you can't spend the night in them.

Kneipe is a colloquial word which can refer to all the above but also simply a bar; Andy Capp is always down at the **Kneipe**, for example. Although **das Lokal** can also be synonymous with all the above, your regular drinking hole is your **Stammlokal**.

Herberge is literally an 'inn' but any of the above might also be called a **Herberge**. A **Jugendherberge**, however, is a 'youth hostel', a German invention.

to punish

bestrafen, strafen

The everyday word is **bestrafen** when you are punished for an offence, e.g. **Wer zu spät kommt, den bestraft das Leben** 'He who arrives late, will be punished' (said by Gorbatchov of Erich Honecker when he refused to introduce reforms), **vorbestraft sein** 'to have a prior conviction'. **Strafen**, on the other hand, suggests something more elevated such as divine punishment, e.g. **Er wird gestraft werden** 'He will be punished' (i.e. the gods will administer justice).

to put

hängen, legen, setzen, stecken, stellen, tun

'To put' is one of the trickiest verbs to translate into German. We'll look at more literal contexts

before attempting to give some guidance in the translation of figurative forms of 'to put'.

These word couplets need to be learned: **hängen** (reg.)/**hängen** (irreg.), **legen/liegen**, **setzen/sitzen**, **stecken/stecken**, **stellen/stehen**. In each case the first verb renders 'to put' and the second indicates the position that the object ends up in as a result of being put. The correct choice of verb to render 'to put' depends on whether the object concerned is upright, flat or is being put into something.

Something that ends up in a lying position requires **legen**, e.g. **Er hat das Buch auf den Tisch (hin)gelegt** 'He put the book (down) on the table', and thus **Das Buch liegt auf dem Tisch** 'The book is (lying) on the table'. If you 'put' a book on a shelf in a standing position, the verb required would be **stellen**, e.g. **Er hat das Buch in das Regal zurückgestellt** 'He put the book back on the shelf'. A chair, which naturally stands, always requires **stellen**, e.g. **Er hat den Stuhl in die Ecke gestellt** 'He put the chair in the corner'; **Er legte den Stuhl auf den Boden** means the chair was laid on the floor, i.e. put in a position not typical of s.t. that otherwise stands. Exactly where the German draws the line between things that stand and things that lie and thus things that require **stellen** instead of **legen** is not always absolutely clear; a saucer **steht auf dem Tisch** and thus requires **stellen**, whereas a knife **liegt auf dem Tisch** and thus requires **legen**. Note that 'down' in 'to put down' is rendered by **hin**, i.e. **hinlegen, hinstellen**.

But the German word for 'word order' is **Wortstellung**, and thus **stellen** is used for 'putting' a word in a certain position in a sentence, e.g. **Das Verb wird ans Ende des Satzes gestellt** 'The verb is put at the end of the sentence'.

When s.t. is 'put' into s.t. else, **stecken** is used, e.g. **Steck dies in deine Tasche!** 'Put this in your pocket', **Steck den Schlüssel in das Schlüsselloch!** 'Put the key in the keyhole'. But **stecken** also describes the result of this action, e.g. **Der**

Schlüssel steckt in der Tür 'The key is in the door'. But when 'putting' s.t. into the oven or fridge, for example, **stellen** is required, e.g. **Sie hat's in den Backofen/Kühlschrank gestellt.**

In spoken German **tun** is commonly used in place of **legen, setzen, stecken** and **stellen** where these verbs mean 'to put', e.g. **Wo hast du die Zeitung hingetan?** (= **hinlegen**) 'Where did you put the paper (down)?', **Tu die Kekse bitte in eine Tüte (rein!)** (= **reinstecken**) 'Please put the biscuits in a bag'. But there are cases where 'to put' can only be rendered by **tun**, e.g. **Tu bitte einen Löffel Zucker in meinen Kaffee!** 'Please put one spoon of sugar in my coffee', **Ich habe eine andere Kassette in den Kassettenrecorder getan** 'I've put another cassette in the cassette player'.

If you 'put' s.t. on the wall, German uses the regular verb **hängen**, e.g. **Ich habe das Gemälde an die Wand gehängt** 'I put/hung the picture on the wall'. The resulting position is rendered by the irregular verb **hängen**, e.g. **Das Bild hat jahrelang an dieser Wand gehangen** 'The picture hung on this wall for years'.

The hardest of all the alternatives given above to prescribe the correct use of is **setzen**. It can be literal, e.g. **Setz den Deckel auf den Topf** 'Put the lid on the pot', **Die Mutter hat ihr Kind auf das Sofa gesetzt** 'The mother put her child on the sofa'; it is always used with reference to people, e.g. **Die Asylbewerber sind in ein Flugzeug gesetzt und abgeschoben worden** 'The asylum seekers were put in a plane and deported'. But more often than not **setzen** renders 'to put' in more figurative contexts, e.g. **Der Arzt hat meine Frau auf Diät gesetzt** 'The doctor has put my wife on a diet', **Er setzt Vertrauen in mich** 'He's putting his trust in me'.

to put off, postpone

aufschieben, hinausschieben, verschieben

'To put off' s.t. till a given time in the future is **verschieben auf** + acc., e.g. **Wir haben es auf morgen verschoben** 'We've postponed it till tomorrow'. When the period of time is not mentioned, **hinausschieben** is used, e.g. **Das dürfen Sie nicht länger hinausschieben** 'You mustn't put that off any longer'. Aufschieben too means 'to put off' with no connotation of resumption at some time in the future, e.g. **Wir haben die Party aufschieben müssen** 'We had to put/call the party off'. This verb is possibly most commonly heard in the expression **Aufgeschoben ist nicht aufgehoben** 'Putting something off doesn't solve it'.

quite

etwas, ganz, sehr, ziemlich

'Quite' is ambiguous in English. When it qualifies an adjective or adverb it can be either very positive or be used to tone the following word down. German **ganz** too has both meanings but is most usually used with the former meaning, which means it is often synonymous with **sehr**, e.g. **Dieses Kleid war ganz teuer** 'This dress was quite (= very) expensive', **Der Film war ganz gut** 'The film was quite good' (down-toner). The other meaning can be unambiguously rendered by **etwas** (somewhat) or **ziemlich** (rather), but English 'rather' can be as ambiguous as **ganz**, whereas **ziemlich** is a definite down-toner, e.g. **Dieses Kleid war etwas/ziemlich teuer** 'This dress was quite (= but not excessively so) expensive'.

to rain, pour

gießen, regnen, schütten, verregnen

Regnen is of course the usual word but **verregnen** renders 'to be spoilt/ruined by rain', 'to be rained out', e.g. **Das Fußballspiel war verregnet** 'The football match was spoilt by rain'.

'To pour (with rain)' can either be expressed by **schütten** or otherwise **gießen** in a couple of set idioms, e.g. **In der Nacht wird es kräftig schütten** 'During the night it will pour', **Es gießt in Strömen/Es hat wie aus Eimern gegossen** 'It is/was raining cats and dogs'.

to raise, rise (*see* TO SINK)

anheben, ansteigen, aufgehen, erhöhen, steigen, steigern, zunehmen

One of the problems here has to do with the distinction between the tr. verb 'raise' and the intr. verb 'rise'; **anheben, steigern** and **erhöhen** are all tr. and **aufgehen, (an)steigen** and **zunehmen** are all intr., e.g. **Die Grünen wollen den Benzinpreis auf €2,50 über 5 Jahre anheben** 'The Greens want to raise the price of petrol to €2.50 over 5 years', but **Der Wechselkurs ist in den letzten Tagen (an)gestiegen** 'The exchange rate has risen in the last few days'.

The most usual way of rendering 'to rise' is with **(an)steigen**, where use of the prefix **an** seems to be optional, e.g. **Die Temperatur steigt noch (an)** 'The temperature is still rising'. **Aufgehen** is used for dough rising and the sun, e.g. **Die Pizza ist beim Backen schön aufgegangen** 'The pizza rose nicely while cooking', **Wie spät geht die Sonne im März auf?** 'At what time does the sun rise in March?'.

Zunehmen translates 'to rise' where it is synonymous with to increase, e.g. **Die Zahl der Einwohner hat zugenommen (= ist [an]gestiegen)** 'The number of inhabitants has increased'. Note that this verb takes **haben**, unlike **(an)steigen** and **aufgehen**.

Erhöhen (lit. to heighten) is used for 'raising' the height of a wall, for example, but is also used fig. for prices and wages, e.g. **Unser Chef weigert sich, unsere Gehälter zu erhöhen** 'Our boss refuses to raise our salaries'.

rather, sooner

eher, lieber, ziemlich

Where 'rather' qualifies an adjective or adverb, **ziemlich** is required, e.g. **Die Familie ist ziemlich arm** 'The family is rather poor' (*see* QUITE). If you would 'rather' *do* s.t., **lieber** is the word, e.g. **Ich bleibe lieber zu Hause** 'I'd rather stay at home' (*see* TO PREFER). Somewhat higher style than **lieber** is **eher** (compare 'sooner' in Eng.), e.g. **Das würde ich schon eher sagen** 'I'd rather/sooner put it that way'. But **eher** is not interchangeable with **lieber** in the following construction, e.g. **Sie ist eher faul als dumm** 'She is lazy rather than stupid'.

to read

ablesen, lesen, (sich) verlesen, vorlesen

The usual word is of course **lesen**, which requires no explanation, but 'to read/call *out*' s.t. is **verlesen**, e.g. **Die Namen aller Preisträger wurden verlesen** 'The names of all the prizewinners were read out'. Note, however, that **sich verlesen** renders 'to make a mistake in reading/to misread', e.g. **Ich habe mich wohl verlesen** 'I probably misread it/read it wrongly'. **Vorlesen**, on the other hand, means 'to read out aloud' or 'to read s.t. *to* s.o'., e.g. **Jeden Abend lese ich meinen Kindern ein Märchen vor** 'Every night I read my kids a fairytale'.

Ablesen means 'to read from the page', e.g. **Er hat seine ganze Rede abgelesen** 'He read his whole speech' (i.e. did not know any of it by heart). **Ablesen** is also used for reading lips, e.g. **Er kann von den Lippen ablesen** 'He can lip-read', **Ich habe es ihm von den Lippen/vom Mund abgelesen** 'I read it from his lips'.

to realise

sich bewusst sein/werden, begreifen, merken, feststellen

'To realise' when it means 'to be/become aware' is **sich bewusst sein/werden**, e.g. **Ich war mir nicht bewusst, dass er das Land schon verlassen hatte** 'I didn't realise that he had already left the country', **Er ist sich auf einmal (dessen) bewusst geworden, dass der Kleine ihm nicht mehr folgte** 'He suddenly realised that the little one was no longer following him'.

Where 'to realise' is synonymous with 'to understand/comprehend' it is best rendered by **begreifen**, e.g. **Er scheint nicht zu begreifen, dass er schuld daran ist** 'He doesn't seem to realise that it is his fault'.

Where 'to realise' is synonymous with 'to discover/ascertain/establish' use **feststellen**, e.g. **Wir haben endlich festgestellt, dass es hier zu kalt für Rebstöcke ist** 'We have finally realised that it is too cold for grapevines here'.

'To realise' can be synonymous with 'to notice', in which case it can be translated by **merken** (*see* TO NOTICE).

really, actually

eigentlich, tatsächlich, wirklich

'Really' as an intensifier of adjectives and adverbs is **wirklich**, e.g. **Er ist wirklich dumm** 'He is really stupid', but also **Ist er wirklich so dumm?** 'Is he really so stupid?'.

Where 'really' can be substituted by 'actually', use **eigentlich**, e.g. **Ich wollte eigentlich nur zehn Minuten bleiben** 'I really/actually only wanted to stay ten minutes'.

Where 'really' is synonymous with 'indeed' or 'in actual fact', use **tatsächlich**, e.g. **Hat er es tatsächlich gemacht?** 'Did he really (and truly) do it?', **Tatsächlich kennt das gesetzestreue Judentum weder die Erbsünde noch das Zölibat** 'Traditional Judaism really recognises neither original sin nor celibacy'.

Remember that 'actually' is often a notorious, meaningless filler in English, in which case it should not be translated into German, e.g. **Wir wohnen schon lange hier** 'We've actually lived here for a long time'.

recently (*see* AS)

kürzlich, in letzter Zeit, neuerdings, neulich, seit/vor kurzem, unlängst, vorhin

How you translate 'recently' depends on how recent the event was – the actual time designated by 'recently' is very vague in English. You will probably mostly require **vor kurzem**[31] which refers to the not too distant past and with which **kürzlich** is synonymous, as is **unlängst**, but this is a more elevated word, e.g. **Sie war vor kurzem/kürzlich bei uns auf Besuch** 'She recently visited us'. **Neulich** is very close in meaning to the above but is vaguer and is possibly further back in the past. Note that only **seit kurzem** can be used if the action started in the recent past and continues into the present, e.g. **Er lernt seit kurzem Russisch** 'He recently started to learn Russian' (*see* FOR).

In letzter Zeit and its synonym **neuerdings** refer to a period of time leading up to the present, e.g. **Die Kontrollen an der Grenze sind in letzter Zeit/neuerdings strenger geworden** 'The checks on the border have got stricter recently/lately'.

Vorhin, being the most recent of all, refers to just now, just a moment ago, earlier on today.

---

[31] Note too **bis vor kurzem** 'until recently'.

to recognise

anerkennen, erkennen, wiedererkennen

'To recognise' s.o. or s.t. after a period of absence is **(wieder)erkennen**, e.g. **Er hat seinen Bruder/das Haus nach so vielen Jahren kaum (wieder)erkannt** 'He scarcely recognised his brother/the house after so many years'. German often uses this verb where we use the adjective 'unrecognisable', e.g. **Er war gar nicht wiederzuerkennen** 'He was not at all recognisable'. **Wieder** is optional where the person or thing referred to was previously known to you, but otherwise it must be omitted, e.g. **Ich habe die Sprache, die beiden gesprochen haben, nicht erkannt** 'I didn't recognise the language the two were speaking'.

'To recognise' in the sense of 'to identify' is simply **erkennen**, e.g. **Der Täter wäre an der Tätowierung auf der Stirn leicht zu erkennen** 'The perpetrator would be easy to recognise by the tattoo on his forehead', **Erkennst du diese Musik?** 'Do you recognise this music?' (= do you know what it is?).

Anerkennen renders 'to recognise' when it means 'to acknowledge', particularly but not only in the political sense, e.g. **Die Bundesrepublik wollte die DDR nicht anerkennen** 'West Germany did not want to recognise East Germany', **Dieses Diplom wird in West-Europa nicht anerkannt** 'This degree is not recognised in Western Europe'.

Where 'recognise' means 'admit', translate it with **zugeben** or **eingestehen**, e.g. **Er muss zugeben, dass er Unrecht hatte** 'He needs to recognise that he was wrong' (*see* TO ADMIT).

to reconcile; the reconciliation

(sich) aussöhnen, (sich) versöhnen;
die Aussöhnung, die Versöhnung

When two *people* in dispute become reconciled **sich versöhnen** is required, e.g. **Sie haben sich versöhnt** 'They became/were reconciled'. **Sich aussöhnen/Aussöhnung** refer rather to groups; **sich versöhnen/Versöhnung** are more emotional than **sich aussöhnen/Aussöhnung** and thus the latter is used for example in political contexts, e.g. **die polnisch–deutsche Stiftung für Aussöhnung** 'the Polish–German Foundation for Reconciliation'. **Versöhnen** is the verb required when fig. 'reconciling' s.t. with s.t. else, e.g. **Man kann die beiden Theorien mit einander versöhnen** 'The two theories can be reconciled with each other'.

to refuse

ablehnen, abschlagen, verweigern,
sich weigern, nicht wollen

'To refuse/reject/deny' s.t., i.e. the tr. verb, is **verweigern**, e.g. **Warum verweigern immer mehr junge Männer den Wehrdienst?** 'Why do ever more young men reject conscription', **Er hat's mir verweigert** 'He refused/denied me it', **Die Länder verweigern der Bundesregierung die Mitarbeit** 'The states refuse the federal government cooperation'. As the last two examples illustrate, this is the verb required when you refuse some*one* some*thing* and the person stands in the dat.

'To refuse' to *do* s.t., i.e. the intr. verb, is **sich weigern** or can be expressed simply by **nicht wollen**, e.g. **Er weigert sich/Er will nicht** '(I asked him to help but) he refuses', **Sie weigern sich mitzuarbeiten/Sie wollen nicht mitarbeiten** 'They refuse to cooperate'.

'To refuse' a request is both **abschlagen** and **ablehnen**, the choice depending partially on syntax, e.g. **Er hat ihr die Bitte um Geld abgeschlagen/Er hat ihre Bitte um Geld abgelehnt** 'He refused her request for money'; the presence of the personal object in the dat. requires the use of **abschlagen**, whereas when this is omitted, **ablehnen** is the appropriate verb. **Ablehnen** is also used 'to refuse/reject/decline' a job, an offer, a suggestion but it can also render 'to refuse' to *do* s.t. so long as it is provided with **es** as its object, e.g. **Er hat es abgelehnt mitzuarbeiten** 'He refused to cooperate'.

to regret

bedauern, bereuen

'To regret' a mistake is **bedauern**, e.g. **Die SED hat den Bau der Berliner Mauer nie bedauert** 'The SED never regretted building the Berlin Wall'. **Bedauern** can be followed by an object or a **dass** clause, e.g. **Wir bedauern, dass . . .** 'We regret that . . .'. Rather than expressing verbally that you 'regret' s.t., German often prefers to use the phrase **zu meinem** (etc.) **Bedauern**, e.g. **(Sehr) zu unserem Bedauern werden wir nicht anwesend sein können** 'We regret (very much) we will not be able to be present'.

Bereuen smacks more of repenting for sins and guilt, e.g. **Er wird's irgendwann bereuen** 'Some day he'll regret it' (= be sorry about it), **Er bereut schon, ihr das Geld verweigert zu haben** 'He already regrets having refused her the money'; **bedauern** could be used here too if the connotation were one of regretting a mistake rather than repenting.

the relationship

die Beziehung, das Verhältnis, die Verwandtschaft

'Relationship' in the sense of being related is **Verwandtschaft** (*see* RELATIVE). The distinction between **Verhältnis** and **Beziehung** is subtle and the two can be interchangeable, the latter often being pluralised. A sexual 'relationship' is usually a **Verhältnis**, but can also be a **Beziehung**, e.g. **Die beiden haben ein Verhältnis/eine Beziehung** 'Those two have a relationship going'. But a **Verhältnis** is not necessarily sexual, e.g. **Ich habe ein gutes Verhältnis zu ihm** 'I have a good relationship with him' (note the use of **zu** for 'with'); **gute Beziehungen zu jdm haben** is synonymous with **ein gutes Verhältnis**. Relations between countries are **Beziehungen** (usually pl.), e.g. **diplomatische Beziehungen** 'diplomatic relations', **die deutsch–französischen Beziehungen** 'the Franco–German relationship/Franco–German relations', **Deutschland will seine Beziehungen zu Kuba verbessern** 'Germany wants to improve its relationship/relations with Cuba'.

Verhältnis must also be used when 'relation' refers to ratio or proportion, e.g. **Die Kosten waren zu hoch im Verhältnis zum Ergebnis** 'The costs were too high in relation to the results'.

the relative, relation

der/die Angehörige, der/die Verwandte, die Verwandtschaft

Der/die Familienangehörige means 'the member of the family/family member', e.g. **In diesen Wikingerhütten schliefen im Schnitt 15 Familienangehörige** 'On average fifteen family members slept in these Viking huts'. The prefix **Familien-** can be dropped if context makes the meaning clear, e.g. **Der Kanzler wandte sich an die Angehörigen der Umgekommenen** 'The chancellor turned to the relatives of the deceased'. **Der nächste Angehörige** expresses 'the next of kin'.

Der/die Verwandte means 'relative/relation', e.g. **meine Verwandten** 'my relatives', but **die Verwandtschaft** is also used as a collective for 'relatives', e.g. **Er hat seine ganze Verwandtschaft eingeladen** 'He invited all his relatives'. The following idioms express the concept adjectivally rather than nominally, e.g. **Er ist (nicht) mit mir verwandt** 'He is (not) a relative of mine', **Wie ist er mit dir verwandt?** 'What relation is he to you?'.

See also **Verhältnis** under 'relationship'.

to remember

denken an, einfallen, sich entsinnen, sich erinnern an, sich merken, wissen

German makes an important distinction with regard to 'to remember' that English does not. German distinguishes between 'recalling' s.t. and 'noting' s.t. for future reference; the former is rendered by **sich erinnern** (plus **an** + acc. before the object) and the latter by **sich merken**, e.g. **Ich kann mich nicht mehr an seinen Namen erinnern** 'I cannot remember his name', **Ich muss mir seinen Namen merken** 'I must remember his name', **Merk dir dies!** 'Remember this'. When instead of an object a **dass** clause follows, **daran** is optional, e.g. **Ich erinnere mich (daran), dass er sehr groß war** 'I remember that he was very tall'.[32] Colloquially **wissen** is commonly used instead of **sich erinnern an**, which is quite a mouthful, e.g. **A: Weißt du noch? (= Erinnerst du dich noch daran?) B: Nein, das weiß ich nicht mehr** 'A: Do you remember? B: No, I don't remember'.

When 'to remember' means 'to bear in mind/don't forget', particularly as an imperative, it is rendered by **denken an**, e.g. **Denk daran, dass du versprochen hast, mir zu helfen** 'Remember that you promised to help me', **Ich habe nicht daran gedacht, das Fenster zuzumachen** 'I didn't remember to shut the window', **Denk daran, dass du . . .** 'Bear in mind that . . ./Don't forget to . . .'.

Einfallen, meaning 'to occur to s.o.' is a common way of expressing 'to remember/recall', but it requires different syntax from the other verbs discussed here, e.g. **Es fällt mir eben ein, dass ich vergessen habe, den Arzt anzurufen** 'I have just remembered (= it occurs to me) I forgot to ring the doctor'. This verb can also render 'to remember' meaning 'to think of s.t. on the spot', e.g. **Mir**

fällt ihre Adresse momentan nicht ein = ich kann mich im Moment nicht an ihre Adresse erinnern 'I can't remember her address right now'.

Sich entsinnen an is an elevated synonym of **sich erinnern an** but tends to be used predominantly in the fixed expression **Wenn ich mich recht entsinne** 'If I remember correctly/If my memory serves me right'.

to rent (out), hire (out), lease, let; tenant, landlord

anheuern, anmieten, mieten, leasen, leihen, verleihen, vermieten; der Mieter, der Vermieter

When you 'rent' a car or a flat the verb is **mieten**; when the firm 'rents (out)' to you, the verb is **vermieten**, e.g. **Zimmer zu vermieten** 'Room to let/for rent'. You, the tenant or renter, are the **Mieter** and the person renting to you is the **Vermieter**, and what you pay is **die Miete**. **Verleihen** is a more elevated word for **vermieten**, usually seen in nominal form, e.g. **Autoverleih/Bootsverleih** 'car/boot rental'. **Leihen** is to **verleihen** what **mieten** is to **vermieten**, but is more commonly used in the sense of 'borrowing/lending' (*see* TO LEND).

Of course in English we call renting 'hiring', which is also rendered by **mieten**. But when a firm 'hires' people to fill jobs, the word used is **anheuern** or **einstellen**. e.g. **Diese Fabrik hat vor kurzem eine Menge neue Kräfte angeheuert/eingestellt** 'This factory hired a lot of new people recently'.

Leasen/Leasing are relatively recent loanwords that are only used in the commercial world and in particular of 'leasing' cars. Otherwise where 'lease' in English is synonymous with 'renting', then **mieten** is used, e.g. **Die Universität mietet diese Gebäude von der Stadt** 'The university is leasing this building from the city'. You may

---

[32] Note that **erinnern** means 'to remind' and is thus a totally separate verb from **sich erinnern**, e.g. **Du erinnerst mich an meine Mutter** 'You remind me of my mother'.

occasioanlly encounter **anmieten,** where the connotation is renting for a limited period of time for a specific purpose; for example, the previous example with **mieten** means the university is renting the building on an on-going basis, but **anmieten** would imply it is only temporary, e.g. **Die Universität will zusätzliche Gebäude für das erste Semester von der Stadt anmieten** 'The university wants to rent/lease additonal buildings from the city for the first semester'.

the report

der Bericht, das Gutachten, die Reportage, das Zeugnis

A 'school report' is **ein (Schul)zeugnis.**

A written or oral 'report' is a **Bericht,** e.g. **Wir haben einen Bericht von einem Terroranschlag in Berlin bekommen** 'We have received a report of a terrorist attack in Berlin'. The 'weather report' on television or radio is both **der Wetterbericht** and **die Wettervorhersage** (lit. weather forecast). A media 'report', synonymous with **Bericht,** can also be a **Reportage.** 'Reporting' is **Berichterstattung,** derived from **Bericht erstatten** (**über etwas** acc.) 'to report/give a report (on s.t.)'.

For **Gutachten** see OPINION.

responsible; the responsibility

verantwortlich, zuständig; die Verantwortlichkeit, die Verantwortung, die Zuständigkeit

'Responsible for s.t.' is ambiguous in Eng. It can either mean who caused s.t. to happen or whose domain s.t. is; the former is **verantwortlich für** and the latter **zuständig für,** e.g. **Wer ist verantwortlich für den Unfall?** 'Who is responsible for the accident?', **Er ist der dafür zuständige Beamte**

'He is the officer responsible for that (= in charge of)'. The noun derived from **zuständig** is **die Zuständigkeit,** which is not problematical, but both **Verantwortlichkeit** and **Verantwortung** are derived from the other root and the distinction is subtle. The 'responsibility/liability' for s.t., in line with the above meaning of **verantwortlich,** is **Verantwortlichkeit,** but it is more usual to express this adjectivally in German, e.g. **Wer ist dafür verantwortlich?** 'Who bears the responsibility for it?'. If expressing this nominally, **Verantwortung** is more likely to be used than **Verantwortlichkeit,** e.g. **Wer trägt dafür die Verantwortung?** 'Who bears the responsibility for it?'.

To do s.t. on your own 'responsibility' requires **Verantwortung,** e.g. **Auf deine/eigene Veranwortung!** 'It's your responsibility/The onus is on you!', **Ich übernehme die volle Verantwortung dafür** 'I'll assume complete responsibility for it'.

the restaurant, café , coffeeshop, baker's, cakeshop, snackbar

die Bäckerei, das Café, die Konditorei, das Restaurant, das Stehcafé

Restaurant corresponds in meaning to the same English word. Remember, however, that it is also possible to partake of meals in **Gaststätten** etc. (see PUB) and these can thus fulfil the functions of often somewhat more down-market restaurants.

A **Café** renders 'coffee-shop' and as such is not problematical, but the difference between a **Café** and a **Konditorei** can be tricky. A **Konditorei**[33] is in fact a 'cake-shop', where the cakes and biscuits are made on the premises, but in many it is also possible to sit down to consume the cake with tea or coffee, in which case **Konditoreien** fulfil the

---

[33] A 'pastry chef' is called a **Konditor,** with the stress on the i, whereas **Konditorei** bears the stress on the final syllable, like all words in -ei.

same function as **Cafés**, but the latter do not normally make their own cakes and may not sell cake(s) to take away.

A **Stehcafé** is a very German concept. It is very common in Europe to have to pay through the nose to consume eats and drinks if you sit down, but if you are prepared to consume while standing, and thus presumably not linger unduly, you can get a cup of coffee and a modest nibble in a **Stehcafé**, best illustrated in Germany by the chains run by Eduscho and Tschibo.

A **Bäckerei** of course sells bread but most also sell a variety of cakes and biscuits, and thus overlap in their offerings with **Konditoreien**, but you cannot sit down to consume in a **Bäckerei**. Note that you can say either **Ich hab's in der Bäckerei gekauft** or **beim Bäcker gekauft** 'I bought it at the bakery/baker's'.

to retire; the retiree

pensionieren, sich pensionieren lassen, in den Ruhestand gehen/treten/versetzen; der Pensionär, der/die Pensionierte, der Rentner, der Ruheständler, die Senioren

'To retire' from your job is either **in den Ruhestand gehen** or **treten**, e.g. **Ende diesen Jahres geht/tritt mein Vater in den Ruhestand** 'My father is retiring at the end of this year'. Synonymous with the above is **in Pension gehen**[34] and **sich pensionieren lassen**. 'To take early retirement' is **in den Vorruhestand gehen/treten**. 'To be retired' is **im Ruhestand sein**, e.g. **Er ist (Lehrer) im Ruhestand** 'He is retired (a retired teacher)'. All these are of course intr. verbs; if s.o. 'is retired' (i.e. being pensioned off), the tr. equivalents **in den Ruhestand versetzen** or **pensionieren** must be

used, e.g. **Mein Vater wird mit 55 in den Ruhestand versetzt/wird mit 55 pensioniert** 'My father is being pensioned off at 55'.

Following on from the above, a 'retiree' is either **der Ruheständler** (**Vorruheständler** 'early retiree'), **der/die Pensionierte** or **der Pensionär**. All three words of course also translate 'pensioner', as does **Senioren** (always pl.), e.g. **die Seniorenkarte** 'senior citizen's ticket/pensioners' concession card'. A very common word for 'pensioner' is **der Rentner**, derived from the word **die Rente** (the pension).

to ring

anrufen, klingeln, läuten, telefonieren

For cases where 'to ring' means 'to telephone' s.o., i.e. **anrufen** and **telefonieren**, see 'to call'. This leaves **klingeln** and **läuten** to be dealt with here. In keeping with 'the (door)bell' being **die Klingel**, **klingeln** refers to a ring at the door, e.g. **Es klingelt an der Tür** 'There's a ring at the door'. This verb can also refer to the phone ringing, but in this case **klingeln** is interchangeable with **läuten**, e.g. **Das Telefon hat geklingelt/geläutet** 'The phone rang'. **Läuten** is also used for the ringing of bells, e.g. **Sonntags läuten alle Glocken im Dorf** 'On Sundays all the bells in the village ring'.

the river, stream

der Bach, der Fluss, der Strom

The usual word for a 'river' is **Fluss**, but large rivers like the Rhine and the Danube, can also be called a **Strom**. **Strom** only translates 'stream' in a figurative sense, e.g. **ein Strom von Besuchern/ Besucherstrom** 'a stream of visitors'. A 'stream', 'brook' or 'creek' is a **Bach**.

---

[34] Note that **Pension** and its derivatives are pronounced as if the word were written 'Pansion' and with the stress on the final syllable.

the road, street, path, way

die Allee, der Bürgersteig, die Gasse,
der Gehsteig, der Pfad, die Straße, der
Straßenzug, das Trottoir, der Weg

Straße translates both 'street' and 'road', e.g. **Er
wohnt in dieser Straße** 'He lives in this street', **Die
Kinder spielen immer auf der Straße** 'The kids
always play on the road'.

German freeways (**Autobahnen**) and federal roads
have names like **A3** and **A40** – such road names
are feminine, e.g. **Es ist ein Stau von 4 Kilometern
auf der A43 zwischen Münster und Dülmen**
'There is a traffic jam on the A43 between
Münster and Dülmen'.

Straßenzug is another word for 'street' that
emphasises the complete streetscape, e.g. **Durch
die Explosion sind ganze Straßenzüge verschwunden** 'As a result of the explosion whole
streets have disappeared'.

A **Gasse** is a small 'street' or 'alley/lane(way)' in
north Germany but in the south, and particularly
in Austria, it simply means 'street' and occurs in
many street names, e.g. **die Kochgasse**. It also
occurs in the expression (**mit dem Hund**) **Gassi
gehen** 'to go walkies (with the dog)'.

Allee, despite appearances, renders an avenue and
is thus something quite grand.

In street names the word **Weg** more or less renders
'road', e.g. **der Langenkampsweg** 'Langenkamps
Rd', but otherwise it renders 'path', 'way' or
'track', e.g. **ein Weg durch den Wald** 'a way/path
through the forest', **der Weg zurück** 'the way
back', **ein Wanderweg** 'a walking track'. Note
that a **Fußweg** is not a paved footpath in a city,
but a track for walkers, for example through a
park or forest, as opposed to (**Fahr**)**radweg**
'bicycle track'. A paved 'footpath' in a town
(Br. pavement, Am. sidewalk) is **der Geh-** or
Bürgersteig or **das Trottoir**.

the room, space

die Kammer, der Platz, der Raum, der Saal,
die Stube, das Zimmer

Zimmer is the basic word. A house consists of a
number of **Zimmer**, e.g. **Badezimmer** 'bathroom',
Schlafzimmer 'bedroom', **Wohnzimmer** 'loungeroom'. When travelling through the German
countryside 'bed and breakfast' places hang out a
sign with **Zimmer frei** on it.

A large 'room' in a public building is a **Raum** or
Saal (pl. **Säle**). What is an **Esszimmer** (dining
room) in a house, is a **Speisesaal** at a boarding
school, station or hospital; likewise with
Schlafzimmer (bedroom) and **Schlafsaal** (dormi-
tory); a doctor's surgery has a **Wartezimmer**, but
a station has a **Wartesaal** or **Warteraum**. But **Saal**
can also translate 'hall' in a public building, e.g.
Konzertsaal 'concert hall'. **Saal** and **Raum** are
more or less synonymous but are not interchangeable in all compounds. **Raum** commonly
refers to rooms in public buildings in general;
although a 'classroom' is a **Klassenzimmer**, you
might say when speaking about the school as a
whole **Die Räume können nicht beheizt werden**
'The rooms can't be heated'. Generally speaking
Räume are bigger than **Zimmer**.

Stube sounds a bit old-fashioned these days but
when it *is* used for a room in a house, it refers to
a loungeroom and implies homeliness and cosi-
ness.

Kammer is small and not commonly used any
more except in certain standard compounds, e.g.,
Dach-/Rumpel-/Speisekammer 'attic/junk room/
pantry'.

'Room' meaning 'space' is **Platz**, e.g. **Gibt es noch
Platz für mich?** 'Is there still room for me', **Es gibt
keinen Platz mehr** 'There is no more room'. **Raum**
can have this meaning too; compare **geräumig**
'roomy, spacious'.

'Space' meaning 'outer space' is **der Weltraum** or **das Weltall**.

the rubbish (bin), garbage (bin), trash (can), waste-paper basket

der Abfall, die Abfälle, der Müll; der Mülleimer, die Mülltonne, der Papierkorb

The 'rubbish' that gets collected on a weekly basis is **der Müll**. The large 'bin' put out in the street is **die Mülltonne** and it is all collected by a **Müllwagen** and taken to the **Mülldeponie** (rubbish tip). Bulky 'rubbish' (old refrigerators, furniture etc.), collected less regularly, is called **Sperrmüll**. The smaller, bucket-sized 'bin' found in kitchens, for example, is a **Mülleimer**, a synonym of which is **Abfalleimer** (**Küchenabfälle** 'kitchen scraps'); this word also refers to a 'rubbish/litter bin' in a public place, which may have written on it **Abfälle** (litter). A 'waste-paper basket' in an office, for example, is a **Papierkorb**.

to run (*see* TO GO)

laufen, rennen

Laufen generally means 'to run' but there are contexts where it can mean 'to walk' (*see* TO WALK). For example, in **Er lief nach Hause, um seine Fußballschuhe zu holen** the emphasis is not so much on the literal act of running but going home (perhaps quickly), **A: Fahren wir in die Stadt? B: Nein, wir laufen** 'A: Shall we drive into town? B: No, we'll walk'. Using **rennen** cuts out all ambiguity as it can only refer to 'running', e.g. **Er rannte nach Hause** 'He ran home'.

More figurative meanings of 'run', as in a machine that 'runs' well, are rendered by **laufen**, e.g. **Der Rasenmäher/Fernseher läuft** 'The lawnmower/ television is running (= is on)', **Das Geschäft läuft reibungslos** 'The business is running smoothly', and even **Seine Nase läuft** 'His nose is running'.

same

gleich(-), selb-

The adjective 'same' is **gleich-** or **selb-**, but the latter differs from all other adjectives in German by being written together with the definite article, e.g. **Wir wohnen alle in der gleichen/derselben Stadt** 'We all live in the same city'. But where the definite article is combined with a preceding preposition, this is not possible, e.g. **im selben Augenblick** 'at the same moment'.

Gleich- and **selb-** are not necessarily interchangeable, the basic meaning of **gleich(-)** being 'similar' and **selb-** being 'one and the same', e.g. **Ich habe den gleichen Computer** 'I've got the same computer' (i.e. same sort), but **Ich arbeite am selben Computer wie er** 'I work on the same computer as he' (i.e. we share it). It has to be admitted that the distinction between these two words is no longer made by many Germans.

Selb- must always be used together with the definite article, but **gleich** can stand alone in the meaning of 'same', e.g. **Die beiden Buben sehen absolut gleich aus** 'The two boys look absolutely the same'.

to save, spare

einsparen, ersparen, retten, schonen, sparen, speichern, verschonen, wahren

'To save' money, water etc. is **sparen**, e.g. **Sie spart für ihren kommenden Urlaub in der Türkei** 'She is saving for her forthcoming holiday in Turkey'. **Einsparen** means to save by cutting back, e.g. **Der Minister hofft dadurch drei Millionen Euro einzusparen** 'The minister hopes to save 3 million euros by doing that'.

When you wish to spare s.o. pain, anguish etc., **ersparen** is required, e.g. **Er will seinem Land den Krieg ersparen** 'He wants to spare his country war', **Die Einzelheiten möchte ich Ihnen ersparen** 'I'd like to spare you the details'.

'To save' s.o. from death or 'to save' their life is **retten**, e.g. **Er hat mich gerettet** 'He saved me' (lit. and fig.), **Er hat mein Leben gerettet** 'He saved my life'.

Where 'saving' s.o.'s life is synonymous with 'sparing' their life, **schonen** is used, e.g. **Die Angriffe aus der Luft wurden eingestellt, um das Leben der Einwohner zu schonen** 'The attacks from the air were stopped in order to spare the lives of the inhabitants'. When it is not lives that are being 'spared', but people or things, **verschonen** is the word, e.g. **Ihr Haus blieb von den Bomben verschont** 'Their house was spared the bombs/saved from the bombs', **Beim Massaker wurde niemand verschont** 'No one was spared in the massacre'.

'To save face' is **das Gesicht wahren**, e.g. **Sie musste unbedingt das Gesicht wahren** 'She simply had to save face'.

'To save' in the computer world is **speichern** (*see* MEMORY), e.g. **Hast du es auf deiner Festplatte oder auf einer Diskette gespeichert?** 'Did you save it on(to) your harddisk or on(to) a floppy disk?'.

to say

besagen, sagen

Sagen is the most usual word, but this very often translates 'to tell' (*see* TO TELL). To express 'to say s.t. *to* s.o.' the dat. normally suffices, but it is possible to use **zu** here too, e.g. **Was hat er (zu) dir gesagt?** 'What did he say to you?'.

Besagen is used where 'to say' is synonymous with 'to mean (to say)', e.g. **Das besagt nichts/viel** 'That says nothing/a lot' (= that means nothing/a lot), **Das besagt nicht, dass** . . . 'That doesn't mean (to say) that . . .'.

the school

die Berufsschule, die Fachhochschule, die Gesamtschule, die Grundschule, die Handelsschule, die Hauptschule, die Hochschule, die Oberschule, die Realschule, das Schulzentrum, die Volkshochschule, die Volksschule

For Anglo-Saxons who basically have a school system consisting of three levels, primary, secondary and tertiary, the German system seems bewildering, mainly because of the choices available at the secondary level. What follows is a brief summary of the types of school that exist with broad definitions to be able to equate them with those in English-speaking societies. As education is not a federal responsibility, there are slight variations in the schools system from Bundesland to Bundesland.

Schule is a general word, as in English, but it is never used to refer to university as is common in America.

'Primary/elementary school', which in Germany starts at age 6, is called the **Grundschule** and includes classes 1 to 4, but in some states goes to the 6th class. You then progress to either the **Hauptschule** (till the 9th class, leading to the general leaving certificate called **der Hauptschulabschluss**)[35] or the **Realschule** (till the 10th class, age 16). These are both a junior high school which you attend prior to continuing with the **Berufsschule** (technical college, i.e. for a trade, normally done in combination with an apprenticeship, an **Ausbildung**, *see* EDUCATION) if you go to the **Hauptschule** or the **Handelsschule** or **Fachschule** if you go to the **Realschule**. The **Handelsschule** is for those seeking office employment (e.g. typing, book-keeping) and the

[35] The **Volksschule**, now outdated, formally covered what is now the **Grund-** and **Hauptschule** combined, i.e. classes 1–9.

Fachschule for those seeking work as a kinder-garten teacher or social worker, for example. Both these schools go for two years after the **Mittlere Reife/Realschulabschluss** done at the conclusion of the **Realschule** (see below).

The more academically inclined intending to go on to university, progress from the **Grundschule** after year 4 to the **Gymnasium** (classes 5–13), previously called **Oberschule**; one might equate **Gymnasium** with grammar school.

At the end of the **Hauptschule** one does **der Abschluss**, which means nothing more than 'final exam'. It in itself is a qualification for nothing. The **Berufsschule** is also completed with an **Abschluss**. You can say **die Haupt-/Berufsschule abschließen** 'to complete the **Haupt-** or **Berufs-schule**'.

The exam done at the conclusion of the **Realschule** is called **die Mittlere Reife**, which is the first public exam done at high school and thus in Britain equivalent to O-Levels. Note the expression **die Realschule absolvieren**, e.g. **Er hat die Realschule absolviert = Er hat die Mittlere Reife.**

The exam done at the conclusion of the **Gymnasium** is called **das Abitur** (or **Abi** for short), which is the school leaving examination on the basis of which one gains admission to uni-versity, thus A-Levels in Britain.

These days several of the above school types may be housed under the one roof and the aggregate of them all is called a **Gesamtschule** or **Schulzentrum** (comprehensive school), but these terms can vary in meaning depending on the Bundesland.

The word **Hochschule** in German refers to tertiary level, not 'high school', thus a **technische Hochschule** is a tertiary level technical college, and can be the equivalent of a university (*see* UNI-VERSITY). A **Fachhochschule** is tertiary but not as

illustrious as a university and is more practically and vocationally orientated.

The **Volkshochschule**, on the other hand, is the term used for 'adult evening school' or 'adult education'.

the sea, ocean, lake

das Meer, der Ozean, der See, die See

Counter-intuitively 'sea' is **die See** while **der See** means a 'lake'. **Das Meer** is synonymous with **See** with reference to the 'sea' in general (e.g. **die sieben Weltmeere** 'the seven seas'), but the official names of the seas of the world use one or the other, depending on convention, e.g. **das Japanische Meer** 'the Sea of Japan', **das Kaspische Meer** 'Caspian Sea', **das Schwarze Meer** 'Black Sea', **das Mittelmeer** 'Mediterranean (Sea)', **das Nordmeer** 'Barent Sea', but **die Nordsee** 'North Sea', **die Ostsee** 'Baltic (Sea)'. Some seas omit the word 'sea' altogether, e.g. **die Adria** 'Adriatic', **die Ägis** 'Aegean'.

The word for 'ocean' is **Ozean** and the three great oceans are called **der Indische Ozean**, **der Atlantische Ozean** and **der Stille Ozean** but the last two are also called **der Atlantik** and **der Pazifik**.[36] The 'South Pacific' or 'South Seas' are **die Südsee**.

the seed

der Kern, das Korn, die Saat, das Saatgut, der Samen, der Stein

Saat is a collective, as bought and planted by farmers, although **Saatgut** is more commonly heard in this sense. An individual 'seed' in the

---

[36] Note the masculine gender. This is unusual as words ending in -ik are otherwise feminine.

botanical sense is a **Samen** and this is also used as a collective for the 'seed' of a given plant, e.g. **zwei Nelkensamen** 'two carnation seeds', **Wie sieht der Samen dieser Pflanze aus?** 'What does the seed of this plant look like?'. **Wirst du den Samen von dieser Blume für mich sammeln?** 'Will you please collect the seed of this flower for me?'.

The 'seed' (i.e. pip or stone) of a piece of fruit is a **Kern**, e.g. **Die neuesten Mandarinen haben keine Kerne (= sind kernlos)** 'The latest mandarins don't have pips', but the word is not limited to fruit, e.g. **Sonnenblumenkerne** 'sunflower seeds'.

'Seed' meaning 'grain' (also poppy and sesame seed) is rendered by **Korn**, as is 'bird seed', e.g. **Geben Sie mir bitte fünf von diesen Brötchen mit den Körnern!** 'Please give me five of these rolls with seeds on them', **Ich muss heute Vogelkörner kaufen** 'I'd better buy bird seed today'.

'Stone fruit' is **das Steinobst**, which contains a **Stein**, as in English.

self

selber, selbst, sich

The reflexive pronoun 'myself', 'yourself', 'himself' etc. is expressed by the accusative of the personal pronoun, i.e. **mich, dich, uns** and **euch**, except for **er, sie, es** and **Sie/sie** which all require **sich**, e.g. **ich kenne mich** 'I know myself', but **er kennt sich** 'he knows himself'. **Selbst** is only added to these reflexive forms where emphasis is required, e.g. **Das kann sein, dass du mich kennst, aber kennst du dich selbst?** 'That may be so that you know me, but do you know yourself?'.

But the reflexive forms 'myself' etc. are used independently of reflexive verbs in English and in such cases they must be rendered in German by either **selbst** or **selber**, with no distinction in meaning between the two and with both bearing stress, e.g. **Hast du den Staubsauger selbst/selber repariert?** 'Did you repair the vacuum cleaner yourself?'.

to send

abschicken, aussenden, entsenden, schicken, senden, verschicken, versenden, zuschicken

The most usual translation of 'to send' is **schicken**. 'To send' s.t. *to* s.o. can be expressed either by the simple dat. or by **an** + acc., e.g. **Sie hat ihrer Mutter einen Brief geschickt/einen Brief an ihre Mutter geschickt** 'She sent her mother a letter/a letter to her mother' (note the change in word order in both languages).

Zuschicken + dat. is a variant of **schicken** + dat./**an** + acc. where the recipient is emphasised, e.g. **Wir haben es Ihnen schon zugeschickt** 'We have already sent it to you'.

'To send for s.o.', i.e. to have s.o. come, is **nach jdm schicken**, e.g. **Wir haben sofort nach dem Arzt geschickt** 'We sent for the doctor immediately'.

'To send *out*' s.t. or s.o. is **ausschicken** (more formally **aussenden**), e.g. **Ein Feuerwehrwagen wurde ausgeschickt** 'A firetruck was sent out'.

'To send on' or 'forward' of mail, for example, is **nachschicken**, e.g. **Werden Sie meine Post bitte nachschicken?** 'Will you please send my mail on?'.

Senden is more elevated than **schicken** and is used for 'sending' people and things of importance, e.g. **Er wird von seiner Firma nach Australien gesandt** 'He is being sent by his firm to Australia', **Die Firma Bender sendet Ihnen seiner Zeit ihren neuen Katalog** 'The Bender Firm will be sending you its latest catalogue in the course of time'.[37] **Entsenden** is even more official sounding than **senden** (compare TO DISPATCH) but is used exclusively of people, e.g. **Die USA wollten keine Truppen nach Osttimor entsenden** 'The USA did not want to send troops to East Timor'.

---

[37] Note that **sandte/gesandt** are the past tenses of **senden** meaning 'to send' but **aussenden** 'to broadcast' is regular (**sendete . . . aus/ausgesendet**).

Verschicken and **versenden** are synonymous and are particularly used for sending items to people commercially (compare once again TO DIS-PATCH), e.g. **Die Kataloge sind alle verschickt/versandt worden** 'The catalogues have all been sent (off)'. **Verschicken**, unlike **versenden**, can also be used of people being evacuated, e.g. **Im zweiten Weltkrieg wurden viele britische Kinder aufs Land verschickt** 'In the Second World War many British children were sent to the country'.

Abschicken, like **verschicken** and **versenden**, also means 'to send off', but is a more everyday way of expressing the concept, e.g. **Ich muss all meine Weihnachtskarten noch abschicken** 'I still have to send off all my Christmas cards'.

It is usual in Germany to write the sender's name and address on the back of an envelope. In this case 'the sender' is **der Absender**, often abbreviated to **Abs.** and written before the name.

serious

ernst, Ernst, ernsthaft, seriös

When a situation, problem or illness is 'serious', it is **ernst**, e.g. **1994 war die Lage in Ruanda ernst** 'In 1994 the situation in Rwanda was serious', **Die Frau hat ernste Kopfwunden** 'The woman has serious head wounds'; also **ein ernster Mann** 'a serious man' (by nature not light-hearted), **ernste Musik** 'serious music'. A 'serious' accident or storm is **schwer** whereas 'serious' damage or injury is **schlimm** (*see* BAD).

To be 'serious' about doing s.t. requires **im Ernst**, e.g. **Er will im Ernst Deutsch lernen** 'He seriously wants to learn German'.

The exclamation 'You can't be serious' can be expressed adjectivally or nominally, e.g. **Das meinst du doch nicht ernst!/Das kann doch nicht dein Ernst sein! But Ist das dein Ernst?** 'Are you serious?', **Das ist mein Ernst** 'I'm quite serious'.

Despite the above, the distinction between **ernst** and **im Ernst** is not always clear-cut, e.g. **Sie meint es ernst mit ihm** 'She is serious about him'. **Ernst** is seldom used as an adverb.

Ernsthaft can only be used as an attributive adj. and refers above all to s.t. that has the appearance of being 'serious', 'sincere' or even 'conscientious', e.g. **ein ernsthaftes Angebot** 'a serious offer', **Der Diplomat streitet dafür, als ernsthafter Friedensemissär anerkannt zu werden** 'The diplomat is fighting to be recognised as a serious peace emissary'.

Seriös means 'to be taken seriously' and thus also translates 'respectable/reputable', e.g. **ein seriöses Angebot** 'an offer you can trust', **ein seriöser Rechtsanwalt** 'a reputable lawyer'.

When the adverb 'seriously' qualifies a following adj., this is best expressed by **schwer**, e.g. **schwer behindert/krank** 'seriously handicapped/ill'.

to serve

bedienen, dienen

Bedienen is used for 'serving' customers, e.g. **Der Kellner hat uns immer noch nicht bedient** 'The waiter still hasn't served us', **Danke, ich werde schon bedient** 'I'm already being served, thanks', **sich selbst bedienen** 'to serve yourself' and thus **der Selbstbedienungsladen** 'self-service shop'. But a shop assistant is likely to ask you **Womit kann ich Ihnen dienen?** 'How can I help you?'.

Dienen, whose object takes the dat., refers to 'serving' a superior or a cause or 'serving' in the armed forces, e.g. **Der Hund hat seinem Herrn treu gedient** 'The dog served his master faithfully', **Unsere Tochter dient in der Bundeswehr** 'Our daughter is serving in the (German) army', **Das soll als Warnung dienen** 'That is meant to serve as a warning'.

the (civil/public, military) service

der Dienst, der öffentliche Dienst, der
Wehrdienst, die Wehrpflicht, der Zivildienst

The civil/public service is **der öffentliche Dienst**,
although you would normally say you are a
civil/public servant rather than that you work
for the civil service, i.e. **Ich bin Beamter** (*see*
OFFICIAL).

Zivildienst exists but refers to the 'service' done
by those young men (**Zivildienstleistende**) who
opt not to do military service and is best translated as 'community service'. 'Military service' is
der Wehr- or **Militärdienst**, and 'conscription', in
as far as there is a difference in either language,
is **die Wehrpflicht**.

A 'service' on a car is best expressed verbally, e.g.
**Ich muss morgen mein Auto warten lassen/zur
Inspektion geben** 'I have to put my car in for a
service tomorrow/have it serviced'.

For 'self-service' see TO SERVE.

to shit, pee

defäkieren, den Darm entleeren, groß
machen, kacken, scheißen; harnen, Wasser
lassen, klein machen, Pipi machen, müssen,
pinkeln, urinieren

The problem here revolves around hitting the
right tone for the company you are in. As vulgar
as 'to shit'[38] and 'to piss' are **scheißen** and **pissen**;
kacken and **pinkeln** are less so, corresponding
more to 'to crap' and 'to piddle', e.g. **Ich muss
mal pinkeln** 'I need (to take) a pee' (*see* TOILET).

Pipi machen is used chiefly by and to children, e.g.
Mama, ich muss Pipi machen 'Mummy, I want to
wee'. **Groß/klein machen** are a similar euphemism
to 'to do a number one/two', e.g. **Hast du groß
oder klein gemacht?** 'Did you do a poo or a wee?'.

A good general, not crude but not over-
euphemistic way of expressing that you need to
go to the toilet is to say **Ich muss aufs Klo (gehen)**
'I have to go to the loo'. Simply **Ich muss** (= I have
to go) also has this meaning.

There is a series of less common euphemisms
which can be directly compared with their
English translations, e.g. **den Darm entleeren** 'to
empty your bowels', **defäkieren** 'to defecate',
Wasser lassen 'to pass water', **urinieren/harnen**
'to urinate'.

to shoot

anschießen, (sich) beschießen, erschießen,
schießen

Erschießen means 'to shoot dead' (*see* TO KILL),
e.g. **Ihr Vater ist erschossen worden** 'Her father
was shot' (and died from it). If a person or animal
is hit by a shot, but has not succumbed to it,
anschießen is used, e.g. **Er ist angeschossen
worden** 'He has been shot'. 'To shoot at' s.o. or
s.t. is **schießen auf** + acc., e.g. **Man hat auf den
Feind geschossen** 'They fired at the enemy', but
'to shoot at' can also be expressed by the tr. verb
beschießen where the meaning is synonymous
with 'to fire at/on' randomly,[39] e.g. **Die Soldaten
beschossen die Panzer aus der Ferne** 'The soldiers
shot at/fired on the tanks from a distance'. 'To
shoot at each other' is expressed by using this verb
reflexively, e.g. **Sie haben sich mit Raketen
beschossen** 'They fired rockets at each other'.

---

38   The exclamation **Scheiße** on the other hand is even
more liberally used in German than in English, commonly
being no more forceful than 'damned' or 'bloody', e.g.
Verdammte Scheiße 'Oh, damn', **Es ist ein Scheißfilm** 'It's
a lousy film'.

---

39   The notion of 'at random' is important here. You could
not say for example **Der Jäger beschoss den Hasen** 'The
hunter shot at the hare' unless he kept on shooting; this
context really requires **schießen auf**.

Beschießen is also used fig. for 'firing' questions at s.o., e.g. **Sie beschoss mich mit Fragen** 'She bombarded me with questions'.

'To shoot' o.s/s.o. in the head/foot etc. is **sich (dat.)/jdm in den Kopf/Fuß schießen**, e.g. **Er versuchte dem Reh in den Kopf zu schießen** 'He tried to shoot the deer in the head'.

should (have)

müsste(n), sollte(n); hätte(n) . . . müssen, hätte(n) . . . sollen

'Should' is usually rendered by **sollte(n)**, the past subjunctive of **sollen**, e.g. **Du solltest ihnen helfen** 'You should help them', i.e. you are not obliged to but it would be nice/advisable if you did. But German can also express 'should' with **müsste(n)**, the past subjunctive of **müssen**, when an obligation to do s.t. is implied – the subtlety of this distinction cannot be expressed in English, e.g. **Es gibt noch etwas, was Sie interessieren müsste** 'There is something else which should interest you' (= I know it will); compare **Es gibt noch etwas, was Sie interessieren sollte** 'There is something else which should interest you' (= I assume it will).

The same distinction between **sollen** and **müssen** meaning 'should' applies to the following perfect constructions with 'should have', e.g. **Du hättest uns anrufen sollen** 'You should have rung us', with a connotation of 'it would have been nice if you had, but it doesn't matter that you didn't', whereas **Du hättest uns anrufen müssen** 'You should have rung us', with a connotation of 'and it is unfortunate that you didn't'.

'Should' as a stylistic variant of 'were to' is **sollte**, e.g. **Sollte sie mich einladen, würde ich akzeptieren** 'Should she invite me (= were she to), I would accept'; **sollte** can be used in this way in a wenn-clause too, e.g. **Wenn sie mich einladen sollte . . .** – here it is interchangeable with **würde**.

the shop

das Geschäft, das Kaufhaus, der Laden, der Shop, das Warenhaus

The most neutral word for a 'shop' is **Geschäft**, e.g. **Wie lange bleiben die Geschäfte samstags offen?** 'How long do the shops stay open on Saturdays?'. Shops for specific wares are best referred to as **das Geschäft**, e.g. **das Lebensmittelgeschäft** 'grocery store/shop', **das Elektrogeschäft** 'electrical appliance store'.

Where in English we might say 'the butcher('s) shop' or 'the baker's shop', you can say in German either **(beim) Metzger/Bäcker** (i.e. at the butcher's/baker's) or refer to the shops as **die Metzgerei/Bäckerei** (*see* CHEMIST).

A 'department store' is a **Kaufhaus** or **Warenhaus** and both are completely synonymous although the latter is a little archaic (*see* DEPARTMENT).

A **Laden** tends to be a smaller shop, classically illustrated in **der Tante-Emma-Laden**, 'corner shop', **der Kramladen** 'junk shop'.

These days it is trendy for the names of certain shops to incorporate the word **Shop**, but it is not otherwise used as a generic term, e.g. **Party-Shop**.

Geschäft can mean 'business' too, thus the generic term for a 'shop' is **Laden**, and therefore the law governing trading hours is called **das Ladenschlussgesetz**.

sick

erkrankt, krank, schlecht

The usual word is **krank**, which can occur in compounds that are strange to English, e.g. **zuckerkrank** 'diabetic', **krebskrank** 'suffering from cancer/sick with cancer'. More elevated than **krank sein** is **erkrankt sein** which must be used when the illness is mentioned, e.g. **Er ist** krank/erkrankt 'He is ill', Er ist an Krebs erkrankt 'He is sick with cancer' (an + dat. = with). 'Seriously sick/ill' is schwer krank/erkrankt.

'To feel sick', i.e. not well, is sich krank fühlen, but to feel you are going to be sick, i.e. vomit, is expressed by einem schlecht sein/werden, e.g. Es ist/wird mir schlecht 'I am going to be sick'. Where 'to be sick' actually means 'to vomit', use sich erbrechen, e.g. Er hat sich im Zug erbrochen 'He was sick in the train'.

the sign

das Anzeichen, das Schild, das Zeichen

A 'sign(post)' is a Schild, e.g. Er hat nicht auf das Stoppschild geachtet 'He took no notice of the stop sign', but a 'traffic sign' can be either a Verkehrsschild or a Verkehrszeichen. A 'sign' made with the hand, eyes etc., i.e. a gesture, is a Zeichen but so is a written sign or symbol, e.g. Er hat mir ein Zeichen gegeben/gemacht 'He gave me a sign/made a sign to me', € ist das Zeichen für Euro '€ is the sign/symbol for euro'.

Anzeichen renders 'sign' when it means indication, e.g. Es gibt Anzeichen dafür, dass die Welt wieder in einen Krieg verwickelt wird 'There are signs that the world is to be involved in a war again'.

silent, quiet, peaceful

friedlich, leise, still, ruhig; sich ausschweigen, schweigen, verschweigen

Still means 'quiet' or 'silent' whereas ruhig means 'quiet', 'peaceful' or 'calm', which means that in the sense of 'quiet' the two are usually interchangeable, e.g. Wir wohnen in einer stillen/ruhigen Straße 'We live in a quiet street', Sei (doch) still/ruhig! 'Be quiet!' (= don't make any noise/shut up), but Stille Nacht 'Silent Night', Das Meer war ruhig 'The sea was calm'. 'Peaceful' in the literal sense of 'peace prevailing' is friedlich, e.g. Die beiden Völker leben jetzt friedlich nebeneinander 'The two peoples now live peacefully side by side'.

As in English there are a number of ways of expressing 'to be quiet' meaning 'to shut up', the one blunter than the other, e.g. schweig/schweigen Sie!, Halt den Mund/die Klappe/das Maul!

'Silent' can be expressed by schweigen (to be silent/to say nothing) and its derivative sich ausschweigen, e.g. Sie antwortete, aber er schwieg (= blieb still) 'She answered but he remained silent', die schweigende Mehrheit 'the silent majority'. Sich ausschweigen (to remain silent) is used instead of schweigen when you remain silent about s.t. (= über + acc. or zu), e.g. Wie er so reich geworden ist, darüber hat er sich lange ausgeschwiegen 'He remained silent for a long time about how he had got so rich'. There is also a verb verschweigen but this means 'to hide/conceal', i.e. not reveal by telling, e.g. Er hat die Tatsachen verschwiegen 'He concealed the facts'.

Leise is the opposite of laut and means making little noise, e.g. Redet bitte leiser! 'Please talk more quietly/softly', Mach das Fernsehen bitte leiser 'Please turn the television down', Mach die Tür leise zu! 'Close the door quietly!', mit leiser Stimme 'in a quiet voice'.

since

da, seit, seitdem, seither

The difficulty here lies in the fact that English 'since' can be a preposition, a conjunction or an adverb; to translate it in German it is crucial to understand the difference.

Seit is first and foremost a preposition that takes the dative case, e.g. **Er hat seinen Vater seit dem Krieg nicht gesehen** 'He hasn't seen his father since the war'. It can also be used as a conjunction, introducing a new clause, but in this function **seitdem** is more commonly used, e.g. **Er hat seinen Vater nicht gesehen, seit(dem) der Krieg angefangen hat** 'He hasn't seen his father since the war began'.

Seitdem, in addition to being a conjunction, as just illustrated, is also an adverb, e.g. **Er hat seinen Vater seitdem nicht wiedergesehen** 'He hasn't seen his father again since'. In this function it is interchangeable with **seither**, but **seitdem** is more usual.

All the above have a connotation of time but there is also a conjunction 'since' in English that is synonymous with 'because'; this 'since' is strictly speaking **da** in German, but is most usually rendered simply by **weil**, e.g. **Da/weil er nicht geholfen hat, ist er nicht eingeladen worden** 'Since/as/because he didn't help, he hasn't been invited'.

to sink

absinken, senken, sinken, versenken,
versinken

Part of the problem here has to do with whether the verb 'to sink' is used transitively or not, e.g. **Das Schiff sinkt** 'The ship is sinking' (intr.) and **Die Piraten versenken das Schiff** 'The pirates are sinking the ship (tr.)'. The difference between the two is further emphasised in the perfect tense where the former, being intr. and a verb of motion, takes **sein** and the latter, being tr., takes **haben**, e.g. **Das Schiff ist gesunken, Die Piraten haben das Schiff versenkt. Senken** is used more fig. corresponding to 'to reduce/lower', e.g. **Man hat den Preis gesenkt** 'They have reduced the price' (tr.); compare **Der Preis ist gesunken** 'The price has dropped' (intr.) (*see* TO RAISE).

Both **absinken** and **versinken** are used with reference to ships 'sinking' but the former is slower and does not necessarily mean a ship sinks to the bottom, which **versinken** expresses, e.g. **Das Schiff sank ab** 'The ship was sinking', **ein versunkenes Schiff** 'a sunken/submerged ship'. Otherwise **versinken** renders 'to sink' in a figurative sense, e.g. **Das Land versinkt in Bürgerkrieg** 'The country is sinking into civil war'. **Versenken**, on the other hand, means 'to lower' (e.g. a coffin) and with reference to a ship 'to scuttle' or 'to send to the bottom', e.g. **Er hat sein eigenes Boot versenkt** 'He scuttled his own boat'.

to sit (down)

sitzen, (sich) hinsetzen, (sich) niedersetzen

'To sit', an intr. verb, is quite simply **sitzen** which in southern Germany takes **sein** in the perfect, but in standard German **haben**, e.g. **Er ist/hat stundenlang auf der Bank im Park gesessen** 'He sat on the bench in the park for hours'.

'To sit down' is either **sich setzen** or **sich hin-** or **niedersetzen** with no significant difference in meaning between all three, e.g. **Er setzte sich auf die Parkbank (hin/nieder)** 'He sat down on the park bench'. Note that **sitzen auf** takes a dative, as it expresses place, whereas **sich setzen auf** takes an accusative as it is seen to express a motion. The addition of the verbal prefix **hin-** or **nieder-** is optional but use of it emphasises the motion involved, e.g. **Setz dich hin!** 'Sit *down*!', **Er war müde und setzte sich hin** 'He was tired and sat down'.

Setzen can be seen as the tr. counterpart to **sitzen**. In the previous examples, where there is no direct object as such, you can regard the **sich** as the object, i.e. 'you sit yourself down' or 'seat yourself'. For this reason 'to sit a child down' is **ein Kind (hin-/nieder)setzen**, e.g. **Er setzte das Kind auf das Sofa (hin/nieder)** 'He sat/put the child down on the couch' (*see* TO PUT).

There is a complete parallel here with the way **liegen** (to lie) and **sich hin-/niederlegen** (to lie down) are used (*see* TO LIE).

the skin

das Fell, die Haut

People have **Haut** as do animals that have a 'hide', thus cows, pigs and elephants, and certainly fish and snakes, but a horse's 'hide' might be called either **Haut** or **Fell**, the latter word being used where there is a reasonable layer of hair. **Dünnhäutig** is both literally and figuratively 'thin-skinned', whereas a 'thick-skinned' (fig.) person has **eine dicke Haut/ein dickes Fell**. Note that **der Dickhäuter** renders quite literally 'the pachyderm' (elephant).

to sleep, to fall asleep, to oversleep, to sleep in, to sleep on

ausschlafen, dösen, eindösen, einnicken, einschlafen, nicken, pennen, schlafen, überschlafen, (sich) verschlafen

'To sleep' is **schlafen** and poses no problem, nor does **einschlafen** 'to fall asleep', except that the latter takes **sein** in the perfect, e.g. **Er hat lange geschlafen** 'He slept for a long time', but **Er ist während des Films eingeschlafen** 'He fell asleep during the film'.

A rather colloquial word for 'sleeping' is **pennen** (compare 'to have a zizz'), e.g. **Er pennt immer während der Deutsch-Stunde** 'He always nods off during the German lesson'. This word has given rise to **der Penner** 'the tramp', i.e. one who sleeps in the streets.

Another colloquial word for 'sleeping' is **dösen** (to doze) from which **eindösen** (to doze off) is derived, which, like **einschlafen**, requires **sein** in the perfect, unlike **dösen**. **(Ein)nicken** too is colloquial for 'to doze (off)'.

'To sleep in' is ambiguous. If you sleep in, as on a Sunday morning, the verb required is **ausschlafen**, which takes **haben**, e.g. **Ich möchte morgen ausschlafen** 'I'd like to sleep in tomorrow'; note too **Bist du ausgeschlafen?** 'Did you get enough sleep?'; **ausgeschlafen** is used as an adjective here and thus **sein** is used. A Deutsche Bundesbahn advertisement advocating taking a sleeper car on long distance train travel once read **Abends eingeschlafen, morgens ausgeschlafen** which means something like 'Fall asleep in the evening and wake up all refreshed'. The ambiguity associated with 'sleeping in' is that you can 'sleep in' by accident not by design, the latter being what **ausschlafen** renders. If you 'sleep in' in the sense of 'to oversleep', the verb required is **(sich) verschlafen** where the prefix **ver-** means 'by accident', e.g. **Der Student kam zu spät zur Vorlesung, weil er (sich) verschlafen hatte** 'The student arrived at the lecture late as he had slept in/overslept'.

'To sleep on' s.t., as in to ponder it, is **überschlafen** (insep.), e.g. **Ich habe den Vorschlag überschlafen und habe mich entschieden, nicht daran teilzunehmen** 'I have slept on the suggestion and decided not to take part in it'.

'To feel sleepy' is **schläfrig sein**.

SO

also, darum, das, deshalb, deswegen, dermaßen, es, schon, so

Where 'so' means 'therefore' or 'thus' German has a whole range of synonymous options: **darum, deshalb, deswegen**.[40] e.g. **Er hat vor kurzem**

---

[40]   These three words have synonymous interrogative parallels, all meaning 'why', i.e. **warum, weshalb, weswegen**.

geerbt, und darum hat er sich das neue Haus leisten können 'He recently inherited and so he was able to afford the new house'.

'So' as an intensifier of adjectives and adverbs is so or **dermaßen**, e.g. **Er ist so/dermaßen faul** 'He is so lazy'.

'So' as a conjunction, i.e. meaning 'so as to/that', is **damit**, e.g. **Der Arzt hat Türkisch gelernt, damit er seinen Patienten besser dienen könnte** 'The doctor learnt Turkish so he could better serve his patients'.

'So' in the expression 'I think so' is rendered by **schon**, e.g. **Ich glaube schon**, but in 'I hope so' by **es** or **das**, e.g. **Ich hoffe es/Das hoffe ich.**

Also is possibly the most common filler used in German, in which case it often remains untranslatable, but it also commonly translates 'so'. 'So' meaning 'well', as a sort of exclamation, is **also**, e.g. **Also, was willst du heute Abend machen?** 'So, what do you want to do tonight?'. But it can also render 'so' meaning 'thus/therefore', e.g. **Was, du hast kein Geld? Du kommst also nicht mit, oder?** 'What, you haven't any dough? So you won't be coming along, will you?', **Sie ist Australierin, also sonnengebräunt** 'She is an Australian, thus suntanned'.

so that

damit, so dass

'So that' has two meanings, each being expressed differently in German. Where it means 'with the result that', you need **so dass** and where it means 'with the purpose that', you need **damit**, e.g. **Sie hatte ihren Schirm zu Hause gelassen, so dass sie patschnass geworden ist** 'She left her umbrella at home so that she got soaking wet', **Sie hat ihren Schirm mitgenommen, damit sie nicht nass würde** 'She took her umbrella with her so that she would not get wet'.

some, a few (*see* ANY, A LITTLE)

ein paar, einige/-es, etwas, irgend, manche/-es, mehrere, welche/-es

'Some' followed by a mass noun is most usually left untranslated, e.g. **Ich muss Brot/Milch kaufen** 'I must buy some bread/milk', **Mein Sohn will Geld verdienen** 'My son wants to earn some money'. 'Some' with reference to such quantities when the nouns themselves are omitted, can be rendered by either **etwas** or **welch-**, e.g. **Brauchst du Milch? Nein danke, ich hab' schon etwas/welche** 'Do you need any[41] milk? No thanks, I've already got some'.

But even a 'some' followed by a plural noun is commonly left untranslated, e.g. **Ich habe Freunde von mir mit einem Haus auf dem Lande besucht** 'I visited some friends of mine with a house in the country'. If you felt compelled to translate this 'some', it would be most appropriately rendered by **ein paar**, which is the German equivalent of 'a few' or 'a couple of', e.g. **Er hat nur ein paar Freunde** 'He only has a few friends'.

It is probably safest to leave 'some' untranslated wherever context permits it. Thus the trick is to know where it must be translated when followed by a plural noun. When a contrast is directly stated or implied, the usual translation is **einige**, e.g. **Nur einige der Studenten haben das Lehrbuch gekauft, (andere aber nicht)** 'Only *some* of the students have bought the textbook (but others haven't)'.

The above use of **welches** with reference to a mass noun also has a parallel with reference to a plural, e.g. **A: Er hat Anteile an BMW gekauft. B: Ich habe auch welche** 'A: He has bought (some)

---

[41] Note that it is an idiosyncrasy of English that 'some' is replaced by 'any' in questions and in combination with negatives, e.g. I need some money, Do you need any money?, I don't need any money? No such distinction is made in German.

shares in BMW. B: I have some too'; **einige** could be used here too, despite the lack of contrast.

In the following example **einiges** could be omitted but its inclusion adds the connotation of life 'of some sort or another', e.g. **In den Ästen des Baumes ist noch einiges Leben** 'There is still some life in the tree's branches'.

Manch literally means 'many a' and can render 'some' where the connotation is 'a fair number but by no means all', e.g. **Manche Leute mögen ihn** 'Some people like him', **Manche mögen es heiß** 'Some Like it Hot' (the Hollywood classic).

Mehrere is always followed by a plural and really means 'several' and thus translates 'some' where this connotation is present, e.g. **Ich kenne auch mehrere (Schauspieler)** 'I also know some (actors)'. Where the connotation of 'several' is not necessary, one could use **einige**, e.g. **Ich kenne auch einige (Schauspieler)**; this final form, not followed by the noun, could equally be expressed by **welche**, e.g. **Ich kenne auch welche.**

'Someone' and 'something' are most usually expressed by **jemand** and **etwas** but can be emphasised by being used in combination with **irgend**, e.g. **Jemand wird ihm helfen/Irgendjemand wird ihm helfen** 'Someone (or other) will help him', **Etwas ist passiert/Irgendetwas ist passiert** 'Something (or other) has happened', **Viele Altautos landen auf Schrottplätzen in irgendwelchen Hinterhöfen** 'Many disused cars end up in scrapyards in some back corner or other'. Note too the compulsory use of **irgend** with **irgendwo** (somewhere) and **irgendwann** (some time).

the sort, kind

allerlei, die Art, die Sorte, was für ein

'Sort' meaning kind or type is **Art**, e.g. **Diese Art Leute/Bücher finde ich stinklangweilig** 'I find this sort of person/book terribly boring'. Note that

with reference to animals **Art** also translates species, e.g. **diese Art Katze** 'this species of cat'. **Sorte** translates 'sort' where it means variety, e.g. **In diesem Laden werden verschiedene Sorten exotischer Früchte verkauft** 'Various sorts of exotic fruit are sold in this shop', **Hast du diese Sorte Mango schon gekostet?** 'Have you ever tried this sort/kind of mango?'.

The indeclinable adj. **allerlei** is a handy way of expressing 'all sorts of', e.g. **Wir bauen allerlei Obstsorten in unserem Garten an** 'We grow all sorts of fruit varieties in our garden', **Man muss allerlei Gemüse essen** 'You have to eat all sorts of vegetables'.

When asking s.o. 'what sort of' a car/house/dog etc. they have, use the expression **was für ein** which occurs in two synonymous syntactical constructions, e.g. **Was für einen Hund hast du?/Was hast du für einen Hund?**

the sound, noise

das Geräusch, der Klang, der Knall, der Krach, der Lärm, der Laut, die Lautstärke, das Rauschen, der Schall, der Ton

Unpleasant 'noise' is **Lärm** or **Krach**, e.g. **Die neuen Nachbarn machen viel zu viel Lärm/Krach** 'The new neighbours make far too much noise'. The former word is somewhat more formal, e.g. **die Lärmbelästigung** 'noise pollution'. A **Knall** is a loud sound, bang or crack, e.g. **der Knall eines Schusses** 'the sound of a shot'.

As the previous example illustrates, a problem arises when 'noise' is synonymous with 'sound', e.g. **Er hat ein Geräusch gehört** 'He heard a noise/sound (not a pleasant sound)'.

The pleasant 'sound' of music, bells, glasses knocking together is **der Klang.**

The most neutral word meaning 'sound' is **Laut**, e.g. **Er machte keinen Laut** 'He didn't make a sound'. This word also renders the 'sounds' of a language, e.g. **Ich kann den englischen th-Laut nicht aussprechen** 'I cannot pronounce the English th-sound'.

The 'sound' or 'volume' button on a radio or television is called **die Lautstärke**, adjusted when the **Ton** is not right, e.g. **Der Ton des Films war so schlecht, dass ich kaum was verstanden habe** 'The sound(track) of that film was so bad that I hardly understood anything'.

Schall renders 'sound' in more technical contexts, e.g. **die Schallmauer durchbrechen** 'to break the sound barrier', **das Überschallflugzeug** 'supersonic plane', **schalldicht** 'soundproof'.

The sound or roar of waves, rustling or swishing sounds, as well as the hissing of radios and loudspeakers and swooshing down of rain are all described by the word **Rauschen**.

to speak, talk, discuss, gossip

besprechen, diskutieren, klatschen, können, plaudern, reden, schnacken, sprechen, schwätzen, sich unterhalten

Generally speaking you can say that **sprechen** translates 'to speak' and **reden** 'to talk', e.g. **Er spricht eine Menge Sprachen** 'He speaks a lot of languages', **Politiker reden viel aber sagen wenig** 'Politicians talk a lot but say little'. Note that **reden** is often used in southern Germany and Austria where northerners would favour **sprechen**. There are several other synonymous words typical of certain regions (e.g. **schwätzen** in the south-west and **schnacken** in the far north), but **sprechen** and **reden** are both considered High German.

'To speak/talk about' s.t. can be rendered either by **sprechen von/über** + acc. or **reden von/über** + acc.

'To speak to' s.o. is **sprechen mit** although in formal contexts **mit** is commonly omitted, e.g. **Mit wem spreche ich?** 'Who am I speaking to?' (on phone), **Darf ich Herrn Würth bitte sprechen?** 'May I please speak to Mr Würth?'.

Können alone suffices to express 'to be able to speak (= to know)' a language, e.g. **Kann er Deutsch?** 'Can he speak German/Does he know German?'.

'To discuss' can be rendered by both **sprechen über** + acc. and **besprechen**, an elevated synonym of which is **diskutieren**, e.g. **Wir haben schon darüber gesprochen/Wir haben es schon besprochen/Wir haben es schon diskutiert** 'We have already discussed it'.

Sich unterhalten über expresses 'to talk/have a chat about' s.t., e.g. **Er hat sich mit mir über seine Kinder unterhalten** 'He talked to me about his children', **Wir haben uns stundenlang über unsere Kinder unterhalten** 'We talked about our children for hours'. **Reden** could have been used here too, as above.

Plaudern means 'to chat' and **klatschen (über jdn/etwas)** 'to gossip (about s.o./s.t.)'.

the spelling; to spell

die Orthographie, die Rechtschreibung; buchstabieren, schreiben

'Spelling' is either **Orthographie** or **Rechtschreibung**, which are synonymous. The latest controversial 'spelling reform' is called **die Rechtschreibreform**. **Buchstabieren** means 'to spell out (aloud)' (< **der Buchstabe** 'letter of the alphabet'), e.g. **Buchstabieren Sie bitte Ihren Namen!** 'Please spell your name', whereas **Wie schreibt man das?** is the way one expresses 'How do you spell that?'

to spend

ausgeben, verbringen

'To spend money (on s.t.)' is **Geld ausgeben (für etwas)**, e.g. **Die beiden geben viel zu viel Geld für Alkohol aus** 'Those two spend far too much money on alcohol'.

'To spend' with reference to time is expressed by **verbringen**, e.g. **Meine Nachbarn haben drei Wochen auf den Philippinen verbracht** 'My neighbours spent three weeks in the Philippines'.

the state (*see* COUNTRY)

das Bundesland, der Bundesstaat,
die Provinz, der Staat

The 16 'states' that form the Federal Republic of Germany (*see* GERMANY) are called **Bundesländer**, e.g. **Er wohnt im Bundesland Niedersachsen** 'He lives in the state of Lower Saxony'; in certain contexts **Land** alone suffices, e.g. **Er wohnt im Land Hessen** 'He lives in the state of Hesse'. The 'states' of the USA (**die Vereinigten Staaten**) or Australia, however, are best referred to as **Bundesstaaten**, e.g. **Er wohnt im Bundesstaat Louisiana/Neusüdwales** 'He lives in the state of Louisiana/New South Wales'. Some countries, like Canada for example, refer to their constituent states as provinces. Although you could say **Er wohnt in der Provinz Ontario**, in a German context the word **Provinz** refers to 'regional areas', usually with the connotation of being backward, e.g. **Er wohnt in der Provinz** 'He lives in the backblocks'.

to stay, remain

sich aufhalten, bleiben, übernachten,
verbleiben, wohnen

'To stay' in the sense of 'to remain' is **bleiben**, e.g. **Wie lange bist du auf der Feier geblieben?** 'How long did you stay at the party?'. Where 'to stay' means 'to spend the night' it is rendered by either **wohnen** or **übernachten**, e.g. **Wo habt ihr in Lüttich gewohnt/übernachtet?** 'Where did you stay in Liège?'. The fact that **wohnen** is somewhat ambiguous here, does not worry the German; context makes it clear that you are not asking where the person 'lived' in Liège, e.g. **In welchem Hotel habt ihr gewohnt?** 'What hotel were you staying in?'.

Sich aufhalten is an elevated verb meaning 'stay' or 'to stop over', e.g. **Der Flüchtling hält sich in der britischen Botschaft in Moskau auf** 'The refugee is staying in the British embassy in Moscow', **Wir haben uns zwei Wochen in Wien aufgehalten** 'We stayed in Vienna for two weeks'. Its use is limited but the noun **Aufenthalt**, 'a stay' in a resort for example, is a commonly used word, e.g. **Ich wünsche Ihnen einen angenehmen Aufenthalt in unserer Stadt** 'I wish you a pleasant stay in our city'.

'To remain' when it means 'to be left' is **verbleiben**, e.g. **20 Sekunden verbleiben bis der Computer sich abschaltet** 'Twenty seconds remain till the computer shuts down'.

to steam, evaporate

dampfen, dämpfen, dunsten, dünsten,
verdampfen, verdunsten

'To steam' food, i.e. the tr. verb, is either **dämpfen** or **dünsten**, e.g. **Die Chinesen dämpfen/dünsten ihr Gemüse in einem Wok** 'The Chinese steam their vegetables in a wok'. **Dampfen** and **dunsten** are the intr. equivalents meaning 'to give off steam', e.g. **Das verhältnismäßig warme Wasser des Sees dampfte/dunstete so schön in der kalten Nachtluft** 'The relatively warm water of the lake steamed so beautifully in the cold night air'. **Dunsten**, unlike **dampfen**, also renders 'to give off a smell'. From these verbs are derived in turn

verdampfen and **verdunsten** which mean 'to evaporate' of liquids; **verdampfen** is when steam is given off, i.e. when s.t. is boiling, whereas **verdunsten** refers to a more gradual process, e.g. **Über 100 Grad Celsius verdampft Wasser** 'Water evaporates at over 100 degrees centigrade', **Das Wasser ist verdunstet** 'The water has evaporated'.

still

immer noch, nach wie vor, noch

Although **noch** on its own means 'still', it is commonly used in combination with the intensifier **immer**, which is usally placed before, but can be placed after **noch**,[42] e.g. **Er ist noch krank/Er ist immer noch krank/Er ist noch immer krank** 'He is still sick'. Somewhat more elevated but synonymous is **nach wie vor**, e.g. **Sie fahren nach wie vor in den Sommerferien in die Schweiz** 'They still go to Switzerland for the summer holidays'.

the stomach, tummy, belly

der Bauch, der Magen

As in English, German is careless when it comes to making a clear distinction between the 'stomach' (**Magen**) and the 'belly' (**Bauch**). You hear both, e.g. **Ich habe Magenschmerzen/ Bauchschmerzen** 'I have a stomach/belly ache', but **Bauch** here does not sound as colloquial as 'belly' or 'tummy' does in English. But the German only says **Er liegt auf dem Bauch** where we might say 'He's lying on his stomach/ tummy/belly'; similarly **Der Mann hat einen besonders dicken Bauch** 'That man has a particularly fat stomach/belly'. When referring to the

---

[42]   There is a parallel here with the way **noch** is used as an intensifier of **nie** (*see* NEVER).

'stomach' as an organ, both German and English use only the one word, e.g. **Der Magen verarbeitet, was gegessen und getrunken wird** 'The stomach processes what is eaten and drunk'.

the stone, rock, gravel, pebble, brick

der Fels, der Felsbrocken, der Felsen, das Gestein, der Kies, der Kiesel, der Stein, der Ziegel, der Ziegelstein

Stein refers to both 'a stone' and 'stone' as a material, e.g. **Ein Haus aus Stein/ein steinernes Haus** 'a house made of stone/a stone house'. Note that a 'brick' is a **Backstein** or **Ziegel(stein)** but if context makes it clear, **Stein** too can translate brick, e.g. **Wir müssen mehr Steine bestellen** 'We must order more bricks'. Where a clear distinction has to be drawn between 'brick' and 'stone', **Naturstein** renders 'stone' as a material.

Where the word 'rock' is synonymous with '(a) stone', both as an individual item and as a material, **Stein** translates this too.

'Rocks' as found in the sea or a rockface/cliff are **der Fels** or **der Felsen**, e.g. **der Felsen von Gibraltar** 'The rock of Gibraltar', **die Felsen von Dover** 'the cliffs of Dover', **Die Fähre nach Rhodos lief auf ein Felsen auf** 'The ferry to Rhodes ran onto rocks/a rock'. A very large 'rock' or 'boulder' might be called a **großer Stein** or a **Felsbrocken**, the latter being bigger than the former.

Gestein is a geologists' term and renders 'stone', 'rock' and 'rocks' as a collective.

Kies means 'gravel' and is commonly found in compounds, e.g. **ein Kiesweg** 'a gravel path'. Derived from this is **Kiesel** or **Kieselstein** meaning 'pebble'.

to stop

anhalten, aufhalten, aufhören, einstellen, halten, stehen bleiben, stoppen

Anhalten is used as an intr. verb with reference to vehicles, e.g. **Er hielt an der Ampel an** 'He stopped at the traffic light'. A bus, for example, **hält an** only where the stop is not scheduled (e.g. to avoid hitting s.t.) but otherwise **halten** is used, e.g. **Der Bus hat an der Ecke angehalten, damit die alte Dame einsteigen konnte** 'The bus stopped at the corner so that the old lady could get on', **Hält der Zweier hier?** 'Does Line 2 stop here?' (thus **die Haltestelle** 'bus stop'). **Halten** is also the verb required for the idiom **Haltet den Dieb!** 'Stop the thief'.

But **anhalten** is also used transitively when you 'stop' a vehicle being driven by s.o. else, e.g. **Der Zollbeamte hat mich angehalten** 'The customs officer stopped me'. From this is derived one of the several words for 'to hitch-hike', **per Anhalter fahren**, also called **per Autostopp fahren**.

If in doubt as to which word to use to render 'to stop', you will seldom go wrong by using **stoppen**, which is both a tr. and an intr. verb, e.g. **Der Autobus stoppte an der Ecke** 'The bus stopped at the corner', **Es ist ihm gelungen, den Zug zu stoppen** 'He succeeded in stopping the train' (both driver and observer). **Stoppen** can also have connotations of 'putting an end to', e.g. **die Rechtschreibreform stoppen** 'to stop the spelling reform', **Die USA haben ihre Entwicklungshilfe an das Land gestoppt** 'The US have stopped their development aid to that country'. This comes very close to the functions of **beenden** 'to end/cease' (*see* TO FINISH).

'To stop' in the sense of 'to call off/discontinue' is **einstellen**, a rather official sounding word, e.g. **Mehrere Gesellschaften haben ihre Flüge nach Afrika eingestellt** 'Several airlines have stopped their flights to Africa'.

Stehen bleiben[43] is used of people when walking, but also vehicles when the implication is one of stopping momentarily before proceeding on, e.g. **Er/das Auto blieb einen Augenblick vor dem Postamt stehen** 'He/the car stopped in front of the post office for a moment'.

'Stop!' on traffic signs is **Halt** or **Stop**, but if you were driving with s.o. you would call out **Halt an!** 'Stop (the car)'; you could also say **Bleib stehen**, which is what you must say if the person being addressed is walking (see previous paragraph).

Aufhören is an indispensable word for expressing 'to stop' in the meaning of 'to cease doing something', e.g. **Er hat aufgehört zu rauchen** 'He has stopped smoking', **Es hat aufgehört zu regnen** 'It has stopped raining', **Der Regen hat aufgehört** 'The rain has stopped', **Hör auf!** 'Stop it' (i.e. pestering me, tapping your fingers etc.).

'To stop' meaning 'to hold back/delay' of progress, development etc. is **aufhalten** , e.g. **Die elektronische Kommunikation ist nicht mehr aufzuhalten** 'Electronic communication can't be stopped any more' (*see* TO STAY).

For 'to stop/prevent' s.o. from doing s.t. see **hindern** under TO PREVENT.

the storm

die Bö, das Gewitter, der Orkan, der Sturm, das Unwetter, der Zyklon

A 'storm' involving gales, without thunder and lightening, is a **Sturm** (*see* TO STORM), whereas a 'thunder storm' is an **Unwetter** or a **Gewitter**, thus **Es gewittert** 'It is thundering'. A **Bö** is a 'gust of wind' but also renders a 'squall' with rain involved. An **Orkan** is a 'hurricane' and a **Zyklon** a 'cyclone'. **Sturm** is also used fig., e.g. **ein Sturm der Entrüstung** 'a storm of indignation'.

---

[43] Under the old spelling this was written as one word.

to storm

anstürmen, bestürmen, erstürmen, stürmen

Stürmen means 'to be blowing a gale', e.g. **Es stürmt** 'There's a storm on', but this word can also be used fig. for 'storming' a bank or some military target, e.g. **Die Bürger von Venezuela haben das Parlamentsgebäude gestürmt** 'The citizens of Venezuela stormed the buildings of parliament'.

Erstürmen, in keeping with the perfective function of the prefix **er-**, means 'to take by storm' and is generally speaking thus limited to military undertakings, e.g. **Die Wikinger haben mit Schwert und Axt die Abteien erstürmt** 'The Vikings took the abbeys by storm with swords and axes'.

Bestürmen is used chiefly fig. with the meaning of 'to inundate', e.g. **Der Bürgermeister ist mit tausenden Protestbriefen bestürmt worden** 'The mayor was inundated with thousands of letters of protest'.

Use of **anstürmen** is pretty well limited to the idiom **angestürmt kommen** 'to come storming along', e.g. **Er kam angestürmt (kam auf mich zugestürmt) und schrie 'Hilfe!'** 'He stormed in (stormed towards me) and screamed "Help!"'.

the story

die Erzählung, die Geschichte, das Märchen, die Story

The most usual word for a 'story' is **Geschichte**, which also happens to mean 'history'. **Erzählung** means 'tale', which like its English counterpart, is perhaps a more bookish word, but a 'fairy-tale' is a **Märchen**. The loanword **Story** is not uncommon and is synonymous with **Geschichte** in this sense.

strange, funny

fremd, komisch, merkwürdig, seltsam, sonderbar, ungewöhnlich, unheimlich

Komisch means both 'funny ha-ha' and 'funny peculiar', e.g. **Er sieht ein bisschen komisch aus** 'He looks a bit strange/funny/peculiar/weird'. In the literal meaning of 'funny ha-ha' you will seldom go wrong if you stick to **komisch** but **skurril** and **lustig** are common synonyms.

In the meaning of 'funny peculiar' or 'strange' **merkwürdig** is a common synonym, e.g. **Er sieht ein bisschen merkwürdig aus**.

Unheimlich (lit. 'uncanny[ily]') and **ungewöhnlich** (lit. unusual[ly]) are commonly used as adverbs to qualify adjectives with the meaning of 'strangely', e.g. **unheimlich/ungewöhnlich still** 'strangely quiet'.

Fremd (*see* FOREIGNER) renders 'strange' in the sense of 'unknown to one', e.g. **Das ist mir völlig fremd** 'That is completely strange to me', **Ich bin völlig fremd in dieser Stadt** 'I am a total stranger in this town'.

to strive for

anstreben, das Bestreben, nachstreben, streben

'To strive for' s.t. is most usually **anstreben**, a tr. verb, e.g. **Die Provinz strebte eine Abspaltung von dem Rest des Landes an** 'The province was striving for separation from the rest of the country'.

Streben nach, an intr. verb, is required when you 'strive' to *do* s.t., e.g. **Die Provinz strebte danach, sich vom Rest des Landes abzuspalten** 'The province was striving to separate from the rest of the country'.

Nachstreben (+ dat. object) means 'to emulate' s.o. but also 'to strive *after*' s.t., e.g. **Er hat immer**

versucht, seinem Vater nachzustreben 'He always tried to emulate his father', **Er strebt schon Jahre einem Leben auf dem Lande nach** 'He has strived for a life in the country for years'.

Bestreben does not occur as a verb but does as a noun and an adjective, **bestrebt**. Both express 'endeavouring to do s.t.', e.g. **In seinem Bestreben zu helfen hat er großen Schaden verursacht** 'In his endeavour to help he caused great harm', **Sein ganzes Leben lang war er bestrebt, ihr zu helfen** 'He endeavoured to help her his whole life long'.

to study; the student

lernen, studieren; der/die Auszubildende/Azubi, der Lehrling, der Schüler, das Schulkind, der Student, der/die Studierende

'To study' s.t. at university is **studieren**, e.g. **Ich studiere Deutsch an der Universität Köln** 'I am studying German at the University of Cologne', but 'studying' in the sense of doing homework must be rendered by **lernen**, e.g. **Ich kann leider nicht mitkommen, denn ich muss lernen** 'Unfortunately I can't come with you because I have to study'. If you are 'studying' German, for example off your own bat, not at a tertiary institution, you must also use **lernen**, e.g. **Ich lerne Deutsch** 'I'm studying (= learning) German' (*see* TO LEARN). 'To study' s.t. in the figurative sense, i.e. of looking closely at it, can be rendered by **studieren**, e.g. **Er studierte den Fahrplan** 'He studied the timetable'.

In keeping with **studieren** being used for university level learning, **Student(in)** can only refer to s.o. studying at that level too and thus 'school student' must be rendered by **Schüler(in)** or **Schulkind** (= school child, pupil). **Der/die Studierende** is an elevated synonym of **Student(in)**, meaning quite literally 's.o. who is studying', e.g. **Die meisten**

Studierenden in Deutschland kriegen kein Bafög 'Most people studying/students in Germany don't get a study grant'.

Der/die Auszubildende, or **Azubi** for short, refers to a 'trainee' or 'apprentice' in any post-school enterprise, the word **Lehrling** now being regarded as dated.

stupid, crazy, mad

albern, bekloppt, bescheuert, blöd(e), dämlich, doof, dumm, närrisch, spinnen, töricht, verrückt

Just as we in English have a whole range of words to express 'crazy', so do the Germans. They are all more or less synonymous. **Töricht** is now rather dated, while **bescheuert** is particularly in vogue and **doof** and **bekloppt** are both limited to the north (NB: **Dick und Doof** 'Laurel and Hardy', i.e. the Fat One and the Stupid One), whereas **närrisch** is heard more in the south. The most common, neutral words are **dumm, blöd(e)**, e.g. **Was bist du dumm/blöd** 'How stupid you are'. To do s.t. like 'mad/crazy' is expressed by **wie verrückt**, e.g. **Er rannte wie verrückt die Treppe rauf** 'He ran like mad up the stairs', **Wir trennen unseren Müll wie die Verrückten** 'We sort our garbage like madmen' (= as if it is going out of fashion). The exclamation 'Are you mad?' is commonly expressed verbally by **spinnen**, e.g. **Spinnst du?**

to support

befürworten, spenden, stützen, unterstützen

Physically 'supporting' s.t. in the sense of bearing (**tragen**), is **stützen**, e.g. **Diese sechs Säulen stützen/tragen das ganze Gebäude** 'These six columns support the whole building'.

Figuratively 'supporting' s.t. in the sense of backing it, is rendered by **unterstützen** (insep.), e.g. **Der Chef unterstützt meine Kandidatur** 'The boss is supporting my candidature'.

'Supporting' in the sense of donating is **spenden,** thus **der Spender** 'supporter/sponsor/donor'.

Where 'to support' is synonymous with 'to approve of', **befürworten** can be used, e.g. **Nur 31% der Bevölkerung befürworten den Krieg gegen ihren Nachbarstaat** 'Only 31% of the population support the war against their neighbouring state'.

sure, certain

bestimmt, gewiss, sicher, sicherlich

If s.o. is 'sure' or 'certain' of s.t. the word is **sicher,** e.g. **Bist du sicher? Sicher** is optionally but very commonly idiomatically used in combination with the dative of the reflexive pronoun, e.g. **Ich bin (mir) sicher, dass er kommt** 'I'm sure he's coming'. To be certain 'of it' is colloquially expressed by **da,** e.g. **Da bin ich mir sicher** 'I'm certain (of it)', **Sind Sie (sich) da sicher?** 'Are you sure (about that)?'.

'Certain' which is not synonymous with 'sure' and does not refer to people being 'certain/sure of s.t.' is **gewiss**; it commonly renders 'certainly/for sure' too, e.g. **Ja, gewiss** 'Yes, certainly', however **sicher** is also possible here but not in the following example, e.g. **Das Schicksal der Geiseln ist ungewiss** 'The fate of the hostages is uncertain' (= up in the air). **Gewiss** is the word required to express the following figurative meaning of 'certain': **Ein gewisser Herr Reuter war eben hier** 'A certain Mr Reuter was just here'. It also occurs in the word **gewissermaßen** 'to a certain extent'.

Although German rarely makes a distinction between adjectives and adverbs, the adverbial form of **sicher, sicherlich,** is frequently used where

an adverb is required often meaning both 'of course' and 'definitely', in which latter case it can be synonymous with **bestimmt,** e.g. **Er wird mir sicherlich/bestimmt helfen können** 'He's sure to be able to help me/He'll certainly/definitely be able to help me'.

to surprise, surprising; to be surprised

erstaunen, staunen, überraschen, verwundern, sich wundern

'To take s.o. by surprise' is **überraschen,** e.g. **Ich war überrascht** 'I was surprised' (= taken by surprise), **Die Soldaten haben den Feind mit dem Angriff überrascht** 'The soldiers surprised the enemy with the attack', **Das war vielleicht eine Überraschung** 'That really was a surprise'.

But more often than not English 'surprise' refers to astonishment in which case forms of **erstaunen** are required, e.g. **Ich war erstaunt zu erfahren, dass er schon geschieden ist** 'I was surprised to learn he is already divorced'. Compare **Er hat mich überrascht angesehen** and **Er hat mich erstaunt angesehen** where the former means 'He looked at me as if taken by surprise' and the latter 'He looked at me with astonishment/amazement'.

Rather than using the adjectival form **erstaunt,** the same can be achieved by using the verb **sich wundern,** which despite appearances does not mean 'to wonder', e.g. **Sie wunderte sich (= war erstaunt), dass Großmutter gar nichts sagte** 'She was surprised that Grandmother said nothing'. **Verwundern** is a less common synonym of **sich wundern,** but **verwundern** is a tr. verb that expresses 'to surprise/amaze/astonish' s.o., e.g. **Das verwundert mich** 'That surprises me'. And finally there is also a verb **staunen,** whose use is rather limited, e.g. **Ich staune** 'Well I never', **Man staunt, wie er trotzdem vorankommt** 'One is astonished at the progress he's making in spite of everything'.

to swim, bathe

baden, schwimmen (gehen)

Baden means both 'to bath' and 'to bathe' (*see* TO TAKE) and in the latter sense is thus synonymous with **schwimmen** but is more commonly used than 'to bathe' in English, e.g. **Ich habe noch nie in der Ostsee gebadet/geschwommen** 'I have never swum in the Baltic Sea'. As with 'swim/ bathe' in English, when 'swimming' from A to B only **schwimmen** can be used, e.g. **Ich bin zu der Insel in der Mitte des Sees geschwommen** 'I swam to the island in the middle of the lake'.

'To go for a swim/swimming' or 'to have a swim' are both **schwimmen gehen** and **baden gehen**, e.g. **Da sind wir mal schwimmen/baden gegangen** 'We had a swim there once'. 'Swimmers' at a swim- ming pool (**das Schwimmbad**) or seaside resort (**der Badeort**) are called **Badegäste**, but if s.o. is 'a good swimmer' he is a **ein guter Schwimmer**.

to take

aushalten, bringen, dauern, ertragen, mitnehmen, nehmen, vertragen

Generally speaking **bringen** and **nehmen** corre- spond with 'bring' and 'take' in English respec- tively, but when 'taking' s.o. or s.t. *somewhere* German uses **bringen**, not **nehmen**, e.g. **Ich bringe dich nach Hause/zum Bahnhof** 'I'll take you home/to the station', **Bringe dies bitte zu deinem Onkel!** 'Please take this to your uncle'. **Mitnehmen** can be used instead but with the added connotation of 'taking' s.t. or s.o. along with you as you are going anyway, e.g. **Nimm dies bitte zu deinem Onkel mit!**

'To take' a bus, train, taxi or tram can be trans- lated by **nehmen**, but is commonly rendered by **fahren mit**, e.g. **Er hat die Straßenbahn nach Hause genommen/Er ist mit der Straßenbahn** nach Hause gefahren 'He took the tram home/He went home by tram'.

'To take a photo of' s.t. or s.o. is **ein Foto machen von**, but **knipsen** is common too, e.g. **Sie hat viele Fotos von der Landschaft gemacht** 'She took a lot of photos of the scenery', **Er hat sie geknipst** 'He took a photo of her'.

'To take/have a bath' is expressed either by **ein Bad nehmen** or simply **baden** (*see* TO SWIM), e.g. **Ich nehme ein Bad** 'I'm taking/having a bath', **Hast du schon gebadet?** 'Have you had a bath yet?'. Likewise **eine Dusche nehmen/ (sich) duschen** 'to take/have a shower' (*see* TO WASH).

Where 'take' means 'last' you require **dauern**, e.g. **Es dauerte eine Weile, bis er zu sich kam** 'It took a while till he regained his senses' (*see* TO LAST).

'To take' meaning 'to stand' or 'to tolerate' is expressed by four verbs, **aushalten**, **ausstehen**, **ertragen** and **vertragen** (*see* TO BEAR).

to take care of, care for, look after

aufpassen auf, betreuen, sich kümmern um, pflegen, sorgen für, versorgen

'To take care of' s.o. in need is **sorgen für**, but this also renders the expression 'to see to', e.g. **Ihre Nachbarin sorgte für sie, als sie krank war** 'Her neighbour cared for her when she was sick', **Ich sorge für das Bier, wenn du für den Wein sorgst** 'I'll take care of the beer if you see to/look after the wine'. The first meaning of **sorgen für** is also rendered by **sich kümmern um**, e.g. **Niemand kümmert sich um ihn** 'There is no one taking care of him'.

'To look after', meaning 'to watch over' (e.g. a child), is **aufpassen auf**, e.g. **Wer passt auf die Kinder auf, während du bei der Arbeit bist?** 'Who looks after the kids while you are at work?'.

Pflegen means 'to look after' where there are connotations of to nurse, to tend, or to maintain, e.g. **In diesem Krankenhaus wird man als Patient sehr gut gepflegt** 'You get well looked after in this hospital as a patient', **Das Denkmal wird gut gepflegt** 'The monument is well looked after/maintained'.

to take part in

sich beteiligen an, mitmachen, teilnehmen an

Sich beteiligen an + dat. and **teilnehmen an** + dat. are synonymous expressions meaning 'to take part/participate in' s.t., e.g. **Die Deutschen wollten sich nicht an diesem Krieg beteiligen/Die Deutschen wollten nicht an diesem Krieg teilnehmen** 'The Germans did not want to take part in this war'. The nouns (i.e. 'participation in') corresponding to these two verbs are **die Beteiligung an** and **die Teilnahme an** respectively.

Mitmachen, with connotations of 'to join in', is another common synonym which you can use when the activity is not mentioned, e.g. **Deutschland will dabei nicht mitmachen** 'Germany does not want to be part of it', **Machst du mit?** 'Are you taking part?' (*see* TO EXPERIENCE).

to taste

kosten, probieren, schmecken

Schmecken is the verb you need in an intr. context, e.g. **Diese Wurst schmeckt ausgezeichnet** 'This sausage tastes delicious'. 'To taste of' s.t. is **schmecken nach**, e.g. **Dies schmeckt nach Nelken** 'This tastes of cloves'. **Schmecken** is also used as a tr. verb when 'taste' means 'to have the taste of', e.g. **Man schmeckt nur einen Hauch Zitrone** 'You can taste just a hint of lemon', **Die Vorspeise war**

so scharf, dass ich danach nichts mehr schmecken konnte 'The entree was so spicy that I couldn't taste anything after that'.

The tr. verb 'to taste' s.t. in the sense of trying it, is **kosten** or **probieren** (*see* TO TRY).

to tax

besteuern, versteuern

Versteuern is what you have to do with money you have earnt, e.g. **Das Geld, das ich mit Nachhilfestunden verdient habe, muss ich leider versteuern** 'The money I earnt from coaching I will unfortunately have to pay tax on' (= to declare). When the government puts a tax on things, **besteuern** is the word, e.g. **Alkoholische Getränke werden in Skandinavien hoch besteuert** 'Alcoholic beverages are highly taxed in Scandinavia'.

to teach

beibringen, dozieren, eine Lektion erteilen, lehren, lernen, unterrichten

Lehren is used for both school and university teaching, and can thus also translate lecturing, e.g. **Er lehrt Management/Deutsch** 'He teaches/ lectures in Management/German'. **Dozieren** is synonymous with **lehren** when it means 'to lecture (in)', e.g. **Er doziert Philosophie** 'He lectures in philosophy'. **Lehren** also renders 'to teach' s.o. s.t. or 'to teach' s.o. to *do* s.t., e.g. **Er hat mich Deutsch gelehrt**[44] 'He taught me German', **Er hat mich schwimmen gelehrt** 'He taught me to swim'.

---

[44] **Lehren** is one of a handful of verbs that take a double object in the acc. but coll. you will hear **jdm etwas lehren**. Compare **beibringen** where the person taught must be in the dat. Coll. you will also hear **jdm/jdn etwas lernen** but this is considered substandard.

The most general word for 'to teach' is **unterrichten**, e.g. **A: Was tun Sie beruflich? B: Ich unterrichte** 'What do you do for a living? B: I teach' (this intr. use of 'teach' could not be rendered by **lehren**), **A: Was/wo unterrichtet er? B: Er unterrichtet Französisch an einem Gymnasium** 'A: What/where does he teach? B: He teaches French at a high school', **Ich unterrichte die sechste Klasse** 'I teach the sixth grade; in this example too **lehren** is not possible' (*see* LESSON).

Beibringen can be synonymous with **lehren** but is always accompanied by the thing and the person taught and is commonly used of skills not necessarily acquired through formal instruction, e.g. **Meine Mutter hat mir Deutsch beigebracht** 'My mother taught me German', **A: Wer hat dir das beigebracht? B: Das hab' ich mir selber beigebracht** 'A: Who taught you to do that? B: I taught myself'.

Jdm eine Lektion erteilen renders the fig. expression 'to teach s.o. a lesson', e.g. **Ich habe ihm eine Lektion erteilt, die er nie vergessen wird,** 'I taught him a lesson he will never forget'.

to tell (*see* TO [TELL A] LIE)

erzählen, sagen

'To tell' is both **sagen** and **erzählen** and the choice depends on how much you have to say. Keeping in mind that **erzählen** means 'to narrate', if what you have to say entails detail, this is the word you require, whereas if it is only a few words, **sagen** is appropriate, e.g. **Erzähl mir, was du in den Ferien gemacht hast!** 'Tell me what you did in the holidays', **Sag mir, wie du heißt/wo du warst!** 'Tell me what your name is/where you were', **A: Du bist zuckerkrank, nicht? B: Wer hat dir das gesagt?** 'A: You are diabetic, aren't you? B: Who told you that?' (*see* TO SAY).

the television

das Fernsehen, der Fernseher, das Fernsehgerät, die Glotze, der Glotzkasten

Fernsehen means both 'television' as a medium as well as a 'television set', whereas **Fernseher** and **Fernsehgerät** can only refer to the latter, e.g. **Es gibt noch kein Fernsehen in dem Land** 'There is still no television in that country', **Wir haben ein neues Fernsehen/ein neues Fernsehgerät/einen neuen Fernseher gekauft** 'We have bought a new television (set)'. **Im zweiten (deutschen Fernsehen)** is the way one expresses 'on channel two', for example. Note the idiom **Ich habe es im Fernsehen gesehen/im Radio gehört** 'I saw it on television/heard it on the radio'.

Die Glotze or **der Glotzkasten** are two colloquial ways of referring to television comparable to our 'the box/telly/tube', e.g. **Ich hab's gestern in der Glotze/im Glotzkasten gesehen** 'I saw it on the box yesterday'.

tender

empfindlich, zart, zärtlich

A part of the body that is tender in the sense of easily hurt or sensitive is **empfindlich**, e.g. **Mein Oberarm ist wegen der Impfung noch etwas empfindlich** 'My upper arm is still a bit tender as a result of the injection'.

'Tender' meaning delicate or fragile is **zart**, but this word is also used of meat, e.g. **Diese Art Geranium ist sehr zart** 'This species of geranium is very tender/delicate', **zartes Fleisch** 'tender meat'.

Zärtlich means 'tender' when s.t. is affectionate or loving, e.g. **Sie sah ihn zärtlich an** 'She looked at him affectionately', **ein zärtlicher Kuss** 'a tender kiss'.

terrible(ly), horrible(ly), awful(ly), dreadful(ly)

furchtbar, ganz, irrsinnig, sagenhaft, scheußlich, schrecklich, ungeheuer, wahnsinnig

Such words are used in German as in English before an adjective to intensify the meaning of that adjective, but whereas **furchtbar** and **schrecklich** can be followed by either positive or negative adjectives, **scheußlich** and **ungeheuer** can only be used with negative adjectives, e.g. **schrecklich gerne/teuer** 'I'd love to/horribly expensive', **furchtbar nett/teuer** 'frightfully nice/expensive', **scheußlich teuer** 'dreadfully expensive', **ungeheuer groß** 'enormously large'.

Irrsinnig and **wahnsinnig**, both of which literally mean 'mad', can qualify both positive or negative adjectives, e.g. **irrsinnig hässlich** 'terribly ugly', **wahnsinnig schön** 'terribly beautiful'. Likewise with **sagenhaft**.

See QUITE for **ganz**.

to test (*see* EXAM)

abfragen, prüfen, auf die Probe stellen, testen

'To test' meaning 'to check' s.t. is both **testen** or **prüfen**, e.g. **Der Fernseher ist repariert worden, muss aber noch getestet/geprüft werden** 'The television set has been repaired but still has to be tested'.

'To test/examine' schoolwork in a written test or examination is **prüfen**, but if conducted orally is **abfragen**, e.g. **Vater, wirst du mir bitte meine Vokabeln abfragen?** 'Dad, will you please test my vocabulary?'.

'To test' in the fig. sense, i.e. 'to put s.o. or s.t. to the test', is **auf die Probe stellen**, e.g. **Ich habe gestern meinen Wagenheber zum erstenmal auf die Probe stellen müssen und er hat mich Gott sei Dank nicht im Stich gelassen** 'I had to put my car jack to the test for the fist time yesterday and thank God it did not let me down'.

to thank, say thank you

sich bedanken, danken, verdanken

'Thank you' can be expressed in several ways, comparable to 'thanks', 'thanks a lot', 'many thanks' etc., e.g. **danke schön/sehr, danke (vielmals), besten/vielen Dank, recht herzlichen/vielen Dank**. You need to be aware that if you're asked if you want a cup of coffee, for example, the answer **danke** means 'no thanks', whereas an affirmative answer requires **bitte sehr** or **ja, gerne**. When thanking s.o. more formally than in the expressions above, you might say **Ich bedanke mich** or **ich danke dir/Ihnen**. Note the use of **bei** with the person being thanked when **sich bedanken** is used: **Der Schriftsteller bedankte sich bei seinen Lesern** 'The writer thanked his readers'. 'I thank you for [doing s.t.]' is expressed as **Ich danke Ihnen (dafür), dass Sie. . . .**

Having s.o. to thank for s.t. in the figurative sense requires **verdanken**, e.g. **Die Panamaer haben den Amerikanern den Kanal zu verdanken** 'The Panamanians have the Americans to thank for the Canal', **Ihm habe ich mein ganzes Unglück zu verdanken** 'I have him to thank for all my misfortune'.

Note that 'Don't mention it/you're welcome' in reply to s.o. for whom you have just done a favour is expressed by **nicht zu danken** or **gern geschehen**.

that/those

dass, der/die/das, dies-, jen-

In spoken German **der/die/das** in all their case forms express both 'the' and 'that/those' as it is possible to pronounce them with emphasis to indicate that they mean the latter, e.g. **Er wohnt in *dem* Haus**[45] 'He lives in *that* house'. As indicating stress in writing is not easy, it is very common for the Germans, in both speech and writing, to use **dies-** to mean 'that/those', which means that it might be interpreted as 'this/these' but the distinction is not important to the German if there is not a contrast being made between 'this/these' and 'that/those', e.g. **Diesen Mikrowellenherd habe ich nie gern benutzt** 'I have never liked using that microwave oven'.

In sentences like the example that follows, 'those' is rendered by **das**, as there is at that point in the sentence no noun to refer back to, unlike the second 'those' which refers back to 'Italians', e.g. **Das sind Italiener, die beiden** 'Those are Italians, those two'.

'That' is also a relative pronoun, corresponding to 'who' or 'which' (*see* WHO).

then

damals, damalig, dann, denn

A temporal 'then' will usually be expressed by **dann**, e.g. **Dann will/wollte ich nach Hause gehen** 'Then (= at that time) I want/wanted to go home'. But a 'then' which is not temporal is **denn**, e.g. **Was willst denn machen?** 'What do you want to do then?'. It is not in fact impossible to hear **dann** being used in such cases either.

A 'then' in the remote past, i.e. one which is synonymous with 'at that time', is **damals**, e.g. **Wilhelm war damals der deutsche Kaiser** 'Wilhelm was the German emperor then'. There is even an adjective derived from **damals, damalig**, e.g. **Der damalige deutsche Kaiser war Wilhelm** 'The then emperor of Germany was Wilhelm'. A

synonym of **damals** is **zu der Zeit**, pronounced stressing **der**.

'Since then' is **seitdem** or **seither** (*see* SINCE), and '(up) till then' is **bis dahin**.

there

da, dort, dahin/dorthin, daher/dorther

In Standard German **da** and **dort** are synonymous in the sense of 'there'. In the south **da** can be synonymous with **hier**, e.g. **Wie lange wohnen Sie schon da?** 'How long have you been living here for?'. But throughout Germany **da** can equate to 'here' in certain set expressions, e.g. **Da bin ich** 'Here I am', **Endlich ist er da, der lang ersehnte Sommer** 'Finally it is here, the long longed-for summer'.

When used with verbs of motion indicating a direction away from the speaker, they must either have **-hin** suffixed to them or be used in combination with a **hin** placed at the end of the clause, e.g. **Unser Sohn wohnt in Ostfriesland. Er wohnt schon Jahre da/dort. Wir fahren übrigens morgen dahin/dorthin** 'Our son lives in East Friesland. He's been living there for years. We're going there tomorrow incidentally' or **Da/dort fahren wir übrigens morgen hin.**

Da and **dort** also occur with **-her** suffixed to them. In common with the somewhat archaic 'thence', **daher** and **dorther** can mean 'from there' but most usually render 'thus/therefore' (*see* SO), in which sense **daher** is the more usual[46] of the two but **darum** and **deshalb** are even more common, e.g. **Wie weit is es dorther von Göttigen? (= von dort nach G.)** 'How far is it from there to Göttingen?'.

---

[45] Note that German shows emphasis in writing by spacing.

[46] It is very common to hear **daher** with this meaning prefixed by a superfluous **von**, e.g. **Wir sind pleite und von daher fahren wir dieses Jahr nicht in Urlaub** 'We are broke and thus won't be going on holiday this year'.

there is/are

es gibt, es ist/sind, es hängt/hängen, es liegt/liegen, es steht/stehen, es sitzt/sitzen

The difference between **es gibt** and **es ist/sind** can be difficult to grasp. Firstly there are important syntactical differences to note: **es gibt** can be followed by either a sing. or pl. noun and that noun is in the acc., e.g. **Es gibt wunderbare Seen/einen wunderbaren See am Rande dieses Dorfes** 'There are wonderful lakes/is a wonderful lake on the edge of this village'. **Es ist/sind** agree in number with the noun that follows and that noun is in the nom., e.g. **Es ist ein Mann hier aus den Niederlanden** 'There is one man here from the Netherlands', **Es sind sehr viele Leute hier aus den Niederlanden** 'There are a lot of people here from the Netherlands'.

The semantic difference between **es gibt** and **es ist/sind** hinges chiefly on permanent existence[47] or temporarily being in a place. In the first example above, the lake or lakes are permanently there, but in the next examples, the man or people are simply present for the time being, as is the case with **Es ist jemand an der Tür** 'There is s.o. at the door'. But **es gibt** is also the required expression that denotes general existence not referring to a particular place, e.g. **Es gibt zu viele Feiertage** 'There are too many public holidays'. Sentences with **es gibt** do not necessarily have to contain an expression of place but those with **es ist/sind** do. Note, however, that in the latter case, the **es** is dropped if the sentence starts with an expression of place or time, e.g. **Es ist ein Eichhörnchen im Schornstein > Im Schornstein ist ein Eichhörnchen** 'There is a squirrel in the chimney', **Letztes Jahr war ein Erdbeben in der Türkei** 'Last year there was an earthquake in Turkey'.

The previous sentence is an example of why this issue is not always clear-cut because with an event, as is the case in that sentence, it is also possible to use **es gibt**, e.g. **Es gab letztes Jahr ein Erdbeben in der Türkei.** (See Durrell 2002, page 372 for more on this complex issue.)

A sentence like **Es wohnt ein alter Mann in diesem Haus** can be translated into English in three ways: 'An old man lives in this house', 'There is an old man living in this house', 'There lives an old man in this house'. The last alternative sounds rather bookish, but is the one that corresponds closest to the German. Although German could say here **Ein alter Mann wohnt in diesem Haus**, the construction with **es** is preferable. Here too, as with **es ist/sind**, the verb must of course stand in the plural if the noun that follows (i.e. the real, as opposed to the dummy subject of the verb) is plural, e.g. **Es wohnen zwei alte Männer in diesem Haus.**

The sort of construction illustrated in the previous paragraph is very common in German with several verbs which can all be rendered by 'there is/are' in English, e.g. **Es steht eine große Eiche vor dem Haus** 'There is a large oak-tree in front of the house'; this can of course be rendered 'There is a large oak tree standing in front of the house', but we are just as likely to omit the 'standing'. German could of course use **es gibt** here. **Es hängt/hängen** and **es liegt/liegen**, which also refer to place, are commonly used in this way, e.g. **Es hing ein schönes Gemälde an der Wand** 'There was a beautiful painting (hanging) on the wall', **Es lagen überall Ahornblätter** 'There were maple leaves (lying) all over the place'. Such verbs, like **es ist/sind**, have separate sing. and pl. forms and are always followed by the nom.

Note that the past tense forms of **es gibt** are **es gab** and **es hat gegeben** and those of **es ist/sind** are **es war/waren** and **es ist/sind gewesen**, e.g. **Es hat zu viel Krach gegeben** 'There was too much noise', **Es ist ein Orkan in Oklahoma gewesen** 'There has been a hurricane in Oklahoma'.

---

[47] Nevertheless there are idiomatic uses of **es gibt** where the notion of permanent existence is not present, e.g. **Was gibt's heute Abend zu essen/im Fernsehen?** 'What is there to eat tonight/on television?', **Es gibt viel zu tun** 'There is a lot to be done'.

the thing

das Ding, eines/eins, die Sache

A concrete object is a **Ding**, but in the plural this word can mean 'matters', e.g. **Was ist das für ein Ding?** 'What sort of a thing is that?', **Diese Dinge gehen dich nicht an** 'These things/matters don't concern you'. **Ding** can also be used affectionately or pejoratively of people, as can 'thing' in English, e.g. **Sie ist ein niedliches, kleines Ding** 'She's a cute little thing'.

In the sing. 'thing' meaning 'matter/issue' is **Sache**, e.g. **Steuerhinterziehung ist eine ernste Sache** 'Tax evasion is a serious thing/matter'. **Sache** can also refer to concrete things, but in very general terms, e.g. **Wirst du bitte deine Sachen aufräumen? Auch das Ding da auf dem Sofa** 'Will you please put your things away? That thing there on the sofa too', **Wir haben in Anatolien tolle Sachen gesehen** 'We saw wonderful things in Anatolia'. In the plural, when it translates 'matters', these matters are not as serious as **Dinge**, e.g. **Solche Sachen interessieren mich nicht** 'I'm not interested in such things/matters'.

There are cases where neither **Ding** nor **Sache** are the appropriate words but where German expresses 'thing' by means of a neuter adj. or the indefinite pronoun **eines/eins**, e.g. **Das Interessanteste ist, dass er endlich verheiratet ist** 'The most interesting thing is that he is finally married', **Eines ist sicher; er tut's nicht wieder** 'One thing is certain; he won't do it again'.

to think

ausdenken, bedenken, denken an/über/von, glauben, halten für/von, sich Gedanken machen über, meinen, nachdenken über, überdenken, (sich) überlegen

Although **denken** is normally the first word you think of when it comes to translating 'to think',

it is not the most usual way of rendering 'to think'. More often than not 'to think' is used to express an opinion, is thus synonymous with 'to believe' and is thus rendered in German by **glauben**, e.g. **Ich glaube, dass er in Mainz wohnt** 'I think he lives in Mainz'. **Meinen**, meaning 'to be of the opinion', is not uncommonly used as a somewhat more formal synonym of **glauben**, e.g. **Ich meine, dass du recht hast** 'I think you are right', but don't hesitate to use **meinen** if 'to think' has the connotation of 'to have an opinion', e.g. **Was meinst du?** 'What do you think/reckon?' (= What is your opinion about it?).

Denken is generally speaking only used when your thoughts are devoted to s.o. or s.t.; it is connected to its object by **an** or **von**, e.g. **Woran denkst du jetzt?** 'What are you thinking about at the moment?', **Sie hat die ganze Zeit an ihre Mutter gedacht** 'She was continually thinking about her mother', **Sie hat kein einziges Mal daran gedacht** 'She did not think about it one single time'. **Denken von** relates to having an opinion about s.o. or s.t., e.g. **Was denkst du davon?** 'What do you think about it?' (see **meinen** above). In certain expressions **denken** in this sense may be followed by **über**, e.g. **Ich denke heute ganz anders darüber** 'These days I have quite a different opinion of it'.

Bedenken means 'to think' in the sense of 'to take into consideration', e.g. **Wenn man bedenkt, was die ökonomische Lage 1945 war . . .** 'When you think of what the economic situation was in 1945 . . .'.

Both **ausdenken** and **erdenken** mean 'to think of' in the sense of 'to think up/devise', e.g. **Hast du eine gute Ausrede ausgedacht/erdacht?** 'Have you thought of/up a good excuse?'.

'To think about s.t. again', i.e. to reconsider s.t., is **überdenken** (insep.), e.g. **Die Regierung wird ihre Drogenpolitik überdenken** 'The government will reconsider its policy on drugs'.

Nachdenken über + acc. is very common and a very handy way of expressing prolonged thinking about s.t., e.g. **Er hat darüber nachgedacht und ist zum Schluss gekommen, dass er nicht auswandern will** 'He has thought about it and has come to the conclusion that he does not want to emigrate'. This expression is very close in meaning to the next item with which it is commonly interchangeable.

'To think about' some*thing* in the sense of 'to deliberate on' is **überlegen**, which is used reflexively if there is an object, e.g. **Sie haben es gemacht, ohne zu überlegen** 'They did it without thinking (about it)', **Ich will es mir mal überlegen** 'I want to think about it for a while', which can also be expressed as follows: **Ich werde es mir durch den Kopf gehen lassen.**

'To think about' or 'to ponder on' s.t. for a prolonged period of time can also be expressed by sich (dat.) **Gedanken machen über** + acc., e.g. **Ich habe mir Gedanken darüber gemacht** 'I have been thinking about it'. This expression can also have a negative connotation but there will usually be some indication of this, e.g. **Ich habe mir ernsthaft Gedanken darüber gemacht** 'I have been very worried about that'.

Halten von means 'to think of' people and things in the sense of having an opinion about them (*see* TO FIND), e.g. **Was hältst du von dem neuesten Film von Peter Weir?** 'What do you think of Peter Weir's most recent film?'.

Halten für renders 'to think' in the sense of considering s.o. or s.t. as being s.t., e.g. **Wir halten es nicht für klug, dagegen zu demonstrieren** 'We do not consider/think it wise to demonstrate against it', **Ich halte ihn für dumm** 'I think he is stupid/I consider him stupid', **Wofür hältst du mich?** 'What do you think I am/What do you take me for?'.

to threaten

androhen, bedrohen, drohen, gefährden

The transitive verb is **bedrohen**, e.g. **Er bedrohte sie mit einem Dolch** 'He threatened her with a dagger', **Die Firma ist von Konkurs bedroht** 'The business is threatened with bankruptcy', **sich bedroht fühlen** 'to feel threatened', **eine bedrohte/gefährdete Tierart** 'a threatened species', the latter being derived from **gefährden** (to endanger) which can be synonymous in both English and German with 'to threaten'.

When things 'threaten' to happen, the verb is **drohen**, an intransitive verb, e.g. **Das Boot drohte zu kentern** 'The boat threatened to capsize', **Ein Sturm drohte** 'A storm was threatening', **ein drohender Sturm** 'a threatening storm', **Es droht Gefahr** 'There is a threat of danger'. It is possible for a person to be the object of **drohen** but the object must be in the dative case, e.g. **Er drohte ihr mit einem Dolch** 'He threatened her with a dagger', **Während der Gefechte sollen sich die Erzfeinde mit dem Atomschlag gedroht haben** (< sich drohen 'to threaten each other') 'During the fighting the arch enemies are supposed to have threatened each other with nuclear attack', **Todesdrohungen erhalten** 'to receive death threats'.

'To threaten with/to do' can be expressed in one word in more elevated contexts by **androhen**, e.g. **Die Armee hat neue Angriffe auf den Süden des Landes angedroht** (= . . . hat mit neuen Angriffen gedroht) 'The army threatened with new attacks on the south of the country, **Dann machten die Rebellen, was sie bis dahin nur angedroht hatten** (= . . . was sie bis dahin zu tun gedroht hatten) 'Then the rebels did what they till that point in time had only threatened to do'.

the throat, neck

der Hals, die Kehle

Strictly speaking **Kehle** means 'throat' and refers only to that part inside the mouth and **Hals** means 'neck' but also refers to the external throat, whereas the '(back/nape of the) neck' is **der Nacken**. Curiously enough **Er hat es am/im Hals** renders 'He has a sore throat' (**Halsentzündung** 'sore throat') although this ailment affects the internal, not the external throat.

to throw

bewerfen, schmeißen, werfen

'To throw' is **werfen** (tr.), a colloquial synonym of which is **schmeißen** (compare 'to chuck' in English). If you 'throw s.t. at s.o.' this must be expressed by **jdn mit etwas bewerfen**, e.g. **Die Bürger haben die Soldaten mit Steinen beworfen** 'The civilians threw stones at the soldiers'; **beschmeißen** is similarly used to render 'to pelt/bombard with'.

the ticket

das Billett, die Fahrkarte, der Fahrschein,
die Flugkarte, der Flugschein, der Strafzettel,
das Ticket

A tram, train, bus or cinema/museum/theatre etc. 'ticket' is a **Karte**, that for transport being rendered by **Fahrkarte**, if the context requires it, and otherwise by **Eintrittskarte**. A more official sounding word for modes of transport is **Fahrschein**, a word you will often see written.

A 'plane ticket' can be a **Flugkarte** (or alternatively **Flugschein**, as above with **Fahrschein**), but because it takes the form of a small booklet (as can train tickets for international travel in Europe), the word **Flugticket** is commonly heard.

It is not, however, impossible for other tickets to be referred to by this word, e.g. **Die Tickets für die Fußballweltmeisterschaft gehen weg wie warme Semmeln** 'The tickets to the Football World Cup are selling like hot cakes'.

Billet(t) is a relatively rare synonym these days of **(Fahr-/Eintritts-)karte**.

A 'parking/speeding ticket', meaning a fine, is **der Strafzettel**.

the time

bis, lange, das Mal, die Uhr, die Zeit,
der Zeitpunkt

Zeit is 'time' is the sense of the passing of 'Father Time', e.g. **Wie die Zeit vergeht** 'How time passes'. Note too **jederzeit/zu jeder Zeit** 'at any time', e.g. **Wenn er wollte, könnte der Papst jederzeit von seinem Amt zurücktreten** 'If he wanted to, the pope could resign his office at any time', **zu DDR-Zeiten/zu Zeiten Karl des Großen** 'at the time of the GDR/Charlemagne'. 'At that (point in) time' is rendered either by **zu dieser/der Zeit** or **zu dem Zeitpunkt**, e.g. **Zu der Zeit/zu dem Zeitpunkt wohnten sie noch in Korea** 'At that time/point in time they still lived in Korea'.

The most common mistake made here is using **Zeit** where **Mal** (= occasion) is required, e.g. **Das höre ich jetzt zum ersten Mal** (also **zum erstenmal**) 'This is the first time I've heard that'. **Erstmals** is synonymous with **zum erstenmal**, e.g. **Die SPD musste nach 44 Jahren erstmals in die Opposition** 'The SPD had to go into opposition for the first time in forty-four years'. Expressions containing **Mal/mal** do not always correspond directly with English 'time' (*see* LAST), e.g. **einmal/zweimal/mehrmals/vielmals** 'once/twice/several times/many times', **ein paarmal** 'a few times/on several occasions', **Wann habe ich dich zum letztenmal gesehen?** 'When did I last see you?', **Ich komme vielleicht ein andermal/noch** einmal 'I might come at some other time/one more time', **diesmal/dieses Mal** 'this time', **nächstes Mal/das nächste Mal** 'next time', **letztes Mal/das letzte Mal** 'last time'. 'Time and time again' is best expressed by **immer wieder**, e.g. **Er fährt immer wieder in seine Heimat zurück** 'He goes back to his homeland time and time again'.

'For the time being' is rendered by **vorerst**, e.g. **Vorerst bleibt er in Kalifornien wohnen** 'For the time being he is going to keep living in California'.

'Time' with reference to the clock is **Uhr**, e.g. **Mein Kind kennt die Uhr noch nicht** 'My child can't yet tell the time', **Wie viel Uhr ist es?** 'What time is it?', which is however just as commonly expressed as **Wie spät ist es?**, e.g. **Ich habe keine Ahnung, wei viel Uhr es ist/wie spät es ist** 'I have no idea what time it is'.

'For a long time' (see FOR with expressions of time) is rendered by the adverb **lange**, e.g. **Er hat lange im Ausland gelebt** 'He lived abroad for a long time'. But **lange** is also used in combination with various other adverbs and prepositions to render a number of expressions incorporating the word 'time', e.g. **Wie lange wohnst du (schon) in England?** 'How long have you lived in England?', **Wir wohnen (schon) seit langem/schon lange in diesem Land** 'We have lived in this country for a long time', **Auf wie lange fahrt ihr nach Korsika?** 'How long are you going to Corsica for?'.

One of the various meanings of **bis** (see UNTIL) is 'by the time (that)', e.g. **Bis es dunkel wird, müssen wir zu Hause sein** 'By the time it gets dark we have to be home', **Bis er ankommt, . . .** 'By the time he arrives . . .'.

to

an, auf, in, nach, zu

Going 'to' places is most usually rendered by **nach** or **zu**. You go **nach** (+ dat.) countries and cities,

e.g. **Wir fahren morgen nach Berlin/Holland** 'We're driving to Berlin/Holland tomorrow'. If you are going 'to' a country or region that requires a definite article, you go **in** (+ acc.) that country, e.g. **Wir fliegen in die Schweiz/Niederlande/Bretagne** 'We're flying to Switzerland/the Netherlands/Brittany'. When any country is qualified by an adjective, the definite article must be used (i.e. **das** for all countries that do not otherwise have an article) and you must then also go **in** these countries, e.g. **Die Kambodschaner sind ins benachbarte Thailand geflohen** 'The Cambodians fled (in)to neighbouring Thailand'. Note how 'to' a country is rendered in the following: **Bist du jemals in Deutschland gewesen?** 'Have you ever been to Germany?'.

Note that 'welcome to' a town or country requires **in** (+ dat.), e.g. **Willkommen in Wien/der Schweiz/Deutschland** 'Welcome to Vienna/Switzerland/Germany'.

In the following sentence 'to' a country is rendered by **an** (+ acc.) as 'to' here is analogous to sending or writing something 'to 'someone (see below), not physically going there, which would require **nach**: **Die Australier verkaufen Autos an Japan** 'The Australians are selling cars to Japan'. Someone explaining the world weather map, for example, will say **Und jetzt kommen wir zu Nordamerika** 'And now we come to North America', where there is clearly no question of physically going there either.

Generally speaking, all other places, and particularly people, you go **zu** (+ dat.), e.g. **Ich bin unterwegs zu Aldi** 'I'm on my way to Aldi' (a supermarket chain), **Sie geht zur Post/zum Markt/zum Bahnhof/zum Metzger/zu ihrem Onkel** 'She's going to the post office/market/station/butcher's/her uncle's place' (see HOME for **nach/zu Hause**). There is a variety of places that you can either go **zu** (+ dat.) or **in** (+ acc.), e.g. **zur/in die Schule/Universität/Stadt** 'to school/

university/town'.[48] On rare occasions **an** (+ acc.) renders a physical movement 'to', but **zu** should also usually be correct, e.g. **Er ging ans/zum Fenster** 'He walked to the window'.

Auf (+ acc.) is sometimes used instead of **zu** to render 'to' public buildings, e.g. **Wir gehen auf den Markt/die Bank/die Post. Sie geht auf eine Party** is also possible (*see* AT).

Going 'to' school or university can present problems. **Mein Sohn geht schon zur Schule** 'My son is already going to school'; this means he is old enough to go to school while **in die Schule gehen** means 'to go to/leave for school'. The same distinction in meaning applies to **zur** and **in die Universität gehen**, e.g. **Er ist schon in die Uni gegangen** 'He has already gone to [the] university' (= left for) (*see* AT). 'To' **Gymnasium** (*see* SCHOOL) can be expressed with either **auf** or **in**, e.g. **Er geht aufs/ins Gymnasium** 'He goes to high school'.

But **an** (+ acc.) is the preposition required for rendering sending and writing 'to' people, e.g. **Sie hat einen Brief an ihre Oma geschickt/geschrieben** 'She sent/wrote a letter to her granny'. This can, however, be expressed by means of a simple dative with no preposition, but then the word order changes (compare the English translations of the above and the following), e.g. **Sie hat ihrer Oma einen Brief geschickt/geschrieben** 'She sent/wrote her granny a letter'. Note that with **geben** only the option with the simple dative is possible, e.g. **Sie hat ihrer Oma Geld gegeben** 'She gave some money to her granny'.

To say s.t. 'to' s.o. is also rendered usually by the simple dative but **zu** (+ dat.) does occur, e.g. **Was hat er (zu) dir gesagt?** 'What did he say to you?'.

---

[48] The distinction here, if any, is that with **in** you are thinking more of the building and with **zu** more of the purpose.

the toilet (*see* TO SHIT)

der Abort, das Klo, das Pissoir, die Toilette, das WC

The choice of word here depends on the degree of formality, rather than that there is necessarily a difference in meaning between them. Germans do not insist on using euphemisms (e.g. bathroom, restroom etc.) in this instance, however formal the situation, but a totally innocuous way of stating you need to relieve yourself is to say **Ich muss austreten**. Otherwise the most neutral word is **Toilette** (pron. twalette), e.g. **Sie ist auf die Toilette gegangen** 'She's gone to the toilet', **Sie ist auf/in der Toilette** 'She is on/in the toilet'. Colloquially, and comparable to 'lav' and 'loo', the word **Klo** is very commonly heard, e.g. **aufs Klo gehen, Ich bin auf'm Klo** 'I'm on the loo'. The full forms **Klosett** and **WC** (< **Wasserklosett**) are dated. A **Pissoir** is a 'urinal' but they are not common in Germany. Now quite dated but still occasionally seen on signs is the word **Abort**.

the top

der Gipfel, oben, die Spitze, der Wipfel

Gipfel is the 'top' or 'summit' of a mountain, whereas **Wipfel** is the 'top' of a tree, e.g. **Diese Affen leben in den Wipfeln der Bäume** 'These monkeys live in the tops of the trees/in the treetops'. The 'top' of anything that ends in a point, thus also a mountain or a tree, is called a **Spitze**, e.g. **die Spitze des Turms/der Pyramide** 'the top of the tower/pyramid'.

The adverb **oben** (on/at the top) will often translate 'top' when referring to the position of s.t., e.g. **Es liegt oben auf dem Schrank** 'It's lying on top of the cupboard', **Es steht auf Seite 10, oben links** 'It is on page 10, at the top on the left'.

to touch

abtasten, anfassen, anrühren, antasten, berühren, rühren, tasten

Berühren is 'to touch' s.o. or part of s.o lightly, even by accident., e.g. **Ich habe ihren Arm berührt** 'I touched her arm', **Bitte Berühren** 'Please press' (on crosswalk button).

Anfassen is 'to touch' more deliberately and physically than **berühren**, i.e. to take hold of, e.g. **Nicht anfassen** 'Don't touch', **Warum hast du sie so angefasst?** 'Why did you touch her/grab hold of her like that?'.

Anrühren is more or less synonymous with both **berühren** and **anfassen**, but is nearly always used in the negative, **Er hat sein Schnitzel nicht angerührt** 'He hasn't touched his schnitzel'.

Rühren means 'to touch' s.o. emotionally, but **berühren** has this meaning too, e.g. **Sie hat mir Geld angeboten, was mich sehr gerührt/berührt hat, aber ich habe es nicht angenommen** 'She offered me money, which touched me greatly, but I didn't accept it'.

Betasten means 'to touch/feel' s.t. in order to inspect it, e.g. **Der Zahnarzt betastete die geschwollenen Drüsen in ihrem Hals** 'The dentist touched the swollen glands in her neck'.

'To touch on' a topic, especially in the negative, is **antasten** or **berühren**, e.g. **Wir haben dieses Thema kaum angetastet/berührt** 'We scarcely touched that topic'.

Abtasten is also used when s.o. or s.t. is 'touched' all over while looking for s.t., but seldom translates as 'touch' in such cases, e.g. **Der Polizist hat den Jugendlichen nach Rauschgift abgetastet** 'The policeman searched the young man for drugs'.

the town, city, village

die City, das Dorf, die Großstadt, die Kleinstadt, der Ort, die Ortschaft, die Stadt, der Wohnort, das Zentrum

A 'town' or 'city' in general is a **Stadt**, e.g. **Ich gehe jetzt in die Stadt** 'I'm going to town/downtown now'. A **Großstadt** is a 'city' (more than 100,000 inhabitants) whereas the word **City** is sometimes used in German instead of das **Zentrum** for 'city centre'. Nevertheless, the very fast train connecting European cities is called der **ICE** (= Inter-City-Express). A 'small town' is **Kleinstadt** but in both cases **eine kleine/große Stadt** is also possible instead of the compounded forms.

Dorf means 'village', but one horse towns in the New World might also be called **Dörfer**; **Kuhdorf** is used with a pejorative connotation for such places. A 'small town' or 'village' can also be called an **Ortschaft**, e.g. **Mehrere Ortschaften in der Nähe des Ätna drohten in den Lavamassen zu verschwinden** 'Several (small) towns in the vicinity of Etna threatened to disappear in the lava flows'. You may even hear **Ort** (lit. 'place') being used where '(small) town' is appropriate in English, e.g. **Er wohnt in einem kleinen Ort in Niederbayern** 'He lives in a village/small town/place in Lower Bavaria'. On official forms where your 'town' is asked for, you will read **Wohnort** (lit. 'place of residence').

to travel

bereisen, fahren, reisen

Reisen renders 'to travel' if speaking of s.o. who is undertaking a long journey or voyage (see **Reise** under TRIP), e.g. **Er ist sehr viel in seinem Leben gereist** 'He has travelled a lot in his life' (i.e. gone to many exotic places), whereas **fahren** refers to more mundane travel, e.g. **Ich habe immer in Köln gewohnt und in Essen gearbeitet und habe also viel**

fahren müssen 'I have always lived in Cologne and worked in Essen so I have had to travel a lot'. Note **Er ist weit gereist/Er ist ein weitgereister Mann** 'He is well-travelled/He is a well-travelled man'.

The difference in meaning between these two verbs is paralleled in **abreisen** and **abfahren**, both meaning 'to leave/depart', the one on a **Reise** and the other on a **Fahrt** (*see* TRIP and TO LEAVE).

Bereisen is a tr. verb and thus must have a direct object as in 'to travel the world', e.g. **Er hat ganz Südamerika bereist** 'He has travelled throughout South America'.

the trip

der Ausflug, die Fahrt, die Reise, der Trip

A 'trip' in the sense of an overseas trip or voyage is a **Reise**, in keeping with the verb **reisen** meaning 'to travel'. A shorter 'trip' by car or train is a **Fahrt**, e.g. **Wie lange dauert die Fahrt von Bremen nach Hamburg?** 'How long does the trip from Bremen to Hamburg take?'. Compare **Gute Reise** 'Bon voyage' and **Gute Fahrt** 'Drive safely'. If 'trip' has the connotation of an 'excursion', **Ausflug** can be used, e.g. **Wir haben früher jeden Sonntag mit unseren Eltern einen Ausflug aufs Land gemacht** 'We used to make a trip into the country every Sunday with our parents'. **Trip** is an informal synonym of both **Fahrt** and **Ausflug**, but not of **Reise**, which meaning it can have in English, e.g. **Sie machten einen Erkundungstrip in die Berge** 'They made a reconnaissance trip into the mountains'.

the trouble

die Mühe, das Problem, die Schwierigkeit(en)

'Trouble' meaning a problem is expressed by either **Problem(e)** or **Schwierigkeiten** (latter always plural), thus to have 'trouble' with your car, computer etc. can be expressed in any of the following ways: **Ich habe Schwierigkeiten/ Probleme/ein Problem mit meinem Auto.**

'Trouble' meaning effort is **Mühe** and thus **sich die Mühe machen/nehmen** renders 'to take/go to the trouble' to do s.t., e.g. **Er hat sich sehr viel Mühe gemacht/genommen (, mir zu helfen)** 'He took a lot of trouble/He went to a lot of trouble (to help me)', **(Machen Sie sich) keine Mühe!** 'Don't go to any trouble'. This can also be expressed by **sich bemühen** but the accompanying syntax differs, e.g. **Er hat sich sehr bemüht (, mir zu helfen).**

(Nicht) die/der Mühe wert expresses the idiom '(not) worth the trouble/effort', e.g. **Es war nicht die/der Mühe wert**, where either the acc. or the gen. is possible. Note also **Es lohnt die Mühe**, 'It is worth the trouble/effort'.

Mühe can also have connotations of 'bother', e.g. **Er hatte viel/wenig/keine Mühe, es zu tun** 'He had a lot of/little/no trouble doing it'.

to trust

anvertrauen, misstrauen, trauen, vertrauen, zutrauen

'To trust' or have confidence in s.o. or s.t. is **trauen**, which takes a dat. object, e.g. **Ich traue ihm nicht** 'I do not trust him' (*see* TO BELIEVE and TO DARE). 'To not trust/mistrust' is **misstrauen** (+ dat.), e.g. **Der PDS (Partei des Demokratischen Sozialismus) wird im Westen misstraut** 'The PDS is not trusted in the west'.

'To trust s.o. to do s.t.' requires **vertrauen**, e.g. **Ich vertraue ihm, dass er das Geld zurückzahlen wird** 'I trust him to pay the money back', **Ich vertraue darauf, dass er das Geld zurückzahlen wird** 'I trust he'll pay the money back'.

'To entrust s.t. to s.o.' is **jdm etwas anvertrauen**, e.g. **Er hat mir sein Testament anvertraut** 'He has entrusted me with his will'.

Zutrauen does not translate 'trust' but means 'to believe s.o. capable of doing s.t.', e.g. **Das hätte ich ihm nicht zugetraut** 'I would not have thought him capable of that'.

to try

ausprobieren, kosten, probieren, versuchen

Probieren and **versuchen** are completely synonymous in the sense of 'to try' but the former, a loanword from French, would seem curiously enough to be more commonly used than the indigenous word. 'To try out/test' is always **ausprobieren**. 'To try' with reference to food can be expressed by both **probieren** and **kosten** (*see* TO TASTE), e.g. **Probiere/koste es mal!** 'Try it'.

to turn

abbiegen, biegen, drehen, einbiegen, kehren, (sich) umdrehen, umkehren, wenden

'To turn' right around in a car, i.e. to make a U-turn is **wenden**, e.g. **Ich kann hier nicht wenden. Weißt du, wo die nächste Wendemöglichkeit ist?** 'I can't turn (around) here. Do you know where the next opportunity to turn is?'. A 'turncoat' is a **Wendehals** as he has done a complete about-turn.

If you need 'to turn' left or right in a car, use **abbiegen**, e.g. **Du musst an der nächsten Ecke rechts abbiegen** 'You have to turn right at the next corner'. Use **einbiegen** when 'turning into' a street, e.g. **Bieg in die nächste Straße rechts ein!** 'Turn into the next street on the right'.

If a person 'turns around', you need **sich umdrehen**, e.g. **Er drehte sich nicht einmal um, als ich ins Zimmer kam** 'He didn't even turn around when I came into the room'. 'To turn s.t. around' is simply **umdrehen**, e.g. **Dreh deinen Sessel bitte um!** 'Please turn your armchair around'.

If you are on your way somewhere and turn around to return to where you've come from, you need **umkehren**, e.g. **Wir waren schon halbwegs zu unserem Urlaubsziel, als wir umkehrten, weil meine Frau krank geworden ist** 'We were already halfway to our holiday destination when we turned around (= turned back) as my wife fell ill'.

When it is s.o.'s 'turn' to do s.t. use a variant of either of the following idioms, e.g. **Jetzt sind Sie dran/an der Reihe** 'Now it's your turn', **Wann bin ich dran/an der Reihe?** 'When is it my turn?'.

to turn on/off, switch on/off

andrehen/zudrehen, anmachen/ausmachen, anschalten/ausschalten, anstellen/abstellen, antörnen/anturnen

'To turn on/off' of lights and electrical appliances is **an-/ausschalten** but colloquially **an-/ausmachen** are commonly heard too (*see* TO OPEN/SHUT). 'To turn a tap on or off' is expressed by **einen Hahn an-/zudrehen**.

Antörnen (also spelt **anturnen**) is inspired by the English figurative expression 'to turn on' (e.g. sexually), e.g. **Sie hat ihn immer angetörnt** 'She has always turned him on'.

You can forget **anstellen** as a verb for 'turning on' s.t. but **abstellen** is the verb used for 'turning off' the gas or electricity, but it can also used of radios, stereos etc.

to understand

begreifen, fassen, kapieren, nachvollziehen, Verständnis haben für etwas, verstehen

The most usual word is of course **verstehen** and must be used for 'understanding' foreign languages, e.g. **Er hat Griechisch gesprochen und ich habe kein Wort verstanden** 'He was speaking

Greek and I didn't understand a word'. 'Understanding' in the sense of not being able to hear s.o. is also always **verstehen**, e.g. **Sprich bitte lauter. Ich kann dich nicht verstehen** 'Please speak up. I can't understand you'.

When it comes to comprehending ideas, **verstehen** can be replaced by **begreifen**, e.g. **Ich verstehe/ begreife nicht, was er meint** 'I don't understand what he means'. **Kapieren** is a coll. stylistic variant, as is **nachvollziehen**, but this is quite high style.

Fassen, which is always used together with a negative, expresses strong inability to comprehend s.t., e.g. **Das ist nicht zu fassen** 'It is incomprehensible', **Ich kann's nicht fassen** 'I don't understand it' (= it is beyond my comprehension, which can be literally expressed by **Das geht über mein Verständnis**). **Verständnis haben für etwas** renders 'to understand' in the sense of being sympathetic to an issue, e.g. **Ich habe Verständnis für das, was sie erreichen wollen** 'I understand what they are trying to achieve'.

the union

die Gewerkschaft, die Union, die Vereinigung

A **Gewerkschaft** is a 'trade union'. Other unions (i.e. organisations) are **Unionen**, e.g. **die EU (Europäische Union)**, **die CDU (Christlich-Demokratische Union)** 'the German conservative party'. The act of creating a 'union' is **Vereinigung**, e.g. **Eine Vereinigung der arabischen Staaten ist ausgeschlossen** 'A union (= unification) of Arab states is out of the question'.

united

vereint, vereinigt, wiedervereinigt

'United' in the names of countries is always **vereinigt**, from the verb **vereinigen** 'to unite', e.g. **die**

Vereinigten Staaten 'the United States' (also called **die USA**), **das Vereinigte Königreich** 'the United Kingdom', **die Vereinigten Arabischen Emirate** 'the United Arab Emirates'. Only in **die Vereinten Nationen** (the United Nations) is **vereint** required. It has become the custom since 1990 to talk of German reunification (**die Wiedervereinigung Deutschlands**), rather than simply 'unification', and thus **wiedervereinigt** is used in that context, **das wiedervereinigte Deutschland** 'reunited Germany'.

the university degree (*see* SCHOOL and PROFESSOR)

Diplom-, der Doktorand, die Dissertation, der Magister (Artium), das Staatsexamen; promovieren

A basic Arts or Science degree at a German university takes a minimum of four years, so whether it is the equal of a BA with honours or an MA depends on where you live in the English-speaking world. Someone going into teaching, medicine or the law will acquire **das Staatsexamen** at the end of their university training, whereas a general Arts degree is **der Magister (Artium)** 'Master of Arts'. In the exact sciences, having done the basic degree in whatever field, you end up a **Diplomingenieur, Diplombiologe, Diplomphysiker** etc. depending on the discipline; these titles are the equivalent of having a Bachelor/Masters of Engineering or Science, e.g. **Mein Vater ist Diplomchemiker** 'My father has a BSc/MSc in chemistry'.

After any of these basic degrees you go on to a doctorate if you study further, i.e. you become a **Doktorand** (doctoral postgraduate); this can also be expressed verbally by means of the verb **promovieren**, e.g. **Ich bin Doktorand/Ich promoviere** 'I am doing my doctorate'. Your 'doctoral thesis' is your **Dissertation** (*see* PROFESSOR for the next degree).

until, till

bis, erst

'Until' is normally **bis**, e.g. **Er hat bis Montag, das Geld zurückzubezahlen** 'He has till Monday to pay the money back', but note that **bis** also renders 'by' in temporal expressions, e.g. **Er will das Geld bis Montag von dir kriegen** 'He wants to get the money from you by Monday' (*see* TIME for more on **bis**.) But 'not until', where 'not' and 'until' are often several words apart, is rendered by **erst** (literally 'only', *see* ONLY), e.g. **Er gibt dir das Geld erst am Montag** 'He won't give you the money until Monday = He will only give you the money on Monday'.

upstairs/downstairs

herauf-/herunterkommen, hinauf-/
hinuntergehen, hoch-/runtergehen, hoch-/
runterrennen, (nach) oben/unten gehen

Being 'upstairs/downstairs' is expressed by **oben/unten**, e.g. **Wo sind die Kinder? Torsten ist oben und Felix ist unten** 'Where are the children? Torsten is upstairs and Felix is downstairs'. 'To go upstairs/downstairs' can be rendered either by **hinaufgehen/hinuntergehen** or by **nach oben/unten gehen**, e.g. **Er ist sofort hinaufgegangen/nach oben gegangen** 'He went upstairs straight away'. As you would expect, 'to come upstairs/downstairs' is expressed by **heraufkommen/herunterkommen** or by **nach oben/unten kommen**, e.g. **Komm bitte herunter/nach unten!** 'Please come downstairs'.[49]

'To run upstairs/downstairs' is **hoch-/runterrennen** but **hoch-** and **runter-** can also be prefixed to **gehen** to render 'to go upstairs/downstairs', e.g.

---

[49]   Note that in spoken German both **rauf** and **runter** occur and can mean both **herauf/hinauf** and **herunter/hinunter** respectively, e.g. **Geh bitte rauf und hilf ihm!** 'Please go up(stairs) and help him' (*see* footnote to OUTSIDE).

Renn bitte schnell mal hoch und hole meine Pantoffeln! 'Please run upstairs and fetch my slippers'.

'To go up/down *the* stairs' is **die Treppe hinauf-/hinuntergehen**, e.g. **Er ist vor einigen Minuten die Treppe hinaufgegangen** (or **raufgegangen**) 'He went up the stairs a few minutes ago'.

to use

anwenden, benutzen, benützen,
gebrauchen, nutzen, nützen, verbrauchen,
verwenden

'To use' is especially tricky. There are contexts where some of these words are interchangeable but the following explanations will serve as some help to understanding the distinctions between them. **Benutzen** indicates using s.t. or s.o. for the specific purpose for which it was intended, e.g. **Aufzug im Brandfall nicht benutzen** 'Do not use the lift in case of fire', **Dieses Besteck ist schon benutzt worden** 'This cutlery has been used' (= is dirty), **Diese Säge ist schwer zu benutzen** 'This saw is difficult to use', **Darf ich deinen Computer benutzen?** 'May I use your computer?', **Ich benutze den Computer nur als Schreibmaschine** 'I use the computer simply as a typewriter'.

Gebrauchen means 'to find/see some use for s.t.', e.g. **A: Kannst du dies gebrauchen? B: Ja, das kann ich gut gebrauchen** 'Can you use this? Yes, I can use that/make good use of that' (i.e. I have a use for it in mind). **Gebrauchen** is the appropriate verb for things you own and regularly use, e.g. **Was für Waschpulver gebrauchst du?** 'What sort of washing powder do you use?'. **Den Topf gebrauche ich nicht mehr** 'I don't use that pot any more'. It is however a fact that **benutzen** is possible in all these exampes as well, which is why you are best to stick to that verb if ever in doubt. **Gebrauchen** can emphasise the effect on the person or thing being used, e.g. **Sie gebrauchen**

mich 'They are using me' (= exploiting). When s.t. is used for its intended purpose **gebrauchen** is also appropriate. Note too **der Gebrauchtwagen** 'the used car'.

Verbrauchen means 'to use up/consume', particularly of energy and time, e.g. **Unser Golf verbraucht sehr wenig Benzin** 'Our Golf uses very little petrol', **A: Haben wir noch Waschpulver? B: Nein, das haben wir verbraucht** 'Have we got any washing powder left? No, we've used it (up)'.

Verwenden means 'to deploy', with which it is similar in style, and emphasises the purpose for which s.t. is being used, for which reason it is often interchangeable with **benutzen**, e.g. **Dieses Plakat darf nicht im Wahlkampf verwendet werden** 'This poster may not be used in the election campaign', **Binnen eines Jahres will die Firma aufhören, für ihre Produkte Fischöl zu verwenden** 'Within a year the firm wants to cease using fish oil for their products', **Ich würde in diesem Fall ein anderes Wort verwenden** 'I would use a different word in this case'.

Anwenden is used with reference to using methods, means, techniques etc. where 'to use' is close in meaning to 'to apply', another possible translation of the word, e.g. **Man hat letztendlich Gewalt anwenden müssen** 'In the end force had to be used/applied', **Diese Regel kann man nicht auf alle Fälle anwenden** 'You can't use this rule in all cases' (= apply it to all cases).

Nutzen and its derivatives all also occur with an umlaut, but only in the south. **Nutzen** emphasises making use of opportunities, e.g. **Als wir in Hamburg waren, haben wir die Gelegenheit genutzt, meine Tante zu besuchen** 'When we were in Hamburg we used the opportunity to visit my aunt', **Nutzen Sie unser Ferienangebot!** 'Make use of/the most of our holiday offer!'. But **nutzen** also means 'to be useful/to be of use', e.g. **Wozu nützt das?** 'What's the use/point of that?', **Es nützt (mir) nichts** 'It is useless/of no use (to me)'. **Nützlich**

(useful) and **nutzlos** (useless) are both derived from this root. **Ausnutzen** means 'to use/make use of' in the sense of 'to exploit', e.g. **Sie haben ihn/seine Leichtgläubigkeit ausgenutzt** 'They used him/exploited his gullibility'.

used to

sich angewöhnen, sich gewöhnen, gewohnt/gewöhnt sein, pflegen

'To get used to s.t.' is **sich an etwas** (acc.) **gewöhnen**, e.g. **Er hat sich an das deutsche Klima gewöhnt** 'He has got used to the German climate'. 'To be used to s.t.' is **gewöhnt sein an** (+ acc.), e.g. **Er ist jetzt an das Klima gewöhnt** 'He is now used to the climate'; it is however possible to omit **an** and use a direct object, e.g. **Er ist das Klima jetzt gewöhnt**, but if you are used to *doing* s.t., the former expression must be used, e.g. **Er ist daran gewöhnt, allein zu wohnen** 'He is used to living alone'.

But there is also an alternative synonymous expression, **etwas gewohnt sein**, e.g. **Das ist er nicht gewohnt (= Daran ist er nicht gewöhnt)** 'He is not used to it', **Er ist gewohnt, früh ins Bett zu gehen (= Er ist daran gewöhnt, . . .)** 'He is used to going to bed early'. Where a clause follows, as in the previous example, the first clause can include an optional **es**, e.g. **Soldaten sind (es) gewohnt, im Freien schlafen zu müssen** 'Soldiers are used to having to sleep in the open'.

'To get into the habit of doing s.t.', as opposed to 'to be used to doing s.t.', is **sich (es)/etwas angewöhnen, etwas zu tun**, e.g. **Er hat (es) sich angewöhnt, früh ins Bett zu gehen** 'He has got into the habit of going to bed early'.

'Used to' meaning 'to be in the habit of doing' s.t. in more formal style is rendered by **pflegen**, e.g. **Der Diktator pflegte Vorträge von über sechs Stunden zu halten** 'The dictator used to give speeches of over six hours' duration'.

to visit; the visitor

besuchen, auf/zu Besuch sein; der Besuch, der Besucher, der Gast

Besuchen covers most contexts, but note that it also renders 'to come/go and visit', e.g. **Er besucht jeden Sonntag seine Tante in Bremen** 'He visits/goes and visits his aunt in Bremen every Sunday'. A common alternative to **besuchen** is **auf/zu Besuch bei jdm sein** – **Er geht jeden Sonntag bei seiner Tante auf Besuch. Zu Besuch,** although synonymous, seems to be limited to more formal contexts, e.g. **Der Außenminister ist zur Zeit zu Besuch in Japan** 'The minister for foreign affairs is visiting Japan at the moment'.

'Visitors' in the sense of 'company' is also **Besuch,** e.g. **Wir haben Besuch** 'We have visitors/company', **Wir bekommnen viel Besuch** 'We have/get a lot of visitors'. If you need to refer to 'visitors' as individuals, **Gast** is best used, e.g. **Vier der fünf Gäste waren erkältet** 'Four of the five visitors had a cold'.

Besucher is not commonly used for 'visitors' in the above sense, where **Besuch** is preferred, but it is used where 'visitors' is synonymous with patrons, e.g. **Das Museum hatte letztes Jahr zehntausend Besucher** 'The museum had ten thousand visitors last year'.

to/the vomit

sich erbrechen, kotzen, spucken, sich übergeben; das Erbrochene, die Kotze

Sich erbrechen and **sich übergeben** (insep.) are synonymous and are both respectable ways of expressing the concept. **Spucken,** which also means 'to spit', is a colloquial way to express 'to vomit' (compare 'to chuck/spew' etc.), as is **kotzen,** which is the cruder of the two; this is the word required for the figurative meaning in

the following idioms: **Du bist zum Kotzen** 'You make me sick', **Es ist zum Kotzen** 'It makes me sick/It makes me want to throw up'. **Das Erbrochene** (adj. noun) and **die Kotze** are the corresponding nouns.

to vote

abstimmen, stimmen, wählen

'To vote for' s.o. in an election is **wählen,** which is also the verb 'to choose', e.g. **Wir haben ihn/die CDU gewählt** 'We voted for him/the CDU'. 'To vote for/against' s.t. is **für/gegen etwas stimmen,** e.g. **Ich habe für die CDU gestimmt** 'I voted for the CDU', **Das Land hat für den Beitritt in die EU gestimmt** 'The country voted to join the EU', **Ich stimme immer ungültig** 'I always vote informal', but **Ich gehe jetzt wählen** 'I'm off to vote now'.

'To vote on' an issue is **abstimmen über** (+ acc.), e.g. **Der Bundestag muss noch darüber abstimmen** 'The Upper House still has to vote on it'.

to wait (for), await

abwarten, erwarten, warten

'To wait for' s.o. or s.t. is **warten auf** + acc., e.g. **Er hat zehn Jahre auf diese Gelegenheit gewartet** 'He waited for this opportunity for ten years', **Wie lange hast du gewartet?** 'How long did you wait (for)?'.

Although **erwarten** normally means 'to expect', it also renders 'to wait for' in the figurative sense of 'to await', e.g. **Was erwartet uns in Berlin?** 'What is waiting for us (= awaits us) in Berlin?'. In combination with **können** and **nicht** or **kaum, erwarten** renders that meaning of 'to wait' that implies excitement or impatience, e.g. **Die Kinder können nicht/kaum erwarten, bis ihr Vater aus**

Mexico zurückkommt 'The kids can't/can hardly wait for their father to return from Mexico'.

'To wait' till s.t. occurs, i.e. 'to wait' for s.t. to happen or 'to wait and see', requires **abwarten**, e.g. **Ich kann noch nichts machen. Ich muss abwarten** 'I can't do anything yet. I have to wait (and see)', **Warten wir mal ab!** 'Let's wait and see', **Europa wartet die Entwicklung in dem Land ab, bevor es der EU beitreten darf** 'The EU is waiting for development in that country before it is allowed to join the EU'. This is using the verb intransitively, but it can also take a direct object, e.g. **Wir haben den Sturm einfach abwarten müssen** 'We simply had to wait the storm out' (= till the storm was over).

to wake up, awake

aufwachen, aufwecken, erwachen, erwecken, wach liegen/sein/werden, wachen, wecken

'To wake up' as an intransitive verb, i.e. when you wake up of your own accord, is **aufwachen**, e.g. **Ich wache jeden Morgen um halb sieben auf** 'I wake up every morning at half past six'. This can also be expressed by **wach werden**, e.g. **Wann wirst du normalerweise wach?** 'When do you normally wake up?'.

Erwachen is a rather literary sounding synonym of the two previous expressions (compare 'to awake[n]'); the name of that well-known publication of the Jehova's Witnesses, for example, is **Erwachet** 'Awake'.

There is a verb **wachen** that is synonymous with **wach liegen/sein** (to lie/be awake) but you are advised to stick to the latter.

'To wake' s.o. else up, i.e. the tr. verb, is **wecken**, e.g. **Weck mich bitte um sieben!** 'Please wake me at seven'. The difference between **wecken** and **aufwecken** is identical to that between 'to wake'

and 'to wake up' as tr. verbs in English, e.g. **Warum hast du mich nicht (auf)geweckt?** 'Why didn't you wake me (up)?'. The above explains why an 'alarm clock' is **der Wecker**.

Erwecken, a tr. verb, is as poetic sounding as **erwachen**, so avoid it.

to/the walk, to go for a walk (*see* TO GO and TO RUN)

(zu Fuß) gehen, laufen, spazieren gehen, einen Spaziergang machen, eine Wanderung machen, wandern

'To walk' is usually rendered simply by **gehen**, e.g. **Ich gehe jeden Tag an der Kirche vorbei** 'I walk past the church every day'; this can, however, be interpreted as 'I go past the church every day'. If you want to make it obvious that s.o. 'is walking' use **zu Fuß gehen**, e.g. **Meine Kinder gehen zu Fuß in die Schule** 'My kids walk to school'.

Laufen (literally 'to run', *see* TO RUN) is used to render the physical skill of 'walking', e.g. **Das Kind läuft schon** 'The child has already started walking', **Er läuft sehr unsicher** 'He doesn't walk too well' (= is not steady on his feet).

'To walk around' some obstacle is either **herumgehen** or **herumlaufen**, e.g. **Er ist um den Tisch herumgegangen/-gelaufen** 'He walked around the table', but 'to go walking around aimlessly' is **herumlaufen**, e.g. **Er ist stundenlang im Park herumgelaufen** 'He walked around in the park for hours'. The division between **gehen** and **laufen** is a tricky one. Watch out for it.

'To go for a walk' in the sense of a leisurely stroll, is rendered either by **spazieren gehen** or **einen Spaziergang machen**, e.g. **Jeden Abend gehen die beiden im Park spazieren/machen die beiden einen Spaziergang im Park** 'Every night those two go a for a walk in the park'. There is also a verb **spazieren fahren** used when one goes for a leisurely drive.

'Walking' in the sense of hiking, i.e. a more strenuous pastime, is rendered by a similar couplet to the above, i.e. **wandern (gehen)** or **eine Wanderung machen**, e.g. **Wir sind am Wochenende in den Bergen gewandert/wandern gegangen** or **Wir haben am Wochenende eine Wanderung in den Bergen gemacht** 'We went walking/hiking in the mountains on the weekend'. Thus a 'walker', 'walking club' and 'walking shoes' are **der Wanderer, der Wanderverein** and **die Wanderschuhe**.

the wall

die Mauer, der Wall, die Wand

The 'wall' of a building, inside and out, is **die Wand**. A 'wall' built around a garden or town, i.e. as a barrier, is **die Mauer**, thus **die Berliner Mauer** 'the Berlin Wall'. That is the theory, but there are individual cases where the distinction is not always so clear. For example, the noise barriers built along freeways these days are called **Schallschutzwände**, where one might have expected **Mauer** to be more appropriate. **Der Wall** equates more with 'rampart' or 'embankment', but can be translated in some contexts by 'wall'; for example, the old East German regime used to refer to the Wall as **der antifaschistische Schutzwall** 'the antifascist protective wall/barrier'.

to wash (up), shower

abspülen, abwaschen, (sich) duschen, spülen, (sich) waschen

Waschen is a verb that always needs an object, thus a sentence like 'He never washes' has to utilise a reflexive pronoun to show the object of the washing, in this case 'himself', e.g. **Er wäscht sich nie**. 'To shower', on the other hand, is optionally reflexive, e.g. **Er duscht (sich) jeden Morgen** 'He showers every morning'. If the action of

washing is being performed on s.o. or s.t. else, there is no problem as that person or thing is the object, e.g. **Ich muss das Auto noch waschen** 'I still have to wash the car'. If washing parts of your body, it is most usual to use the dat. of the reflexive pronoun[50] in combination with the definite article, e.g. **Ich muss mir die Hände waschen** 'I must wash my hands'. Possessives can be used if a certain emphasis is present, e.g. **A: Wascht euch die Hände! B: Ich habe meine Hände schon gewaschen**. 'A: Wash your hands. B: I've already washed *my* hands'. Note how you express washing the hands of another person, also avoiding a possessive adjective: **Ich habe ihm die Hände gewaschen** 'I washed his hands'.

'To wash up' or 'to do the washing up' is **abwaschen** or **den Abwasch machen**, e.g. **Hast du schon abgewaschen?** 'Have you done the washing up yet?'. Although **abspülen** strictly speaking means 'to rinse (off)', this verb is commonly used as a synonym of **abwaschen**, as is **spülen**, and a 'dishwasher' is always a **Spülmaschine**, whereas a 'washing machine' (i.e. for clothes) is a **Waschmaschine**.

to water

begießen, besprengen, bewässern, gießen, sprengen

'To water' the garden or lawn requires **(be)sprengen** (to sprinkle/spray), whether you do this with a hose or a sprinkler (**der Rasensprenger**), e.g. **Der Rasen muss gesprengt/besprengt werden** 'The lawn must be watered'. The **be-** prefix is optional.

If 'watering' plants, use **(be)gießen**, where once again the prefix is optional, e.g. **Wirst du bitte meine Blumentöpfe (be)gießen, während ich im**

---

[50] The dat. forms of the reflexive pronoun only differ from the usual reflexive pronoun in the first and second persons sing., e.g. **mir, dir, sich, uns, euch, sich**.

Urlaub bin? 'Will you please water my flower pots while I am on holidays?'.

Bewässern equates more with 'to irrigate' and is best use for fields and the like.

to welcome

begrüßen, willkommen heißen

'To welcome' a guest ist **jdn begrüßen** (note it contains a long vowel), e.g. **Die Familie hat mich sehr herzlich begrüßt** 'The family welcomed me heartily/gave me a very hearty welcome'. When 'welcoming' s.o. in a formal speech, you can use **begrüßen** or **willkommen heißen**, e.g. **Es ist mir eine Ehre, Sie hier begrüßen zu dürfen** 'It is an honour for me (to be able) to welcome you here', **Ich heiße Sie herzlich willkommen bei uns** 'I sincerely welcome you here'. Of course, as in English, it may be sufficient to say simply **(Herzlich) willkommen** (stress on **kommen**) 'Welcome'.

In the figurative sense of 'welcoming' the fact that something has occurred, **begrüßen** is also used, e.g. **Er begrüßte die Nachricht** 'He welcomed the news'.

when

als, wann, wenn

In a question **wann** must be used, e.g. **Wann ist er angekommen?** 'When did he arrive?'. Take note that **wann** is also required in indirect questions, e.g. **Ich habe keine Ahnung, wann er angekommen ist** 'I have no idea when he arrived'.

Otherwise the word you will normally need is **wenn**, e.g. **Ich sag's ihm, wenn er zurückkommt** 'I'll tell him when he gets back'. Note, however, that **wenn** can also mean 'if' (*see* IF).

When the action in the when-clause took place on one particular occasion in the past, the conjunction required is **als**, not **wenn**, e.g. **Das Kind fing an zu weinen, als es von der Schaukel fiel** 'The child began to cry when it fell off the swing'. But when the action occurred regularly in the past, i.e. where 'when' means 'whenever', **wenn** must be used, e.g. **Das Kind hat nie geweint, wenn es von der Schaukel gefallen ist** 'The child never cried when it fell off the swing'.

In the construction 'hardly/scarcely . . . when', 'when' is rendered by **so** or **da**, e.g. **Kaum war er weg, so/da tauchte seine Frau unerwartet auf** 'Scarcely had he left, when his wife turned up unexpectedly' (consisting of two main clauses), but it is also possible to translate 'when' here with **als**, e.g. **Kaum war er weg, als seine Frau unerwartet auftauchte** (consisting of a main clause and a subordinate clause).

where

wo, woher, wohin

German has preserved the distinction previously made in English between 'where', 'whence' and 'whither'. Whenever 'where' is used together with any verb of motion, you need to ask where the person is coming *from*, by means of **woher**, or where they are going *to*, by means of **wohin**. The former really only occurs with **kommen**, e.g. **Woher kommen Sie?** 'Where do you come from?'. This would normally be taken to mean where do you hail from, i.e. from what town or country, but you could also say **Woher kommst du jetzt?** referring to where the person has just been.[51] **Wohin** must be used with all verbs like **gehen**,

---

[51] Note that 'from' in the answers to these two questions differs. In the first case, when referring to one's town or country of origin, one replies **Ich komme aus Warschau/Polen** 'I come from Warsaw/Poland', but in the second case one replies **Ich komme jetzt gerade von Köln** 'I've just now come from Cologne'.

fahren, laufen, fliegen etc. when enquiring where s.o. is going to, the trouble being that we in English usually omit the 'to', e.g. **Wohin gehst du?** 'Where are you going?'. Particularly in speech, but also permissible in writing, is the custom of placing **her** and **hin** at the end of the clause, e.g. **Wo kommen Sie her?, Wo gehst du hin?**

'Wherever' is expressed by **wo immer**, e.g. **Es gibt Umweltverschmutzung, wo immer man sich in der Welt befindet** 'There is environmental pollution wherever you are in the world'.

who

der/die/das etc., wer/wen/wem

The difference between these two sets of words is that between relative and interrogative pronouns. In questions **wer, wen** or **wem** is required depending on the case in which 'who' stands, thus in other words **wer** is 'who', **wen** is 'whom' and **wem** is 'to whom', e.g. **Wer hat's gemacht?** 'Who did it?', **Wen hast du gesehen** 'Who(m) did you see?', **Wem hast du das Geld gegeben?** 'To whom did you give the money?' = 'Who did you give the money to?'. Remember that the same forms are required in indirect questions too, e.g. **Er weiß nicht mehr, wem er das Geld gegeben hat** 'He no longer remembers who he gave the money to'.

The other set of forms is used when the 'who(m)' introduces a relative clause and is thus often interchangeable with 'that' or may even be omitted in English, but never in German, e.g. **Die Leute, die nebenan wohnen, kommen aus Lettland** 'The people who/that live next-door come from Latvia' (nom. pl.), **Die Leute, denen wir Weihnachtskarten geschickt haben, haben nie wieder von sich hören lassen** 'The people (who, whom, that, –) we sent Christmas cards to, have never been heard from again' (dat. pl.).

The full paradigm for the relative pronoun is:

	M	F	N	PL
N	der	die	das	die
A	den	die	das	die
G	dessen	deren	dessen	deren (*see* WHOSE)
D	dem	der	dem	denen

whose

dessen/deren, wessen

Grammatically speaking these forms belong with the forms given under 'who' but will be dealt with separately here. The distinction between **wessen** and **dessen** etc. is basically the same as that between **wer** and **der** etc., i.e. the former translates 'whose' in both a direct and an indirect question and the latter in a relative clause, e.g. **Wessen Frau ist sie?** 'Whose wife is she?', **Das ist der Mann, dessen Frau die Lehrerin meines Sohns ist** 'That's the man whose wife is my son's teacher'. The full paradigm of the genitive of the relative is:

M	F	N	PL
dessen	deren	dessen	deren

The appropriate form is determined by the gender or number of the noun which precedes 'whose', i.e. which the 'whose' relates back to, e.g. **Die Frau, deren Mann** . . . because she is feminine and **der Mann, dessen Frau** . . . because he is masculine and **Die Kinder, deren Mutter** . . . because **Kinder** is plural; the choice of the correct form has nothing to do with the gender of the noun that follows the 'whose'.

Note the following less stilted way of expressing 'whose' by avoiding use of **wessen**, e.g. **Wem gehört dieses Buch?** 'Whose book is this this?' (lit. Who does this book belong to?).

will

werden, wollen

'Will' (i.e. **werden**) as a marker of the future tense is used somewhat less in German than in English. If the future is otherwise indicated by means of an adverb of time, it is usual in German to leave the verb in the present tense, e.g. **Das mache ich morgen** 'I'll do it tomorrow', **Er kommt nächste Woche** 'He'll be coming next week', but in both these cases it is of course also possible to use the present in English too, e.g. I'm doing it tomorrow, He's coming next week, but in German this is the preferred construction.

Sometimes 'will' does not refer to the future but is used in requests. In such cases German can use **wollen**, e.g. **Willst du bitte das Fenster zumachen?** 'Will you please shut the window?'. It is however possible to use **werden** here too, e.g. **Wirst du bitte das Fenster zumachen?**, and as in English, you can make this sound a little more polite by using 'would', e.g. **Würden Sie bitte das Fenster zumachen?** Even more polite would be **Seien Sie bitte so nett, und machen Sie das Fenster zu!**

the window

das Fenster, die Fensterscheibe, das Schaufenster

The normal word for 'window' is **Fenster**. In English we sometimes use 'window' when we mean 'window pane', in which case the German uses **Fensterscheibe**, e.g. **Felix hat die Fensterscheibe beim Fußballspielen zerbrochen** 'Felix broke the window while playing football'.

A 'shop window' is a **Schaufenster**, e.g. **Ich hab's im Schaufenster bei Karstadt gesehen** 'I saw it in the window at Karstadt'.

the woman, girl

die Dame, die Dirne, die Frau, das Fräulein, die Göre, Jungfern-, die Jungfrau, das Mädchen, das Mädel, das Weib

Dame is used in all contexts where 'lady' is used in English, e.g. **meine Damen und Herren** 'ladies and gentlemen'. **Frau** is the equivalent of 'woman' but also renders 'wife', e.g. **eine Frauenbewegung** 'a women's movement', **Darf ich meine Frau vorstellen?** 'May I introduce my wife?'. **Frau** is also used as a title before surnames the way 'Mrs' and 'Miss' are in English, e.g. **Frau Würth** 'Miss/Mrs/Ms Würth'.

Fräulein is used to render 'Miss' as a title but women's liberation targeted the old distinction between **Frau** and **Fräulein** and now **Frau** is used for both. You can still use this word if needing to get the attention of a waitress or shop assistant, e.g. **Fräulein, würden Sie mir bitte helfen?** 'Miss, would you please help me?'.

A 'girl' is a **Mädchen**, a common southern variant of which is **Mädel** (pl. -s), while colloquial forms heard in the north are **die Deern** (pl. -s) and **die Göre** (little girl), but **das Gör** (pl. -en) is a northern word for 'child/brat' and in the plural falls together with **die Göre**.

Weib is usually a derogatory word for a woman (compare 'broad') but is acceptable in certain idioms, e.g. **Wein, Weib und Gesang** 'wine, women and song', **Sie ist ein tolles Weib** 'She is quite a woman/a great bird'; also **Fischweib** 'fishwife'.

Jungfrau means virgin (**die Jungfräulichkeit** 'virginity') but the 'Virgin Islands' and a 'maiden voyage' are **die Jungferninseln** and **die Jungfernfahrt** respectively.

wonderful, terrific, awesome, great

cool, geil, herrlich, prächtig, super, toll,
wunderbar, wunderschön

A good general word for 'wonderful' is **wunderbar**. Certainly where s.t. is **sehr schön**, it is appropriate to call it **wunderschön**, but this word has a wider application than just physical beauty, e.g. **Seine Tochter ist wunderschön** 'His daughter is really beautiful', **Das Leben in Amerika ist wunderbar/wunderschön** 'Life in America is wonderful/marvellous'. **Prächtig** means 'splendid' or 'magnificent' with reference to physical beauty but also renders 'wonderful' in general, e.g. **Diese Landschaft ist prächtig** 'This countryside is magnificent/beautiful', **Das Leben ist prächtig** 'Life is wonderful/great'.

'Wonderful' with reference to the taste of foods is **herrlich** 'delicious' (*see* NICE).

Adjectives extolling one's enthusiasm for things are subject to fashion in both German and English (compare 'awesome', 'cool', 'grouse', 'fab' etc.). **Cool** is used in German these days more or less where it is used in English, but other fashionable adjectives are **geil** (lit. randy), with an intensified form **affengeil**, as well as **super** and **toll**, e.g. **Der Typ ist cool/geil** 'That chap is cool/way-out', **Der Film/die Party war super/toll** 'The film/the party was awesome/terrific'.

words, vocabulary

die Worte/Wörter; das Lexikon, die Vokabel,
das Vokabular, der Wortschatz

Wort has two plural forms, **Wörter** and **Worte**. Individual 'words' are **Wörter**, e.g. **Er verwendet immer ganz schwierige Wörter** 'He's always using quite difficult words'. A dictionary is a **Wörterbuch** because it is a collection of independent words. **Worte**, on the other hand, is used as a collective noun for 'words' when they refer to something said, i.e. as a whole not individually, e.g. **Der Minister wird bald schon seine Worte bereuen** 'The minister will soon regret his words'.

When learning 'words' as items of vocabulary, the term **Vokabeln** (sing. **eine Vokabel** 'one item of vocabulary' or one 'word') is customary, e.g. **Felix muss bis Montag alle diese lateinischen Vokabeln lernen** 'Felix has to learn all these Latin words by Monday', **der Vokabeltest** 'the vocabulary test', **das Vokabelheft** 'the vocabulary book'.

The technical term for the 'vocabulary' of a language is **das Lexikon**, e.g. **Das holländische Lexikon beinhaltet mehr Wörter französischer Abstammung als das deutsche** 'The vocabulary of Dutch contains more words of French origin than that of German'. The everyday word for this, but also used for an individual's 'vocabulary', is **Wortschatz**, e.g. **Emil hat schon einen ausgezeichneten Wortschatz für ein vierjähriges Kind** 'Emil already has an excellent vocabulary for a four-year-old child'. A more learned synonym of **Wortschatz** is **Vokabular**.

to work; the work

arbeiten, bearbeiten, erarbeiten,
funktionieren, wirken; die Arbeit, beruflich,
berufstätig

'To work' in the most usual sense is **arbeiten**, e.g. **Wo arbeitest du?** 'Where do you work?'. 'To go to work', by the way, is **arbeiten gehen** or **zur Arbeit gehen**. **Wir müssen jetzt an die Arbeit gehen** renders 'We must now get (down) to work'. And 'at (your place of) work' is **bei der Arbeit**, e.g. **Wo ist Karl heute? Er ist bei der Arbeit** 'Where is Karl today? He's at work' (*see* JOB).

If a farmer 'works' his fields, **bearbeiten** is the verb required (i.e. a transitive verb).

If an appliance doesn't 'work', the best verb to use is **funktionieren** but **gehen** is also possible, e.g.

Meine Festplatte funktioniert/geht nicht mehr 'My hard disk isn't working any more'.

'It's working', meaning that s.t. is having an effect, is **wirken**, e.g. **Mein Hausarzt hat Kamillentee empfohlen, und er hat gewirkt** 'My GP recommended camomile tea and it has worked'.

There are derivatives of **arbeiten** (e.g. **ausarbeiten, bearbeiten** and **erarbeiten**) but these only rarely equate with meanings of English 'to work'. 'To work out' a plan or strategy, for example, is **erarbeiten**, e.g. **Er hat diesen Plan erarbeitet** 'He worked out this plan', i.e. it was his idea, whereas 'to rework/revise/adapt' s.t. is **(neu) bearbeiten**, e.g. **Er hat seine deutsche Grammatik neu bearbeitet** 'He has revised his German grammar'.

The adjectives **beruflich** (professionally) and **berufstätig** ([gainfully] employed) are commonly used in contexts where in English we might use the noun or verb 'work', e.g. **Was machen Sie beruflich?** 'What sort of work do you do?', **Meine Frau ist auch berufstätig** 'My wife works too'.

(to be) worth

sich lohnen, sich rentieren, wert sein

'To be worth' doing (s.t.) is most usually rendered by **sich lohnen**, e.g. **Es lohnt sich, Fremdsprachen zu lernen** 'It is worth learning foreign languages', **Das lohnt sich nicht** 'That's not worth doing'. **Es lohnt sich nicht** only renders 'It's not worth it' in the sense of it is not worth the effort of doing something; if you mean that something is too expensive, this must be expressed as follows: **Was, dreißig Euro für dieses Buch? Das ist es nicht wert** 'What, 30 euros for that book? It is not worth it'.

Sich rentieren is an elevated synonym of **sich lohnen**.

A statement like 'Berlin is worth a visit' is expressed as **Berlin ist eine Reise wert**, with **wert** following the noun; compare also **Die Halskette**

ist mehr als tausend Euro wert 'The necklace is worth more than €1000'. But **wert** in 'It is (not) worth the trouble' governs either the nom. or the gen., e.g. **Es ist (nicht) die/der Mühe wert** (*see* TROUBLE).

wrong, right

falsch, nicht richtig, sich irren, los, nicht stimmen, verkehrt, (Un)recht haben

When people are 'right/wrong' **Recht/Unrecht haben** is used, e.g. **Du hast Recht, und sie hat Unrecht** 'You are right and she is wrong'. Where 'wrong' has connotations of 'to be mistaken' **sich irren** is possible, e.g. **Jeder kann sich mal irren** 'Anyone can make a mistake'. This is also used to express the idiom 'If I am not mistaken . . . (= if I remember correctly), i.e. **Wenn ich mich nicht irre. . . .**

If s.t. as opposed to s.o. is 'right' or 'wrong', **richtig** and **falsch/verkehrt** are used, e.g. **Was du da sagst, ist völlig falsch/verkehrt** 'What you are saying is utterly wrong', **Die Adresse ist richtig/falsch/verkehrt** 'The address is correct/wrong'. But 'wrong' in such contexts is quite frequently rendered by **nicht richtig**. 'To be right (wrong)', not of people, is commonly expressed by **stimmen (nicht)**, e.g. **Diese Adresse stimmt nicht** 'This address is wrong', **Stimmt das, was du sagst?** 'Is that correct, what you are saying?'.

'Wrong' as in 'There's something wrong with the car' or 'What's wrong with the car?' is best expressed with **los**, e.g. **Es ist was los mit dem Auto, Was ist mit dem Auto los?** (*see* TROUBLE). If you see s.o. with a worried look on their face where you would ask in English 'What's wrong?', **los** is used in German, **Was ist los (mit dir)?** 'What's wrong (with you)?'.

In the idiom **eine Fehlentscheidung treffen** (to make a wrong decision) we find 'wrong' being rendered idiomatically.

yes, no

doch, ja, jawohl, nein

'Yes' and 'no' are of course usually simply **ja** and **nein,** but 'yes' in reply to a question in the negative is **doch,** e.g. **A: Er hat keine Kinder, oder? B: Doch. Zwei** 'A: He doesn't have any kids, does he? B: Yes (he does). Two.'

Take note of **Ich glaube ja/nein** 'Yes, I think so/No, I don't think so'. Synonymous with **ich glaube ja** is **ich glaube schon.**

Jawohl renders a very emphatic 'yes', i.e. 'yes indeed', but has a rather military or comical ring to it these days and is best avoided.

Bibliography

Beaton, K. B. *A Dictionary of German Usage*, Oxford, 1998.

Donaldson, B. C. *Beyond the Dictionary in Dutch*, Coutinho, Muiderberg, 1990.

Durrell, M. *Hammer's German Grammar and Usage*, Arnold, London, 2002 (4th ed.).

Durrell, M. *Using German Synonyms*, CUP, 2000.

Eggeling, H. F. *A Dictionary of Modern German Prose Usage*, Clarendon, Oxford, 1961.

Farrell, R. *A Dictionary of German Synonyms*, CUP, Cambridge, 1953.

Parkes, G. and A. Cornell *NTC's Dictionary of German False Cognates*, NTC Publishing Group, Lincoln, 1996.

Schmitz, W. *Übungen zu synonymen Verben*, Hueber, Munich, n.d.

Schmitz, W. *Übungen zu Präpositionen und synonymen Verben*, Hueber, Munich, 1984 (7th ed.).

Turneaure, B. M. *Der treffende Ausdruck*, Norton, New York/London, 1996 (2nd ed.).

English–English Index

abbreviate	*abbreviate*	any	*any*
about (to be –)	*deal with*	anybody	*any*
about	*about*	anyone	*any, no*
abridge	*abbreviate*	anything	*any*
accept	*accept*	anywhere	*any*
accident	*accident*	apart from	*except (for)*
according to	*according to*	apartment	*house*
accuse	*accuse*	apparatus	*appliance*
ache	*hurt*	apparently	*obviously*
actually	*really*	appear	*appear*
admit	*admit*	appliance	*appliance*
advertise	*advertisement*	application	*apply for*
advertisement	*advertisement*	apply for	*apply for*
advise	*advise*	appointment	*date*
afraid (of)	*fear (for)*	approach	*approach*
after that	*after*	area	*area*
after	*after*	army	*army*
afternoon	*periods of the day*	arrive	*arrive*
afterwards	*after*	arts	*arts*
age	*age*	as	*as*
ago	*ago*	ask	*ask*
agree	*agree*	assistant professor	*professor*
agreement	*agree*	associate professor	*professor*
alive	*alive*	at	*at*
all	*all*	attack	*attack*
allow	*permit*	attract	*attract*
announce	*announce*	avoid	*avoid*
another	*another*	await	*wait (for)*
answer	*answer*	awake	*wake up*
		awesome	*wonderful*
		awful(ly)	*terrible(ly)*

*The words on the left are dealt with under those on the right which occur alphabetically in the book.

far	*far*	gossip	*speak*
farm	*farm*	government	*government*
farmer	*farm*	graduate	*university*
fat	*big*	grain	*grain*
fear (for)	*fear (for)*	gravel	*stone*
feel	*feel*	great	*wonderful*
few (a)	*some*	ground	*ground*
fight	*fight*	grow	*grow*
finally	*last(ly) (at)*	guard	*guard*
find	*find*	guess	*guess*
finish	*finish*	gun	*gun*
fire	*fire*	habit	*custom*
first(ly)	*first(ly)*	handle	*handle*
flee	*flee*	hang	*hang*
floor	*floor, ground*	happen	*happen*
follow	*follow*	happy	*happy*
food	*food*	hard	*hard*
for	*for*	have to	*must*
force	*force*	head	*boss*
forceful	*force*	heal	*heal*
foreign	*foreigner*	hear	*hear*
foreigner	*foreigner*	heat	*heat*
free	*free*	heater	*heater*
freeze	*freeze*	heating	*heater*
freezer	*freezer*	hello	*hello*
friend	*friend*	hide	*hide*
front door	*door*	hire (out)	*rent (out)*
frozen	*freeze*	holiday(s)	*holiday(s)*
fry	*cook*	home (at)	*house*
funny	*strange*	hope	*hope*
garage	*garage*	horrible(ly)	*terrible(ly)*
garbage (bin)	*rubbish (bin)*	hospital	*hospital*
gate(way)	*door*	hotel	*pub*
German language	*German language*	hour	*hour*
Germany	*Germany*	house	*house*
get in/out	*get in/out*	humid	*humid*
get on/off	*get in/out*	hurry	*hurry*
get	*get*	hurt	*hurt*
girl	*woman*	if	*if*
give	*give*	imagine	*imagine*
go for a walk	*walk*	immediate(ly)	*immediate(ly)*
go	*go*	immigrant	*immigrate*
goodbye	*goodbye*	immigrate	*immigrate*

German–English Index

abbiegen	*turn*	abschicken	*send*
abbrennen	*burn*	abschlagen	*refuse*
Abend	*periods of the day*	abschließen	*close*
Abendbrot	*lunch*	Absicht	*intend*
Abendbrot	*meal(time)*	absinken	*sink*
Abendessen	*meal(time)*	absolvieren	*finish*
abends	*periods of the day*	abspülen	*wash*
aber	*but*	Abstand	*distance*
abfahren	*leave*	abstellen	*turn on/off*
Abfall	*rubbish*	abstimmen	*vote*
Abfälle	*rubbish*	Absturz	*accident*
abfinden (sich)	*cope (with)*	abstürzen	*freeze*
abfliegen	*leave*	abtasten	*feel, touch*
abfragen	*test*	Abteilung	*department*
abgehen	*leave*	abwandern	*immigrate*
abgesehen von	*except*	abwarten	*wait (for)*
abhängen	*depend on*	abwaschen	*wash*
abkaufen	*buy*	ähneln	*look like*
Abkommen	*agree*	ähnlich sehen	*look like*
abkürzen	*abbreviate*	ähnlich sein	*look like*
ablehnen	*refuse*	Aktie	*part*
ablesen	*read*	akzeptieren	*accept*
Abort	*toilet*	albern	*stupid*
abputzen	*clean*	all	*all*
abraten	*advise*	all-	*all*
abreisen	*leave*	Allee	*road*
abriegeln	*close*	allerlei	*sort*
absagen	*cancel*	allmächtig	*force*
		als	*as*

*The German words on the left are dealt with under the English keywords on the right which occur alphabetically in the book.

also	*so*
Alter	*age*

Ampel	*light*	anheuern	*rent*
Amt	*office*	anhören (sich)	*listen to*
amüsieren (sich)	*enjoy*	anklagen	*accuse*
an	*about, at, on, to*	ankommen (darauf –)	*depend on*
anbauen	*grow*	ankommen in/bei	*arrive*
anbelangen	*concern*	ankündigen	*announce*
anbetreffen	*concern*	anlachen	*laugh*
anbieten	*offer*	anlächeln	*laugh*
anbrennen	*burn*	Anlage	*appliance*
andauern	*last*	anlangen	*concern*
ander	*different*	anleiten	*lead*
ändern (sich)	*change*	Anlieger	*inhabitant*
anders	*different*	anlocken	*attract*
anders	*otherwise*	anlügen	*lie*
andrehen	*turn on/off*	anmachen	*turn on/off*
androhen	*threaten*	anmalen	*paint*
anerkennen	*recognise*	anmerken	*notice*
Anfall	*attack*	anmieten	*rent*
anfallen	*attack*	annähern (sich)	*approach*
Anfang	*begin*	annehmen	*accept*
anfangen	*begin*	anpflanzen	*grow*
anfassen	*touch*	Anrainer	*inhabitant*
anfordern	*ask*	Anruf	*cry*
anfreunden (sich)	*friend*	anrufen	*call, ring*
anfühlen	*feel*	anrühren	*touch*
Anführer	*lead*	anschaffen (sich)	*buy*
angehen	*concern*	anschalten	*turn on/off*
angehören	*belong*	anschauen (sich)	*look*
Angehörige	*relative*	anscheinend	*obviously*
angenehm	*nice*	anschießen	*shoot*
Angestellte	*employee*	Anschlag	*attack*
angewöhnen (sich)	*used to*	anschuldigen	*accuse*
Angewohnheit	*custom*	Anschuldigung	*accuse*
angezogen	*dress*	ansehen (sich)	*look*
Angreif	*attack*	Ansicht	*opinion*
angreifen	*attack*	ansonsten	*otherwise*
Angst haben um/vor	*fear*	ansteigen	*raise*
Angst machen	*fear*	anstellen	*employee,*
Ängstigen (sich)	*fear*		*turn on/off*
angucken (sich)	*look*	Anstellung	*job*
anhalten	*stop*	anstreben	*strive for*
anheben	*raise*	anstreichen	*paint*
anheiraten	*marry*	Anstreicher	*paint*

anstürmen	storm	auf	at, on, open, to
antasten	touch	auf Wiederhören	goodbye
Anteil	part	auf Wiederschauen	goodbye
antörnen	turn on/off	auf Wiedersehen	goodbye
Antrag	apply	aufbewahren	keep
Antrag (einen – stellen)	apply	aufdrehen	open
antreten	begin	aufessen	eat
anturnen	turn on/off	Auffassung	opinion
antworten	answer	auffinden	find
anvertrauen	trust	aufgehen	raise
anwachsen	grow	aufhalten	stop
anwenden	use	aufhalten (sich)	stay
Anwohner	inhabitant	aufhängen (sich)	hang
Anwohnerschaft	inhabitant	aufheben	keep
Anzahl	number	aufhören	finish, stop
Anzeichen	sign	auflegen	hang
Anzeige	advertisement	aufmachen	agree, open
anziehen	attract	aufpassen auf	look after,
anziehen (sich)	dress		take care of
anzweifeln	doubt	aufschieben	put off
Apartment	apartment	aufschließen	open
Apotheke	chemist	Aufschnitt	meats
Apotheker	chemist	aufsuchen	look up
Apparat	appliance	aufwachen	wake up
Ära	age	aufwachsen	grow
Arbeit	job, work	aufwärmen	heat
arbeiten	work	aufwecken	wake up
Arbeitgeber	employee	aufziehen	education
Arbeitnehmer	employee	Augenblick (im –)	(at the) moment
Arbeitsplatz	job	augenblicklich	(at the) moment
Arbeitszimmer	office	ausbilden	education
Armbanduhr	clock	Ausbildung	education
Armee	army	ausbuddeln	dig
arrivieren	arrive	ausdenken	think
Art	sort	Ausflug	trip
Arzneimittel	medicine	ausgeben	spend
Assistent	professor	ausgenommen für	except
Assistent (der wissenschaftliche –)	professor	ausgraben	dig
		aushalten	bear, take
Ast	branch	ausheben	dig
Asylant	immigrate	ausheilen	heal
Asylbewerber	immigrate	auskennen (sich)	know
auch	even	auskurieren	heal

auslachen	*laugh*	bangen um	*fear*
Ausland	*country*	Bank	*chair*
Ausländer	*foreigner*	Bau	*building*
ausländisch	*foreigner*	Bauch	*stomach*
auslaufen	*leave*	bauen	*build*
ausleihen	*lend*	Bauer	*farm*
ausmachen	*turn on/off*	Bauernhof	*farm*
ausmalen	*paint*	beabsichtigen	*intend*
auspacken	*pack*	Beamter	*official*
ausprobieren	*try*	Beamtin	*official*
ausreichen	*enough*	beanspruchen	*claim*
ausreichen	*last*	beantragen	*apply*
Ausruf	*cry*	beantworten	*answer*
ausrufen	*cry*	bearbeiten	*work*
ausschalten	*turn on/off*	bedanken (sich)	*thank*
ausschlafen	*sleep*	Bedarf	*need*
ausschreiben	*advertisement*	bedauern	*regret*
Ausschuss	*committee*	bedeckt	*cloudy*
ausschweigen (sich)	*silent*	Bedenken	*doubt*
aussehen	*look like*	bedenken	*think*
aussenden	*send*	bedeuten	*mean*
außer	*except*	bedienen	*serve*
außerdem	*except*	Bedienstete	*official*
außerhalb	*outside*	Bedingung	*condition*
äußerst	*most*	bedrohen	*threaten*
Aussiedler	*immigrate*	bedürfen	*need*
aussöhnen (sich)	*reconcile*	Bedürfnis	*need*
Aussöhnung	*reconcile*	bedürftig	*need*
ausstehen	*bear*	beeilen (sich)	*hurry*
aussteigen	*get in/out*	beeindrucken	*impress*
austauschen	*change*	beeindruckend	*impress*
Auswanderer	*immigrate*	beenden	*finish*
auswandern	*immigrate*	beerben	*inherit*
auszahlen (sich)	*pay*	beerdigen	*bury*
ausziehen (sich)	*dress*	befolgen	*follow*
Auszubildende	*study*	befragen	*ask*
Auto	*car*	befreunden (sich)	*friend*
Auto fahren	*go*	befürchten	*fear*
Azubi	*study*	begießen	*water*
Bach	*river*	Beginn	*begin*
backen	*cook*	beginnen	*begin*
baden	*swim*	begraben	*bury*
Balance	*balance*	begreifen	*realise, understand*

bewahren	keep		borgen	lend
bewähren (sich)	prove		böse	bad
bewässern	water		Boss	boss
bewegen (sich)	move		Brand	fire
beweinen	cry		braten	cook
beweisen (sich)	prove		Brathähnchen	chicken, meats
bewerben um (sich)	apply		Brathendl	chicken, meats
Bewerbung	apply		Brathühnchen	chicken
bewerfen	throw		brauchen	must
bewohnen	live		brauchen	need
Bewohner	inhabitant		brennen	burn
bewölkt	cloudy		Brief	letter
Bewölkung	cloudy		bringen	take
bewusst sein (sich)	realise		Broiler	chicken
bewusst werden (sich)	realise		Brot	loaf
bezahlen	pay		Brötchen	loaf
bezahlt machen (sich)	pay		Brummi	car
Beziehung	relationship		Bub	boy
Bezirk	municipality		Büchse	box
bezweifeln	doubt		Buchstabe	letter
biegen	turn		buchstabieren	spelling
bieten	offer		buchstäblich	literally
Bilanz	balance		buddeln	dig
Bildung	education		Bundeskanzler	prime minister
Bildungswesen	education		Bundesland	state
Billett	ticket		Bundesländer	Germany
bis	time, until		Bundesrat	government
bis gleich	goodbye		Bundesrepublik	Germany
bis morgen	goodbye		Bundesstaat	state
bis später	goodbye		Bundestag	government
Biskuit	cake		Bundeswehr	army
bitten um	ask		Bungalow	house
blasen	blow		Burg	castle
Blazer	coat		Bürgersteig	road
Bleibe	house		Büro	office
bleiben	stay		Bursche	boy
Bleistift	pen		Café	restaurant
blicken	look		Chance	chance
blöd(e)	stupid		checken	check
bloß	only		Chef	boss
Bö	storm		Chemiker	chemist
Boden	ground		City	town
Bodenbelag	carpet		clean	clean

Eigentum	*property*	Einwanderer	*immigrate*
Eigentümer	*owner*	einwandern	*immigrate*
Eile (in großer – sein)	*hurry*	einwilligen	*agree*
Eile haben	*hurry*	Einwohner	*inhabitant*
eilen	*hurry*	einzahlen	*pay*
eilig (es – haben)	*hurry*	einzig	*only*
ein	*one*	emigrieren	*immigrate*
ein ander	*another*	empfangen	*get*
ein paar	*some*	empfehlen	*advise*
einander	*each other*	empfinden	*feel*
einbiegen	*turn*	empfindlich	*tender*
einbilden (sich)	*imagine*	Ende (zu – gehen)	*finish*
einbuddeln	*bury*	Ende (zu – sein)	*finish*
einchecken	*check*	enden	*die*
eindösen	*sleep*	enden	*finish*
Eindruck (einen – machen auf)	*impress*	endgültig	*last(ly)*
		endlich	*last(ly)*
eindrucksvoll	*impressive*	eng	*narrow*
eines	*one, thing*	Entfernung	*distance*
einfallen	*remember*	entfliehen	*flee*
Einfamilienhaus	*house*	entgegennehmen	*accept*
einfrieren	*freeze*	entkleiden (sich)	*dress*
eingehen	*die*	entleeren (den Darm –)	*shit*
eingestehen	*admit*	entlehnen	*lend*
einhalten	*keep*	entleihen	*lend*
einig sein	*agree*	entscheiden (sich)	*decision*
einige	*some*	Entscheidung	*decision*
einigen (sich)	*agree*	entschlafen	*die*
einiges	*some*	entschließen (sich)	*decision*
Einigung	*agree*	Entschließung	*decision*
einmal	*even, first(ly), once*	Entschluss	*decision*
einnicken	*sleep*	entsenden	*send*
einpacken	*pack*	entsinnen (sich)	*remember*
eins	*thing*	Epoche	*age*
eins	*one*	Erachten	*opinion*
einschätzen	*judge*	erarbeiten	*work*
einschlafen	*sleep*	erbauen	*build*
einsparen	*save*	erben	*inherit*
einst	*once*	erbrechen (sich)	*vomit*
einsteigen	*get in/out*	Erbrochene	*vomit*
einstellen	*employee, stop*	Erde	*ground*
eintreffen	*arrive*	Erdgeschoss	*floor*
einverstanden sein	*agree*	ereignen (sich)	*happen*

erfahren	*experience, hear, learn*	erscheinen	*appear*
		erschießen	*shoot*
Erfahrung	*experience*	ersparen	*save*
erfolgen	*follow*	ersparen (sich)	*save*
erforderlich	*necessary*	erst	*even, first(ly), only, until*
erfordern	*ask*		
erfrieren	*freeze*	erstaunen	*surprise*
ergreifen (die Flucht –)	*flee*	ersteigen	*climb*
erhalten	*get, keep*	erstens	*first(ly)*
erhängen (sich)	*hang*	erstürmen	*storm*
erhitzen	*heat*	ertappen	*catch*
erhoffen (sich)	*hope*	erteilen (eine Lektion –)	*teach*
erhöhen	*raise*	ertragen	*bear, take*
erhören	*hear*	ertränken	*drown*
erinnern an (sich)	*remember*	ertrinken	*drown*
Erinnerung	*memory*	erwachen	*wake up*
erkälten (sich)	*cold*	erwachsen	*grow*
erkältet sein	*cold*	erwärmen (sich)	*heat*
Erkältung	*cold*	erwarten	*wait (for)*
erkämpfen	*fight*	erwecken	*wake up*
erkaufen	*pay*	erweisen (sich)	*prove*
erkennen	*know, recognise*	erwerben	*buy*
Erkenntnis	*knowledge*	erwidern	*answer*
erklettern	*climb*	erwischen	*catch*
erklimmen	*climb*	erzählen	*tell*
erkrankt	*sick*	Erzählung	*story*
erlauben	*permit*	erziehen	*education*
erleben	*experience*	Erziehung	*education*
Erlebnis	*experience*	es	*so*
erlernen	*learn*	essen	*eat*
erliegen	*die*	Essen	*food*
erlügen	*lie*	Etage	*floor*
ermorden	*kill*	etwa	*about*
ermuntern	*encourage*	etwas	*any, quite, some*
ermunternd	*encourage*	Examen	*exam*
ermutigen	*encourage*	Fachhochschule	*school*
ermutigend	*encourage*	fahren	*go, travel*
ernst	*serious*	Fahrgast	*passenger*
Ernst	*serious*	Fahrkarte	*ticket*
ernsthaft	*serious*	Fahrschein	*ticket*
eröffnen	*open*	Fahrt	*trip*
erraten	*guess*	fallen	*find*
erreichen	*arrive*	falsch	*wrong*

fangen	*catch*	Fluss	*river*
Farm	*farm*	folgen	*follow*
Farmer	*farm*	fordern	*ask, claim*
fassen	*understand*	fortbilden	*education*
fechten	*fight*	Fortbildung	*education*
fehlen	*miss*	fortfahren	*continue*
fehlschlagen	*fail*	fortsetzen	*continue*
Feier	*party*	Frage	*ask*
Feierabend machen	*finish*	fragen	*ask*
Feiertag	*holiday(s)*	Frau	*woman*
Fell	*skin*	Fräulein	*woman*
Fels	*stone*	frei	*free*
Felsbrocken	*stone*	fremd	*strange, foreigner*
Felsen	*stone*	Fremder	*foreigner*
Fenster	*window*	fressen	*eat*
Fensterscheibe	*window*	Freund	*friend*
Ferien	*holiday(s)*	Freundin	*friend*
fern	*far*	freundlich	*nice*
Ferne	*distance*	friedlich	*silent*
Fernsehen	*television*	frieren	*freeze*
Fernseher	*television*	fritieren	*cook*
Fernsehgerät	*television*	froh	*happy*
fertig	*finish*	fröhlich	*happy*
fertigwerden	*cope (with)*	früher	*once*
Fest	*party*	Frühstück	*meal(time)*
Festplatte	*disk*	fühlen (sich)	*feel*
feststellen	*realise*	führen	*lead*
fett	*big*	Führer	*lead*
fettig	*big*	Füller	*pen*
feucht	*humid*	Füll(feder)halter	*pen*
Feuer	*fire*	funktionieren	*work*
Filiale	*branch*	furchtbar	*terrible(ly)*
Filzstift	*pen*	fürchten	*fear*
finden	*find, like*	Fußboden	*floor, ground*
Flasche	*bottle*	ganz	*all, quite, terrible(ly)*
Fleck(en)	*mark*	gar	*even*
fleißig	*hard*	Garage	*garage*
fliehen	*flee*	Garnele	*prawn*
Flinte	*gun*	Gasse	*road*
Flucht	*flee*	Gast	*visit*
flüchten (sich)	*flee*	Gastarbeiter	*immigrate*
Flugkarte	*ticket*	Gasthaus	*pub*
Flugschein	*ticket*	Gasthof	*pub*

Gipfel	top	Hammelfleisch	meats
Glas	bottle	handeln um (sich)	deal with
glauben	believe, think	handeln von	deal with
gleich	immediate(ly), same	Handelsschule	school
gleichen (sich)	look like	hängen	hang, put, there is/are
Gleichgewicht	balance		
Glotze	television	harnen	shit
Glotzkasten	television	hart	hard
Glück haben	happy	hätte machen können	could
glücklich	happy	Haupt	boss
Glühbirne	light	Hauptschule	school
Göre	woman	Hause (zu –)	house
graben	dig	Haustür	door
gratis	free	Haut	skin
Gremium	committee	Heer	army
Griff	handle	heilen	heal
grillen	cook	Heim	house
groß	big	Heimat	house
groß machen	shit	heimzahlen	pay
Großstadt	town	Heirat	marriage
großwerden	grow	heiraten	marry
grüezi	hello	heiß machen	heat
Grund	ground	heißen	call, mean
Grundschule	school	heißen (willkommen –)	welcome
Grundstück	ground, property	heizen	heat
grüß dich/euch	hello	Heizkörper	heater
grüß Gott	hello	Heizung	heater
gucken	look	Henkel	handle
guten Abend	hello	Henne	chicken
guten Morgen	hello	her	ago
guten Tag	hello	heranbilden	education
haben (die Absicht –)	intend	heranwachsen	grow
Hackfleisch	meats	heraufkommen	upstairs
Hahn	chicken	heraus	outside
Hähnchen	chicken	Herberge	pub
Hühnchen	chicken	herein	outside
Hallo	hello	Herr	boy
Hals	throat	herrlich	nice, wonderful
halten	stop	herumsehen (um sich –)	look around
halten (sich)	keep	herunterkommen	upstairs
halten für/von	think	heute	periods of the day
halten von	find	heutig	periods of the day
halten	last	heutzutage	now

hinaufgehen	upstairs	Infarkt	attack
hinaus	outside	informieren (sich)	inform
hinausschieben	put off	Inhaber	owner
hindern	prevent	inmitten	middle
hinein	outside	innerhalb	outside
hingehören	belong	Insasse	passenger
hinhören	listen to	Inserat	advertisement
hinkriegen	do	inserieren	advertisement
hinlegen (sich)	lie	Interesse haben an	interested in
hinnehmen	accept	interessieren für (sich)	interested in
hinrichten	kill	interessiert sein an	interested in
hinsehen	look	irgend	some
hinsetzen (sich)	sit	irgendwo	any
hinterlassen	leave	irren (sich)	wrong
Hintertür	door	irrsinnig	terrible(ly)
hinuntergehen	upstairs	ja	yes
hinziehen	attract	Jacke	coat
Hirn	mind	Jackett	coat
hoch	big	jawohl	yes
hochgehen	upstairs	je	ever
hochklettern	climb	jeder	any
hochrennen	upstairs	jemals	ever
Hochschule	school	jemand	any
höchst	most	jener	that/those
Hochzeit	marriage	jetzt	now
Hocker	chair	Job	job
hoffen	hope	Junge	boy
hoffentlich	hope	Jungfern-	woman
hören	hear, listen to	Jungfrau	woman
hören auf	listen to	Jura	law
Hose(n)	pants	Jurist	law
Hotel	pub	Kacken	shit
Huhn	chicken	Kalbfleisch	meats
Hummer	prawn	Kalender	diary
Illustrierte	magazine	Kälte	cold
Imbissstube	restaurant	kalte Platte	meats
immer noch	still	Kamin	heater
immigrieren	immigrate	Kammer	room
Immobilie	property	kämpfen	fight
imponieren	impress	kapieren	understand
imponierend	impressive	Karosse	car
imposant	impressive	Karton	box
in	on, to	Kästchen	box

lohnen (sich)	*worth*		meist	*most*
Lokal	*pub*		meistens	*most*
los	*wrong*		Menschen	*people*
lösen	*buy*		merken	*notice, realise*
losfahren	*leave*		merken (sich)	*remember*
Luftgewehr	*gun*		merkwürdig	*strange*
lügen	*lie*		mieten	*rent*
Lust haben	*feel*		mindestens	*least*
lustig	*strange*		Ministerium	*department*
lustig machen über (sich)	*laugh*		Ministerpräsident	*prime minister*
machen	*do*		missen	*miss*
Macht	*force*		misslingen	*fail*
mächtig	*force*		misstrauen	*trust*
Mädchen	*woman*		Mitfahrer	*passenger*
Mädel	*woman*		mitmachen	*experience, take part in*
Magazin	*magazine*		mitnehmen	*take*
Magen	*stomach*		Mittag	*lunch*
Magister	*university degree*		Mittag essen	*lunch*
Mahlzeit	*meal(time)*		Mittagessen	*lunch, meal(time)*
Mais	*grain*		mittags	*lunch, periods of the day*
Mal	*once, time*			
malen	*paint*		Mitte	*middle*
Maler	*paint*		mitteilen	*inform*
man	*people*		Mittelpunkt	*middle*
Manager	*boss*		mitten in	*middle*
manch-	*some*		mittlere	*middle*
Mann	*boy*		mögen	*like*
Mantel	*coat*		Möglichkeit	*chance*
Märchen	*story*		moin	*hello*
Marke	*mark*		Moment (im –)	*(at the) moment*
Matte	*carpet*		momentan	*(at the) moment*
Mauer	*wall*		Monatsschrift	*magazine*
Medikament	*medicine*		morden	*kill*
Medizin	*medicine*		Morgen	*periods of the day*
Meer	*sea*		morgen	*periods of the day*
mehrere	*some*		morgens	*periods of the day*
meiden	*avoid, mean, think*		morgig	*periods of the day*
Meinung	*mind*		Most	*drink*
Meinung (einer/ anderer – sein)	*agree*		Mühe	*trouble*
			Müll	*rubbish*
Meinung (nach – von)	*according to*		Mülleimer	*rubbish*
Meinung	*opinion*		Mülltonne	*rubbish*

müssen	*must, shit, should (have)*	Neueste	*news*
		neugierig	*curious*
nach	*according to, after, to*	Neuigkeit	*news*
		neulich	*recently*
nach Hause	*house*	nicht durchkommen	*fail*
nach oben gehen	*upstairs*	nicht ein	*no*
nach unten gehen	*upstairs*	nichts	*any*
nach wie vor	*still*	nicken	*sleep*
nachbessern	*improve*	nie zuvor	*before*
nachdem	*after*	nie	*never*
nachdenken über	*think*	niederbrennen	*burn*
nachher	*after*	Niederlassung	*branch*
Nachmittag	*periods of the day*	niederlegen (sich)	*lie*
nachmittags	*periods of the day*	niedersetzen (sich)	*sit*
Nachrichten	*news*	niemals	*never*
nachschlagen	*look up*	niemand	*any*
nachsehen	*check, correct*	nirgends	*any*
nachstreben	*strive for*	nirgendwo	*any*
Nacht	*periods of the day*	Niveau	*level*
nachts	*periods of the day*	noch	*even, still*
Nachts (des –)	*periods of the day*	noch ein	*another*
nachvollziehen	*understand*	noch nie	*never*
nachweisen	*prove*	noch	*ever*
nahe	*near(by)*	Nord	*east*
Nähe (in der –)	*near(by)*	Norden	*east*
nahen	*approach*	Not	*need*
näher kommen	*approach*	Notar	*law*
näher rücken	*approach*	Note	*mark*
nähern (sich)	*approach*	nötig	*necessary*
Nahrung	*food*	nötig haben	*need*
Nahrungsmittel	*food*	notwendig	*necessary*
Napf	*dish*	Nummer	*number*
närrisch	*stupid*	nun	*now*
neben	*near(by)*	nur	*only*
nee	*no*	nutzen	*use*
nehmen	*take*	nützen	*use*
nehmen (in Kauf –)	*accept*	nützlich	*use*
nehmen	*catch*	nutzlos	*use*
nein	*no, yes*	ob	*if*
nennen	*call*	oben	*top, upstairs*
nett	*nice*	Oberhaupt	*boss*
neuerdings	*recently*	Oberschule	*school*
Neues	*news*	Ofen	*heater*

offen	open	Pfeife	pipe
offenbar	obviously	pflegen	take care of, used to
offenkundig	obviously	Pforte	door
offensichtlich	obviously	pfüteuch	goodbye
öffentlicher Dienst	service	pfüti	goodbye
öffnen	open	pinkeln	shit
Ökonom	economy	Pipeline	pipe
Ökonomie	economy	Pipi machen	shit
original	original(ly)	Pissoir	toilet
originell	original(ly)	Pistole	gun
Orkan	storm	PKW	car
Ort	place, town	Platte	dish
Orthographie	spelling	Plattenbau	building
Ortschaft	town	Platz	place, room
Ost	east	platzen	fail
Ostdeutschland	Germany	plaudern	speak
Osten	east	Popcorn	grain
Ozean	sea	prächtig	wonderful
packen	pack	Praktikant	education
Pädagogik	education	Premier	prime minister
Palast	castle	Premierminister	prime minister
Papier	paper(s)	Priester	priest
Papiere	paper(s)	Probe	test
Papierkorb	rubbish	probieren	taste, try
Parkhaus	garage	Problem	trouble
Parlament	government	Professor	professor
Partei	party	promovieren	university degree
Parterre	floor	Proviant	food
Party	party	Provinz	country, state
Parzelle	ground	prüfen	test
Passagier	passenger	Prüfung	exam
passieren	happen	Puder	powder
Pastor	priest	Pulle	bottle
Pegelstand	level	Pulver	powder
pennen	sleep	Pulverkaffee	powder
Pensionär	retire	Pulverschnee	powder
pensionieren	retire	pumpen	lend
pensionieren lassen (sich)	retire	putzen	clean
		Rad fahren	go
Pensionierte	retire	radeln	go
Personen	people	Radiator	heater
Pfad	road	Raststätte	pub
Pfarrer	priest		

Schild	sign	schützen	protect
Schinken	meats	schwätzen	speak
schlafen	sleep	schweigen	silent
schlau	clever	Schwein haben	happy
schlecht	bad	Schweinebraten	meats
schlecht	sick	Schweinefleisch	meats
schließen	close	schwer	hard
schließlich	last(ly)	schwierig	hard
schlimm	bad	Schwierigkeit(en)	trouble
Schlitten	car	schwimmen (gehen)	swim
Schloss	castle	schwinden	disappear
Schluss (zum –)	last(ly)	schwül	humid
schmal	narrow	See	sea
schmecken	like, taste	sehen	look
schmeißen	throw	sehr	quite
Schmerz	hurt	seit	since
Schmerzen	hurt	seitdem	since
Schmerzen	hurt	seither	since
schmoren	cook	selb-	same
schnacken	speak	selber	self
schnappen	catch	selbst	even , self
Schnupfen	cold	selbstständig	independent
Schnupfen bekommen	cold	selbstsicher	confident
Schnupfen haben	cold	seltsam	strange
Schnupfen holen (sich)	cold	Seminar	department, lecture
Schnupfen zuziehen (sich)	cold	Seminarschein	exam
		Semmel	loaf
schön	nice	senden	send
schon	so	Senioren	retire
schonen	save	senken	sink
Schorle	drink	seriös	serious
schrecklich	terrible(ly)	servus	goodbye, hello
Schrei	cry	Sessel	chair
schreiben	spelling	setzen	put
schreien	cry	Shop	shop
Schrippe	loaf	sich	each other, self
Schrotbüchse	gun	sicher	sure
Schüler	study	sicherlich	sure
Schulkind	study	sinken	sink
Schulzentrum	school	Sinn	mind
Schüssel	dish	Sirup	drink
Schusswaffe	gun	Sitte	custom
schütten	rain	sitzen	sit

sitzen	*there is/are*
skurril	*strange*
Slip	*pants*
so	*according to, as, so*
so dass	*so that*
soeben	*just*
Sofa	*chair*
sofern	*as long as*
sofort	*immediate(ly)*
sogar	*even*
solang(e)	*as long as*
sollen	*mean, should (have)*
sonderbar	*strange*
sondern	*but*
sonst	*otherwise*
sonstig	*otherwise*
sorgen für	*take care of, look after*
sorgfältig	*careful(ly)*
Sorte	*sort*
Souterrain	*floor*
sowohl . . . als (auch)	*both*
Sozius	*passenger*
sparen	*save*
spät (zu – kommen)	*late*
spazieren gehen	*walk*
Spaziergang (einen – machen)	*walk*
Speicher	*memory*
speichern	*save*
Speise	*food*
speisen	*eat*
spenden	*support*
spinnen	*stupid*
Spital	*hospital*
Spitze	*top*
Spot	*advertisement*
sprechen	*speak*
sprengen	*water*
Sprudel	*drink*
spucken	*vomit*
spülen	*wash*

spüren	*feel*
Staat	*state*
Staatsexamen	*exam, university degree*
Stadt	*town*
Stadtkern	*middle*
Stammlokal	*pub*
Standuhr	*clock*
stark	*force*
Stärke	*force*
stattfinden	*happen*
staunen	*surprise*
stecken	*put*
Stehcafé	*restaurant*
stehen bleiben	*stop*
stehen	*there is/are*
steigen	*climb, get in/out, raise*
steigern	*raise*
Stein	*seed, stone*
Stelle	*area, job, place*
stellen	*ask, put*
stellen (auf die Probe –)	*test*
stellen (einen Antrag –)	*apply*
Stellung	*job*
sterben	*die*
Stiel	*handle*
Stift	*pen*
still	*silent*
stimmen	*vote, wrong*
Stimmung	*mood*
Stock	*floor*
Stockwerk	*floor*
stoppen	*stop*
Story	*story*
strafen	*punish*
Strafzettel	*ticket*
Straße	*road*
Straßenzug	*road*
streben	*strive for*
streichen	*cancel, paint*
streiten um	*fight*
Strom	*river*

umkommen	die	verbessern (sich)	improve
umschlagen	change	verbleiben	stay
umsehen (sich)	look around	verbrauchen	use
umsonst	free	verbrennen	burn
umsteigen	change, get in/out	verbringen	spend
umtauschen	change	verdampfen	steam
umziehen	dress, move	verdanken	thank
unabhängig	independent	verdunsten	steam
unbedingt	necessary	verehrt	dear
unerhört	hear	vereinbaren	agree
Unfall	accident	Vereinbarung	agree
ungefähr	about	vereinigt	united
ungeheuer	terrible(ly)	Vereinigung	union
ungewöhnich	strange	vereint	united
Unglück	accident	vereisen	freeze
unheimlich	strange	verenden	die
Union	union	vererben	inherit
unlängst	recently	verfahren (sich)	lose (one's way)
unmittelbar	immediate(ly)	verfehlen	miss
Unrecht haben	wrong	verfolgen	follow
unten	upstairs	vergangen	last
unterhalten (sich)	speak	vergehen	pass
Unterhose	pants	vergraben	bury
Unterlagen	paper(s)	verhalten (sich)	behave
Unterricht	lesson	Verhalten	behave
unterrichten	inform, teach	Verhältnis	relationship
unterschiedlich	different	verheilen	heal
unterstützen	support	verheiraten (sich)	marry
unweit	far	verheiratet sein	marry
Unwetter	storm	verhindern	prevent
urinieren	shit	verirren (sich)	lose (one's way)
Urlaub	holiday(s)	verkehrt	wrong
ursprünglich	original(ly)	verkraften	cope (with)
urteilen	judge	verkürzen	abbreviate
Vaterland	country	verlagern (sich)	move
verabredet sein	date	verlangen	ask
Verabredung	date	verlassen	leave
verändern (sich)	change	verlassen auf (sich)	depend on
verantworten (sich)	answer	verlaufen (sich)	lose (one's way)
verantwortlich	responsible	verlegen	cancel
Verantwortlichkeit	responsible	verleihen	rent
Verantwortung	responsible	verleihen	lend
verbergen (sich)	hide	verlernen	learn

verlesen (sich)	read	verstehen	understand
verlieren	lose (one's way)	versteuern	tax
vermachen	leave	versuchen	try
vermählen	marry	verteidigen (sich)	defend
Vermählung	marriage	vertragen	bear, take
vermeiden	avoid	vertrauen	trust
vermieten	rent	verwandeln (sich)	change
vermissen	miss	Verwandte	relative
verpacken	pack	Verwandtschaft	relationship,
verpassen	miss		relative
verrecken	die	verwechseln	confuse
verregnen	rain	verweigern	refuse
verriegeln	close	verwenden	use
verrückt	stupid	verwirren	confuse
versagen	fail	verwundern	surprise
versäumen	fail	Vetter	cousin
versäumen	miss	Viertel	area
verschenken	give	Vokabel	words
verschicken	send	Vokabular	words
verschieben	cancel	Volk	people
verschieben	different, put off	Volkshochschule	school
verschlafen (sich)	sleep	Volksschule	school
verschließen	close	Volkswirt	economy
verschlossen	close	Volkswirtschaft	economy
verschonen	save	vor	ago, before
verschweigen	silent	vor allem	especially
verschwinden	disappear	vorbei	over
versenden	send	vorbeifahren an	pass
versenken	sink	vorbeigehen an	pass
versetzen	move	vorbereiten	prepare
versinken	sink	vorbeugen	prevent
versöhnen (sich)	reconcile	Vordertür	door
Versöhnung	reconcile	vorenthalten	keep
versorgen	take care of	vorgestern	periods of the day
verspäten (sich)	late	vorhaben	intend
verspätet sein	late	vorheizen	heat
Verspätung haben	late	vorher	before, first(ly)
verspeisen	eat	vorhin	recently
Verstand	mind	vorig	last
verständigen (sich)	agree	vorkommen	appear, happen
verständigen	advise, inform	vorlesen	read
Verständnis haben für	understand	Vorlesung	lecture
verstecken (sich)	hide	Vormittag	periods of the day

vormittags	*periods of the day*
Vorsicht	*careful(ly)*
vorsichtig	*careful(ly)*
Vorstand	*committee*
vorstellen (sich)	*imagine*
Vortrag	*lecture*
vorüber	*over*
vorübergehen	*pass*
vorverlegen	*cancel*
vorwärmen	*heat*
vorwerfen	*accuse*
vorziehen	*cancel, prefer*
wach liegen	*wake up*
wach sein	*wake up*
wach werden	*wake up*
wachen	*wake up*
wachsen	*grow*
Wächter	*guard*
wagen (sich)	*dare*
Wagen	*car*
wählen	*vote*
wahnsinnig	*terrible(ly)*
wahren	*keep, save*
Währung	*currency*
Wall	*wall*
Wand	*wall*
wandern	*walk*
Wanderung (eine – machen)	*walk*
Wanduhr	*clock*
Warenhaus	*shop*
warm werden	*heat*
warten	*wait (for)*
Wärter	*guard*
was für ein	*sort*
waschen (sich)	*wash*
Waschpulver	*powder*
Wasser lassen	*shit*
Wasserspiegel	*level*
WC	*toilet*
wechseln	*change*
Wecke	*loaf*
wecken	*wake up*

Wecker	*clock*
Weg	*road*
weggeben	*give*
weggehen	*leave*
Weh	*hurt*
wehen	*blow*
Wehrdienst	*service*
wehren (sich)	*defend*
Wehrmacht	*army*
Wehrpflicht	*army, service*
wehtun	*hurt*
Weib	*woman*
weigern (sich)	*refuse*
weil	*as*
weinen	*cry*
weit (. . . entfernt)	*far*
weiterbilden	*education*
Weiterbildung	*education*
welch-	*some*
wenden	*turn*
wenigsten (am –)	*least*
wenigstens	*least*
wenn	*if*
wer/wen/wem	*who*
Werbespot	*advertisement*
Werbung	*advertisement*
werden	*get, grow, will*
werfen	*throw*
Werk	*job*
Werkstatt	*garage*
wert sein	*worth*
wessen	*whose*
West	*east*
Westdeutschland	*Germany*
Weste	*coat*
Westen	*east*
Wettbewerb	*competition*
Wettkampf	*competition*
Wettstreit	*competition*
wie	*as*
wiedererkennen	*recognise*
wiedervereinigt	*united*
wievielte	*date*

willkommen heißen	welcome	Zeit (in letzter –)	recently
Wipfel	top	Zeitalter	age
wirken	look, look like, work	Zeitpunkt	time
		Zeitschrift	magazine
wirklich	really	Zeitung	paper(s)
Wirtschaft	economy, pub	Zentralheizung	heater
Wirtschaftswissen-schaft	economy	Zentrum	middle, town
		Zettel	paper(s)
Wirtschaftswissen-schaftler	economy	Zeugnis	report
		Ziegel(stein)	stone
Wirtshaus	pub	ziehen	grow, move
Wissen	knowledge	ziemlich	quite, rather
wissen	know	Ziffer	number
wissen	remember	Zimmer	room
Wissenschaft	knowledge	Zivildienst	service
wo	where	zu	at, close, to
Wochenschrift	magazine	zu Hause	house
woher	where	zubereiten	prepare
wohin	where	züchten	grow
wohnen	live, stay	zudrehen	turn on/off
Wohnhaus	house	zuerst	first(ly)
Wohnort	town	Zufall	accident
Wohnung	house	zufolge	according to
Wolken	cloudy	zufrieden	happy
wolkig	cloudy	zufrieren	freeze
wollen	refuse, will	zugeben	admit
Worte	words	zugehören	belong
Wörter	words	zugucken	look
wörtlich	literally	Zuhause	house
Wortschatz	words	zuhören	listen to
wunderbar	wonderful	zulächeln	laugh
wundern (sich)	surprise	zulachen	laugh
wunderschön	wonderful	zulassen	permit
Wurst	meats	zuletzt	last(ly)
Würstchen	meats	zumachen	close
Zahl	number	zumindest	least
zahlen	pay	zumindestens	least
Zahlwort	number	zunächst einmal	first(ly)
zanken (sich)	fight	zunehmen	raise
zart	tender	zurechtkommen	cope
zärtlich	tender	zurücklassen	leave
Zeichen	sign	zurückrufen	call
Zeit	time	zurückzahlen	pay

zurzeit	*(at the) moment*	zutrauen	*trust*
zuschauen	*look*	zuversichtlich	*confident*
zuschicken	*send*	Zuwanderer	*immigrate*
zuschließen	*close*	zuwandern	*immigrate*
zusehen	*look*	Zwang	*force*
Zustand	*condition*	Zweifamilienhaus	*house*
zuständig	*responsible*	Zweifel	*doubt*
Zuständigkeit	*responsible*	zweifeln	*doubt*
zusteigen	*get in/out*	Zweig	*branch*
zustimmen	*agree*	Zweigstelle	*branch*
zustoßen	*happen*	Zyklon	*storm*

eBooks – at www.eBookstore.tandf.co.uk

A library at your fingertips!

eBooks are electronic versions of printed books. You can store them on your PC/laptop or browse them online.

They have advantages for anyone needing rapid access to a wide variety of published, copyright information.

eBooks can help your research by enabling you to bookmark chapters, annotate text and use instant searches to find specific words or phrases. Several eBook files would fit on even a small laptop or PDA.

NEW: Save money by eSubscribing: cheap, online access to any eBook for as long as you need it.

Annual subscription packages

We now offer special low-cost bulk subscriptions to packages of eBooks in certain subject areas. These are available to libraries or to individuals.

For more information please contact webmaster.ebooks@tandf.co.uk

We're continually developing the eBook concept, so keep up to date by visiting the website.

www.eBookstore.tandf.co.uk